Performing Action

Artistry in
Human Behavior and Social Research

Joseph R. Gusfield

Transaction Publishers
New Brunswick (U.S.A.) and London (U.K.)

This book is printed on acid-free paper that meets the American National Standard for Permanence of Paper for Printed Library Materials.

Library of Congress Catalog Number: 00-042309
ISBN: 0-7658-0016-0
Printed in the United States of America

Library of Congress Cataloging-in-Publication Data

Gusfield, Joseph R., 1923-
    Performing action : artistry in human behavior and social research / Joseph Gusfield.
        p. cm.
    Includes bibliographical references and index.
    ISBN 0-7658-0016-0 (alk. paper)
    1. Action research. 2. Sociology—Methodology. 3. Human behavior.
I. Title.

HM571 .G87 2000
301'.01—dc21   00-042309

To the memory of Erving Goffman and Alvin Gouldner—two whose friendship and scholarship added much to my life

Contents

Introduction:
Human Behavior as Performance

I begin with a story and a description. The story was told to me by a friend who had been an undergraduate at the University of California at Los Angeles in the late 1940s. An attractive woman came once a week to take a class on the campus. Her walk was so provocative that her presence was soon known to many men. They would time themselves so as to be able to watch her as she came to class. Several years later, she became, and remains even today, the most famous of American sexual icons—Marilyn Monroe.

The description is part of an essay on women's fashion by the then (1979) fashion critic of the *New Yorker* magazine, Kennedy Fraser. In an analysis of fashions designed for executive women, Fraser remarks on the male suit:

> The suggested fashions for women in business begin with the uniform of men in business—the suit—and then add touches of self-consciousness...it doesn't simply take itself for granted. The traditional business uniform of men—matching jacket and pants of a neutral color, an easily laundered, simply styled shirt...continues in favor not only because of conservatism but because it is eminently practical. *It is a style of dress that can be forgotten about while the people who wear it devote their attention to the work at hand.* (Italics mine. Fraser, 1981: 232-33)

What both of these strips of human behavior have in common, for purposes of this analysis, is the capacity for multiple interpretations, for meanings at different levels and of different dimensions. Monroe's walk was at once both a means of locomotion and an invitation. The male suit is not only a means of covering the body and providing warmth. In its style and material, it also conveys a message of dependability and predictability. It is in the messages conveyed that a great deal of human interaction and observation occurs. There are

1

many ways of walking to and from the same places and many styles for coverage and warmth. That very comparison of possibilities is the background for the creation of meanings in human action.

The Performance Metaphor

In using the metaphor of "performance," I am borrowing from the stage, the movies, the concert hall and, more recently, the world of visual art and entertainment. In short, from the arenas conventionally associated with art. I do this deliberately because one of the goals of this volume, as in much of my past work, is to forge a closer relationship between art and sociology and, at the same time, to mark out the boundaries and differences between them.

In utilizing the concept of behavior as performance, I am pointing to two similarities between the staged or planned actions of the artistic world and that of what the artist and art critic Allen Kaprow calls "non-theatrical performance" (Kaprow, 1993: 163-81). First, the behavior involves a performer and an audience. Somebody engages in action—whether interpersonal interaction or public actions—where the audience is, to some substantial degree, unknown to the performer. Secondly, the performance is open to the interpretations of the audience. Literary, drama, and art critics have long pointed out and exemplified the diverse meanings with which they and audiences interpret performances.

While the two vignettes that began this chapter are simple and their analysis probably already well understood by my readers, it is in the application of the idea of performance to the wide range of interpersonal and public actions that the concept becomes more useful. I shall argue that the process of interpretation of meanings in behavior is a significant part of human life, central to the work of sociological inquiry, and a valuable part of what sociologists do as observers and critics of societies. It constitutes an activity not too unlike that of the literary critic and the art historian but yet distinctive and unique to the analysis of the social scientist.

There is much similarity in the approach taken here to that of the philosopher Paul Ricoeur whose work has been influential to me. In his seminal essay, "The Model of the Text: Meaningful Action Considered as a Text" (Ricoeur, 1979; see also Ricoeur, 1978), Ricoeur advanced the idea that action can be construed in the same frame as written texts. They are capable of being understood through the same methodologies as those used in examining written texts. While much analysis of written texts has focused on the intentions of the writer this has ignored the ways in which a text creates a multiplicity of potential interpretations:

> [T]he meaning of human action is also something which is *addressed* to an indefinite range of possible "readers"...like a text human action is an open work, the meaning of which is "in suspense." It is because it "opens up" new references and receives fresh relevance from them, that human deeds are also waiting fresh interpretations which decide their meaning (Ricoeur, 1979: 86).

There are, of course, many precursors both to Ricoeur and to my orientation. Two whose influence has been great are the philosopher-literary critic Kenneth Burke and the sociologist Erving Goffman. From Burke I have utilized the idea that experience is mediated by language and the perspectives which different modes of thought make possible and probable. Of special importance are those of the attribution of motives, the rhetoric of identification, and the symbolic character of action (Gusfield, 1989).

From Goffman, I have derived the idea of self-presentation, akin to my conception of performance (Goffman, 1959). There is much similarity between his usage and orientation (often called dramaturgical) and mine. The metaphor of literary performance is derived from Goffman. Unlike Goffman, however, my focus is not on the performer and the "arts of impression management," nor on the presentation of self. My focus is more on the process of interpretations and on public events and acts of public officials. The interaction order is only one arena of presentation. My focus is on the performance and the observer rather than the performer.

Elsewhere, as I have written, both Goffman and Burke are frequently grouped together as exponents of a dramaturgical perspective toward human behavior. It is important however to recognize the differences. Burke referred to his viewpoint as "dramatistic," (Burke, 1968) which he defined as

> a method of analysis and a corresponding critique of terminology designed to show that the most direct route to the study of human relations and human motives is via a methodical inquiry into cycles or clusters of terms and their functions. (Burke, 1989: 135)

Burke's use of the metaphor of "drama" was oriented to the substance of literature as analogous to life as drama—as conflict and dialectic understandable through the perspectives of terminology. Goffman's use of the stage as metaphor was on "dramaturgy," on the process of acting. Much of his analyses are of deception in human actions as a means of understanding how it is legitimate selves present themselves as who they claim to be and others accept or reject their presentations. Only much later in his life and work did Goffman and Burke come closer together in Goffman's *Frame Analysis* and in *Forms of Talk* (Goffman, 1974; 1981).

The Limits of the Performance Metaphor

Metaphor serves to surprise, to show similarities where differences or indifferences are conventionally thought to occur. Poets utilize metaphor for aesthetic purposes. Scientists use it to bridge the gap between their thought and popular understandings. Social scientists use it to uncover diverse meanings and perspectives that a strip of action makes possible.

But metaphors can also distort, mislead, and cover as well as uncover. There is considerable difference between the stage and "real life." Goffman has pointed out some eight ways in which the theatrical performance differs from life outside the theatre (Goffman, 1974: 138-45) The theatrical performance, for example, is cut off from a history and spatially bound. The actors know the ending and the conversation is both explicit and uncluttered. It involves, as Coleridge wrote, the "willing suspension of disbelief." The performer is both aware of and oriented toward the audience.

Nevertheless, the similarities are pertinent to the understanding of the meanings and significances of action not only for the performer but, most importantly for the sociologist, to the observer.

Kaprow has noted that many nontheatrical activities can also be construed as performances:

[I]t is not difficult to see the performance aspects of a telephone conversation, digging a trench in the desert, distributing religious tracts on a street corner, gathering and arranging population statistics, and treating one's body to alternating hot and cold immersions. But it is difficult not to conventionalize them...whole situations are brought intact into art galleries, like Duchamp's urinal, or art audiences taken to the performances as theater. The transformed "artification" is the focus; the "cooked" version of nonart, set into a cultural framework, is preferred to its "raw" primary state. (Kaprow, 1993: 174)

Kaprow is concerned with art as an institution and with opening it up to include nonconventionalized events, "Happenings," in the term he developed and in this sense conventionalized.

For the sociologist, the distinction between conventionalized and nonconventionalized activity is less important. Some aspects of behavior are manifestly observed by the actor and the observer as performances, as when a teacher conducts a class. Others have a latent element of meaning. Marilyn Monroe may not have thought of her walk as provocative at the time of her appearance on the UCLA campus, nor do men articulate their wearing of a suit as a performance of self or social duty. Ms. Monroe might have thought she was "just walking," and the wearer of a suit doing so "because it feels right." It is the meanings attributed to action that renders them into performances.

I can illustrate my usage in a reconceptualization of a theme in my 1963 study of the American Temperance movement (Gusfield, 1963: esp. Ch. 7). In analyzing the American movement to outlaw the sale of alcoholic beverages in the late nineteenth and early twentieth centuries, I suggested that the Prohibition efforts, at the state and national levels, could be viewed as attempts to maintain and defend the social status of traditional Protestant middle classes in the United States. Regardless of its legal goals or its enforceability the very passage of laws established social supremacy by acting out and symbolizing the status system of the society. They answer the question: In whose interests and according to whose values is the government operated? Whatever the actions of people, what are the dominant values of the society, in G. H. Mead's term, the "generalized other"? (Mead, 1934).

The Problem of Intentionality

There is an apocryphal tale of an author whose book was reviewed in a literary journal. The author wrote back to the journal complaining about the reviewer's interpretation. "That is not what I meant at all," wrote the author. The reviewer replied in the next issue: "Sir, you do not understand what you have written."

Any author, playwright, or visual artist is prepared for the possibility and, more likely, the probability that what he or she intended has not been received as such; that the audience, the reader, has construed the product in different, sometimes opposite ways. In recent years, in literary theories of "reception theory" and deconstructionism there has been a focus on the diverse meanings that written or artistic matter can entail. It has given rise to the view that the text is in the reader not the writer. Any set of material can produce multiple meanings (Fish, 1980: Isler, 1978).

In seeing behavior as text, we place the emphasis on the viewer, on the diverse meanings that a strip of action can convey. However, students of language have long distinguished between denotative and connotative meanings. There are dimensions of meaning. Kenneth Burke begins his volume, *A Grammar of Motives,* with the question, "What is involved when we say what people are doing and why they are doing it?" (Burke, 1945: 3). To answer that question is not a simple matter.

One response might be to say Ask them. To do so ignores the manifold levels of meaning that are created by action, the "opening up" process about which Ricoeur writes in the above quote. On the denotative, instrumental level we try to gauge the intentions of the actor as goal-oriented in a deliberative fashion. If I drive from my home to my office I am engaged in an act of transportation. I may or may not be conscious of how I appear to others, of how my sense of self is or is not portrayed in my driving.

On the other hand, my act of driving an automobile may be seen by others as a reflection of myself or the entire strip of traffic filled with meanings about American life. It may be seen as replete with symbolic connotations.

Erving Goffman has discussed this issue in his distinction between what is "given" and what is "given off." (Goffman, 1959: 2-5). What is given is closer to the act of communication—a fit between the intentionality of the actor and the interpretation of the viewer. The wearer of the suit may intend to communicate his dependability in a business world. What is given off is not communication in the usual sense—a fit between the actor and the viewer. Here the action creates the occasion and the opportunity for the viewer to interpret the behavior in terms and understandings that can be unrelated, even contradictory, to the intentions of the actor.

Goffman was especially interested in the ways in which actors attempted to control the interpretations of the viewer. This is what he called "impression management."

I assume that when an individual appears before others he will have many motives for trying to control the impression they receive of the situation. This report is concerned with some of the common techniques that persons employ to sustain such impressions and with some of the common contingencies associated with the employment of these techniques...I shall be concerned only with the participant's dramaturgical problems of presenting the activity before others. (Goffman, 1959: 15)

Goffman titled the first chapter of his first book "Performances." His perspective is different from mine. My concern is with the audience, not the actor, with the play, not the playwright; with the play, not the players.

That very diversity of perspective is central to my thesis in this book. The widely quoted passage from Kenneth Burke's *Permanence and Change* is most pertinent: "Every way of seeing is also a way of not seeing" (Burke, 1935: 49).

The Levels of Performance

To this point, I have left unexplicated the distinction between "performance and "non-performance." I do so because what may be for the actor action unrelated to the audience may be filled with connotations for the viewer; what may be "an individualistic choice of clothing" may be for the observer a comment on how a social organization creates the legitimacy of its participants. To quote Goffman once again, "What's play for the golfer is work for the caddy."

Certainly a great deal of human action occurs in an unselfconscious manner and in a one-dimensional form. The wearer of the suit may view it solely in terms of aesthetic tastes and the viewers may also see it in those terms. It becomes "performance" when the audience, the viewer, finds other meanings beyond those that are manifest, as Kennedy Fraser has done in the above quotation.

But actors may often be aware of other, latent meanings, as much of Goffman's discussion of impression management indicates. At still another level, the latent meanings seen by the viewer may be dimly aware in the mind of the actor. The wearer of the suit, on reading Fraser's essay, may recognize his, or her, actions and recognize the motivations and inferences as drawn by the observer.

Much of the concern of this book is in the dimension of the actor's actions as containing unrecognized inferences, even inferences created by the observer. Though bound by the text, the observers can find in it a diversity of meanings. They may bring to it perspectives which are not manifestly and conventionally "there." At least as old as Simmel's *The Metropolis and the Mental Life* (originally published, 1903), this has formed a major part of sociological activity.

Simmel brought to his analysis of the city, as he did in his work on the consequences of a money economy, an interest in the styles of behavior characteristic of modern life. He was especially interested in the development of individuality as an aspect of the self and relations to others. In one part of *The Metropolis and the Mental Life*, he discussed one dimension of that style as a result of the quantitative, large population of urban communities—the disposition to exaggerate and intensify individual differences.

> From one angle, life is made infinitely more easy in the sense that stimulations, interests...present themselves from all sides...which scarcely requires any individual efforts for its ongoing. But from another angle, life is composed more and more of these impersonal cultural elements and existing goods and values which seek to suppress peculiar interests and incomparabilities. As a result, that this most personal element be saved, extremities and peculiarities and individualizations must be produced and they must be over-exaggerated merely to be brought into the awareness even of the individual himself. (Simmel, 1995: 44)

This, Simmel referred to as "the atrophy of individual culture through the hypertrophy of objective culture" (ibid.).

What Simmel can be said to have done in this classic essay was to treat aspects of human behavior as performances of the urban culture, to find meaning in them that converts actions into commentaries on historical and institutional change.

How is such a form of analyzing human life peculiar to the sociologist? Isn't it just "armchair philosophizing" that reduces the sociologist to literary critic without the aid of proper training? In the remainder of this chapter, I shall argue that there is a common element in sociology and the humanities but that there are also some significant differences. There is both a humanistic dimension to sociology and a dimension of science but there is, nevertheless, and dominantly so, a form of understanding and discovery that is neither and both.

The Cultural Turn in Contemporary Sociology

In his analysis of the development of European sociology, Wolf LaPenies argued that in the nineteenth and early twentieth century sociology might well have gone in the direction of literature rather than science. Describing the alternatives, he pointed to Bentham and Coleridge as poles in the conflict:

> Bentham asked, "Is this true?" Coleridge asked, "What does this mean?" In the nineteenth century every Englishman was either a Benthamite or a Coleridgian. (LaPenies, 1988: 104)

In one sense, this diversity between a sociology directed toward factual generalizations (Naturwissenschaften) and a sociology directed toward "understanding" (Verstehen or Geisteswissenschaften) has marked the history of sociology. Yet for much of the twentieth century sociological thought and research has been characterized by a quest for causes and effects, for factual accuracy. Meaning has been subordinated to a search for institutional and group influences. In this sense, "culture," as the consciousness of actions, has been conceptualized as "super-structure" or epiphenomena.

Nowhere has this principle of analysis been stated more succinctly than by Karl Marx in *The German Ideology*: "It is not consciousness that determines life, but life that determines consciousness" (Marx, 1932: 10).

In recent decades there has been a turn away from this focus on social structure to a return to the importance of culture, to a preoccupation with the meanings of actions rather than their causes. This is what is referred to as "the cultural turn." It is a product of the studies and writings in a variety of disciplines—linguistics, literary theory, phenomenological philosophy, ethnomethodology. Many names are connected with it, including Berger and Luckmann, Garfinkel, Schutz, Heidegger, Husserl, Geertz, Foucault, and Ricoeur.

What this new focus on culture implies is the importance of the study of experience—culture as the presuppositions, categories, and perspectives that enable actors to make sense of raw experience. Goffman, who has been one of the main influences in the sociological turn toward an understanding of how experience is shaped and constructed, put it, as follows, in the introduction to his book, *Frame Analysis*:

> This book is about the organization of experience—something that an individual actor can take into his mind—and not the organization of society. I make no claims to be talking about the core matters of sociology—social organization and social structure...I am not addressing the structure of social life but the structure of experience individuals have at any moment of their social lives. (Goffman, 1974: 13)

However, Goffman's formulation ignores the central concern of the sociologist with social structure—the division of society into groups and positions, with aspects of class, status and power. Marx's insistence on the priority of class and economic interests may be misplaced, but the question of how culture and structure are related to each other remains the focus of sociological concerns.

An inquiry into the meanings of performance, especially at the public level, takes on relevance for sociologists, as for me, as it becomes related to group life and social structure. The analysis of performance is then viewed from the perspective of the diversity of meanings attributed to specific parts of society.

The Human Science

In one of his many essays, Kenneth Burke makes a distinction between semantic and poetic meaning (Burke, 1957). Semantic meanings are the language of technical research and analysis in which an act or object has one and only one clear and unambiguous meaning. As Burke puts it, its aim is "to give the name and address of every event in the universe" (Burke, 1957: 123). Poetic meaning utilizes the multiplicity of meanings that a given act can have. To say, as Lenore Weitzman has, in her study of divorce (Weitzman, 1985), that with no-fault divorce poverty was being "feminized" is poetic. It forces us to see poverty through a wider process. It is a form of metaphorical speech. Poverty is presented in the image of a woman. The two kinds of meanings are not irreconcilable. To choose one is not necessarily to eschew the other. But they are different. Poetic meaning opens up new, often unexpected, meanings.

Social Science as an Artform

I distinguish between social science knowledge as technical knowledge invested with the authority of science and that social science knowledge which is unique, being neither science nor art but something of both—what has been called a "human science." The distinction is analogous to that of Robert Bellah, expressed in several papers (Bellah, 1981; 1985), between a technical and a practical reasoning. Each implies different audiences. As Bellah wrote: "The chief audience of practical social science is not 'decision-makers' but the public, and its chief impact on social policy is through influencing the climate of opinion rather than supplying discrete information for those in power" (Bellah, 1981: 22).

I would amend Bellah's description to include the ways in which social science influences opinion and action through conferring meanings via the forms of discourse that it has made available. The cultural product of the social science book or article is now a standard part of the intellectual world of modern societies. Concepts such as Daniel Bell's "post-industrial society" or C. Wright Mills's "power elite" are part of the standard language equipment of many college graduates and others who form a large segment of the politically important publics. It is the nontechnical, less research designed work that has provided the conceptual and discourse material out of which the social sciences and their publics have "made sense" of our world. The names of many come to mind. The Holy Trinity of Durkheim, Marx, and Weber have been followed by a long line of creators of meaning. DeTocqueville and the "tyranny of the masses"; Veblen and "conspicuous consumption," Galbraith and the techno-structure, Olsen and the "free rider," Riesman and "inner- and other-directed"; Rieff and "the triumph of the therapeutic; Bourdieu and "cultural capital," Bellah, et al. and *Habits of the Heart*. Doubtless you can supply many others.

The influence of social science on the meaning of things and events has affected the discourse with which public discussion is conducted. They develop the tools with which modern societies are made understandable.

There is a great stock of such concepts, including anomie, alienation, mobility, and many more. There are also the paired terms which express both historical change and institutional differences. Among these are tradition-modernity; community-society; caste and class; formal and informal; bureaucratic and charismatic. The metaphors of "role" are drawn from the stage, of "stratification" from geology. They add an element of visual imagery to verbal formulations.

Such concepts bring into play vivid and directing metaphors and analogies that make the new or the strange familiar. A concept like "cultural capital" (Bourdieu, 1970; 1984) presents the uses of education and tastes in terms of marketability. In this fashion they take on meanings of competition, making what appears to be the expression of personal preferences into a weapon in a form of struggle between classes.

The existence and persistence of imagery, analogy, and metaphor is more than an admission of rhetorical skill. Metaphor expresses one thing in terms of another but it also enables us to expand the potential meaning by seeing them in another setting. It is part of another reading of the text. Blau and Duncan's use of a path as a way of expressing individual social mobility is one such artform (Blau and Duncan, 1963). Goffman's terms, "frontstage" and "backstage," are another. Metaphor surprises and in surprising expands the meanings of its primary object, the ones for which metaphors are found.

McCloskey remarks : "To say that markets can be represented by supply and demand 'curves' is no less a metaphor than to say that the west wind is 'the breath of autumn's being'" (McCloskey: 74).

To speak of these terminologies as "ideal types," abstracted from the complexities of actual events is to confer a meaning on them different from "fiction" or metaphors. Often they are all three. This literary, imaginative, and creative side of social science has been both unavoidable and a very significant way in which the art and science of the social sciences is conducted.

The Humanities and Sociology

In the model of science there is a clear distinction between the subject and the object. That distinction is blurred in a more humanistic view of human behavior. To a significant extent the subject is the interpreter of his or her objects.

To say that ambiguity and multiple meanings are embedded in human behavior and in the social science is not to maintain that all research, all theory, and all conclusions are equally acceptable in that discourse. Because the social sciences must often rest with "mere plausibility" does not mean that we cannot distinguish between good and bad judges, between pure imagination and the disciplined constraints to which the collection and analysis of data lead. Meanings may be partial, but they may or may not be grounded in observations analyzed in a manner that grants the reader the chance to agree or disagree with the analyst's interpretation, to see other perspectives that reveal other aspects of a complex strip of behavior. Rather than emerging with singular, undeniable answers, the social sciences have been at work developing a body of positive conjecture, which, in dialectical fashion, provides an arena of discourse.

This dialectical quality to the social sciences is a major source of their impact on social thought. Language and thought become ironic when that which is familiar and commonplace is depicted as strange and problematic. The cultural framework within which beliefs are couched is rendered an object of awareness. There is much analogy here to Arthur Danto's view of artistic creation as the "transfiguration of the commonplace" (Danto, 1981). It is in this sense that the social scientist is in the business of manufacturing meaning. In all of the examples chosen above, the couching of the problem is as much a part of the study as is the data.

This matter of seeing something in terms of its opposite or bringing new perspectives to bear on old material is a way of widening the dimensions under which public and private areas are perceived. The social scientist, from this stance, is engaged in accumulating meanings rather than narrowing them. In this, he stands alongside the humanists of history, philosophy, and literary theory. But he is not engaged in the free rein of imagination. The art that is practiced is not devoid of checks, of constraints on what is seen as a "text."

There is an ironic component to much that is done in the art of social science. It consists in rendering problematic what has been taken as nonproblematic. It involves what Richard Brown calls, "the capacity to derealize the present" (Brown, 1987: 190).

I have already called attention to the stream of sociological research and writing in the field of social problems that have challenged the status of the conditions that have defined problems such as alcoholism, mental illness, and child abuse. My own studies of drinking and driving have led me to impute political divergences where consensus was thought to exist (Gusfield, 1981; 1988; 1996). From the perspective of traffic safety, the relation of drinking-driving to auto death is the paramount consideration. Accordingly, the phenomenon is one among a number of safety elements and not necessarily as high on the agenda as are others such as auto design, safer roads, seat belts. For those whose perspective is largely with minimizing alcohol problems, it is in steps to minimize drinking. For those who have pressed for new laws through such movements as MADD (Mothers Against Drunk Driving), drinking-driving is a severe ethical dereliction. As victims they seek justice and retribution. These perspectives are all involved in the drinking-driving public yet each approaches the subject with a different meaning for the action.

It is as a critical ironist that the social scientist performs a fundamentally intellectual and artistic rather than a predominantly scientific role. To do so, however, is to stand outside the institutional structures of the society, to be a critical examiner of the basic frameworks of concept and method by which institutions function. This has considerable repercussions for the place of social science in the social structure. The criminologist worries about how crime is defined and cannot accept the institutional definitions of the justice system. The student of organizations does not accept the statement of goals of the chief executives.

In these respects the sociologist, even when functioning in a more artistic manner, is not akin to the humanities scholar. His or her method is more empirical, more open to doubt and skepticism, even toward his or her own ideas, and less concerned with the aesthetic qualities of his or her reports. Imagination is more restrained, more systematized and more open to factual and logical criticism than is true of art as the artist practices it.

Science, as we have sketched it, operates as an elite whose authority provides certainty and order to a part of the culture. Professions can be based on a science as engineering has done, as medicine strives toward, as guidance and counseling attempt. The claim to valid authority on the part of professions rests on the claim to an existence of a certain body of knowledge, which is not accessible to laymen.

A dialectical, dialogic view of the social sciences departs from this form of authoritative certainty. It presents an arena within which the quest for order is paralleled by a quest for disorder, for alternatives. Mannheim's "free-floating" intellectual offers a partial and contestable view but not the consistency and certainty on which to base a cultural elite in a rationalistic and organized society (Mannheim, 1949: Pt. III).

While such a dialectic of voices presents a rich pluralism it is doubtful that contemporary populations and, especially rationally oriented organizations, can utilize its undermining of institutional structures. The role the social scientist assumes is to be the critic of the assumptions, presuppositions and frameworks within which the discourse of institutional life is conducted and, in that way, contribute to alternative "ways of seeing."

The books that have been the most influential have been those that achieved their influence through their impact on the dominant perspectives of their times. We have already mentioned a number of them. These enter into the arena of public discourse and provide new perspectives. They cannot substitute for choices that entail values nor can they help us avoid politics. But they do give us the awareness of self and others that seems to widen the alternatives to be considered.

Seeing human behavior from a variety of perspectives is inconsistent with an attitude of science that seeks for a one, true answer as the end of scientific activities. Consensus is attained because other answers appear as illogical and disproven by empirical experience-experiment, prediction, or other means such that the doubter cannot but be convinced. If we cannot gain or even seek "truth," what value is there to interpretive analysis, to the study of behavior as performance?

In his analysis of what he calls "signifying acts," R. S. Perinbanayagam has stated my view clearly. Dramatistic analysis, what I call performance study, enables the reader to achieve distance from the conventional perspectives and thus to be able to create and imagine new and different orientations, to think in a broader fashion about the world around him: It exposes people "to the possibilities of playing different roles in different plays, of giving them the vocabularies and strategies to abandon old plays for new ones. Viewed in this way, dramatic ontologies provide us with a safeguard against the sins of reifying existing social structures, as well as confusing historical phenomena as transcendental and transhistorical ones" (Perinbanayagam, 1985: 81).

The focus on sociology as a meaning-creation discipline underlies much of the materials in this volume. more specifically I have organized the materials around three terms: Rhetoric, Reflexivity, and Symbolism—three actions that demonstrate the human element in action.

Rhetoric

Rhetoric has been given a bad name in modern intellectual discussion, equated to propaganda and advertising. Yet much of human action can be seen as a means of persuasion. Much is action before some kind of audience. The presence of the audience makes our behavior self-consciously adjusted to the viewers. Charles Horton Cooley's apt phrase of "the looking-glass self" was a classic form of describing that quality of audience orientation that is part of human interaction (Cooley, 1902: Ch. 5.). From this perspective it is irrelevant if the actor seeks to persuade his/her audience. What is significant is that the action carries with it possible meanings that can persuade the audience to one or another view of the actor and/or the action.

Being oriented to an audience, human interaction is capable of analysis as a form of literature, as a means of creating a response from a reader, observer, or participant in interaction. In recent years, literary theorists have emphasized how the study of literature is also the study of much of human action as well. While many of the chapters in this volume reflect the uses of literary theory in sociological work, this chapter on rhetoric is explicit in its emphasis on rhetorical and artistic methods in understanding human behavior.

The first of these chapters (The "Double Plot" in Institutions) is one of my earliest papers. Published in 1963, it was first presented to an academic audience in 1950. It draws on a concept I first encountered in the work of the British literary critic, William Empson, to analyze a range of ceremonial and ritualistic behavior in a variety of contexts.

Chapter Four applies the idea of rhetoric to analyze the styles and artistic methods of mundane research reports in an area of social science. This mode of perceiving research as literature and scrutinizing it from this perspective is continued in the next chapter, a more detailed analysis of two classic studies in sociology—one highly quantitatived and the other enthnographic in method. The last chapter in this section applies some aspects of literary analysis to the study of sports as an artful performance.

Reflexivity

Of the four chapters in this section, three are chiefly programmatic. They discuss general approaches to the study of social movements and assert the importance of the process of reflection both for movement participants, opponents, and audiences. Reflexive analysis treats the object of study as one that observers reflect upon and interpret. Such an analysis is less concerned with the movement as an entity-seeking objective than it is with the movement seen as a performance given meaning by the interpretations of others.

The last chapter in this section applies the ideas of reflection, interpretation, and performance to a comparative study of how the idea that specific behavior came to be considered as traditional was constructed in several different cultures.

Symbolism

This section brings together the idea and concepts of literary analysis, performance, and the interpretive act in the analysis of human action. The concept of symbolism used is akin to its usage in literary criticism and visual arts. It points to the potential in human behavior for different levels of meaning both for the performers and for the audiences. The distinctions often made between the literal and the figurative, the denotative and the connotative, the manifest and the latent are all recognitions of the pervasive use of symbolic analyses. Sociology has used symbolic analysis in the study of art and religion, but has not made considerable use of it in other areas such as law, politics, and everyday life.

The chapters in this section are illustrative of how analyses of behavior as artful performance can shed light on the meanings of events and their relation to aspects of social differentiation and social control, the abiding questions of social structure that constitute the defining character of sociological analysis.

The first chapter in this section reprints a general discussion of symbolic analysis followed by a review of sociological studies in the decade prior to its publication in 1984.

References

Bellah, Robert. 1981. "Social Science as Practical Reason" (unpublished paper).

Bourdieu, Pierre, and Jean-Claude Passeron. 1970. *Reproduction in Education, Society and Culture*. Beverly Hills: Sage Publications.

Bourdieu, Pierre. 1984. *Distinction*. Cambridge, MA: Harvard University Press.

Brown, Richard H. 1987. *Society as Text*. Chicago: University of Chicago Press.

Burke, Kenneth. 1957. *The Philosophy of Literary Form: Studies in Symbolic Action*. New York: Vintage Books.

Burke, Kenneth. 1965. *Permanence and Change*. Indianapolis: Bobbs-Merrill.

Burke, Kenneth. 1945. *A Grammar of Motives*. New York: Prentice-Hall, Inc.

Cooley, Charles H. 1902. *Human Nature and the Social Order*. New York: Charles Scribner's Sons.

Danto, Arthur. 1981. *The Transfiguration of the Commonplace*. Cambridge, MA: Harvard University Press.

Fish, Stanley. 1980. *Is There a Text in This Class?* Cambridge, MA: Harvard University Press.

Fraser, Kennedy. 1981. *The Fashionable Mind*. New York: Alfred A. Knopf, Inc.

Goffman, Erving. 1981. *Forms of Talk*. Philadelphia: University of Pennsylvania Press.

Goffman, Erving. 1974. *Frame Analysis: An Essay on the Organization of Experience*. Cambridge, MA: Harvard University Press.

Goffman, Erving. 1959. *The Presentation of Self in Everyday Life*. Garden City, NY: Doubleday Anchor Books.

Gusfield, Joseph. 1989. "Introduction" to *Kenneth Burke on Symbols and Society*, edited by Joseph Gusfield. Chicago: University of Chicago Press.

Isler, Wolfgang. 1978. *The Act of Reading*. Baltimore, MD: Johns Hopkins Press.

Kaprow, Allan. 1993. *Essays on the Blurring of Art and Life*. Berkeley and Los Angeles: University of California Press.

LaPenies, Wolf. 1988. *Between Literature and Science: The Rise of Sociology*. Cambridge: Cambridge University Press.

Mannheim, Karl. 1949. *Ideology and Utopia*. New York: Harcourt, Brace and Co.

Marx, Karl. 1932. From "The German Ideology" (1845-46) in *Capital and other Writings*. New York: The Modern Library

McCloskey, Donald. 1985. *The Rhetoric of Economics*. Madison: University of Wisconsin Press.

Mead, George Herbert. 1934. *Mind, Self and Society*. Chicago: University of Chicago Press.

Perinbanayagam, R. S. 1985. *Signifying Acts*. Carbondale: Southern Illinois University Press.

Ricoeur, Paul. 1979. "The Model of the Text: Meaningful Action Considered as a Text." in Paul Rabinow and William M. Sullivan, eds., *Interpretive Social Science: A Reader*. Berkeley and Los Angeles: University of California Press (originally published, 1971).

Simmel, Georg. 1995. "The Metropolis and the Mental Life." In Phillip Kasinetz, ed., *Metropolis: Center and Symbol of Our Times*. New York: New York University Press (originally published, 1903).

Part 1

Rhetoric

2

The "Double Plot" in Institutions

The literary critic, William Empson, has expressed the point of view of this paper in discussing the function of two or more plots in a drama. Empson analyzed the aesthetic value of that literary device which uses one or more comic characters to lampoon the serious or heroic characters in an otherwise serious drama. An example of this is the cowardly Falstaff as a burlesque of the rash Hotspur in Shakespeare's first part of *Henry IV*. Of this device Empson says:

> A clear case of "foil" is given by the play of heroic swashbucklers which has a cowardly swashbuckler, not at all to parody the heroes but to stop you from doing so. (It says in effect) "If you want to laugh at this sort of thing laugh now and get it over...." After you have made an imaginative response of one kind to a situation, you are more completely interested in the play, if the chief other response is called out too. (Empson, 1938: 30)

This "double-plot," as Empson calls it, is evident in many human activities. A situation possesses one meaning, in the form of the socially approved expectations of others or the technical requirements of some major interest of the actor. Yet the actor is ambivalent towards the required behavior. The playing of a social role frequently involves the strain of "shutting off" divergent, yet desired, roles. It is at this point that some form of "role release" is highly useful to the institution and to the role-player.

It is suggested here that this general problem has often been solved through the development of socially approved forms within which the individual can legitimately act contrary to norms and values which otherwise guide his overt conduct. These enable the primary institu-

Reprinted from the *Patna University Journal* 18, 1 (1963): 1-9

tion to maintain stability free from disruptive elements. They enable the individual to deal with an internal problem of conflicting dispositions to act.

It is with this phenomenon, which (paraphrasing Radcliffe-Brown) I shall call "institutionalized licentiousness," that this paper is concerned. We will attempt to point out some of the situations in which such forms have developed and their relation to the social structure. We will discuss comedy as a major form of such license. Lastly, we shall generally qualify our simple hypothesis and discover that license is itself possessed of ambiguity.

One illustration of sanctioned role-release in contemporary Western society is the drinking party. Drinking offers an adequate motive for otherwise illegitimate action. It removes the onus of personal responsibility for deliberate choice and hence reduces conflicting elements in the person.[1] The drinking party, in which drink is not only approved but socially expected, makes the relaxation of the moral censor itself a norm. Attitudes that might disrupt other institutions are allowed some expression and release in a regulated fashion, in a counter-institution. The Hindu festival of Holi has similar attributes.

Dollard's remarks regarding black-white sex relations in previous decades in the American South are highly apropos (Dollard, 1937).[1] The prevalence of black mistresses and concubines in the lives of respected white members of the community was not socially disapproved. Dollard remarks that this provided a release from the sexual restrictiveness with which the white woman, even in marriage, was viewed. The Southern chivalrous concept of white womanhood, which viewed her as a non-erotic object, was kept intact despite the contradiction of sexual desires. Husband-wife and male-female relations were prevented from exposure to a disruptive element.

In his study of joking relationships in primitive tribes, Radcliffe-Brown suggested that the joking relationship frequently found between son-in-law and mother-in-law can be explained by the dual attitude of friendliness and antagonism to a readjusted family situation (Radcliffe-Brown, 1940; Brant, 1948). Disrespect and antagonism is approved in the form of jokes of extreme insult and license. In this way, the antagonism is kept from pervading other aspects of the relationship. Murdock, in a cross-cultural survey of social structures, found that the ceremonial regulation of sex may be permissive, as well as restrictive (Murdock, 1949: 267). A number of societies sanction either general sexual license or a slackening of ordinary sexual restrictions on the occasion of weddings, funerals, festivals, or religious ceremonies. Within American society, the male convention (business, fraternal, or academic) has many aspects of an institutionalized "break" in an otherwise rigidly maintained system of monogamy and responsible adulthood. The American Legion convention is a striking example.[2]

An important element has often been the introduction of burlesque or satire of the sacred through the medium of the clown, fool, or comedian who is permitted to engage in otherwise highly profane behavior. Religion, social stratification, authority, manners, and sexual morals have frequently been objects of such occasions. Festivals, which are by definition breaks in routine, have often provided opportunity for such behavior.

In reports of studies of primitive tribes, some attention has been given to the institution of the sacred clown (E. Parsons and Beals, 1934; Steward, 1930; Bowman, 1937) Although the sacred clowns of the Pueblos played an important role in sacred rituals, their behavior demonstrated license with the customary modes. They ate and drank filth, simulated sexual intercourse, used obscene and insulting language to women. All this was done in a society where bodily contacts are uncommon, people are timid about gossiping, and where sexual expression is very restrained in public. Among the Mayo-Yaqui Indians similar behavior is part of the clown's role. Beals says, "The [clowns] may say and do, and the crowd may laugh at things which are never said or done in every day life. Ordinarily they would be not only offensive but grossly insulting" (E. Parsons and Beals, 1934: 505). In both these tribes the clownish behavior is the element of the ritual most closely watched. It is talked about and the dancer's repute is most dependent upon his abilities as a clown.

In medieval Europe, the Feast of Fools (now our very protestantized April Fools' Day) burlesqued the sacred Mass (Welford, 1935: 72-73; Disher, 1925: xviii-xix: 43-44; Kitchin, 1931). Fool characters, dressed in motley and cap and bells, assumed the role of pope or bishop, played dice, ate pudding on the altar, and burned old shoes in the censer.[3] Sex roles were reversed. Men wore skirts and women trousers. Religious institutions were kept intact through giving rein to the desire for the blasphemous instead of creating a greater threat to authority through papal regulation. In the Greek Saturnalia (which has become the generic name for such ceremonies), the slaves were masters for a day and the masters were slaves.[4] I am told that in certain American Army units, on specified days, officers wait on enlisted men.

We have, in American society, similar kinds of topsy-turvy rituals. In the office party, usually at Christmas time, the boss becomes just one of the gang. The office hierarchy is suspended. *Fortune Magazine* has described the typical office Christmas party (which they call the business bachanal) as follows:

> Many a clerk quakes, the morning after, at a hazy recollection of haranguing the boss on managements' stupidities, the boss himself, for that matter, may suffer a hot flash of regret for having lifted his quavering baritone, at one point, in the strains of the minstrel song of an English king....And what is one to make of the second and third vice-presidents publicly panting after the shapely Miss Schultz, suddenly emerged from the obscurity of the Collections and Audit Dept....or more to the point perhaps, can one make Miss Schultz? (*Fortune Magazine*, 1950, p.91)

A relationship of pure sociability, as Simmel has shown, distills out of that relationship existent social roles and statuses. The sacred barriers of status are relaxed. Frequently, in the outdoor academic, office, or plant affair, some form of athletics is a feature. In these kinds of hierarchies the status structure exists on a continuum of increase with age, while athletic skills run in the opposite direction. Hence, a reversal of hierarchical relations. The objects of laughter at these affairs indicate their function as comic rituals. But the social hierarchy does not collapse. Such ceremonies appear to contain a strong element of catharsis; they effectuate release of some strong emotion or feeling. By taking license with the routine structure of day-to-day social behavior, the socially equalizing dispositions can be divorced from the charisma of status relations, and allowed expression in opposing behavior. The contradictory values which these relations have for us are thus kept from clashing too blatantly. The antagonisms felt toward the institution are released outside of that institution in an approved fashion.

We can consider comic behavior in some of its elements as an important form of institutionalized license. The history of the court-fool is very instructive (Welford, op cit; Disher, op cit). The court-fool first appears as a "natural" fool—mentally subnormal. Imbecility, moronishness, insanity have been, until the advent of humanitarianism, great sources for laughter. The explanation for this lies at the heart of the comic attitude. In Kenneth Burke's phrase, comedy involves taking a "perspective by incongruity." [5] In the serious aspects of life, we build up frames of reference for the understanding and judging of human behavior—basic logical premises, cultural and social norms and values—which give us cues with which to determine what is fit and proper and what is unfit and impious. The mentally abnormal person is comical because he brings a different set of assumptions to bear on familiar situations. This the comic always does. That stock comic figure, the absent-minded professor, is an example. Professors imply wisdom. Absent-mindedness, to many people, implies lack of wisdom, a patent incongruity.

The "natural" fool epitomizes incongruity. Consequently, he was a fit person to be given the liberty to utter improper remarks to be rude, obscene, and to criticize and insult the King. (Shakespeare's Fool in *King Lear* is of this type.) In many of the festivals already mentioned, the Fool was the heroic figure, the symbol of the entire festivity of license, and the arch critic of ecclesiastical and secular authority.[6] By the fourteenth century on the continent, the Fool had become an "artificial" Fool, often a member of the intellectual elite. (Until the eighteenth century, German professors augmented their incomes by playing the Fool at court.) Yet the liberty to be impious and critical far beyond other members of the court or the society still remained an aspect of the office. Fools' societies and masquerades became widespread. In these activities burlesques of authority were practiced by many members of the community. The sottie, the Fools' dramas in which a Fool is the central character, were well known for the great license they took in political criticism. It is suggested that this institution, the Fool, was a major mode of institutionalized licentiousness, which allowed, within this form, the expression of divergent attitudes.

In comedy, the censors of social disapproval and conscience are relaxed. Since comedy is incongruous, comic behavior, like drink, dissolves moral responsibility. This is especially true of the public comic figure. The nature of an audience itself renders license permissive. Thus, we laugh more when a radio comedian has a studio audience than when we laugh alone (Cantril, 1935: 222).

Consider the art of the movie comedian W. C. Fields. One element in his characteristic roles was that of the insulting attitude towards children. "Go away brat, you bother me" was one of his frequent lines. The legend in which Fields is supposed to have poured whiskey into the milk of the child star, an effective "scene-stealer," Baby LeRoy is always a great source of humor. When LeRoy fell asleep and failed to report for his scene, Fields is reputed to have remarked, "You see, kid's no trooper." The authenticity of the remark is unimportant. The character that Fields created for his audience is the important element—aggression toward children is one of the most profane acts a member of Western civilization can commit. Children are to be cherished. Yet, as many will testify, children are frequently annoying even when not committing punishable acts. Fields gave expression to a disposition in an approved fashion. He is the heroic villain, unpunished for his misdeeds. He is the gambler, the drunk, the lazy hero. Groucho Marx, in similar fashion, is the foe of conventional manners, and the exponent of insult. In the piety of the comic form, impiety is given a pious channel of action.

The cathartic effects of humor are further suggested in the permitted satire of twentieth-century authoritarian social structures. In Russia, satirists Ilf and Petrov gained great popularity in the 1930s through lampooning Party organizations and Soviet bureaucracy in their work *The Little Golden Calf* (E, Johnson, ed., 1945: 720-32). In later years the magazine, *Krokodil,* has been a severe satirist of all but the topmost elements in the Party. In Nazi Germany, the Bavarian comics, Weiss Ferdl and Karl Valentin, were allowed to satirize in comic form a great deal of political impieties that more directly political speakers could not (E. Pope, 1941). Here is the institution of court-fool in another guise. These comedians possessed an immense following from all political segments. If you attempt to explain their license on the basis of popularity, it does not explain why other popular, but more directly political, figures were silenced.

In the same manner, self-criticism is more permissible in the form of comedy than in any other guise. Jewish self-criticism, for example, exists almost entirely in the form of jokes and witty epigrams. Many of these picture the Jew in stereotypes associated with anti-Semitic doctrine.

The antithesis of an institutionalized mode of behavior is itself institutionalized, allowed approved existence within channelized routes. However, any such simple hypothesis as the cathartic effects of institutional license seems inadequate as explanation for all cases. We are not saying that humor is always a criticism. We are not saying that license is always functional or that these are its only consequences. By the concept of function we do not imply any "hidden hand." Institution A is functional to Institution B insofar as its consequences are the increased maintenance and stability of Institution B. A given system of behavior need not be functional to anything. It may entail many functions. It may be functional to some institutions and dysfunctional to others. No assumption of necessary occurrence or of causation is implied. Functionalism, in this sense, is not a theory. It is a frame of reference, which supplies the kinds of questions we wish answered about elements in a social system. We are not then postulating the hypothesis that license is always functional. We are only suggesting that at times it seems to have been, and that such a perspective sheds some light on a highly complex phenomenon.

After all, *Krokodil* magazine was mostly devoted to anti-American cartoons. Weiss Ferdl was eventually forced to moderate his satire. The Catholic Church at times attempted to abolish the Feast of Fools and did so in the fifteenth century. Even drunkenness results in dysfunctional hangovers.

If comedy is "perspective by incongruity," it is a new perspective, an object of thought viewed from a new interest or standpoint. Comedy is itself ambiguous; it possesses multiple possibilities. On one hand, it assumes conservatism. Something cannot appear incongruous unless we have a standard of congruity, which is thus reinforced.

On the other hand, comedy is revolutionary, dysfunctional. Kenneth Burke, on whose writings I have leaned heavily for my understanding of comedy, speaks of the comic corrective. This is the opposite to comedy as catharsis. When I first read *The Communist Manifesto*, I was amused that Marx should have called bourgeois marriage a system of legalized prostitution. Yet as I reflected on the nature of prostitution—the exchange of sexual access for financial gain—and on the feminine ideal of middle-class marriage—exchange of sexual access, family duties, and social grace for social status and financial protection—I must admit points of resemblance. New aspects of an old object are pointed out and the possibility exists for the creation of new attitudes.

The solution to this problem of contradictory elements in comedy, I suspect, lies in a more thoroughgoing analysis of institutionalized licenses and their histories. As regards comedy, not only must we know the kinds of situations in which different forms arise and the cultural ethos of the group, but we must be more attentive to the rhetoric of comedy. Whom are we persuaded to identify with and what is the nature of that identification? I do not feel sympathy with nor concern about Groucho Marx. He is always in command and my identification is one of exultant conquest. Chaplin enlists my sympathies against his foes and thus my loyalties. Groucho, to me, stresses the cathartic element in the comic. Charlie stresses the corrective element in the comic.

I have tried to set forth some means by which social structures have dealt with problems developing out of ambiguous attitudes towards situations. It is maintained that the concept of institutionalized license is a useful point from which to orient research. The function of such institutions in any concrete setting is a problem for research. This paper has suggested that one way in which social structures have dealt with the problem of vice has been by allowing it a little play and renaming that play *virtue*.

Notes

1. Some women, who are easily seduced only when drunk, and are aware of this, almost deliberately drink themselves into a state where their inhibitions can be relaxed. The social role of the soldier is similar, providing a sanctioned withdrawal of civilian sex, monetary, and etiquette norms. As many recruiting officers realize, this fact is an important source for the lure of the Army. Further, cultural norms of masculinity, which otherwise are difficult to maintain within civilian social institutions, are rendered capable of action in the military life. (Cf. Talcott Parsons, "Certain Primary Sources and Patterns of Aggression in the Social Structure in the Western World," in *Essays in Sociological Theory*, Glencoe, IL, Free Press, 1949.) A number of observers, including this author, noted an element of distinct gaiety and escape in the college students who entered the Army in 1942–43.

2. *Time Magazine*, reporting on the nineteenth American Legion convention, New York City in 1937, mentions the following types of behavior by conventioneers: Horses ridden into hotels, loud martial music day and night, giant firecrackers set off in streets and department stores, conventioneers sleeping shoeless in hotel lobbies or sleeping drunken on marble floors, taking over traffic policeman's activities with the obvious and successful purpose of tying it into knots, shooting "craps" on Broadway car tracks, and using electric shockers on women. The attendance at this convention, including families, was 110,000. Cf. *Time*, October 4, 1937, pp. 12–14.

3. The Fool's Mass apparently represented survivals of a pagan ritual never completely extinguished. Cf. Robert Briffault, "Festivals," *Encyclopedia of the Social Sciences*, Vol. 6, pp. 198–201; Horbert Thurston, "Fools, Feast," cf. *The Catholic Encyclopedia*, Vol. 6, pp. 132–33.

4 .For detailed description of Roman and other forms of Saturnalia, cf. J. G. Frazer, *The Golden Bough*, Vol. 6 (The Scapegoat), pp. 309–411.

5. The analysis of comedy presented leans heavily on that of Kenneth Burke. Cf. *Performance and Change*, pp. 95–207; *Attitudes towards History*, Vol. 1, pp. 49–55, 213–26.

6. A reflection of this is seen in Jacque's speech in Shakespeare's *As You Like It*,
    Act 2, Scene VII:

> I must have liberty
> Withal, as large a charter, as the wind,
> To blow on whom I please; for so fools have;
> Invest me in my motley; give me leave
> To speak my mind.

References

Bowman, H.A. 1937. "The Humor of Primitive Peoples," in *Studies in the Science of Society* (presented to A. G. Keller).

Brant, C. S. 1948. "On Joking Relationships." *American Anthropologist*, n.s. L. pp.160-62.

Cantril, Hadley. 1935. *The Psychology of Radio*. Harper and Bros.: London and New York.

Disher, M. Wilson. 1925. *Clowns and Pantomimes*. London: Constable & Co.

Dollard, John. 1937. *Caste and Class in a Southern Towns*. New Haven: Yale University Press.

Empson, William. 1938. *English Pastoral Poetry*. New York: W. W. Norton & Co. p. 30.

Fortune Magazine. December 1950, p. 91.

Johnson, Edgar, ed. 1945. *Treasury of Satire* . New York: Simon & Schuster.

Kitchin, G. 1931. *Burlesque & Parody in English* Edinburgh: Oliver and Boyd.

Murdock, G. P. 1949. *Social Structure*, New York: The Macmillan Co.

Parsons, Elsie Crews, and Ralph L. Beals. 1934 "The Sacred Clowns of the Pueblo and Mayo-Yaqui Indians," *American Anthropologist*, Vol. 36, 1934, pp. 491-514.

Pope, Ernest R. 1941. *Munich Playground*. New York: G. P. Putnam's Sons.

Radcliffe-Brown, A.R. 1940. "On Joking Relationships," *Africa*, XIII, pp. 195-210.

Steward, Julian. 1930. "The Ceremonial Buffoon of the American Indian." *Michigan Academy of Science, Arts and Letters*, Vol. 14.

Welford, Enid. 1935. *The Fool*. London: Faber & Faber.

3

The Literary Rhetoric of Science:
Comedy and Pathos in Drinking-Driver Research

Prologue: What It's All About

The Rhetoric of Research! The title imposes an obvious contradiction. Research is Science: the discovery and transmission of a true state of things. Rhetoric is Art. The Aristotelian definition defines it as "the faculty of observing in any given case the available means of persuasion" (Aristotle, 1941:1329). As such, Rhetoric is an art useful for the politician, the journalist, the speaker, the artist—the man or woman who seeks to move people to action. "It is chiefly involved with bringing about a condition, rather than discovering or testing a condition" (Bryant, 1965:18; Winterowd, 1968:14). It was the skill perfected by the Sophists and is associated with such nonscientific and nefarious processes as advertising, propaganda, and politics. It is the artist who needs rhetoric to produce a deliberate effect in the audience. Art is Art and Science and Science and the twain shall not meet. Is it not to replace Rhetoric and Art that Science has come into the world?

It has been customary to distinguish efforts to persuade through language—the activity of the artist—or through logic—the activity of

Reprinted from *American Sociological Review* 41:1 (February 1976):16-34. This paper grew out of research conducted while on a Guggenheim Fellowship. I am indebted to the John Simon Guggenheim Foundation for support. I have also gathered from the comments and advice of Richard Brown, Bennett Berger, Kenneth Donow, Paul Filmer, Frederick Jameson, Mary Johnson, Marcia Millman, and Kingsley Widmer.

the scientist. Albert Hofstadter has made this difference between scientific and literary uses of language the crux of his distinction between the two functions of Art and Science. The literary artist, maintains Hofstadter (1955), uses language as a significant vehicle for his or her activity. How objects and events are described or explained is more important than the subject matter of the narrative or poem. For the scientist this is not the case. Language is only a medium by which the external world is reported. That which is described and analyzed is not itself affected by the language through which it is reported.

> Put generally, the scientist searches for items which are involved with each other in patterns of dependence...the scientist's language is not one of these items...he must not allow his language to become part of the content of his assertion.

> The character of the imaginative object achieved by the artist depends on the character of the language he employs, whereas the language of the scientist does not operate within the involvement pattern he formulates. (Hofstadter, 1955: 294-295)

This is what I call the "windowpane" theory. It insists on the intrinsic irrelevance of language to the enterprise of Science. The aim of presenting ideas and data is to enable the audience to see the external world as it is. In keeping with the normative prescriptions of scientific method, language and style must be chosen that will approximate, as closely as possible, a pane of clear glass. As an empirical reality, the normative order of Science is approximated in this perspective. Scientists do express their procedures, findings, and generalizations in "neutral" language. Their words do not create or construct the very reality they seek to describe and analyze.

From another standpoint, such a neutralized use of language is an impossibility. Idealist philosophy has generally insisted on the important role of the observer to what is observed, but seldom has attention been drawn away from theories and concepts to the language of presentation, to scientific documents as communicating devices and cultural products. For that we have to go to the literary analysts. A viewpoint directly opposite to Hofstadter's is given by Northrop Frye (1957:331):

> Anything which makes a functional use of words will always be involved in all the technical problems of words, including rhetorical problems. The only road from grammar to logic, then, runs through the intermediate territory of rhetoric.

Frye's analysis of scientific work comes at the end of a major analysis of literature and is confined to general discussion. Literary critics have generally limited their art to the analysis of literature. With some major qualifications, discussed below, "the literary analysis of scientific knowledge" does not exist. Yet if words, sentences, paragraphs, and larger units are a major tool for reporting, and therefore persuading, an analysis of the way in which scientific knowledge leads to practical actions cannot ignore the language and literary style of science as an object of study.

That is just what I am going to do in this paper, presented in the form of a staged play, in order to make the metaphor of literature more obvious. My assertion is not that Science *is* Literature, but rather that we can treat Science *as if* it were Literature and that this metaphorical conceit will be productive. It will increase your and my understanding of the product and its implications for practical action. In this process, I may lead both of us to a better understanding of where the metaphor is both applicable and inapplicable (Brown, 1973; Turbayne, 1962). But let's continue the prologue.

The distinction between Science and Literature seems to me to be capable of two dimensions, to each of which I address this paper.

The literary Style of Science (the substance of Act I). The passage from philosopher Hofstadter is testimony to the intuitive hypothesis I've alluded to above. That passage implies that to be scientific is to exercise a definite form over the language in use, to write in a particular way that shows the audience that the writer is "doing science." The writer must persuade the audience that the results of the research are *not* literature, are *not* a product of the style of presentation. The style of nonstyle is itself the style of science. There is a literary art involved in scientific presentation.

The literary Art in Science (the substance of Act II). In this paper, I will look through and look at the content of science in its literary dimension. Frye (1957:74) maintains that in literature, unlike nonliterary prose, the "sign-values of symbols are subordinated to their importance as a structure of interconnected motifs." Yet if there is a literary character to scientific documents they will also display a certain autonomy of language. Efforts to be evocative, interesting, aesthetically pleasing and to make the work relevant and significant will contrast with the "windowpane" functions described by Hofstadter. The content of the research will itself be, in part, a result of its presentation. If all communication entails both an assertive, descriptive level and an aesthetic, artistic level, then the windowpane is never completely clear; there is always a streak of stained glass to capture our imagination and wonder.

The relevance of Art in Science (the substance of Act III). While there is an aesthetic joy in the game of analysis, my intents are not so purely artful. They also include the assertion that such analysis makes a difference, that the artistic side of science is a significant part of the scientist's display of the external world. Not only will I show the artistic side of science, but I will use that exposition to understand the product—the theory, generalization, or conclusion to which the work of the scientist has led. Most importantly, I will use it to shed light on the practical actions that emerge as prescriptive through this process of artful science.

My attention is not fixed on *the* Scientific Enterprise. It is both more modest and more searching. I narrow my vision at one set of windows—the research studies in the area of "driving while under the influence of alcohol." It is in the course of a larger book-length study of knowledge and policy in this area of social control that I was drawn to think about the literary qualities of scientific presentation. Certain aspects of that work led me to undertake a more careful reading of forty-five major research papers which have been alleged to be the bases for much political, legal, and medical policy toward "drinking driving" in the past twenty-three years, in Europe and the United States.

While I will allude to several of the papers in this area, one report has been chosen for a more thorough analysis. My method, especially in treating papers as narratives, is such that I need to analyze the framework of the paper as a unit. To do this for forty-five papers is impossible in a short paper. Accordingly, I have resorted to a literary device common to science—the use of the synecdoche—a literary device of representation in which a part substitutes for the whole. I selected one article for thorough concentration, to represent the system of literary analysis applied to a scientific document. This paper (Waller, 1967), "Identification of Problem-Drinking among Drunken Drivers," was chosen for two conscious reasons: (1) It has been influential, frequently cited by other research persons and in governmental documents as a base for advocating particular policies. (2) It represents a number of studies and papers which, in recent years, have operated as persuasive elements in a transformation of strategy toward the control of auto accidents associated with alcohol use.

Enough procrastination. On with the play!

Act I: Scientific Style: The Rhetoric of Method

How does the scientist proceed to establish his/her claim to be "doing science" and thus to be read in a "scientific" way by the audience? In the frame of the windowpane, the scientist does not ask for that "willing suspension of disbelief" with which Coleridge maintained the theatre audience accepted a stage in London as the Italian balcony of Romeo and Juliet. How does the scientist, however, act as dramatist, setting a stage and persuading his readers to treat his/her work as one type of production rather than another?

In this act of my play, I am developing the literary *genre* of the scientific report and my topic is not its content but its form. I will make use of two literary modes of analysis. Following Kenneth Burke (1945), I will examine the *dramatistic* keys in use, examining the use of scene, act, agent, agency, and purpose. The objective here is to "uncover" the placement of responsibility for describing the action described. With analysts of narrative fiction such as Henry James, Percy Lubbock (1957) and Wayne Booth (1961), I will utilize the concept of *voice* to explicate the relation of observer to observed and observer to audience which influences the point of view or stance of the writer toward his subject and his/her audience.

The Keys of Dramatism

What is the scenic surrounding of the paper? Scientific papers are not published randomly; they appear in a setting. The paper, "Identification of Problem-Drinking among Drunken Drivers," did not appear in *Playboy* magazine, in a collection of American short stories, or in a work on freshman composition. It is "placed" in the *Journal of the American Medical Association* (Waller, 1967). That setting establishes a claim for the paper to be taken as authoritative fact and not as fiction or imaginative writing. All of the forty-five documents were like this one in being found in settings dedicated to research rather than art. Most are in medical journals, some in journals devoted to automobile safety or safety in general. A substantial segment are found in the *Quarterly Journal of Studies on Alcohol,* and still another group are found in the proceedings of scholarly conferences on alcohol problems or specifically on the problem of drinking and driving. The *Journal of the American Medical Association* is not primarily an organ of news or professional advice. It contains accounts of new research in areas of physiology and medical science. In order to play in the game, the scientist must pick the proper field.

Act

What is the action of the paper? I want to show it as a form of narrative, a "story" that has movement with a beginning and an end involving change. The article begins with a title that describes a category, "drunken drivers," and an attribute, "problem-drinking," which is to involve an action, "identification." Following the article appears a summary of the paper to follow. It presents the paper in capsule form—the methods used and "findings"—such as, "High correlation was found between two or more arrests involving drinking and an impression of problem drinking" (Waller, 19670: 124). This summary presentation establishes the inference that what is significant about the paper can be separated from the larger body of language. The audience, if it so wishes, can get the crux of the play from the program. The stage production has a quality of embellishment.

Like a narrative, the first paragraph sets up a tension, which the paper will proceed to resolve. The audience is told that "it is becoming increasingly apparent that a substantial proportion of drivers who get into accidents after drinking or who are arrested for drunken driving are not social drinkers but rather persons with a long-standing drinking problem" (p.124). This assertion sets up a tension between this newer perspective toward drinking drivers and an older, conventional one in which drinking drivers are representative of the general population of drinkers—the social drinkers.

Unlike a short story or poem, the paper reaches out for its material beyond the self-contained confines of its own product. It refers to other studies, including some of the author's, as grounds for some of the assertions. Unlike the artistic product, the author also gives his denouement in the beginning. "This finding necessitates the reevaluation of current methods for preventing driving after drinking" (p.124).

It is in the unfolding of the story that the action of the paper occurs. Having foreshadowed the comment in the first paragraph, the author does not presume to leave the matter unexplicated. He follows a pattern: first, the description of the methods used to identify problem-drinking among drinking drivers; second, the results or findings of this method; last, the comment or significance of the results is placed at the end. This sequential arrangement places policy significance, what is to be done, as the outcome of methods that generate results. The activity supported and/or rejected appears as the culmination of method. This centrality of method and externality of data is the major key to the story. The resolution of the conflict or tension set up in the first paragraph involves a change away from a conventional perspective toward drinking drivers and toward a new perspective both in cognitive understanding and in policies to be espoused. In this sense, the flow, or action, of the paper is dramatic.

Agent

What is salient here and in our fuller discussion of the agent under the rubric of *voice*, below, is the hidden and unassuming posture of the observer. As the theory of the "windowpane" would suggest, the author must not intrude into the product. Yet the observer must also be trusted in a way not called for in artistic works. If the artist does not claim to be a reporter of the factual world but a constructor of imaginative and pleasurable products, his/her claim to veracity is not an essential part of the claim to artistic acceptance. James Joyce need not be accepted as a reliable producer of accounts of Dublin in the early 1900s in order for the reader to appreciate *A Portrait of the Artist as a Young Man*. The reader need not even know the author to appreciate the novel. But where the author attests to a world of real properties, his/her integrity and competence to report is a question.

The dilemma between personalizing and removing the agent seems to be solved in all but one of the forty-five papers by a device of identification through role. In this paper, following the title appear the name and credentials of the author: Julian A. Waller, M.D., M.P.H. At the bottom of the page, in footnote form, the author is described as someone connected with an organization: "From the Bureau of Occupational Health, California Department of Public Health. Dr. Waller is now with the Bureau of Chronic Diseases" (p.124). Thus the agent is described in a role (medical and public health) and in an organization.

Having told the audience about his professional competence and acceptance, the author must now move out of the limelight if the document is to be untainted by the obvious presence of the observer. The language chosen performs this function through an emphasis on the externality of the source of action and through the passive character of the agent. Viz: "It was decided to use this latter method" (Schmidt and Smart, 1959: 632); not: "We decided...." "The test indicates there is a significant difference" (Borkenstein, et al., 1964: 188); not: "Based on the test, we concluded...." "Data...confirm a self-evident fact" (Holcomb, 1938: 1084) and "Recent reports have suggested...." (Waller, 1966: 532) are other examples I culled from a variety of the papers studied.

In Waller's paper (nota bene: I have taken to personalizing the product), such circumlocutions are frequent. The active voice is absent. In the lead sentence, the author (by inference) writes: "It is increasingly becoming apparent...." But to whom? Throughout the paper the conclusion or result is portrayed as emerging from an external world of data or tables. "Differences were found..."; "This finding necessitates the reevaluation."

Agency

What this pattern of rejection of personal terms or active voice does is to place the source of action in the agency or method. Waller's paper creates a style consistent with "windowpane" theory by establishing a reality outside the observer. The style reinforces this externality and provides the basic epistemological assumption; by use of the same method different observers must reach the same conclusions.

Both the identification of the author in the beginning and the passivity of the style support the portrayal of a procedure in which the observer is governed by a method and by the rules of scientific integrity in relation to the method. He continues to make this point throughout the paper by following a regimen of meticulous attention to details and thereby avoiding a judgment by the reader that he has been less than scrupulous in following the method. Thus the percentages are given in decimals, such as 19.3 percent or 6.1 percent for samples ranging from 150 to 19 (Table I, p. 125). Where discretion had to be used, the event is meticulously described to avoid the implication of whimsy or bias:

One nondrinking driver involved in an accident also appeared in the drunken-driver sample. *For purposes of analysis* [italics mine] he was considered as a separate person in each group. (p. 125)

Purpose

That the author means to persuade his audience of certain conclusions is both evident and explicit. The importance of method substantiates the overall style of detachment. He means to persuade, but only by presenting an external world to the audience and allowing that external reality to do the persuading. Thus the language must be emptied of feeling and emotion. The tone must be clinical, detached, depersonalized. His language must not be "interesting," his descriptions colorful or his words a clue to any emotion which might be aroused in the audience. Beginning with the title, "Identification of Problem-Drinking among Drunken Drivers," the language is flat, prosaic, and descriptive without imagery. The title describes an object, "drunken drivers," and a set of attributes—problem-drinking—along with a process to be performed—identification. The title is not flamboyant, puzzling, or funny. Contrast a more journalistic title, "He Couldn't Help Himself," or a more literary one, at once ambiguous and intriguing, "The End of the Road." (The term "drunken driver" seems a contradiction to this style and will be discussed in considerable detail below.)

Let me pull these standards of analysis together. The style of the paper and its setting in a medical journal makes it recognizable not as art but as claiming to be science. The language is deliberate, nonevocative, meticulous, and limited in imagery. It informs the reader that the persuasion is to come from an external reality not from the author or his use of language. The description is minimally metaphorical. The intent is made to seem cognitive and logical rather than affective or emotional. We, the audience, are to think and not to feel. Although the author is not anonymous and is identified as a scientist in a governmental organization, the style of writing grounds the action of the paper in the agency of methodological procedures of data collection and analysis. The agent is minimized and the drama of the paper is presented as flowing from the unfolding of the procedures of method, not from the interests, biases, or language of the author.

Voice and Viewpoint

Literary criticism has been filled in past decades with the problem of point of view, especially in analyses of novels (Freidman, 1969). Since Flaubert and James, novelists have self-consciously attempted to place themselves less and less into their novels, hoping to persuade the reader not by telling him or her about the characters but by showing through action (Booth, 1961: Ch. 1). When the novelist characterizes the protagonists through descriptions of them, he is telling. When he presents the action and lets the audience infer character, then he is showing. "I am a Camera," wrote Christopher Isherwood in the first sentence of *The Berlin Stories*, "with its shutter open, quite passive, recording, not thinking."

The consideration of this problem leads to the analysis of the agent as narrator with a specific presentation of his point of view:

> Whether or not they are involved in the action as agents, narrators and third-person reflectors differ markedly according to the degree and kind of distance that separates them from the author, the reader and the other characters of the story they relate or reflect. (Booth, 1969:180)

Audience-Author Ratios

In emphasizing the passive voice of the author and his absence as a significant mover of events and conclusions, I described the observer as presenting himself as a "windowpane," if not a camera. In that sense, the author does not claim a special vantage point or viewpoint as compared to his audience. He is in the same seat, showing the observations that lead to conclusions. The audience knows as much and as little as the author. They are on an equal plane.

One frequently used device to achieve equality is, of course, the regal or editorial "we." I did not find this in Waller's paper. The consistent absence of any designation of the author is also reinforced by the passive voice by which action is described: "Information was obtained..."; "An impression was ventured...." Although we did not find it in Waller, other authors use the inclusive "we" to put themselves into the audience: "In accident research we [italics mine] are now past the stage...." (Hyman, 1968: 53).

The style of Waller's paper is that of an equivalence ratio between author and audience. The mode of writing reduces distance and avoids claims of authority or superior judgment on the part of the author. He seems to say: "I will give you, the reader, all the knowledge and factual information that I have. We will reason together and achieve a consensus through fact and reason. You, as a rational person, cannot *but* reach the same conclusion as I."

This ratio of author to audience can, of course, be distinguished from others where the ratio is more or less than unitary equivalence. When the author tells instead of showing, he claims authority and distance from a viewpoint above the reader, in command of greater skill or special knowledge, as a scientist addressing a lay public or as Joseph Fielding writing in his novels. When the opposite is the case, the author shows the reader and leaves to him or her to make of it what he or she wishes, as in a Pirandello play or in some modern forms of ethnography. Even in our sample of papers, we found one or two instances where the author presented a set of findings and would not interpret or order them into a set of conclusions (Gerber, 1963).

Distance and Subject

Who is the author in relation to the subjects he studies? Is he one of them? Is he decidedly not among those he describes? What is his stance and distance toward the object of study? The endless discussions of objectivity and political morality in science since Marx have continuously posed the questions of point of view as a major one for the ethics of the scientist. Recently, Robert Merton has posed this question in spatial terms by referring to "insiders" and "outsiders" (Merton, 1972). The problem is analogous to that of distance in literary analysis.

The clinical style of Waller's paper preserves the stance of the outsider by looking at drinking drivers as a group of whom the author, and thus the audience, is not a part. He has neither loyalty nor economic interest in them. They are "objects of study" and not members of the audience. His paper is not addressed to drinking drivers. Nowhere are any of the sampled groups referred to as including the author or the audience. Both author and audience are presented as "outsiders." Not drinking drivers themselves, they take the stance of observers of the nonself.

Is the stance one of equivalence? In the first paragraph, the author speaks of the need to reevaluate "current methods for preventing driving after drinking" (p. 124). Throughout the paper there is no doubt whose "side" he is on. Nor is there any evidence of an effort to persuade the audience of the wisdom of this "side." It is taken for granted. The author, and inferentially the audience, are superior to the subjects in that they are distant from and above the behavior of drinking and driving.

The stance or viewpoint of the author is one of equivalence with his audience but superiority to his subjects. As an appeal to the persuasive power of reason, it is the style of Science to minimize Rhetoric, to negate and downplay evidence of viewpoint. Wayne Booth's characterization of fiction is inconsistent with the "windowpane" theory of Science:

> In short, the author's judgment is always evident to anyone who knows how to look for it....As we begin to deal with this question, we must never forget that though the author can to some extent choose his disguises, he can never choose to disappear. (Booth, 1961: 20)

You, the reader, and I are now at the end point of Act I, where the playwright reveals his dialectical hand. By now you have probably suspected what is the case. I will begin to assert that *A* is *non-A,* that what Wayne Booth has written about Fiction, I will assert about Fact. Art and Rhetoric have not been sent into perpetual exile to live outside the walls of Science and Knowledge. With or without passport, they steal back into the havens of clinical and antiseptic scholarship and operate from underground stations to lead forays into the headquarters of the enemy.

Curtain

End of Act I

Act II: Literary Art: The Rhetoric of Substance

I have shown you the stage. It is time to produce the play itself, to attend to contents after having seen the package. The first act has been the rhetoric of method—the style of Science. The second act is the rhetoric of substance—the presentation of the phenomena revealed by the study.

As a device to facilitate the discussion of Waller's paper, I reproduce the summary that is placed at the beginning of the article. It is a "quick and dirty" overview:

Information about previous contact with community agencies, particularly contact involving drinking problems, was compared for 150 drunken drivers, 33 accident-involved drivers who had been drinking but were not arrested, 117 sober drivers involved in accidents, 131 drivers with moving violations, 19 drivers with citations plus arrest warrants, and 150 incident-free drivers. Screening criteria for problem drinkers were two or more previous arrests involving drinking or identification by a community agency as a problem drinker. These criteria were met by the following: drunken drivers, 63%; drivers with an accident after drinking, 50%; drivers with warrants, 30%; nondrinking drivers with an accident, 14%; persons with driving violations, 8%; and drivers with no incidents, 3%. High correlation was found between two or more arrests involving drinking and an impression of problem drinking. Eighty-seven percent of the drunken drivers were known to community agencies, most with multiple contacts starting before age 30. (p. 124)

Reduction to Substance: The Whatness of the Object

Let me begin at the beginning—the title and the first sentence. What is the object of study as it is described by the author? The title contains a significant term that contrasts with the nonemotive and clinical character of the paper and the general tone of the title: "Drunken." This is a specific image, far more concrete than the "weaker" and more general term "drinking." A "drunken driver" is not only a more opprobrious figure, it is also a more visual image joined to the commonsense experience and imagination of the audience with drunkenness. It may, as it does to me, convey the sense of a reeling, incoherent, unreasonable and thus unpredictable and dangerous person. Yet the first sentence shows the reader a somewhat different object, less specific and less of a specific image. What was studied were "...drivers who get into accidents after drinking or who are arrested for drunken driving" (p. 124). While Waller consistently refers to "drunken drivers," what he studies were persons arrested for violating legal restrictions against "driving under the influence of alcohol." Generally, this is evidenced by a chemo-mechanical test, which measures the blood-alcohol count. In Oakland, California, where the study was conducted, the maximum count considered "legal" is 0.10 milligrams per milliliter of blood. The point of this is that arrests with or without accidents are not evidence of "drunkenness" in a commonsense or lay conception.

With the first sentence and the title, the author has already converted "fact" into imagery; he has changed or reduced the data to something else. He has determined which aspects of the events—accidents after drinking—shall be highlighted. The issue of reductionism is crucial, both to Science and to this paper. It is a major way in which the research scientist makes sense or relevance out of his work. "Metonymy," wrote Kenneth Burke, "is a device of 'poetic realism' but its partner 'reduction' is a device of 'scientific realism'" (Burke, 1945: 506). The terms in which the object is described has, in Waller's paper, already involved a reduction in one direction and a rejection of others.

The issue of the object has other levels of analysis significant for the ultimate conclusions and policy advised. Here Waller's usage is similar to that of most of the work in the field of "drinking driving." It attempts to uncover the substantial attributes of the driver as a relatively permanent component of personality and/or social habits. In defining and analyzing the "drinking driver," Waller, like others, narrows the range of matters connected with the events being studied. The language used leads toward one particular channel of narrowing and away from others.

The concept of "drinking driver" emphasizes the agent and minimizes the scene or the act or the agency as possible elements in accidents. "Drinking driver" imputes, as I see it, an attribute of selves. There are drinking drivers and nondrinking drivers as there are male and female drivers, old and young drivers, competent and incompetent drivers. Both "drinking driver" and "drunken driver" lead to the search for attributes of the person which exist and extend before, during, and after the action of driving. Even within the terminology of "driver" other circumlocutions in use, though less frequent, direct attention toward aspects of the driving situation. "The alcohol-impaired driver" or the "intoxicated driver" place the driver in a context and make the extensiveness of the attributes less certain and more ambiguous.

It is possible also to dispense with the "driver" as an object and to describe the "same" phenomena with terms that indicate placement or scene or act. The phrase "persons engaged in drinking driving" or even "drinking driving" contrast with "drinking driver" by underlining the situational character of the event being examined.

These differences between "driver" and "driving" are not random choices of grammar. They reflect the significant perspectives of psychology and sociology, respectively—the difference between a drama of agent and a drama of scene. In his title and in his opening sentence, Waller has pulled the audience into the perspective of psychology and into a search for abiding characteristics of the personalities of persons.

Metaphor: The Transformation of the Drinking Driver

Waller's paper is one of several major research studies that have resulted in a transformed perspective toward the drinking driver in governmental and legal circles. His study design influences which of two major perspectives should be utilized in thinking about drinking drivers and in developing policies to minimize drinking driving. These perspectives are expressed through two central terms or metaphors: the *social drinker* and the *problem drinker*. What is happening in this paper can be expressed as the dramatic reconceptualization of the drinking driver from the metaphor of the social drinker to the metaphor of the problem drinker.

I refer to these as "metaphors" because they are used to extend the meaning of primary data. They are not descriptions of the factual information collected but are instead presentations of that data in a form that creates linkages to something already known by the audience. They heighten perception by extending the primary data into another realm. Utilizing Max Black's interaction theory of metaphor (Black, 1962), Mary Hesse has stated the view of metaphor I used here:

> The metaphor works by transferring the associated ideas and implications of the secondary to the primary system. These select, emphasize or suppress features of the primary; new slants on the primary are illuminated; the primary is seen through the frame of the secondary. (Hesse, 1966: 232)

It is the major conclusion of Waller's paper that, contrary to the then conventionally held view, "a substantial proportion" of drinking drivers are problem drinkers and not, as formerly believed, social drinkers. A "large" number of drinking drivers also had arrest records involving the use of alcohol or had been diagnosed by one or more community service agencies as having a problem involving alcohol use. Such records and/or diagnoses were found only among a "small" proportion of the nondrinking drivers.

It is again the first paragraph in which the author tells his audience the nature of the two types found among drinking drivers: the drinking driver qua social drinker and drinking driver qua problem drinker. Present methods for diminishing drinking driving assume, he says, that "the erring driver has committed his act *rationally but foolishly* " (p.124). The opposite type, the problem drinker as drinking driver, is contrasted with this social drinker as "psychosocial *pathology* rather than social misjudgment" [italics mine].

In this paragraph and throughout the paper, Waller touches the central issue of knowledge and policy toward drinking driving: Are such drivers who threaten to cause accidents to be seen as ordinary citizens whose habits of alcohol use are "normal" for American life? Or are they extraordinary people whose drinking habits are "abnormal" for American life? If the former is the case, then the drinking driver can be seen as a generally conforming person whose occasional lapse is not a sign of a basic attribute connected with antisocial behavior. He or she is not a deviant person. Insofar as the latter is the case, the drinking driver is less controllable, more compulsive, and less amenable to change through reason and persuasion.

The contrast is continued in the manner of description. The actions of the ordinary citizen are not venal. He is "social": conforming and not compulsive. He may act foolishly, but there is a basic attribute of rational capacity and attitude. He is "not likely to repeat his indiscretion" (p. 126), unlike the problem drinking driver who "does not learn from a punitive experience" (p. 129). He is "engulfed in the deluge of alcohol-related problems" (p.12).

The "root metaphor"—the basic metaphorical system around which the distinctions are drawn—is essentially organic-medical (Bruyn, 1966:137; Brown, 1973). The population of drinking drivers is seen through the lenses of medical language. Some are "normal" and others are "pathological." Both terms are repeated in describing, respectively, the two types of drivers and the two types of drinkers in the society. Social drinkers are normal citizens and their drinking driving is not symptomatic of deviation from attributes of the *healthy* person. Problem drinkers are *unhealthy* and their drinking driving emanates from a flawed and unhealthy personality.

Myth and Archetype: The Production of the Morality Play

Literary critics have frequently pointed out the recurrent use of certain stock characters and types as the basis for themes and patterns in contemporary literature. Such archetypes constitute a major device by which the artist enables the reader to identify the new through the form of the old. Sociologists, using a literary metaphor, have expressed the same idea in concepts of "social role," "social types" and "ideal typology." Frye refers to such common patterns of typology as "myths" in that they draw upon already shared images, stories, and events:

> Realism, or the art of verisimilitude, evokes the response "How like that is to what we know." When what is written is *like* what is known, we have an art of extended or implied simile. And as realism is an art of implicit simile, myth is an art of implicit metaphorical identity. (Frye, 1957: 136)

In order to create theoretical and generalizable knowledge, the author must link the specific objects of his/her study to more universal categories of persons and events with which the audience is already familiar (Gusfield, 1975). Unless he chooses such types, the knowledge will exist at the level of history or ethnography; descriptive of a particular time, a particular place, a particular set of people. Social roles, such as "the father" or literary myths, such as the story of Œdipus, become conventionalized forms through which the objects can be described. Such myths and archetypes bear a distinct relation to scientific models. The model of a frictionless system enables physicists to "talk about" motion; the model of a "primary group" enables the sociologist to "talk about" human relationships. The similarity between this analogical process in science and in literature led Max Black (1962: 241), in his discussion of models, to refer to them as "conceptual archetypes."

It is in the light of types seen as myths that we can again analyze the major contrasts in Waller's paper between drinking drivers and nondrinking drivers and between "social drinkers" and "problem drinkers." All of these are types with which there is familiarity, in actual or vicarious experiences, or both. They constitute stock themes in popular literature and drama as well as in news and common talk. The idea of the "killer drunk" is one such character whose irresponsibility and commitment to an hedonistic style of life creates tragedy for others. The very use of the term "drunken" in the title constitutes an invocation of the theme in the context of persons who have come to official attention equally through arrest for drinking driving or through accidents in which the offense is uncovered. So too, the usage "social drinker" carries an implication of contrasts to "drunken." Suppose Waller had referred to "problem drinkers" and "social drunks"? In this alternative usage, he would have referred to that category of persons who, on occasion, drink to drunkenness but whose action does not express an addictive problem. This behavior is quite common in a large segment of Americans (Cahalan, et al., 1969).

The typology thus operates to label and stigmatize drinking drivers as "problem drinkers" and to exonerate and label the "social drinkers" as responsible citizens who have slipped but whose dereliction is not a reflection of a personal flaw. The root term of "normal" and "pathological" continues to place these groups in the image of the archetypal forms. The drinking drivers are analogized to the problem drinkers and characterized within the terms of the myth of the drinker as deviant, outcast, and stigmatized. "Engulfed in the deluge of alcohol-related problems" they are described in the following way:

> The central theme in the lives of the drunken drivers seems to be alcohol. Almost three-quarters of their many arrests involved drinking. Their marriages often were in a state of dissolution because of excessive drinking. Among drunken drivers, arrest reports commonly observed that the person had been arrested for assaulting his wife when he arrived home intoxicated and she began scolding him for his alcoholic pattern. (p.129)

Waller has given the audience a strong depiction of the stock figure of the drinker as deviant. Agency workers, whose records Waller utilized, had found drinking problems in only one-fourth of the cases and made a medical judgment of alcoholism in only one-tenth. Waller explained this contradiction to his findings by saying that the agency workers had used the stock image of gross intoxication and the "skid row bum." Nevertheless, his portrayal comes close to that stock figure. Writing of the sample of persons with arrest warrants out for failing to answer citations in nondrinking, moving violations, Waller writes that they "also [italics mine] represent a

population with profound psychosocial pathology" (p. 129). In analyzing the drinking drivers, he refers to a subtype as "sociopathic."
Summing up, the author says that "it is not possible to escape the
conclusion that this group of persons does not learn from a punitive
experience" (p.129).

If the problem drinker has been stigmatized as responsible for
drinking driving and the drinking driver stigmatized as a deviant
drinker, in this process the "social drinker," the "solid citizen" of
conviviality, has been "taken off the hook" and absolved from deviance. The contrasting archetype—the social drinker—is an "erring
driver" when he strays. He is a man of rationality and basic goodwill
who "can be dissuaded." Such men are not very likely to be drinking
drivers. When he is the drinking driver, a "social drinker might
[italics mine] err once in the excessive use of alcohol sufficient to
result in his arrest, but he would not be likely to repeat his indiscretion" (p. 126). If not exactly heroic, the social drinker is neither
villainous nor venal.

The implicit use of stock forms has enabled the author to produce
a morality play in which drinking driving is an arena for the expression of personal and moral character. The social drinker is
Everyman—rational, socially responsible, given to occasional and
human lapses of conduct but basically law abiding, controllable and
controlling, and responsive to norms of social cooperation. The Boy
Scout of the highways, he can be trusted to carry out the dictates of a
rational and interdepending society with a minimum of guidance and
force to keep him from going off the road. Not so the problem
drinker. He is the Juvenile Delinquent of traffic. Irresponsible, compulsive, and irrational, his drinking is part of his social defiance and
deviance.

The Rhetoric of Action

The author is not content to stop before the open window. After
showing the audience, Waller also *tells* them how the study changes
proscribed behavior. Assuming a shared interest between himself and
his audience in minimizing the phenomena of drinking driving, he
draws implications for how the audience should now formulate policies to that end. His message is directed to an audience of policy
makers or advisors to policy makers and not to drinking drivers or to
persons who may be drinking drivers. "This finding necessitates the

reevaluation of current methods for preventing driving after drinking"
(p. 124).

The policy argument of "Identification of Problem-Drinking among
Drunken Drivers" is that the apparatus of law enforcement cannot
control drinking driving effectively because the drinking driver is usually a medical and not a legal problem. The assumptions of law,
according to Waller, are couched in the image of the "social drinker";
they expect that the delinquent or potential delinquent is a rationally
motivated person whose behavior and future behavior can be influenced by fear of punishment. Instead, the drinking driver problem
must confront the "problem drinker," who cannot exercise sufficient
self-control to permit rational considerations to operate. The central
paragraph reads as follows:

> Among the drunken drivers, the 971 previous arrests, 694 of which were due
> to drinking, represent a pathetic monument to the failure of the punitive
> approach to prevent further difficulty with drinking. With the current avail-
> ability of more appropriate methods to treat and rehabilitate those with a
> drinking problem, we must look with utter amazement at the determined
> employment of techniques that have so completely proven their futility. Cur-
> rent methods for treating alcoholism are highly successful in a quarter to a
> third of patients and at least partially successful in a substantial proportion of the
> remainder. (p. 124)

Put in Burke's terms, Waller has produced a transformation of
scene, from the law courts to the hospital or clinic. Having
reconceptualized the drinking driver from a delinquent to a patient, he
has diminished the significance of legal measures as appropriate policy
and increased the importance of medical practice as a major procedure
for solving the problem of drinking and driving. The audience must
now look to themselves—doctors, alcohol treatment personnel, experts on alcoholism—rather than to lawyers and police as the effective
agents of social policy in this arena.

It is noteworthy that as the author proceeds to draw action implications, the "measured cadence" of the scientific style gives way to a
brisker pace and a more emotive, imperative language. Phrases like
"patent failure," "pathetic monument," "look with utter amazement"
appear. As Frye has pointed out, when the author moves to persuade
the audience to action, the "strategic withdrawal from action," which
characterized the reporting of methods and findings, gives way to a
faster rhythm and a more emotive style (Frye, 1957: 327). Most of the

imagery alluded to in this paper has come from the introduction and the final section labeled "Comment."

So we bring the second act to an end on an upbeat. The courts have moved off center and to the side. In their place the medical and paramedical practitioners of alcoholism treatment have taken the starring roles. The audience of the *Journal of the American Medical Association* can paraphrase Pogo and say, "We have found the solution and the solution is us."

Curtain

End of Act II

Act III: The Rhetoric of Social Hierarchies

The drama of drinking driver research, especially as exemplified in Waller's study, may now be seen as a dialectical process in which the main character—the drinking driver—has been transformed from acceptable social drinker to stigmatized problem drinker. In what follows, I assert that this transformation also involved the disestablishment of one form of social hierarchy and its replacement by another. Through the medium of research as drama, the phenomenon of hierarchy is itself re-presented and emerges as something different from its appearance at the opening curtain.

The Hierarchy of Drinkers as Social Hierarchy

The analysis of drinking drivers and their drinking patterns, as signified by Waller's study, has provided the audience with a shift in the hierarchical character of the major actors. In this shift the social drinker has been "upgraded" by being exonerated from the charge of responsibility for auto accidents. The "drinking driver" has been "degraded" by being equated with the "problem drinker." That very equation further stigmatizes the already labeled deviant status of the "problem drinker." As the play has been acted out, what was down has come up and what was up has come down. The social drinker regains the aura of Everyman while the drinking driver is now "pathological"—marginal and deviant. In this fashion the gap between law abider and law avoider has been widened. The social drinker has moved up the hierarchy of deserved esteem while the drinking driver has, in a veritable *double entendre*, been "put down" (Burke, 1945).

The distinction, and its correlative hierarchy, is also one that is congruent to social structure. It is invested with hierarchies of class, race, and ethnic diversities. Akin with many recent studies of drinking driving, Waller does more than locate the drinking driver on a spectrum of drinkers. He also locates the drinking driver, qua problem drinker, in the social structure of American society. Consistent with other studies of the drinking driver, Waller supports the view of drinking drivers and problem drinkers as resident in the lowest income and status levels (Cosper and Mozersky, 1968; Hyman, 1968). He reports that blacks comprised 49 percent of the drunken drivers but only 25 percent of the driver population of Oakland, site of the study. Drivers of Mexican and American Indian descent were 11 percent of the drunken drivers, but 2-4 percent of the total population of drivers. Even though qualified, the image of the low status of the drinking driver emerges. In discussing information about arrest records, Waller writes:

> Nonwhite drivers consistently had larger proportions with arrests, and had more arrests per person. However the differences were not significant at P < 0.05 except for drivers of Mexican or Indian extraction with violations. (p. 128)

In an earlier study (Waller and Turkel, 1966), the authors found a statistically significant difference based on race. Among auto fatalities, blacks were more likely to have had alcohol present in the blood than were whites and were also more likely to have a record of arrests for public intoxication or evidence of cirrhosis of the liver or both. Blood alcohol levels were higher among drinking whites than among drinking blacks, however. Commenting on these findings the authors remarked:

> There is reason to believe that the predominant subculture among American Negroes is fairly tolerant toward the use of alcohol, explaining the observed differences. However, heavy drinking is not over-represented among Negro fatalities. (Waller and Turkel, 1966: 535)

Note that in both papers the image of the black as problem drinker is introduced and then qualified, rather than being presented directly as a qualified or ambiguous image.

What has happened is that the problem of drinking driving has now been located at the bottom of the social structure. As one research report states it (Cosper and Mozersky, 1968: 110), "class differences, although present, are not great except for the marked disparity between the poorest, least educated persons and the rest of the population." Although the equation of social structure and problem drinker is not completely supported by all investigators (nonclass religious and ethnic differences are also viewed as significant), the emergence of the problem drinker as drinking driver and the location of one major source of problem drinkers in the lowest categories of the social hierarchy does place the problem outside the scene of the solid citizen problemless drinkers. As long as the social drinker was the potential source of the problem of auto accidents due to drink, it constituted an impeachment of a prevalent style of stable middle- and working-class drinking habits. Caught between pressures and self-imposed demands for "tough" enforcement and the perception of drinking driving as a "normal" crime of "normal" people, police and courts have had difficulty in response. The findings in Waller's paper provide a happy solution to the moral dilemma posed at the beginning of the paper by the imputation of dereliction as a general trait of ordinary, lawful people. The problem has been shifted to people who are "sick" and quite likely morally suspect anyway. Thus the social structure and the legitimacy of social hierarchy are reinforced and the possibility of degradation dispelled.

Comedy and Tragedy in Social Structures

If this is a literary analysis of a document, what is the mood of the writing? Is it comedy, tragedy, tragicomedy, or farce? I look for the answer in the final character of the main protagonists—the social drinker and the problem drinker. The importance of the question goes beyond closure of a literary analysis. To determine the mood of the writing will help you and me to understand the kind and quality of the emotive response that the writer of the document may attempt to control in the reader.

Whatever the state of the social drinker as an object of feeling in the original scene, at the conclusion, I assert, he has been cast as a comic figure. His is the classic comic drunk: a figure of stability and established position who has temporarily lost his balance. He is not portrayed as being inherently and through personal makeup a menace to community, either on the road, in his familial life, or in his roles as worker and citizen. His drinking, and even his driving after drinking, become comic. They are neither venal, "sociopathic," "pathological," nor recurrent and threatening to the audience. Drunkenness as an unusual, episodic event in the life of a stable person is a comic event, classically introduced in comedic scenes in drama. When the drunken behavior is perceived as a constant, compulsive event, filled with recurrent threat to self and others, the same event becomes frightening and "tragic," in contrast to comic.

But the drinking driver, qua problem drinker, is not the tragic figure of literary history. Victim of his own incapacity to control his drinking and possibly socialized to a lifestyle which prevents a change in his habits of leisure, he cannot change himself even under the sanction of legal punishment and the fear of death through accident. Yet his is not the story of the great man fallen from high places and powerless to regain the seat of power. No Œdipus he. The source of his own and others' destruction, he is a powerless figure whose stigmata are not offset by any ribbons of glory.

The Descent into Pathos and Therapy

Neither major figure of Waller's drama is heroic nor villainous. The social drinker is at worst foolish, at best the rational man. Neither he nor the problem drinker, his contrasting image, is a tiny man caught in large indifferent or malevolent forces, which shape their destinies, "rough hew them though they may." If the problem drinker is tragic, it is in the sense of a low mimetic tragedy, a pathetic soul rather than a tragic one. In his lowly status and his compulsive drives, he is a figure of pathos, outside identification with the audience of readers and the author. His troubles stem from his indulgence and lack even the sense of being the outcome of otherwise laudable motives carried to excess, as Macbeth "o'erleaps" his own ambitiousness.

What deeply distinguishes this drama from many literary tragedies is its "*deus ex machina* "—the intervention of the author, the audience, and the profession of alcoholism treatment. An array of hope, in the form of counselors, screeners, and practitioners, is available to redeem the pathetic drinker through the vehicle of therapy. This Utopian strain of social engineering lifts the drama above the mood of despair and finality that high mimetic tragedy entails. No agency for the blind can help Œdipus nor can old-age assistance restore Lear.

Scientific Feeling: The Union of Form and Substance

I have now pushed myself into a patent contradiction. The style of a nonemotive language has created a whole bucketful of emotions—comic, tragic, pathetic. But the language of science is not quite that of literature and the arousal of feeling is much more ambiguous here than on the stage. While Waller describes the problem drinker he does not tell us, the audience, how we are to feel toward that central character. When I call the drinking driver "pathetic," I do so by reference to my feelings aroused by the paper and those I expect the "ordinary" reader would have, as indicated by my experience with how such people as those likely to read Waller's paper have responded to the problem drinker in other contexts and other places.

It is significant that the language through which the writer has tried to describe his characters is couched in the nonemotive forms already described above, rather than the more direct phrases with which a novelist or playwright might try to arouse feeling in his readers. It is the muting of feeling that is itself the characteristic mood, emotion, or feeling of the paper, viewed as a literary document. In this is its author's stance toward the object of study—the drinking driver—and whatever feeling he might otherwise arouse in the reader. The drinking driver stands as an object outside the emotional ambit of the writer and the reader. In this sense, pathos is to be checked, limited, and even obliterated as a reaction of the audience.

It is important that the only clear use of emotional language appears in the paper when the author describes not the actors—the drinking driver—but those officials who create policy toward the actors. In the quotations above, the author emerges from hiding to score past policy as a "pathetic monument" and to view it with "utter amazement." Here is anger, scorn, and irony.

The avoidance or limitation of feeling provides the writer, and therefore attempts to persuade the reader, with the necessary accompaniment to his identification with the "society" as victim. To see the "problem drinker" in highly differentiated or individual terms or to view him as an object of emotional concern would make the problem of drinking driving less clear and the objective of social control more problematic. To be punitive, as the law has been according to Waller, or benevolent, as an "underdog sociology" might entail (Becker, 1967; Gouldner, 1968), would be to adopt a very different stance: less functional, less efficient, less concerned with rational maximization of benefits and minimization of costs. Waller's critique of law and his support of medical therapy is an argument based on effectiveness for social functioning. The drinking driver is neither villain nor hero. He must be helped because he creates "trouble" for other folks, such as his readers.

Form and substance combine. In placing the drinking driver downward in the social structure and in constructing him as a neutral object, control is enhanced. In order to consider the social costs and benefits, the reader and the policy maker are cautioned to mute their feelings toward the specific and particular qualities—loathsome or appealing—of drinking drivers and see them as types and view them from the stance of the organization and the society. Both language and feeling, imagery and emotion, are those of Olympian hierarchy and organizational logic—*sans passion, sans irae.*

Curtain

End of Act III

Epilogue: What is to be Done?

When I first presented some of these ideas before a faculty seminar at Goldsmith's College, University of London, the question was raised: Am I not also utilizing the devices of Art in my analysis? Is not my critical stance toward the author misplaced since I, too, might similarly "put down" my own performance? This criticism invites me to provide an analysis and a rationale for the status of the scientific document as something purporting to be accepted as a "true" account. By invoking a description of Science as Art, have I now diminished or effaced the claim of Science to be doing Science and not Art?

Another criticism much related to the first came from the editor of the *American Sociological Review* in his letter asking me to revise this paper:

> [D]o you intend your own rhetoric to be a stimulus to action? What sort of action? Should there be any change in the practice of scientific rhetoric? For example, does it have positive or negative functions for "science"?

Both sets of critics ask me to go beyond *showing* that scientific documents can be examined as if they were works of art. They want me to tell readers what I conclude from the performance: to produce a policy. I will try to do that in this final section.

One possible response is that Waller has been deficient as a scientist. Indeed, my critics at Goldsmith's felt that I myself had, through irony, taken a tone of moral and intellectual superiority toward him: that I had been a "smartass." Unfortunately, there is no denying it. The transformation of the author from competence to unawareness is implicit in criticism. But that "deficiency" is not a personal failing, a breach in the author's operation within the standards and canons of scientific method. It is implicit and inherent in the enterprise of defining, describing, and interpreting data through verbal or written communication insofar as conclusions and generalizations imply meanings for action.

This paper is part of a larger study of the way knowledge relates to policy and to strategies for the solution of public issues. What interests me in this case is how it is that knowledge is, and is not, usable and used as a prescription to action. My concern is with the transfer of statements of fact into statements of policy, exactly the procedure used to produce conclusions of action from descriptions of knowledge.

It is precisely in the acts of developing and presenting particular data as classified into general categories, the very nub of theorizing and/or conclusion making, that acts of selection, of nomenclature, artistic presentation, and language emerge. Waller is not accused of "bad" science. His procedure is normal to the effort of scientific procedures to make sense out of the world and to couch that sense in a form related to activity. To be relevant or significant, data must not only be selected, they have to be typified and interpreted. In doing this, language and thought are themselves the vehicles through which such relevance is cast. In Burke's terms they are "modes of action" (Burke, 1941; 1945: xxii). They lead us to conclusions and thus to new perspectives. It is not that Science is "reduced" to Rhetoric, and thus rendered corrupt and useless. It is rather that the rhetorical component *seems* to be unavoidable if the work is to have a theoretical or a policy relevance. Thus an analysis of scientific work *should* also include its rhetorical as well as its empirical component (Gusfield, 1975). Science is thus a form of action with meanings derived from its Art as well as its Science (Geertz, 1973).

This analysis of Science as literature is by no means inconsistent with "normal" science as a truth-begetting instrument. It points, however, to the multiple realities in which and through which it may be construed. Some years ago I was driving across the country with a friend who was then a radio announcer. On hearing a news broadcast with a stirring news event, I remarked, "Did you hear that?" My friend answered, "Yes. His diction is terrible." As Schutz (1970: 245–262) and more recently Goffman (1974) have both shown and told, there are many possible realities within which an event can be framed. At this level, the literary criticism of Science is a way of revealing other processes, other realities at work besides the "normal" method of scientific discovery and verification. What is important and significant at least in the analysis of the drinking driver literature presented here, is that such an analysis heightens our recognition of the ways in which the objects—in this case drinkers and drivers—are being transformed in a dramatic presentation.

But at another level, represented by the sections analyzing the transformations of meaning in the objects of policy, the dramaturgical and artistic components of Science are not so consistent with the view of Science as positive knowledge. Examined reflexively, my own words carry a ring of skepticism toward the policies that are presented by Waller as flowing from an objective body of knowledge. It is not that the author is "wrong" in concluding that drinking drivers can be seen as problem drinkers. It is that his interpretation involves theatre—it involves a performance and a presentation that contains an element of choice and both enlists and generates a context, a set of meanings that give content and imagery to his data. The analysis of the document as a literary performance has revealed the human actions through which the transformation of the social drinker into the problem drinker has occurred. It is not, at least in this analysis, that the data is challenged. What is at stake, however, is the necessity of the interpretation and the close connection between that interpretation and its form of presentation, its artistic element. It is in underlining the tenuousness and ambiguity of conclusions that I cannot blink at having called into question the certainty and stability of scientific interpretation. My perspective here is akin to Peter Gay's depiction of the confidence and "ideological myopia" of the Enlightenment *philosophes*:

> They never wholly discarded that final, most stubborn illusion that bedevils realists—the illusion that they were free from illusions. (Gay, 1966: 27)

I bring this paper to a close with three suggestions of what is potentially available through a development of science as a literary genre. First, it heightens the self-understanding and awareness of what we, social scientists, do as we transform research into written reports, into words which have connotations in action as well as abstract knowledge. Second, it enables the analyst of social issues to appreciate and explore how he or she contributes to what Herbert Blumer (1971) calls "the process of collective definition" through which objective conditions are transformed into public problems and policies.

Last, there is a contribution that such analysis can make to public policy. In being attentive to the elements of language and choice involved in giving meanings to data, the analyst calls attention to the singularity and selective activity through which policy implications are drawn. In doing this, it becomes more likely that social scientists and others can create, explore, and develop the potential variety of other interpretations and policies that would otherwise remain unnoticed and unavailable. It is this capacity to recognize the context of unexamined assumptions and accepted concepts that is among the most valuable contributions through which social science enables human beings to transcend the conventional and create new approaches and policies.

References

Aristotle. 1941. *Basic Works*. Tr. by Richard P. McKeon. New York: Random House.

Becker, Howard. 1967. "Which Side Are You On?" Social Problems 14:239–247.

Black, Max. 1962. *Models and Metaphors*. Ithaca, NY: Cornell University Press.

Blumer, Herbert. 1971. "Social Problems as Collective Behavior." *Social Problems* 18:298–306.

Booth, Wayne. 1961. *The Rhetoric of Fiction*. Chicago: University of Chicago Press.

_____. 1969. "Distance and Viewpoint." In R. M. Davis, ed., *The Novel: Modern Essays in Criticism*. Pp. 171–191. Englewood Cliffs, NJ: Prentice-Hall.

Borkenstein, R. F., R. F. Crowther, R. P. Shumate, W. B. Ziel, and R. Zylman. 1964. *The Role of the Drinking Driver in Traffic Accidents*. Bloomington, IN: Department of Police Administration, Indiana University.

Brown, Richard. 1973. "An Aesthetic for Sociology: Toward a Logic of Discovery for the Human Sciences." Unpublished Ph.D. dissertation, University of California, San Diego.

Bruyn, Severyn. 1966. *The Human Perspective*. Englewood Cliffs, NJ: Prentice-Hall.

Bryant, Donald. 1965. "Rhetoric: Its Function and Scope." In J. Schwartz and J. Rycenga, eds., *The Province of Rhetoric*. Pp. 3–36. New York: Ronald Press.

Burke, Kenneth. 1941. *The Philosophy of Literary Form*. New York: Random House.

_____. 1945. *A Grammar of Motives*. New York: Prentice-Hall.

Cahalan, Don, Ira Cisin, and Helen Crossley. 1969. *American Drinking Practices.* New Brunswick, NJ: Rutgers Center of Alcohol Studies.

Cosper, Ronald, and Kenneth Mozersky. 1968. "Social Correlates of Drinking and Driving." *Quarterly Journal of Studies on Alcohol* (Supp. No. 4):58–117.

Frye, Northrop. 1957. *Anatomy of Criticism.* Princeton, NJ: Princeton University Press.

Freidman, Norman. 1969. "Point-of-View: The Development of a Critical Concept." In R. M. Davis, ed., *The Novel: Modern Essays in Criticism.* Pp. 142–170. Englewood Cliffs, NJ: Prentice-Hall.

Gay, Peter. 1966. *The Enlightenment: An Interpretation.* New York: Vintage.

Geertz, Clifford. 1973. "Thick Description: Toward an Interpretive Theory of Culture." In Clifford Geertz, *The Interpretation of Cultures.* Pp. 3-30 New York: Basic Books.

Gerber, S. R.. 1963. "Vehicular Fatalities in Cuyahoga County, Ohio, 1941–1960." In *Proceedings of the Third International Conference on Alcohol and Road Traffic, 1962.* Pp. 38–44. London: British Medical Association.

Goffman, Erving. 1974. *Frame Analysis: An Essay on the Organization of Experience.* Cambridge, MA: Harvard University Press.

Gouldner, Alvin. 1968. "The Sociologist as Partisan: Sociology and the Welfare State." *The American Sociologist* 3:103–116.

Gusfield, Joseph. 1973. *Utopian Myths and Movements in Modern Societies.* Morristown, NJ: University Programs Modular Studies, General Learning Press.

_____. 1975. *Community: A Critical Response.* London: Basil Blackwell.

Habermas, Jurgen. 1971. "Technology and Science as 'Ideology.'" In Jurgen Habermas, *Toward a Rational Society.* Pp. 81–122. Boston: Beacon.

Hesse, Mary. 1965. "The Explanatory Function of Metaphor." In Y. Bar-Hillel, ed., *Proceedings of the 1964 International Congress for Logic, Methodology and Philosophy of Science.* Pp. 249–259. Amsterdam: North Holland Publishing.

_____. 1966. *Models and Analogies in Science.* Notre Dame, IN: University of Notre Dame Press.

Hofstadter, Albert. 1955. "The Scientific and Literary Uses of Language." In Lyman Bryson, Louis Finkelstein, Hudson Hoagland, and R. M. MacIver, eds., *Symbols and Society.* Pp. 291–335. New York: Conference on Science, Philosophy and Religion in Their Relation to the Democratic Way of Life, Inc.

Holcomb, Richard L. 1938. "Alcohol in Relation to Traffic Accidents." *Journal of the American Medical Association* III:1076–1085.

Hyman, Merton M. 1968. "The Social Characteristics of Persons Arrested for Driving while Intoxicated." *Quarterly Journal of Studies on Alcohol* (Supp. No. 4):138–177.

Lubbock, Percy. 1957. *The Craft of Fiction.* New York: Viking.

Merton, Robert. 1972. "Insiders and Outsiders: A Chapter in the Sociology of Knowledge." *American Journal of Sociology* 78:9–47.

Schutz, Alfred. 1970. *On Phenomenology and Social Relations.* Chicago: University of Chicago Press.

Schmidt, W. S., and R. G. Smart. 1959. "Alcohol Drinking and Traffic Accidents." *Quarterly Journal of Studies on Alcohol* 20:631–644.

Turbayne, Colin. 1962. *The Myth of Metaphor.* New Haven, CT: Yale University Press.

Waller, J. J. 1967. "Identification of Problem-Drinkers among Drunken Drivers." *Journal of the American Medical Association* 200:124–130.

Waller, J. J., and Henry W. Turkel. 1966. "Alcoholism and Traffic Deaths." *New England Journal of Medicine* 275:532–536.

Winterowd, W. Ross. 1968. *Rhetoric: A Synthesis.* New York: Holt, Rinehart and

4

Two Genres of Sociology:
A Literary Analysis of *The American Occupational Structure* and *Tally's Corner*

It is appropriate that I begin with an apocryphal story. Some years ago a novelist responded to the review of his book with a letter to the journal. The reviewer had it all wrong, wrote the author. That was not what he had meant at all. The reviewer wrote back: "Sir, you do not understand what you have written."

The novelist's dilemma is no different than the sociologist's. What we come to know by our studies is only a step in the process of telling our tales of scholarship. The text we write is itself a stage in the process. What the reader does in the act of reading is still another. What is known, what is written, and what is conveyed are by no the means the same.

The movement toward the analysis of research as a text is now slightly more than a decade old. (R. H. Brown, 1977; Gusfield, 1976; Latour and Woolgar, 1979). It is congruent with the general movement in the humanities and the social sciences toward a self-reflexiveness that examines and questions the assumptions on which the methods of the discipline have been based. The rhetorical turn in sociology has meant that the reporting of research in books, monographs, and journal articles is not a neutral process. The act of writing is a further stage in the process of constructing scholarship. The written product is not a transparent window to a world outside, but is instead colored and opaque, reflecting the language and organization of written work.

Sociological writing, like most of social science, is rhetorical in that it presents an argument; it is an effort to persuade. (Perelman and Olbrechts-Tytecka, 1969; Toulmin, 1958). How persuasion is accomplished is a legitimate inquiry. Style, structure, language, metaphors, visual material are as germane to the analysis of "scientific" reports as they have been to literary materials. The very style and organization of a discipline is itself an essential aspect of its conventional rhetoric (Gusfield, 1981: Ch. 2-4; Bazerman, 1989).

Rhetoric, like communication in general, is more than a one-sided affair. As Kenneth Burke recognized many years ago and as literary theory has come to realize in recent years, reading is a relationship between text and reader (Burke, 1950; Iser, 1978 ; Suleiman and Crosman, 1980). The reader is not a passive slate on which the author may inscribe. I return to the story with which I began. The text that the novelist experienced was not the text that the reviewer experienced. What constitutes the text for any particular reader and in any particular context is not given by the search for a fixed meaning that has conventionally occupied professors of literature. Much depends on the interaction between the reader and the "text" (Iser, 1978). The experience of the reader is constructed in the process of reading in a particular context (Fish, 1980; Smith, 1981).

The writer and others involved in the production of the product, such as the publishers, editors, and designers are aware of their audiences. Being aware, they are concerned with influencing the reception their work will have on their readers. The text can be examined as a means of potential control over how the reader will read. Does the text attempt to ready the reader for the nature of the argument that the author appears to be making?

"His (the interpreter's) object should therefore be, not to explain a work, but to reveal the conditions that bring about its various possible effects...(to clarify) the *potential* of a text" (Iser, 1978: 18).

There is an additional interest in this enterprise beside the joy of playful scholarship. How is it that scientific presentations gain the authority of certain fact? How are audiences and readers led to belief? How do they come to accept and trust the texts that purport to establish fact and to draw credible conclusions from facts?

The Rhetorical Problem of Sociological Texts

Perhaps it may be objected that the texts of sociological studies are not literary works and therefore are not rhetorical works. They are not products of creative imagination. They are attempts to represent a reality, a world of fact and not imagination. The stuff of literature is fictive. Social science, as a cultural product, is mimetic; it represents phenomena that are real.

But central to this paper is just that point. How to maintain the character of sociological work as *not imaginary* will be the crux of much of my examination of these texts. Most sociological texts with which I am familiar are organized to convince the reader that some state of affairs is so and that alternative, imagined states, are not so. Being efforts to persuade, they are analyzable as rhetoric. Being an organization of language, they are capable of being examined as literature.

In this light, most sociological arguments are ways of leading the reader to a conclusion which, given the means used to present the data and its analysis, cannot be denied by its audience. The reader is imagined as part of a universal audience for whom the diversities of interest and community are irrelevant. No matter what the reader desires, the argument will reach undeniable conclusions and will compel the reader to the author's persuasion (Perelman and Olbrechts-Tytecka, 1969; Gusfield, 1981: Ch. 4).

It is this form of argument, and the deviations from it, that occupies my attention in this paper. It, too, is an argument and how successful it is in achieving your assent is, ultimately, in your hands.

In one sense. no writing ever begins at the beginning. It must assume the reader's knowledge of the language and his or her literacy. It must assume some of the conventions of reading as well. In this paper I need to prevent the reader from raising certain difficulties which will act as barriers to his or her willingness to follow the argument. Among these is a way of setting some matters outside of the text of the paper so that the reader will not raise them or will not let them dominate his or her reading.

One is the question of evaluation. My intent is not to evaluate the adequacy of these documents by any criteria of adequacy. This, I know, is a difficult and in the end not a successful attempt. But let me save for a later discussion that gnawing and important question. Let us put it, at least for the time being, outside the frame of the paper.

Let us also place the character of these two studies as truly representative of their respective genres outside the frame, as well. *The American Occupational Structure* and *Tally's Corner* were both published in 1967. Each has become a "classic" example of method: *The American Occupational Structure* of census survey and quantitative analysis and Tally's Corner of field observation and qualitative analysis. Both are still read by sociologists and in use in training students, whatever the current acceptance or rejection of their conclusions. I will treat each as typical of a genre in sociological writing, although I have no warrant resulting from a more thorough examination of other such works. In writing of these two works as examples of genres I recognize that such an assumption is substantiated only by impressions derived from my general experience in reading sociology.

The two genres have been described in various terms although no major effort has been made to define them clearly. The distinction has gone under a variety of terms. Among them are thin-thick description; quantitative-qualitative; experience-far and experience-near; etic-emic; objective-subjective; scientific-humanistic; generalizable-concrete.

Lastly, this is my interpretation and examination of two texts. While I write as if the author intended the consequences I see, that is only a conceit, a metaphor for the analysis of the potential I discover in the text. My data is not the intentions of the authors but the texts as I examine them. The text, however, is available to all that care to examine it.

The American Occupational Structure and Tally's Corner

The paper now has its frame in place and I am ready to lead you onto the canvas. The two books I chose were selected for three reasons. First, each has become a "classic" in its field. Though published twenty-five years ago, they are still read and referred to. Secondly, each represents an example of a distinct and different model. *AOS* (*The American Occupational Structure*) is a quantitative study in the mode I will call the experimental; it is analogous to what is often called the "scientific model." The data drawn on are from a survey of 25,000 persons planned by the authors and conducted by the U.S. Bureau of the Census. *TC* (*Tally's Corner*) is an observational, ethnographic account of the author's participation with a group of black men in a section of Washington, D.C. The data drawn on are the author's observations. Lastly, I knew each of these books reasonably well, having taught *TC* several times and having conducted a study not unlike *AOS*, based on a survey of occupational careers and utilizing the quantitative method pioneered in *AOS*.

Forming the Audience: Controlling Access to Readership

For whom is this book meant and who is likely to read it? Not everyone is a likely reader of every book. Just as American opera, by the expense of tickets, the formality of clothing, and the arrangements of time tells many that it is not for them, so a book, even in its physical appearance, keeps the gates open and accessible to some and repels and rejects others. Granted that a text is a relationship between the author, text, and reader, what is done to influence the composition of the readership?

A folk adage asserts that "you can't judge a book by its cover." A more skeptical perspective suggests that the cover is the initial presentation that the author makes to intended readers. It is the first evidence with which to answer the question: What kind of book is this? Am I part of its readership?

Three aspects of the physical structure of books are clues to their implied and potential reader. The size of a book and the shape of its contents are one form of presentation telling the reader something of its accessibility to him. *The American Occupational Structure* is a big book: eighteen pages of front material, 442 pages of text, and seventy pages of appendices and index. Its type is elite on glossy paper. *Tally's Corner* is a short book; fifteen pages of front material, 230 pages of text ,a twenty-five—page appendix and four pages of references. The type is larger than *AOS* and the paper thicker, of rag quality. Chapter 1 of *Tally's Corner* is twenty-five pages long and contains forty paragraphs and approximately 5,000 lines. Chapter 1 of *The American Occupational Structure* is twenty-one pages long, contains forty-nine paragraphs and is approximately 9,700 lines long. In physical structure, *Tally's Corner* might be a novel. *The American Occupational Structure* would be hard to present as a novel, even if by Umberto Eco.

The same difference in accessibility appears in the titles. *The American Occupational Structure* announces its abstract character. "Structure" is a conceptual term, a metaphor suggesting the solidity and persistence of a building. It is not the ordinary language of most Americans. "The" gives the title a decontextualized appearance, the structure as distinguished from the individuals and individualized cases from which it is drawn (Gusfield, 1986). This is not presented as a book calculated to interest the average reader nor one likely to be understood without some special knowledge. The dust jacket supports this. It is orange and blue. The orange part announces the title and the authors. The blue part seems to be an abstract form. On closer inspection the contours of human figures are discernible.

Tally's Corner announces its lesser technical, "serious" nature by its cover. I am comparing the original hardcover copy of *The American Occupational Structure* and its dust jacket with the paperback *Tally's Corner*. (The paperback copy of *The American Occupational Structure* is unavailable to me.) The hardcover copy of *Tally's Corner* is available and is beside me. The hardcover, now out of print, is also on my desk, but the dust jacket and original binding have been replaced by library binding. The size and shape of the hardcover and paperback copies of *Tally's Corner* are identical. The title is specific and uses the ordinary language of urban imagery—somebody's corner. The subtitle, "a study of street-corner men," testifies to its character as research. The front cover is black along one side and white along the other. The white side announces the full title and the author, with the author's name in larger type than additional matter, including the subtitle. The front cover also includes the information that there is a foreword by Hylan Lewis (a black sociologist) and a quote lauding the study by Daniel Patrick Moynihan, then, as described, Director, Joint Center for Urban Studies, M.I.T. and Harvard University. The black side is a photo of blacks on a street. Three young men are standing around a mailbox, one reading a newspaper. A man some distance away is reading something, standing against a storefront. A fifth man is walking on the sidewalk between the man and the three youths. It is an ordinary moment caught by the camera.

The cover suggests a concrete character to the book. It is about specific people in specific places. The credibility of the author and the importance of the study are supported by the prestigious people (Hylan Lewis and Daniel Moynihan) who vouch for it even before the reader has opened the pages.

The authors, like the star system in movies, may influence the reader's belief that he/she is a fit reader. Who were the authors? Peter Blau and Otis D. Duncan, authors of *The American Occupational Structure*, were both well known to professional sociologists and were professors at major universities. Eliot Liebow, author of *Tally's Corner*, was then unknown outside of a small circle of colleagues. The inside front cover of *The American Occupational Structure* dust jacket describes the authors, indicating their academic positions including major awards, places taught, and books published. Their credentials are "hung on the wall." The back cover describes the book, emphasizing the "most comprehensive set of facts and data on occupational mobility ever assembled for any nation." The back cover of *Tally's Corner* presents quotes from reviews or blurbs praising the book. Three of these are identified by the newspaper in which they appeared: *New York Times, Washington Star, Detroit Free Press*. Three are identified by the names and positions of the reviewers: Special Assistant to the Secretary, Department of Housing and Urban Development; Psychiatrist-in-Chief, Massachusetts Institute of Technology and the same quote from and identification of Moynihan that appears on the front.

Even before the reader opens the books, he has seen a presentation that indicates the differences of access and the credentials of the authors. The relation of *Tally's Corner* to policy questions connected with urban planning has already been suggested. The technical character of *The American Occupational Structure* has been presented and the possible inaccessibility of the book for some audiences has been established. The high repute of its authors is presented. Liebow's book was his doctoral thesis in Anthropology at Catholic University in Washington, D.C. That knowledge is contained in his "acknowledgements" section while the cover "sponsors" the work through eminent persons and institutions.

The table of contents is a second aspect that in the text reveals again the different levels of accessibility characterizing each book. The titles of chapters are ordinary language in *Tally's Corner*, the special vocabulary of sociology in *The American Occupational Structure*. Thus, chapter 2 in Blau and Duncan is entitled "The Occupational Structure: Patterns of Movement." In Liebow's study, it is "Men and Jobs." Despite these differences, however, both works are efforts to persuade the reader to conclusions that explain some phenomena. In that respect they both will have recourse to the cloak of Science and will use the lineaments of Rhetoric to accomplish it.

The language used in the text is a third sign of how the audience of readers may be limited or expanded. Consider the following sentences, with which each book begins its first chapter:

"The objective of this book is to present a systematic analysis of *The American Occupational Structure*, and thus of the major foundation of its stratification system. Processes of social mobility from one generation to the next and from career beginnings to occupational destination are considered to reflect the dynamics of the occupational structure" (*AOS*, p. 1).

"Problems faced by and generated by low-income urban populations in general and low-income urban Negroes in particular have become one of the chief concerns of the nation. We have declared War on Poverty and mobilized public and private resources for a concerted effort to expunge delinquency and dependency from our national life" (*TC*, p. 3).

The first is the language of the professional sociologist. The second is the language of the college-educated reader.

What is implied in the opening of these books is a particular kind of reader and a particular community in which he or she is found. *The American Occupational Structure* is aimed at a more technical audience than is *Tally's Corner*. Blau and Duncan require a reader who understands "sociologese," who knows some rudimentary social statistics and is willing to make a sizable commitment of time. Such an audience is technical in the sense of being drawn from a community of people with special training. *Tally's Corner* is a book for many seasons and many kinds of readers. The more dramatic language of ordinary readers implies that *Tally's Corner* draws a wider community than does *The American Occupational Structure*.

Narrative: The Intellectual Structure

Though they differ in the kind of audience each book presupposes, they are alike in one substantial element of form. Both are narratives. They proceed sequentially through a beginning, middle, and end. The earlier parts of each book are a route toward an end, a conclusion. I mean by "structure" something closer to the sociologist's understanding of parts and wholes and their relationship to each other. I do not mean "structure" in the sense of an underlying, latent paradigm in the sense of French structuralism. It is the relation of chapters and parts to each other and to the whole that is here considered. These books are arguments, not random collections of material. The beginning chapters would make no sense at the end and vice-versa. The middle chapters, although conceivably interchangeable within that section, cannot stand alone or be exchanged with the beginning or the conclusion. In a sense, which will be qualified later, the ending is the aim of each book (Kermode, 1966; Ricoeur, 1984).

Even at the level of content there is great similarity. *The American Occupational Structure* begins with a chapter that discusses, in order, stratification theory and mobility research, methods of data collection, and the organization of the book. *Tally's Corner* begins with a chapter less explicit about its parts but also divided into three very similar sections. The first discusses the problem of the poverty cycle and the then current crisis in black families. It proceeds after this to discuss the methods of study and closes with a description of Tally's corner and the men who make up the group under study. Both books end with a concluding chapter summarizing what they have found and drawing conclusions for wider issues.

In the discussion of their materials, and in the opening parts of chapter 2 in *Tally's Corner*, each presents a body of materials to be explained by the remainder of the work. In the introductory chapter of *Tally's Corner*, Liebow indicates that his study is "an attempt to meet the need for recording and interpreting lower-class life of ordinary people, on their grounds and on their terms" (p. 10). But it is not a hit-or-miss attempt. It is guided by the policy concerns for the cycle of poverty continuing across generations among American urban blacks. *Tally's Corner* is an effort to use its data to explain that cycle.

The American Occupational Structure is also couched in the logic of explanation. In the first paragraph of the book, Blau and Duncan announce that their objective is to conduct a systematic analysis of the occupational structure and through that arrive at the major foundation of the stratification system. "By analyzing the patterns of these occupational movements, the conditions that affect them, and some of their consequences, we attempt to explain part of the dynamics of the stratification system in the United States."

The parts of each book are consistent with these objectives. Having stated the intention, each author discusses what methods are used and then proceeds to describe and analyze the data. Chapter 1 is introductory. In Blau and Duncan, this is followed by two chapters that state the findings that characterize the occupational structure. Following these are two chapters detailing the method that will be used in explaining that structure and a third, which is a transition. The method is used to present the model of the mobility process and, toward the end of the chapter, detailed in a presentation of data on the role of education in that process. Then follow six more data chapters on such matters as inequality of opportunity, especially the role of race, geographical and social mobility, kinship, marriage, and differential fertility. This is the logic of independent variables and their use in explaining the dependent variables—the present occupational position of the respondents and the mobility patterns they displayed. The book ends with a concluding chapter that serves as capstone and goal of the analysis.

In *Tally's Corner* there is a similar middle of discrete topics—jobs, marriage, lovers, children, friends. Similarly, the conclusion is also the playing back of the data on the substantive questions. The greater space given to method in *The American Occupational Structure* than in *Tally's Corner* is significant and will be discussed below.

Framing Devices: The Suspension of Disbelief

In presenting their studies as something other than literature, the social scientist distinguishes a product of imagination from a product of fact. It is the facticity of his or her data that must be established if the reader is to be compelled to accept the conclusions of the author. If the author could, at the very beginning of his or her work, know that the reader will trust the veracity and acumen of the author the recourse to the agency, to method, would be unnecessary.

That is not the case. Instead the character of argument requires a rhetoric directed at a hostile, skeptical, and doubtful reader. The studies examined here, in differing ways and to different degrees, imply a reader who says, in the American vernacular: "I'm from Missouri. Don't tell me; show me."

While this is the case, and is, indeed, the basis of a rhetoric, there are limits to the recalcitrance of the reader. There are assumptions that must be made if the show is to go on at all. Samuel Taylor Coleridge pointed out that the audience at a drama must engage in "a willing suspension of disbelief" if the audience is to treat the actions of actors on a stage in a particular time and space as those of others elsewhere. It is the art of the brilliant soprano, playing Madame Butterfly, that enables a fat and fortyish Italian lady to convince her American audience that she is, for a short time and space, a geisha in her early twenties in Japan of the 1860s.

Until quite recently, and still conventionally, paintings have had frames to tell the viewer where the painting begins and where it ends. The frame is an attempt to lead the viewer, and in this case the reader, toward the kinds of matters worth attention and away from those that will distract. It helps to define what is content and what is not.

In both the documents being analyzed here, the frames are antecedent to the plot and narrative. The narrative structure of the books implies further that the material, the data, are fit sources for the orderliness with which they will be described and analyzed, and truly represents fact and not imagination. Yet each work is only a representation of its study. It is not the actual set of events. As Hayden White has written about narrative in general:

> [E]very narrative, however seemingly "full" is constructed on the basis of a set of events which *might have been included but were left out* ...in which continuity rather than discontinuity governs the articulation of the discourse." (White, 1981: 10)

The American Occupational Structure

What is the unique character of *The American Occupational Structure*? What will it do that other mobility studies have not done? The authors tell the reader that the study is unique in the kind and amount of data used. The size of the sample (20,000) permits kinds of analyses not possible previously. Most importantly, it will enable the authors to investigate the conditions associated with mobility. Past studies have been directed almost exclusively toward the amount of mobility but not the conditions that might explain them. Such studies have also investigated how mobility patterns are affected by various factors—race, education, social origins, etc. The authors will reformulate this problem by decomposing the concept of occupational mobility into its constituent elements: social or career origins and occupational destinations" (p. 9). But instead of asking what effect one variable has on mobility—race for example—they will "ask what influence it exerts on occupational achievements and how it modifies the effects of social origins on those achievements" (p. 9).

The substantive questions about upward mobility in American society are not unique to this study, as the authors recognize. To what extent is the occupational structure characterized by mobility between and within generations? What conditions favor and deter mobility? It is the amount of data and the techniques of analysis that permit new answers to these questions.

In creating a narrative of fact the sociologist is characteristically searching for generalizations beyond the sheer description of material collected. He/she meets the problem of extracting the universal from the particular. The reader must cope with the problem that few studies are able to obtain clear and unambiguous data on which to base conclusions. The author must also cope with the limits, or "impurity" of data so that the reader will utilize the data in the ways the author intends, as if it were purer than it can be. How to deal with the limitations of data is a common problem for the writer.

One facet of the frame lies in the relation between concept and data. In the first paragraph of chapter 1, the authors tell the readers that this is a study based on "a considerable amount of empirical data" from a representative sample of over 20,000 *men* between the ages of twenty and sixty-four. The reader learns that the data are from a national survey planned by the authors and conducted in March 1962 as an adjunct to the monthly Current Population Survey conducted by the U.S. Bureau of the Census. The survey was entitled "Occupational Changes in a Generation."

At the very outset, the audience is asked to believe that *The American Occupational Structure* can be discussed without including women and households. They are asked to share a meaning about "the American occupational structure" that excludes women and treats the meaning of mobility in individual rather than family terms. I shall discuss this later in commenting on the concept of mobility as a shared element between audience and author.

A second aspect of frame is in the adequacy of data. In chapter 1, Blau and Duncan admit several deficiencies in the data. Census Bureau procedures and policies led to a cumbersome time lag between planning and approval of plans that made it difficult to make changes between the pre-test and the final survey. Census policy made them unable to gain data on attitudes. Was the sample adequate? Here the authors go outside the frame and the painting. They refer the reader to a census report on the sample. However, the sample was approximately 25,000, but only approximately 20,000 returned a question-naire that was usable. The sample excluded the institutional popula-tion, including men in the military, thus reducing the universe repre-sented to approximately 85 percent. In two appendices, the authors deal with this problem of missing data, including non-responses to particular questions They do so by a pattern of assumptions and the use of decennial census data that lead to different conclusions about the limited credibility of the data obtained in response to questions about the respondent (male) and his father. In the case of father's occupation they are less sure than in the case of father's education. In both, however, there are disclaimers about the "purity" of the data obtained.

To give a specific example and its use, take the case of the accu-racy of respondent's data about the occupation of the father when the respondent was age sixteen. The authors matched the pre-test sample with the data on the father at approximate son's age sixteen in the raw decennial census returns. In chapter 1, they report that of the 123 matched cases, 30 percent showed a discrepancy between the respondents' designation of their father's occupation and what the census material showed about the father at that time. The appen-dix indicates that of the 570 in the pre-test sample, a match was possible in 123 cases. Another way of reporting that result in the text might have been that of the 570 pre-test sample, the accuracy of designating the father's occupation could be assured in 15 percent of the cases. Even in census post-interview studies (p. 15), the authors point out that occupation is not consistent in 17-22 percent of the cases. (Notice that I have refrained from using a modifying term such as "only" or "at least.")

The problem is a common one in social research. The data are seldom as good as the model of scientific methods would demand. But do deficiencies vitiate the ending? How can the reader be con-vinced that the study is acceptable? The authors must prepare the reader for what will lie inside the frame by argument, which leads the reader to check his doubts for the purposes at hand. He/she must suspend his/her disbelief in the inadequacy of the data.

(The admission of difficulties in the data is itself a show of cred-ibility, establishing the veracity of the authors and their commitment to reveal data. If they are willing to admit flaws in their data then they should be believable and trusted to be honest about other matters.)

The basic argument is, in part, given in the series of reasoned estimates and simulated data such as discussed above. In part that process is developed in appendices, which require a further dilution of the audience, excluding those who lack the training to understand or who are willing to accept the data on the strength of the authors. Even with the efforts to correct for missing data, inaccuracies and limited reliability, the data depart from the model of adequacy. Blau and Duncan argue that while there are sources of error, the data are no worse than government census data in particular and survey research in general. These are conventionally accepted within the profession and so, too, they are a warrant for accepting the adequacy of the present data.

"The conclusion, however, is not that the OCG data on socioeconomic background are free of error but merely that they may be almost as reliable as CPS (Current Population Survey of the U.S. Census) data on current occupational status....it must be conceded that very little was done to estimate the effect of such error on conclusions and inferences. In that respect, unfortunately, our investigation is all too typical of the current standards of social research" (p. 16).

In placing some of the methods for dealing with these problems into appendices, Blau and Duncan further limit the audiences to whom they speak. However, within the text and in the beginning they qualify the "purity" of the data. All this lies outside the frame. When they begin to report the study, such qualifications are not constantly alluded to, although they are not ignored. It is left to the reader to make the necessary discounts and limitations. As we might imagine, a style of writing that constantly reminded the reader of the limits on the data would become even more cumbersome and boring. They lie outside the frame and not in it. It is the reader who must apply a discount, who must willingly suspend disbelief.

Tally's Corner

In one sense, the production of a frame is a set of instructions to the reader about how to read the work. In *Tally's Corner*, both the foreword and the first part of chapter 1 provide the policy direction that orients the author. An argument is made for the usefulness of studying black corner men. Like *The American Occupational Structure,* the comparison with other studies of black lower-class life is made. Past studies of black lower-class life and poverty have largely focused on women and children. The black male as an element in understanding poverty had seldom been studied.

The other consideration that will make the study worthwhile is the extent to which the incidence of poverty is much greater among blacks than among whites. Blau and Duncan assume the reader's agreement with their assessment of the importance of studying occupational mobility. Liebow does not take his reader's agreement for granted. Having convinced the reader he can now go ahead.

At the outset, Liebow, like Blau and Duncan, must face the issue of the validity of his study in a self-conscious manner. In his *Some Versions of Pastoral,* William Empson points to the use of the Fool in *King Lear* as a device often used by playwrights, a comic foil to the tragic character of Lear, an internal critic. Such devices, writes Empson, serve to prevent the audience from dismissing the "argument" of the play by lampooning it before the audience can do so (Empson, 1938; Gusfield, 1963). They rid the playgoer of his disposition to offset the seriousness by the comic and leave the main plot acceptable. They must confront and diminish the unwillingness to suspend belief before the reader does so.

Where Blau and Duncan go to great lengths to establish the worthwhile quality of their data, Liebow treats the matter in several pages and one appendix. The bulk of Liebow's material is drawn from observations of his participation with two dozen black men who "hang out" on a corner in Washington, D.C. The study of these men is defended in several ways. One is as a correction to the emphases on women and children in earlier studies, as we have seen. Another is the belief expressed by the author, and others, that interview and questionnaire methods have either excluded lower-lower-class black men or have not received valid information. What has been learned from these may be a false picture. The present study will correct this by recording and interpreting lower-class life "on their grounds and on their terms" (p. 10).

The method of participant observation also raises problems for the reader. If the focus of the study is on national problems of poverty, why devote a book to some twenty particular men chosen for ease of study? How can you make any general assertions from so special a study? Liebow utilizes a ploy of diminution, of claiming not to attempt to convince the reader of the certainty of his data and his analyses. "The present attempt, then, is not aimed directly at developing generalizations about lower-class life," but in examining one minute segment, "to attempt to make sense of what was seen and heard, and to offer this explanation to others" (p. 16).

Liebow asserts that he deliberately did not develop a research design and hypotheses prior to working in the field. His analyses are therefore post facto. In a footnote quoting Robert Merton's criticism of participant observation, Liebow counters Merton's criticism that conclusions drawn from this data "remain at the level of *plausibility* (low evidential value) rather than leading to 'compelling evidence' (a high degree of confirmation)" (*Social Theory and Social Structure*, pp. 93-95, quoted in *Tally's Corner*, p. 12). Liebow counters by saying that the timing of the hypotheses is unimportant. Whether the hypotheses are developed before or after the data is collected is immaterial. Their validity rests on their future replication. But, like Blau and Duncan's recourse to the limits of conventional procedures, "given the present state of the art, we can ill afford to look 'merely plausible' explanations of human behavior in the mouth" (fn. 6, p.12).

Such a position disarms the critic who may then decide the study is not worth reading or who will no longer look for signs that the author has any point-of-view to which he or she will try to compel the reader's assent. Liebow, like Blau and Duncan, is aware that his conclusion does belie giving us, "Just the facts." He does, however, as I will show later, want the particulars—the observation—to illuminate the universal—the general problem of black ghetto poverty. He does make it necessary to suspend our disbelief in the adequacy of his data for the questions of the study.

There is a further issue arising in *Tally's Corner* from the method of participant observation, one largely dealt with by Liebow in an appendix on fieldwork. Are his accounts of the actions of the men on the street corner accurate? How could an obviously well-educated person (male judging by the name) achieve the necessary rapport with lower-class, poorly educated men? The reader does not know until told that Liebow is white, a major piece of information in a field study of blacks. Liebow's account of his "fitness" is less an argument than a biography. His father owned a grocery store in a black area of Washington and he grew up in a black neighborhood.

Where *The American Occupational Structure* had recourse to method, to agency, in establishing the grounds for belief, *Tally's Corner* uses agent, the character and experience and competence of the author. There is necessarily a different kind of presence in each of these books. Blau and Duncan remain in the shadows and avoid a presence. It is the data applied by method that is the action of *The American Occupational Structure.* The authors are behind the curtains, puppetmasters, perhaps, but invisible to the audience who views their presentation.

In *Tally's Corner,* the agent, Elliott Liebow, is constantly present. Belief in his ability to get the data and to report it honestly is essential to his presentation. The responsibility of the author for selection and conclusions is more evident in *Tally's Corner* than in *The American Occupational Structure.* Like their data, Blau and Duncan are unobtrusive. Like his data, Liebow is a participant.

It is necessary, then, for each of these authors to establish the community of readers and the objects to which they will attend. In order to proceed, the reader must grant the author trust in his accounts and accept the value of the study as worth his or her attention. To achieve this the author needs to persuade the reader to place himself/ herself in the necessary audience, to accept the conventions of judgment, and to suspend doubt and distrust—to share the author's belief in the value of his study. Without such frames, anyone and everyone is a possible reader and the foundations of the community must be reestablished on every page. The willingness to disbelieve and the compulsion to accept and be persuaded depends on the community that the readers share (Fish, 1980). This is a major point in this paper and will be elaborated on throughout.

Plot and Story: Assuming the Community of Readers

I begin this section with a distinction between plot and story. By "plot," I refer to a general scheme that the text utilizes to provide meaning and significance to its parts. It is an abstract statement, as in "boy meets girl; boy loses girl; boy wins girl." This simple and trite narrative is not about any particular boy or particular girl. Stories are concrete; they are particular people doing particular things. The plot of *Hamlet* is its narrative structure and is repeated in other dramas. The story is unique to *Hamlet.*

Social science is mostly a procedure for emplotment. Even Erving Goffman, perhaps the most eminent of sociological storytellers, entitled his major book, *"The" Presentation of the Self in Everyday Life.*

By no means are sociologists adverse to storytelling, but narrativity in the structure of the studies analyzed here makes the relation of plot to story a matter of importance.

Paramount to my discussion of the rhetorical element in social research is the thought that how material is presented (the form) has a close relationship to what is presented (the content). An analysis of these two books must necessarily be attentive to the form as a matter of impact on what is presented to the reader.

Emplotment

In one sense these studies are narratives about narratives. The authors depict the behavior of their subjects in the light of a sequence of events, but that sequence is more than a listing of events, as a chronology might be (White, 1981; Plumb, 1971). It has direction and theme to it. "Emplotment invites us to recognize a traditional class of configurations" (Ricoeur, 1984: 164). In both studies the concept of an occupational career is the central model or metaphor which integrates and gives point to the material presented. These books have the career as their plot.

The American Occupational Structure. The data which Blau and Duncan use as the major material under scrutiny consists of five variables from each respondent. These are the occupation of R's (respondent's) father when R was 16; the highest grade of school R's father completed; the first full-time job of R; the educational attainment of R; and the present job of R. These are perceived as a sequence in which some variables follow others through time. In what is often seen as the major contribution of *AOS*, this is referred to through the metaphor of a "path." Thus first job cannot occur after present job; son's educational attainment cannot occur before father's occupation. The model of a career is imagined in the metaphorical concept of a path and multiple regression coefficients (I am sorry but I cannot explain this within the confines of this paper. Nontechnicians, please hang on. I don't believe my paper depends on this bit of technical training) established between the five variables with the concept of path as the metaphor for careers.

The use of plot enables the authors to talk about "the American stratification system" and mobility. It enables them to use existing data on men as if the plots of groups represented the totality of stratification and occupational status (income plus education); as if it represented the way in which each unique case can be perceived. As a metaphor or model it must necessarily ignore two major categories: women and households. Although they do recognize and use in their data single parents or guardians other than fathers, they do not gather material on women in the labor force, on the institutionalized population, or the military. Nor do they consider the contributions of women and other family members, including extended family, to the respondent's position in the stratification system. Even by 1960, many households achieved middle-class income positions through the occurrence of joint earners.

I have already discussed several qualifications to the "purity" of the data used in *The American Occupational Structure* .The authors are conscious of these infirmities and, from time to time, call them to the attention of the reader. However, the analysis of data is, in the main, conducted with an assumed database in which the "reality" is an abstract and aggregated one. Liebow concentrates on one group of about twenty men. Blau and Duncan are talking about twenty thousand. Such a number cannot be observed by "hanging around," nor can be talked about as specific and particular persons. To talk about them is to create a set of abstractions in which the particularities are dismissed and the aggregated similarities are the matters of attention.

The issue is recognized by the authors. In discussing the basic model of mobility as a path in which educational level attained is prior to the respondent's first job, they realize that this is not always so. In many cases (how many aren't known), the entry-level job may occur before completion of education and/or the first job was only "temporary" and not the beginning of career. This they see as a flaw in their planning of the study. "We are inclined to conclude that their reports were realistic enough" (p. 166). Their error, they say, lay in the meaning that the authors gave to those reports as referring to the same entry-level status.

Blau and Duncan are aware that this uncovers a still more fundamental issue in the means of aggregating the twenty thousand cases, in giving a homogeneous meaning to the responses. They echo Hayden White's description, above (p.12), of the problem of historical narrative:

> The fundamental difficulty here is conceptual. If we insist on any uniform sequence of the events involved in accomplishing the transition to independent adult status, we do violence to reality....As soon as we aggregate individual data for

analytical purposes we are forced into the use of simplifying assumptions. (*The American Occupational Structure*, pp. 166-67)

The authors then decide to adopt the assumption that "first job" has the same significance for all the respondents in its temporal relation to educational attainment and later work experience. Without such an assumption, the measures of association would be impossible since the meanings of the variables would then be diverse. They write, "If this assumption is not strictly correct we doubt that it could be improved by substituting any other *single* measure of initial occupational status" (p. 107).

Tally's Corner. In an interesting manner Liebow makes use of the same plot of the "normal" career of attempted occupational mobility to make his data understandable. Liebow begins the chapter, titled "Men and Jobs," with a graphic description of a white truck driver who stops at the street corner and asks the corner men if they want work. They shake their heads and say *no*. Here is no plot, but a story—a unique occurrence happening to particular people. Liebow, however, sets himself the task of explaining this story through a more general account of the role of jobs in the life of the street-corner men.

The story that Liebow has described makes sense, in his account, by comparison with a "normal" account of careers and the role of jobs in careers. On the corner, "getting a job, keeping a job, and doing well at it is clearly of low priority" (p. 34). Explaining why this is so is the substance of much of *Tally's Corner*. It makes sense to do so only if the reader is already convinced that the street-corner men are not like most others, that in American society the desire for turning jobs into careers, for social mobility, is the norm, and the absence of a career is something to be explained. If fires were normal occurrences, the happening of a fire would not be news.

Again, the attribution of the absence of career and mobility motivation in the corner men will remain at the level of "story," of a concrete, particular set of people whom the author has known unless it can be generalized to more than the corner men. In his foreword, the sociologist Hylan Lewis points out that this is a study of "losers" and does not describe those who have become "winners" and succeeded at legitimate careers or have taken illegitimate careers as successful paths to mobility.

Achieving Reality: The Art of Facticity

In their study of a biochemical laboratory, the sociologists Latour and Woolgar (1979) gave great attention to the processes by which the laboratory's findings achieved an "out-thereness" quality when reported in publication. The rhetoric of scientific presentation must minimize the role of the writer in constructing the reality of "fact." The social scientist stands above the flux of interests and conflicts because what he knows cannot be denied. It does not rest on sentiment or self-interest but on what is truly "out there."

Each of these two books, *The American Occupational Structure* and *Tally's Corner*, wrestles with this problem, from different standpoints and with different mechanisms of coping. But cope they must. Put in the context of the analysis of fiction, each author claims to show and not to tell (Booth, 1961). But as Booth also points out, in literary works it becomes impossible to do one without the other. In this and the following section, I want to amplify this judgment in these non-literary works

Tally's Corner: The Art of Showing

I have already mentioned the problem of the personal relation to material that the participant observer faces. He, or she, rests much of the claim to believability on the reader's willingness to trust the veracity and observational skills of the author. Two questions are posed, the first of which we will analyze in this section. The other is reserved for later. The first question bears on the veracity or accuracy of what has been observed and reported. The second bears on the significance, or meaning, of those reports on the framework or structure of the book, on its conclusions.

By no means is Liebow content only to show what he has heard and seen. He wants to explain it and to advocate that explanation as an aid in understanding something more general—the problem of black poverty. As he points out in the very beginning of the book, one often discussed aspect of that problem has been the absence of the father and /or husband from the family in the black lower class. In chapter 4, "Husbands and Wives," Liebow examines this problem using his observations. The writing consists of descriptive statements, analytic statements, and "protocols" (the notes and quotations used by Liebow— the primary material).

Chapter 4 begins with a descriptive statement about Liebow's subjects: "A few of the street-corner men expect to get married sooner or later. A few are married. Most of the men have tried marriage and found it wanting."

Why should the reader believe Liebow? Has he reported "fact"? Since we know from the appendix that he spent a year observing the corner, at various times of the day and night, what we are given is a selection. There is no survey of the neighborhood. How can we trust his report?

Much of this chapter consists of statements like the above, in which the reader is told something about the corner men and that something is analyzed. Liebow tells a number of stories about specific marriages or consensual unions. These become the basis, the evidence, for the analytic statements. In one part of the chapter, Liebow maintains that corner men clearly distinguish between the demand rights of marriage and the privileges of consensual unions. He then tells a story, concretizing the analytic statement.

"[This] can be seen in the conflict between Stanton and Bernice. Shortly after they began living together, Stanton was arrested and jailed for thirty days. Upon his release, he went to their apartment where he discovered Bernice with another man. Over the next several weeks, Stanton refused to look for work. It *was understood*(italics mine) that he was making Bernice 'pay'....Both men and women said this was a 'terrible' thing for Stanton to do, that maybe Bernice hadn't done the 'right' thing but she had a right to do what she did because they weren't married" (p. 106).

We recognize that these statements, paraphrasing what Liebow heard, are not the verbatim report of what was said or the contexts in which it was said, that they are the end product of a process. Why should we believe that this is an interpretation that is credible? What Liebow does, as most field work reports do, is to utilize his protocols from time to time. (I am doing the same thing when I quote from Liebow or from Blau and Duncan) Consider the following use of protocol in the same chapter. Here Liebow is describing what he claims is a common justification for marital breakup, used by the corner men he observed: the theory of sexual infidelity as a manly flaw. "Men are just dogs! We shouldn't call ourselves human, we're just dog, dogs, dogs! They call me a dog, 'cause that's what I am, but so is everybody else-hopping around from woman to woman, just like a dog" (p. 121).

This protocol, like most used in *Tally's Corner*, is indented as a quotation and single-spaced. It is, in some respect, "outside" the text. The shift in language and style further gives it a reality that separates it from the paraphrased statements of the author. It has the ring of reality although we do not know to what remarks it was a response nor the difference between what was said and what was recorded in Liebow's notes. As an illustration, however, the reader can use it to check his or her interpretation of the statement against the use that Liebow makes of it. Agreement with the interpretation of the protocol heightens the trust of the reader in the other statements he makes.

The American Occupational Structure: The Rhetorical Uses of Statistical Presentation

The use of numerical forms and visual devices, such as charts, tables, and graphs, and in this case path coefficient models, serves additional functions beyond the analytical mechanism. The numerical form has a precision and a definiteness that verbalized measures lack. It enables comparison to occur between classes. Thus, on page 154, a table (Table 4.5) is presented showing the percentage differences between men of different mobility scores both in the observed data and on the hypothesis that Father's Occupational Status and Respondent's Occupational Status are statistically independent within categories of education. The mobility score measures the distance "traveled" between the father's occupation and the son's on an interval scale on which every occupation has a status score. Thus, movement upward from 26-96 is a long distance, although the authors point out that the distributions (long or short) are arbitrary. What is not arbitrary, they assert, is that, *on the average*, the respondent's own occupational status is higher than that of the father's.

This is a typical pattern in quantitative studies carefully done and carefully explicated. Given the assumptions that of necessity had to be made, however, the reader might be expected to take the operations with a proverbial grain of skeptical salt. How can the data be accepted as a summarization of a factual world?

The use of numbers is itself a device which demonstrates that the results are a product of labor and care. To refer to observations of 24.9 percent and 15.5 percent grants a definiteness to the data. It converts "maybes" into "certainlys."

So, too, does the use of visual devices. Here the analogy to Liebow's use of protocols is apparent. Tables and other visual material are "outside" the text. They can then be referred to as the source of commentary in text. A frequent usage is as follows in reference to the same table.

"Comparing the observed with the expected A distribution, *we see* (italics mine) that there is considerably more relative stability in actual fact than the hypothesis of perfect mobility predicts" (p. 154).

The table has become the data. "The chances of upward mobility are directly related to education, *as Table 4.5 shows*" (italics mine).

Another way in which the data become "real" is through the continuous use of the closed world which has been built. As we shall see, Blau and Duncan fluctuate between couching their statements in measurement terms or making assertions about the experiences of the entire aggregate. Thus, compare the statement about measurement, "The proportion of men who experience some upward mobility increases steadily with education" (p. 157) with the statement about persons, "it is the social composition of men on this educational level that accounts for their downward mobility" (p. 161). Each group very seldom, if ever, yields uniform results. Even if sons on the average have higher occupational status than their fathers, many have lower occupational status. The disposition to treat the data as uniform by ignoring the qualifications is ever present and, as we will show, throws onto the reader the burden of moving from plot to story.

Style and Its Deviation: Looking through Different Glasses

In a brilliant analysis of the rhetoric of news in Israeli radio, Itzhak Roeh describes a useful device for examining the use of words and word patterns in these two studies (Roeh, 1982). Roeh finds that in the straight news broadcast, where most items describe official and elite acts and statements, the typical form of the sentence is assertive. Subject, verb, and object follow in that order. Viz. "The leader of the Left in Lebanon says that Lebanon is approaching a civil war." Here an event is described without limitations. In the news magazine, which follows the news broadcast, sentences are more likely to begin with subordinate clauses. Viz. "In the western parts of the town of Tiberias the police have fixed check posts." Here the event is limited to a specific place.

Roeh's examination of these differences leads him to conclude that the first form, what I call assertive style, conveys respect and objectivity. The latter style permits greater creativity and implies a less "factual," more tentative existence. Roeh uses the metaphor of glass to convey these differences. The form of language that asserts fact without becoming reflexive is called *transparent*. The contrast is *opaque*.

I have already made a number of references to how patterns of language use in these two works affects their status as factual accounts. Here I want to analyze the language of these two studies with concern for how "facticity" is, or is not, established.

Style as Cadence: The Function of Dullness

I have already remarked on the dull quality of the language in *The American Occupational Structure*. Sentences are long and the language other than ordinary. The style is marked by a deliberate lack of style. What I mean by this is a reference to the seeming lack of concern for unique, unconventional, or surprising uses of language. The very coventionality of the language is like the male suit of clothes. Its very uniformity conveys the stereotype that makes trust in the wearer believable (Fraser, 1981: 227-34). It presents the message, "I don't spend time and thought on fashionable appearance." There is an even cadence and rhythm to the sentences which detract from attention to the language. (As my colleague Bennett Berger has expressed it, the most desirable state of things appears to be one without words, if that were possible.) Much of this is accomplished through lengthy sentences with long subordinate clauses. Viz.:"The importance of the type of community in which a man was brought up for his occupational success can only mean that more urbanized environments prepare youngsters better for high-status occupations" (p. 263). A succession of sentences like this, not atypical in *The American Occupational Structure*, has something of the effect of continuous monotonic drumming.

Tally's Corner is a sharp contrast. The use of ordinary language makes for images that are concrete and distinct. Viz., "Few married men, however, do, in fact, support their families over sustained periods of time. Money is chronically in short supply and chronically a source of dissension in the home" (p. 131). The repetition of the word "chronically" in the second sentence gives a rhythmic change and a "surprise" that may make a reader conscious of the language. The use of verbatim and vernacular passages from the speech of the corner men contributes as well to unexpected language. *Tally's Corner* has a literary "feel" to it. In contrast *The American Occupational Structure* seems to guard its monotonic style as a means of shoring up the sense of a real rather than an imagined set of "facts." The style seems to say that this is hard material to get and to analyze and therefore the accounts are more reliable.

Here style and access are not unrelated. *Tally's Corner* holds the interest of the reader and does not exclude those uninitiated into sociology. By the same token, it is an easy read. It demands much less of the reader's attention and scrutiny than does *The American Occupational Structure*. The very boredom that The American Occupational Structure may induce shuts out the lesser-trained and interested reader. In turn, the dull quality of the language requires the reader to pay close attention to what is a careful and complex argument. The danger of one is the safety of the other. Liebow's readers may be more likely to follow the sequence from start to finish, but do so casually. The reader of *The American Occupational Structure* may be inclined to skip around in it, but to do so with close attention.

Shifts in Style

Each of these studies is reported in several different "languages." A major distinction in *The American Occupational Structure* is between verbal and visual material. I have already written, above, about the significance of the use of visual forms. Within the verbal materials, I shall examine some distinctions between sentence forms and their possible affects.

Tally's Corner utilizes three distinct forms. I have already described and discussed the distinction between the ordinary language of the author and the vernacular talk of the street-corner men and women. Here I will concentrate on the distinction in *Tally's Corner* between the author's language in describing and analyzing his "people" and the language used when he discusses "social science." In problems of style each of the three authors faces the central problem to which I have alluded throughout this paper—the argumentative and thus rhetorical character of the study.

Within the text of *Tally's Corner,* Liebow varies between describing and analyzing. Even when analyzing, however, Liebow sticks close to ordinary language. Viz., "The streetcorner is, among other things, a sanctuary for those who can no longer endure the experience or prospect of failure" (p. 214). Much of the discussion of implications of the study for theories of lower-lower-class behavior and Liebow's response to other sociologists is contained in footnotes. In *The American Occupational Structure* most of this is found in the text.

In first teaching *Tally's Corner*, in a methods course, I was surprised to find that much of the argument addressed to sociologists rather than lay people was found in the footnotes. Here the language is less likely to be "ordinary." In this quotation from a footnote Liebow discusses his qualifications to another theory with which he states much agreement.

"The first is that the stretched or alternative value systems are not the same order of values, either phenomenologically or operationally, as the parent or general system of values: They are derivative, subsidiary in nature, thinner and less weighty, less completely internalized, and seem to be value images reflected by forced or adaptive behavior rather than real values with a positive determining influence on behavior of choice" (p. 213).

This bifurcation of text and footnote seems a device that separates the audiences or readers. It keeps the style of *Tally's Corner* clear and, in the same study, also gives Liebow credibility as a social scientist by showing that he, too, can make the proper "noises." It has more significance than a union card display, however, and that will be discussed below.

Despite the general rejection of self-consciousness about their use of language, Blau and Duncan evidence at least two important shifts in language in addition to the verbal-visual dimension. Both are forms of what I will call the assertive-qualified dimension. They are analogous to Roeh's distinction between the transparent and the opaque.

Roeh's usage has pertinence for this paper in two ways. In *The American Occupational Structure* there are at least two kinds of statements: those that summarize, examine, or describe the collected data and those that present interpretations derived from the examinations, descriptions, and summations of the data. This is a distinction based on content. Within these differences there are also matters of form. Assertions can be made in qualified as well as assertive forms and interpretations can be made in similar fashion.

Blau and Duncan do more in *The American Occupational Structure* than report how they did their study and what they found. A great many paragraphs contain interpretations of data in which the authors shift into dramatic language. This is language that imputes motives, purposes, emotions, and other concrete elements to agents, to persons. Thus, from the final sentence in the chapter on analysis of the case of education:

> The relative deprivation of social status implicit in downward mobility is suffered most often by men in the intermediate educational brackets, and their exposure to this greater risk of deprivation *may well* (italics mine) make them a potentially explosive force in periods of economic crisis. (p. 161)

The use of the qualifying term "may well" is a means of putting the reader on guard that this sentence does not have the same evidentiary value as others. From the same section, here is a more assertive statement describing the data: "Downward mobility, however, does not exhibit a corresponding linear association with education" (p. 157). This is technical language. The downward mobility is nobody's particular mobility and is not a product of any human act but an abstracted concept.

In general, and more impressionistically, there appears to be a pattern to these usages. In some chapters, the assertive statements are contained within paragraphs which have discussed the method involved in reaching the assertion and which qualify the assertive strength of the statement. In others there appears to be a greater use of short assertive sentences to introduce the paragraph. The concluding chapter is especially given to this latter effect. Some chapters engage in more shifts from technical to dramatic language than do others.

The following are instances of what I refer to as assertive and qualified statements. Both are taken from lead sentences in paragraphs, but from different chapters:

Assertive: (from the concluding chapter) "Upwardly mobile couples tend to have fewer children than others with the same social origins" (p. 414).

Qualified: (from the chapter on differential fertility) "In sum, although the additive model cannot be accepted without reservation, it comes very close to predicting all the effects produced by a simple classification of couples as mobile or nonmobile" (p. 379).

It is difficult to know how to explain such seeming patterns. They appear to me to be related to the different authors. Substantive chapters and sections, as well as those on method, seem more qualified in their assertions and less likely to shift into dramatic language than do those specifically, like the conclusion, devoted to advancing a theory. Nevertheless, the distinction also seems to hold for substantive chapters written by the theorist, Blau, and those written by the methodologist, Duncan. To what extent these reflect general differences in style between the qualified assertions of methodologists and the assertive style of theorists or between Otis Duncan and Peter Blau is well beyond this paper.

Two aspects of style are, however, common throughout *The American Occupational Structure*. First, the general use of social science language in the verbal text is consistent. Unlike *Tally's Corner,* there is no shift from social science to ordinary language, although there are shifts from statistical analysis to social science language. Second, although to varying degrees, there is a general use of dramatic language when the authors move beyond data to concretize and give added significance to their material.

Polemical Nexus and the Altered Audience: Creating Moral Significance

It will be useful to raise a further query about these books: What do they appear to ask the reader to do? Is he or she to be the same person with the same beliefs and desires as before? Is there a praxis, a practical implication to these studies? If there is, and I believe there is, how do the authors try to accomplish it?

Both *The American Occupational Structure* and *Tally's Corner* have been important works in their fields. The Blau-Duncan volume has had an importance for the development of a method-path analysis. Yet if a method did not lead to worthwhile substantive significance it would be an empty agency. Each study did produce substantive findings of importance. In this section, I examine the two studies as ways of compelling belief in their significance. Another way of putting this question is to ask: What is it that the authors are trying to convince the reader is both true and important in their study? What difference should it make that things are as the authors have found them?

The Polemical Nexus

In *Tally's Corner,* Elliot Liebow does not go to much length to convince readers that the American black has experienced much discrimination and that such patterns of racial relations ought not to exist. Blau and Duncan do not attempt to argue the general virtue of achievement as a worthy tenet of social stratification.

"In a liberal democratic society *we* (italics mine) think of the more basic principle as being that of achievement. Some ascriptive features of the system may be regarded as vestiges of an earlier epoch, to be extirpated as rapidly as possible" (p. 161).

Insofar as the reader is seen as antithetical and hostile to the ideas being presented, the work has a polemical quality. It seeks to convert those who are initially in disagreement with the "message" of the work. But each also assumes some knowledge and belief shared by the community of their readers which makes the selection and analysis of materials sensible and significant.

The polemic, however, is not against the symbolic hostile reader. It is also addressed to a specific other; to social science works which are contradicted by the present work. It is here that the direction and relevance of the book is made clear to its readers. Hayden White, again:

> [E]very historical narrative has as its latent or manifest purpose the desire to *moralize* the events of which it treats. (White, 1981: 14)

In *Tally's Corner,* the polemic is directed against a then current mode of explaining black poverty. That explanation is found both in popular thought and also, in another form, in the writings of other social scientists. It is sometimes called the "culture of poverty," sometimes the class values approach. In the story of the truck driver and the reluctance of the corner men to work, Liebow writes as if he could read the mind of the truck driver, who has been able to recruit only two or three men after twenty to fifty contacts:

> To him, it is clear that the others simply do not choose to work...these men wouldn't take a job if it was handed to them on a platter. (p. 30)

Both in the chapter, "Men and Jobs" and in the concluding chapter, Liebow refers to social scientists who explain black poverty as, in part, a result of cultural characteristics. Improving the work productivity of the lower-class black is a problem of improving his motivation to achieve higher goals, of changing "work habits and motivation" (quoted from Allison Davis, "The Motivation of the Underprivileged Worker, p. 90 in Liebow, p. 30).

Put in Burkean terms, the key dramatistic concept in this account is that of the agent. With a theory that emphasizes the limited ambitions of the agent, the act of work rejection is understandable. It fits the reader's assumed understanding of how "such people" would act differently from you and me. Liebow's rhetoric assumes a different dramatistic concept in his explanation of the identical action. As is true of most sociological studies, his emphasis is on the scene as providing the motivation for the act. Analyzing the stories which he relates through paraphrase and protocol leads Liebow to see the action of the corner men as appropriate behavior given the skills they possess, their limited education, and the character of the menial jobs available to them.

Consider the issue of "deferred gratification" or "present-time"orientation, which had been accepted by many sociologists as a distinction between middle and lower-class people. One of Liebow's "stories" illustrates his thesis. Tally has asked him to hold eighty dollars of his pay. When Tally retrieves the money, Liebow asks why Tally doesn't put his money in a bank, since there are many close by. Tally responds:

> No, man...you don't understand. They closed at two o'clock and they closed Saturday and Sunday. Suppose I get into trouble and I got to make it [leave]. Me get out of town and everything I got layin' up there in that bank? No good! No good! (p. 69)

It is not that the corner men and the reader have different future orientations. They have different futures.

I emphasize this part of *Tally's Corner* because it is important to the rhetoric of fieldwork and, as we will see, to Blau and Duncan as well. In her study, *Rhetoric in Sociology,* Ricca Edmonson (1984) suggests that field studies utilize one or both of two enthymemes (an enthymeme is a truncated syllogism in which one of the premises is understood but unstated): the ordinary man and/or the rational man. Liebow's usage in the analysis of the corner men and their work life is of this character. He is saying to his readers: "You and the corner men are no different in your values and goals. If you were faced by their situation you would behave in the same manner." The scene explains the act, once you, the reader, understand the scene. There is a vicious cycle of poverty but it is not a result of historical continuities or cultural values. Sons behave like fathers because they face the same situations. Once the reader perceives the scene he or she can truly understand the "fitness" of the act in that scene.

The same appeal to a background knowledge of the reader appears in Liebow's account of marriage among the corner men. Liebow uses his stories of the corner men to demonstrate the contradictions between their account of why their marriages break up—the theory of manly flaws—and what is "truly" at work. The first theory, echoed in many social science writings, is that lower-lower class males do not value monogamy. Not so, writes Liebow. They give many indications of placing a high value on marriage and stable families. The problem, and the ubiquitous marital breakups, are results of the corner man's inability to play the role of breadwinner in a fashion adequate to him and to "normal" American standards. When these phenomena are viewed against the scene, the life situation of the corner men then:

> both "serial monogamy" and cultural distinctiveness tend to disappear. In their place is the same pattern of monogamous marriage found elsewhere *in our* (italics mine) society but one that is characterized by failure. (p. 220)

The appeal is again to the background knowledge of the reader in conjunction with the material presented about the corner men. The reader must agree with Liebow in his description of conventional American marriage patterns and with his understanding of the corner men .The generalizability of field work, in this instance as elsewhere, lies in this reconstruction of the logic of action of those studied. Edmondson is, I believe, correct about the rhetoric of field studies within the sociological paradigm. In sociology, the scene-act ratio is dominant. The act—behavior—has been shown to be "appropriate" to the scene (Burke, 1945: Ch. 1). With anthropologists and psychologists it may well differ. Almost by definition, cultures differ and individuals differ. The appeal to the "ordinary man" or the "rational man" may not be as much in use in those disciplines as in sociology where it is paramount.

The American Occupational Structure and Its Social Significance

Blau and Duncan make no case for the direct relevance of their study to matters of public policy. Nor are they as explicit in the early parts of the book about versions of social stratification with which they disagree. The posture of authorial absence would not permit any indication that the authors knew ahead of time what versions of American stratification were being contradicted by their book. At the outset, in chapter 1, the authors present their targets of revision in methodological terms. What they will do that others have not done is to relate variables to each other. They are less interested in the association between father's occupation and son's than in the influence of one variable on another and the co-joint influence of the two on son's contemporary occupational status. Thus father's origin has an influence but it has that influence, in part, by influencing the kind and amount of education that, in turn, has an influence on son's occupational status.

However, this methodological polemic against single-variable associations leads to conclusions of a substantive nature. These are foreshadowed by remarks in chapter 1 about a previous study by Lipset and Bendix (Lipset and Bendix, 1959). The reader is told that the Lipset-Bendix study is the most extensive secondary study of social mobility in several industrial societies and, on the final page of that chapter, that in the conclusion the authors will suggest reformulations of the theories presented in the prior study. Indeed, that study and its generalizations will emerge as a major foil against which *The American Occupational Structure* is to be seen.

Perhaps the central problem of mobility and stratification studies among sociologists in the late 1950s and early 1960s was that of the extent of opportunity for social mobility in the United States. Was it the case that America was an open society in which people could overcome the detriments of social origins and climb to higher places on the stratification ladder? Lipset and Bendix, using secondary analysis of survey data, had concluded that mobility in the United States, though considerable, was no greater than in other industrial societies (Lipset and Bendix, 1959). Further they had supported the conception of a "vicious circle" of poverty such that occupational and social status tended to be self-perpetuating. In describing that concept, Blau and Duncan use the Lipset-Bendix study as the best statement of the theory (pp. 199-200). Their quarrel with it rests on two conclusions, which they derive from their data and analysis.

1. A considerable amount of occupational mobility does occur in the United States.

2. While father's status is significant to son's, its effect is largely that of influencing the degree of education achieved by the son. How-

ever, and this is explicitly stated as a major conclusion of the study: "Far from serving in the main as a factor perpetuating initial status, education serves primarily to induce variation in occupational status that is independent of initial status" (p. 201).

The exception to their conclusion, however, is the case of the American black. Here Blau and Duncan agree with Liebow in finding that the "vicious circle" theory of poverty applies. They find its source in racial discrimination.

The Scene-Act Ratio

At bottom, Liebow and Blau-Duncan are sociologists or social anthropologists. Their basic paradigm is that of scene. The relatively high levels of mobility in American society are not, as Blau and Duncan find it, a matter of the capacities of the individuals who overcome their initial social origins. It is instead the influence of an institutional structure, the school, and its cultural principles which creates the opportunity structure making mobility possible. In concluding the book, the authors take the leap from a set of measured findings to conclusions about American society and its stratification system. Explicitly labeling their conclusions as "speculations," they see the role of education in supporting high mobility rates as evidence of a fluid rather than a rigid class structure. The causes of America's high rate of occupational mobility lies in the universalistic principles of "our industrialized society" (p. 431). The weakening of kin and communal ties and internal migration, in conjunction with education, all contradict the particularistic and ascriptive barriers to mobility. The act, mobility, is congruent with the scene. The existence of the scene is itself reflected in the action of occupational mobility.

Significance and the Normative "We"

It does not take a great amount of imagination to recognize the political significance of *The American Occupational Structure*. From one standpoint, the logic of the book might have been followed had they not written a conclusion but were content with a summary of findings. The findings alone, however, do not instruct the reader as to the direction that the findings might lead. The facts do not speak for themselves. They do not instruct the reader what to do or to feel about the facts shown. A summary of findings lacks moral significance.

Blau and Duncan are again explicit in their appeal to a set of standards by which the findings are to be judged. At various times they find it necessary to provide the reader with some vantage point, some stance from which to give importance to their study by linking it to something known and supposedly accepted by the reader. In the beginning to chapter 5, perhaps the major chapter describing the concepts and methods of the study, they distinguish between ascriptive and achievement systems, as "pure" types. They write, "In a liberal democratic society *we* think of the more basic principle as being that of achievement" (p.163). Like Liebow, the interpretations involve an appeal to "what everyone knows, "to the normative "we".

In this respect, the absence of women and households in the sample of persons studied, conventional as it was for sociology in the early 1960s, implies a readership which assumes the insignificance of women, either as members of the society, or as significant to the occupational work-force. Their absence, either as "father's occupation" or as "respondents," was not deemed a matter important enough to be extensively justified. Here the audience and the authors seem to have shared a particular version of mobility on which consensus occurred. It is doubtful if an American sociologist doing a similar study in this year (1989) could make such an assumption about the concepts of "occupational structure" or "social mobility."

The Two Genres

To some extent there is a dialectic of genres in these two books. The concrete, particular, and dramatic character of *Tally's Corner* does not prevent its opposite from occurring. Both in the footnotes and in text where Liebow must describe the general situation of blacks and of the lower-lower class (an abstract term itself) he must assume the aggregative, abstract "society" that Blau and Duncan study. Where the authors of *The American Occupational Structure* are limited by their data, they also express a need to convey a more concrete and particular account, even if speculative.

Yet it would be grossly misleading to say that each becomes the other. The styles, the methods, the authorial presence of Liebow are not that of Blau and Duncan. The dramatistic genre of Liebow makes different demands on its readers than does the technical genre of Blau and Duncan. Both ask the reader to follow them in sequence, not to read the conclusion before the introduction or the section on methods after the substantive chapters. Each throws onto the reader the burden of the background knowledge necessary to make sense of the materials. Each throws onto the reader the burden of discount. Blau and Duncan ask the reader to ignore, for the extent of the study, the limitations that the collected data impose on facticity. Liebow, despite the disclaimer of provability, develops an argument couched in terms of reflecting a factually existent world encompassing far more than *Tally's Corner*. In this sense, the books do become each other. Liebow begins in doubt, uncertainty, and the plausible, but ends with definiteness and certainty. Blau and Duncan begin with certainty and provability and end in plausability.

Nevertheless, the differences between the two studies, possibly the two genres, lies in what the reading experience seems to be for its readers. In reading Blau and Duncan, the reader is the equal of the writer. Once admitted into the "fratority" of admissible readers, he or she is in the same place as the author. The data the writer has gathered is presented to the reader. The questions a skeptical reader would make are made by the authors, and the agency—the methodology—governs both writer and audience. The reader must come to the same conclusion as the author because the reader, like the author, is a rational being who is exposed to the same data and, in part, a member of the same cognitive community as the author.

The methodology of *The American Occupational Structure* is like the scaffolding of a building. It is essential to erect the structure but once erected it may be dispensed with. The conclusions are the end product and all else, including the analysis, are only stations on the way to the end of the line. Once the reader has become convinced of the validity or invalidity of the study, his or her task is done and the means used to reach the end become irrelevant, no longer needed.

What does remain, over and above the findings and conclusions, is the image of stratification conveyed by the metaphor of the "path". Such imagery, akin to the concreteness of story, exercises the imagination of the reader. The picture of the factory system in Marx, of the bureaucracy in Weber, of the folk community in Toennies; these have been a major source of the power of sociologists in intellectual life (Nisbet, 1976). The image of the path provides a standard of "career" to the life cycle that contrasts with the shortened image of the respondent stepping into the shoes of the father.

Yet the organization of *The American Occupational Structure* is, in its emphasis on plot, not oriented toward change through the process of reading. Not so with *Tally's Corner*. Here the audience cannot readily separate the means from the ends of the study. A bald resume of *Hamlet*, in a page or so, would sound like many other plots. Reading an abstract or summary of *Hamlet* is not the same as reading *Hamlet*. Reading a summary of Veblen is a poor substitute for reading Veblen. The empathic response of putting oneself in the "role of the other" is elicited by the concreteness of the stories. It is through these that the reader can *appreciate* the reasonableness and ordinariness of the corner men's attitudes.

Creating Meaning and Changing Facts

Another way of stating the differences between these two genres is in recognizing what seems to occur in the process of reading each. Blau and Duncan are intent on proving the accuracy of a state of fact. The meaning of social mobility is taken for granted as something shared with their readers, as I have pointed out in discussing the absence of women and households. The general framework of perception and understanding is assumed. Thus the absence of women in the sample is not something that has to be defended. The use of the experimental report as model can proceed. The behaviors being reported on—occupations, stratification, mobility—have meanings that are assumed as fixed.

Liebow's task, or function, is quite different. He takes behavior that has been given a common meaning and attempts to change the reader's perception of it, to create a new perspective within which the meaning of the action is changed. The orientation to career and to marriage are now to be seen as no different from that of the reader. What is different is the scene within which they act.

What Liebow can accomplish is a change in the reader's evaluation and understanding of behavior. The end product is an appreciation of the behavior of the corner men by understanding why they act as they do. Blau and Duncan cannot provide new meanings, do not instruct the reader into new meanings, although the concept of path is a new metaphor. What they can do is compel an alteration in what is believed within the structure of already existent meanings. Liebow cannot support an aggregative sense about his twenty people that can apply to a large population. What he can do is to render an existent meaning of behavior that the reader holds as no longer the only, or even the most plausible, meaning available.

The problem of sampling is a crucial one for Blau and Duncan because they are claiming to describe aggregative facts, about central tendencies. They assume a reader who shares their interpretation of the meanings of events and actions—the status value of an occupation, for example. Given the problem of their study it could not be done with a sample of twenty men.

Liebow's study is not vitiated by the small size and particularity of his subjects. His object is the interpretation of behavior; the creation of meaning. Having shown that the corner men are not to be understood by conventional interpretations, he has cast doubt about generalization based on large samples that assume the conventional interpretations.

Writing social science appears to depend upon an assumed community of fact and meaning. But reading is more than the outcome of already given frameworks of understanding. It can, and does, lead to shifts and ruptures with what has gone before (Leenhardt, 1980). New facts are assimilated; new meanings emerge. The discovery of general facts and the interpretation of specific meanings are not necessarily accomplished in the same manner nor do they persuade the reader in the same way.

References

Bazerman, Charles. 1989. *The Shaping of Written Knowledge*. Madison: University of Wisconsin Press.

Blau, Peter, and Otis Duncan. 1967. *The American Occupational Structure*. New York: John Wiley and Sons.

Booth, Wayne. 1961. *The Rhetoric of Fiction*. Chicago: University of Chicago Press.

Brown, Richard Harvey. 1977. *A Poetic for Sociology*. Cambridge: Cambridge University Press.

Burke, Kenneth. 1945. *A Grammar of Motives*. New York: Prentice-Hall, Inc.

Edmonson, Ricca. 1984. *Rhetoric in Sociology*. London: Macmillan.

Empson, William. 1938. *English Pastoral Poetry*. New York: W. W. Norton.

Fish, Stanley. 1980. *Is There a Text in This Class?* Cambridge, MA: Harvard University Press.

Fraser, Kennedy. 1981. *The Fashionable Mind*. New York: Alfred A. Knopf, Inc.

Gusfield, Joseph. 1963. "The 'Double Plot' in Institutions." Patna University Journal 18, (January): 1-9.

_____. 1986. "Science as a Form of Bureaucratic Discourse: Rhetoric and Style in Formal Organizations." In T. Bungarten, ed., *Wissenschaft-Sprache und Gesellschaft*. Hamburg: Edition Akademion.

_____. 1981. *The Culture of Public Problems: Drinking-Driving and the Symbolic Order*. Chicago: University of Chicago Press.

_____. 1976. "The Literary Rhetoric of Science: Comedy and Pathos in Drinking-Driving Research." *American Sociological Review*, 41 (February).

Iser, Wolfgang. 1978. *The Act of Reading* .Baltimore: Johns Hopkins Press.

Kermode, Frank. 1966. *The Sense of an Ending: Studies in the Theory of Fiction*. London: Oxford University Press.

Latour, Bruno, and Steven Woolgar. 1979. *Laboratory Life: The Social Construction of Scientific Fact*. Los Angeles: Sage Publications.

Leenhardt, Jacques. 1980. "Toward a Sociology of Reading." In Susan Suleiman, and Inge Crosman, eds., *The Reader in the Text*. Princeton, NJ: Princeton University Press. Liebow, Elliot. 1967. *Tally's Corner*. New York: Little, Brown and Co.

Lipset, Seymour, and Reinhard Bendix. 1959. *Social Mobility in Industrial Society*. Berkeley: University of California Press.

Nisbet, Robert. 1976. *Sociology as an Art Form*. London: Oxford University Press.

Perelman, Chaim, and L. Olbrachts-Tytecka. 1969. *The New Rhetoric*. South Bend, IN: University of Notre Dame Press.

Plumb, J. H. 1971. *The Death of the Past*. Boston, MA: Houghton Mifflin.

Ricoeur, Paul. 1984. *Time and Narrative*. Vol. 1. Chicago: University of Chicago Press.

Roeh, Itzhak. 1982. *The Rhetoric of News in the Israel Radio*. Bochum: Studienverlag Dr. N. Brockmeyer.

Smith, Barbara Herrnstein. 1981. "Narrative Versions, Narrative Theories" In W. J. T. Mitchell, ed., *On Narrative*. Chicago: University of Chicago Press.

Suleiman, Susan, and Inge Crosman, eds. 1980. *The Reader in the Text*. Princeton, NJ: Princeton University Press.

Toulmin, Stephen. 1958. *The Uses of Argument*. Cambridge: Cambridge University Press.

White, Hayden. 1981. "The Value of Narrativity in the Representation of Reality." In W. J. T. Mitchell, ed. *On Narrative*. Chicago: University of Chicago Press.

5

Sport as Story:
Form and Content in Agonistic Games

In the 1984 Olympics, the Women's marathon was won easily by
Joan Benoit, but many of the 90,000 who witnessed the final lap were
more impressed and absorbed by one contestant who finished far back
from the leaders. This Danish runner entered the Coliseum in visible
pain, staggering, obviously weakened and possibly delirious. Among
the spectators, and later in the television commentaries, the sight of
her suffering aroused an intense debate. Would she be able to complete the lap of the stadium track needed to complete the marathon
without incurring permanent damage to her body or her mind? Should
authorities intervene to stop her? Should she be left alone to make that
decision? The crowd understood the importance to her of completing
the race, but also understood the potential danger she faced. Watching
from the Coliseum audience, I recalled the lines of a poem by Yeats,
"An Irish Airman Foresees His Death" (Yeats, 1962: 55-56):

> I balanced all, brought all to mind,
> The years to come seemed waste of breath,
> A waste of breath the years behind
> In balance with this life, this death.

The analogy between Yeats' airman and the Danish runner is undoubtedly overly melodramatic yet in other arenas and at other times
the stories of both are repeated manyfold in the daily lives of the
audience. It is the story of Heroism versus Prudence; of Honor versus
Safety; of Hotspur versus Falstaff. It was the bravery and determination of the runner to complete the task despite the risks and costs that

so moved the spectators, including myself and those around me in the stands.

From one perspective, the story of the 1984 Marathon is unique, a singular event. It will not happen again to the same people, in the same way, in the same place and time. From another viewpoint, it is a story repeated at many times and in many places. As Freud used the Oedipus drama to describe the recurrent cycle of parent-child dynamics, sports events replay, in mythical fashion, a spectrum of common experiences, dilemmas and conflicts with which the audiences that watch them can identify. In a symbolic relationship they can evoke memories and emotions. The story of the Marathon becomes a metaphor for many experiences in the lives of the audience.

Seen in this way, the events of spectator sports can be described in the language of Art, as narrative performances akin to Literature and Drama. In this paper, I want to analyze spectator athletic events from the vantage of that metaphor, seeing what is similar and what is distinct in the narrative performances of sports, literature, and nonspectator life.

This is not just an exercise in playful thought, an "idle" conceit. Metaphors reveal what is otherwise hidden, but they also hide what other metaphors may reveal. Metaphors of Business, Entertainment, Education, or Mass Media events reveal many, often hidden, attributes of modern professional, spectator sports, but they ignore the understanding of the "text," the activity itself, and the meanings it possesses for its audience. They explain much, but the excitement and intensity with which the spectator watches is lost. The cultural understanding eludes us. We cannot see what all the shouting is about.

Sociologists have often played the role of foreigner in literary and artistic analysis. For many in literary theory or art criticism the sociologist has been the unwelcome and unsavory interloper, sullying the purity of Literature and Art by an historicist reduction of the noble to the common. For many others the sociologist has been the stranger who is able by the detachment of the outside to bring a welcome realism to the trained incapacities of a discipline. In both guises the sociologist has become associated with an emphasis on the institutional and structural elements that affect art and literature (Becker, 1982). Class, organization, mass media. occupation, market are a few of the salient concepts of sociological analysis that have been used both by sociologists and those who borrow from their stock of armaments. This paper is not in that tradition.

I want to walk a different one-way street here. In recent decades, social scientists have turned toward literary and artistic analysis as a source of theories and methods for the understanding of human behavior as "text," as embodying in its fullness aspects of attention and interest that capture significant elements (Geertz, 1973; 1983). In this analysis of sports, I want to treat spectator sports as a matter of culture. In so doing, I am considering the sports event as a performance of a particular kind—an activity that is attended as an aesthetic experience by the spectator. I want to bring to the study of this human behavior some of the analytic procedures of the literary and artistic analyst for whom the text has an integrity and meaning, which cannot be given completely, nor even significantly, by recourse to its historical and institutional settings. Sociological methods and theories explain a great deal, but what is left untouched, unexplained, is often what is so central that it cannot be reduced or transformed into something else. But they frequently fail to explain or understand the activity itself.

An analysis of sports as a cultural object seeks to find the meanings of the action itself as perceived by its audiences. In this sense, I am reversing conventional sociological procedure. Rather than analyzing Art as a species of social behavior, I am analyzing behavior as a species of Art. [1]

Sociological Reductionism and Sports

In an old movie of the 1930s, *College Rhythm,* Hollywood presented the then popular view of undergraduate life in the United States. Amidst the activities of dating and sports appeared the unflattering portrait of the college radical. Short and unattractive, wearing thick glasses, he denounced football as "a capitalistic device instigated by the meat-packing barons to promote the sale of pigskins."

This is a caricature of the sociologist, to be sure. Yet it is not without its continuity to a common intellectual disposition to transform the spectator sport into an industrial enterprise, from "It's only a game" to "It's only a business." Such analyses have stressed both the structural, institutional sides of athletic events and the cultural, symbolic aspects of the games themselves. Consider the following from two analyses of communications:

> Televised sports, too, is best understood as an entertainment genre, one of the most powerful. What we know as professional sports today is inseparably intertwined with the networks development of the sports market. (Gitlin, 1982: 439)

The structural values of the Super Bowl can be summarized succinctly: *American football is an aggressive, strictly regulated team game fought between males who use both violence and technology to win monopoly control of property for the economic gain of individuals within a nationalistic entertainment context.* (Real, 1982: 238)

There are two problems with the usual sociological analysis of professional spectator sports. It is not that they are wrong or that they do not shed light on the context in which sports occurs or on many aspects of its symbolism. They do so, however, with two consequences:

1. In reducing the event to a non-sports realm—capitalism, professionalism, military combat—they produce a rhetoric that disparages and transforms the subject. The very term "reductionism" suggests a transformation that demeans its subject. It leaves the implication that the spectator is being manipulated into an experience that is false. The spectator is being used for ulterior purposes of which he or she is unaware. They make the consumer into what Garfinkel has called a "cultural dope." The resultant rhetoric depreciates what spectators appreciate.

Any analysis involving metaphors, as do most social analyses, is a form of reductionism. The difficulty with many is that they assume there is only one reduction that is feasible or that contradictory metaphors are not possible. I am asserting here that one way of seeing many sports events is through the conflict of routine and regulation, on the one hand, and unpredictability and transcendence on the other. This comes closer to the character of the experience of watching. It is an experience which other analyses, valuable as they may be, should not eradicate if we are to understand the activity of watching.

2. The second difficulty with such analyses is that they do not explain or understand the text itself—the elements to which the spectator is attentive, or at least not all of them. In his analysis of the American football spectacle, the Super Bowl (which I have quoted above), Michael Real brings his insightful essay near its close with the following paragraph:

While the critics may overstate their case, viewing the Super Bowl can be seen as a highly questionable symbolic ritual and an unflattering revelation of inner characterstics of mass-mediated culture in North America. Nevertheless, to be honest, for many of us it still may be a most enjoyable activity. (Real, 1982: p. 238)

It is this quality of athletic event in spectator sports that typical sociological analyses miss. This is what I refer to in discussing the story form of sports. The suspense and the excitement that comes with

the lack of prediction and the capacity for transcending the technological and the regulated, ruled character of many areas of life is a
contrast to much of everyday life. It is noteworthy that sports is the
one activity which regularly destroys and disrupts the routines of mass
media—radio and television. Even though efforts are made to provide
for commercials and to create time-bound segments, as in football and
basketball, both the pace of the game and the possibility of overtime
make programming unpredictable. Tennis and baseball, games in which
the length is not regulated by time periods, are even more difficult.
The mass media have been unable to change this central feature of
sports. Without it the story would be meaningless.

While contemporary sports is closely connected to the mass media
in its institutional settings, the form and much of the content has not
changed radically since its appearance in the late nineteenth century
before the appearance of radio, television, and movies. Computers
have led to a proliferation of statistics about sports, but the "numbers
nut" has long been a feature of sports fans.

I have been delayed in finishing this paper because, in part, I was
drawn away from it to watch the 1992 Winter Olympic games on
television. That quality of absorption is not given by any analysis of
the structure of the mass media industry. As William James said, "To
miss the joy is to miss all."

Agonistic Sports as a Literary Form

By "spectator sports," I refer to the professionalized, athletic event
performed before mass audiences in modern stadia or observed on
radio or television and reported in the press. The preoccupation of
large segments of modern populations with spectator sports is an important aspect of daily life. Emerging in the nineteenth century and
vastly expanded by the rise of mass media, commercialized and public
sports are a feature of modern urban societies (Barth, 1980: Ch.5;
Betts, 1969; Huizinga, 1950: Ch. 12). They differ considerably from
the elite sports and folk games of agricultural communities and, in
their commercialized and professional characteristics, from the Greek
and Roman ones as well (P. Burke, 1978).

Analyses of games, play. and athletic events have generally con-
centrated on the players, the athletes in athletic contests. My angle of
interest in this paper is on the audience, the spectators. It is from this

angle that what is game and a form of play to the performers is performance to the observers. Athletic events are one type of entertainment for their audiences. It is in its character as performance that the dramatic quality of sports competitions become a type of Art.

Of course, a view of action as inherently dramatic can be extended toward much of human behavior, as a number of sociologists have maintained (K. Burke, 1945; Goffman, 1956; E. Burns, 1972; Gusfield, 1963;1981). What I maintain in this paper is that the form of sports events heightens the intensity and dramatic impact of its performances. Athletic contests differ, in significant ways, both from the daily life of the audiences and from the staged occasions of professional theatre, the written forms of Literature and the visually fixed forms of painting, or even current performance art. Sports events are, from the standpoint of the spectators, a particular form of Art. As such, the spectators bring to them the frames of meaning they have developed, which enable them to order the sensations and events they observe. The game is itself staged by the players and the organizers of play, but it is done within certain constraints that constitute its form.

The Constraints of the Script

Sociologists have used the concept of "role" as a way of designating the expectations, duties, and privileges that accrue to the holder of a position in the social organization. To be a mother or a father or a child is to assume a set of opportunities and responsibilities connected with those statuses. The concept is, however, at best an abstract version of situated events. As many have pointed out, human action is not so fixed and constrained (Cicourel, 1973; McHugh, 1968; Perinbanayagam, 1985). The metaphor of the stage is limited (Goffman, 1974: Ch. 5). The role that governs an event is often chosen from among diverse possibilities in defining the situation. The situated experience must be provided with a meaning. Human beings transform roles, adapt them to specific persons, to specific situations. In many ways, they play with roles and with rules; they obey them, ignore them, avoid them, and transform them.

This is the case with games. Participants in friendly card games bend rules, change rules for the occasion or for longer periods. Sandlot teams decide to adopt new rules for the occasion of the game. Tennis players decide the match will consist of fewer games per set or fewer sets per match. Beginnings, middles, endings are not so fixed that the participants, though competitors, cannot cooperate and change the rules, create handicaps to aid some of the players, or make decisions that depart from the constraints of the script. Where the play is not the object of audience attention, the players are freed to enjoy the action of the game itself with less concern for winning or losing. Human behavior undergoes a continuous and continuing unpatterning of revisions, reforms, and even revolts.

Spectator sports are more formalized and hence closer to script than much of human behavior. Not only are times of occurrence relatively fixed, the rules of the game are clear and cannot be tampered with in specific situations. Imagine a group of runners who, minutes before the Olympics race, decide that the 100-meter dash should, for that day, be shortened to 80 meters, or that one of the runners, having just twisted his ankle, should be given a head start. The script, having been written, the players adhere to it. They do not "break frame."

But while athletic contests take place within a frame, it is not the same as the frame of literary and visual Art. Once in the frame of the athletic contest, the content is still uncertain. Works of Art are reproducible and/or fixed. Revisit the museum after thirty years and Rembrandt's *The Night Watch* will be the same, minus wear and weathering: Day will not have come; the good burghers will not have changed clothes, nor will any of them have gone to breakfast.

To be sure, some forms of art allow for some improvisation. The musical score can be performed differently by instrumentalists or conductors. But the general script is adhered to. Mozart cannot sound like Debussy unless the performers break the frame and revolt against their bonds. *Hamlet* can be performed in many different ways, but in none of them will he kill Claudius, marry Ophelia, or be murdered by Polonious.[2] Keats said it when, in his "Ode on a Grecian Urn," he wrote: "Forever wilt thou love and she be fair." Neither can the Ode itself be rewritten. Rereading it after many years, it is as constant as the figures on the urn.

It is essential to the form of drama constituting sports that the content is never assured. The race, the game, the match is never the same. The outcome is never certain. The annals of life are replete with the tragedies created by the spectator who has bet on a "sure thing." Each event is a unique action. It will not happen again, in the same way and the same situation.

It is this characteristic of the athletic performance that is essential to its characteristic form. It is a real and non-reproducible event. It is neither planned nor a staged performance. Like life, it has similarities to the stage but it is not an artificial world. As such, it contains the same tension of risk, uncertainty, and chance that is synonymous with life. What the audience observes is the life action of the athlete. Unlike the stage or film, it is real action. When the audience comes to believe that it is staged, as in American wrestling matches, the tension and crisis is lost and the performance becomes of another type. The spectators must believe that what they see is unrehearsed and thus uncorrupted, that each contestant is performing as best he or she can at that moment. That is the essence of contest.

The Contest as Drama

It is difficult to imagine, at least in Western culture, the staged drama that lacks tension resulting from conflict, as well as uncertainty. Whether it is Oedipus struggling against the Fates or Lear against his daughters and his own foolishness, the principle of *agon*, of competition and contest, is a major form of spectator sports. The footrace, the soccer game, the tennis match, the boxing match, the baseball game are all clear instances of the agonistic principle. There is a winner or winning team. There are losers or losing teams.

This does not necessarily mean that competition is a zero sum situation. Being less than first may not be complete loss for the second or third in a footrace, for those close to the finalist in a tournament, such as tennis, or for a nation gathering points and medals in the Olympics.

What is the case, however, is that the uncertainty and the competition creates the dramatic tension of the athletic event. In much of modern sports, the spectator, while appreciative of the skill and beauty of sheer motion and action, is not primarily attendant on such as the focus of attention. A narrative form is imposed which grants the action significance and meaning in a context of opposition, conflict, and contest. A competitive form can be imposed even when it might otherwise be seen as pure *ludus*, play per se, to follow Caillois' usage of Huizinga's term (Caillois, 1979: pp. 30-33). Caillois points to the game of yo-yo playing as often conducted so that one player attempts to do better than another or to surpass his or another's prior record (Caillois, pp. 29-30). Certainly many individualistic sports, where competition is not direct and face-to-face, are, nevertheless, governed by agonistic forms. Weight-lifting, pole-vaulting, high jumping, gymnastics are instances of this. So, too, and especially in Olympic sports, the conflict may also be between the individual and the past, in the shape of the Olympic or world record.

As a principle of the form of athletics, the contest is not itself unrestricted and formless. There must be at least partial equality of skill, otherwise the contest is meaningless since there is no margin for unpredictability. In horse-racing, at least in the United States, care is taken by the organizers of horse-races to create races in which horses of similar racing quality are pitted against each other. This system of "handicapping" is a way of trying to assure spectators and others that it is "true" contest. As Caillois describes agonistic games, they are

> like a combat in which equality of chances is artificially created, in order that the adversaries should confront each other under ideal conditions, susceptible of giving precise and *incontestable* (nota bene) value to the winner's triumph. (Caillois, 1979: 14)

Seen from this standpoint the absence of male-female sports conflict is a means of assuring the integrity of the contest. A boxing match between two males, one a flyweight and the other a heavyweight, would lack the drama of competition. (However, this does not explain the absence of either female boxing divisions or of matches between a female heavyweight and a male flyweight.) Victory for the contestant of excessive advantage lacks sweetness.[3]

The Athletic Form of Agonistic Sports

Many games contain most of the elements of athletic contests, but are not classifiable as athletic sports. They lack the quality of physical skill and prowess. Among these are games that arouse interest, excitement, and drama, but which depend on skills that are chiefly intellectual or depend largely on the operation of chance, or on both. Chess, checkers, parchesi, dice, bridge, and most games of chance fall into this category. Chess and bridge are two examples of games in which conflict, competition, uncertainty, and rule-governed behavior create very high drama. There is an international organization of these games and they have a wide audience of followers. They are newsworthy events. They are certainly forms of play but must be distinguished from sports, as the term is used in common practice.

The athletic contest does involve chance, but in the limited sense that all of life involves chance. Other games, such as dicing, "blackjack," roulette and such are closer to pure chance although here, too, degrees of skill exist. In such games, the conflict or competition is between the individual player and the house," but the tension and drama of such games is often great for spectators as well as players (Sagan, 1984: Ch. 2). Yet they do not engage the mass spectator audiences . Chess may be the marginal exception in East Europe where it may assume mass attention.

The athletic contest involves the body—its capacities, its limits, its beauty, its operation. Running, jumping, diving, swimming, tumbling, kicking, throwing, lifting, hitting are elemental actions that all cultures experience. It is the nature of the athletic contest as a physical encounter that the spectators bring to it their experience with the limits which physical abilities and endurance entail. The body is a universal experience of human beings as biological species.

Youth versus experience, age versus bodily capacities, the limits which human capabilities and natural barriers pose—these are foundations on which are raised the stories of sports events. The individual tests the physical dimensions of his skills against those of others and the triumphs and defeats rebound to the sense of power and character of the nations, territories, or social designations they symbolize.

The relationship of the physical to the capacity of the contender to overcome, or to use the capacities and limitations of his biological self, is essential to the story of the athletic event. Winning, within the confines of the fair contest, is the contest between athletes of similar abilities and thus the triumph of how it is used, of character, discipline, intelligence and aspiration. When the contest is less than equal, where experience and will contend against physical limits and powers, the conflict between Biology and Culture, Nature and Will is accentuated. The dramas of athletic contests are dramas of achievement that touch on basic conflicts within the self of the spectator and between his or her environment. It is because the achievements of the athletes contain such meanings that victory or defeat can symbolize the achievements of nations as well as individuals.

Transcendence and Routine

The physical aspect of athletics introduces another element, akin to unpredictability, and not necessarily narrative. This is the phenomena of transcendence, the quality of going beyond what seems possible. The great feat of endurance, the broken record, the "impossible" catch provide thrills and excitement apart from the contest and conflict of an agonistic character. In a recent review of a book on the famous hitting streak of the baseball "hero," Joe DiMaggio[4] the geologist and historian of science, Stephen Gould, points out that streaks in games can be predicted on the basis of individual past achievements. However, he maintains, DiMaggio's streak was beyond what prediction would have led us to expect. That is its greatness. He concluded the review by writing:

> DiMaggio's hitting streak is the finest of legitimate legends because it embodies the essence of the battle that truly defines our lives. DiMaggio activated the greatest and most unattainable dream of all humanity, the hope and chimera of all sages and shamans; he cheated death, at least for a while. (Gould, 1988: 12)

The Bounded Character of the Athletic Event

In his essay on contests, including casino gambling and commercialized spectator sports, Erving Goffman suggested that such events are similar to life in the characteristic of fatefulness. But it is unlike the "reality" of the spectator's routine life in its short span and bounded character.

> Everyday life is usually quite different...ordinarily the determination phase— the period during which the consequences of his bet are determined—will be long, sometimes extending over decades, followed by disclosure and settlement phases that are themselves lengthy. The distinctive property of games and contests is that once the bet has been made, *outcome is determined and payoff awarded all in the same breath of experience.* A single sharp focus of awareness is sustained at high pitch during the full span of the play. (Goffman, 1967: 155-56)

In the routine experience of the spectator, the major decisions of life and career are made and his fate determined over the long span. Marriage, education, occupation, children, and the various transformations that these involve subject us all to the exigencies and vicissitudes of choice and chance. We do not, and seldom can, see these events as a performance. They are not visible to an audience and cannot be presented in a short enough form to constitute a performance of "real-life" events.

The opposite is the case when the audience watches the sports contest. There is fatefulness and a real experience, but it occurs to others, to the contestants. It is their experience, their fate, that is the object of observation. But it is encompassed in a form that is short enough for the beginning, the middle and, so essential, the ending. The rewards and the punishments can be viewed during a single sitting or over a short season of several months.

The Dramatic Content of Agonistic Sports

Literature and Art can be seen as a relation between the observer/ reader and the artistic product. The text is a construction of the reader as well as the writer (Iser, 1978; Fisch, 1980). So, too, while the uncertainty and transcendent character of sports are central elements and inherent in the events, the meanings are dependent on the spectator's understandings of them. The form of the art is given content by its viewers.

Sports as Object

Central to the frame within which spectator sports occurs is the distinction between spectators and players, between Art and Life. For the players, the game is life. Their reputation, their livelihood, their futures are represented by their performance. It may be peak moment, tragic Fate, or ignominious defeat. A. E. Housman has given voice to this in his poem, "To an Athlete Dying Young" (Housman, *Collected Poems*, p. 32):

> Now you will not swell the rout
> Of lads that wore their honors out,
> Runners whom renown outran
> And the name died before the man.

For the audiences that watch the contest the distance between what they observe and their own lives is paramount. In this sense, the athletic performance is a form of what Art has come to mean in many countries and in many cultures in the modern era. It can exist to the spectator as a story, a narrative to be observed. Here the recent paper by the literary analyst, M. H. Abrams sheds much light on the social setting and cultural frame within which sports, as a form of Art, depends (Abrams, 1985). Abrams was concerned with the change in visual and literary Art which developed in Western societies, beginning in the seventeenth century and coming to dominance in the nineteenth. That change replaced the sense of artistic objects as related to some outside end—religious, decorative, instructive, etc., with the attitude that such objects are to be appreciated "for their own sake."

> What defines a work of art is its status as an object to be "contemplated" and contemplated "disinterestedly"—that is, attended to "as such" for its own sake. (Abrams, 1984: 8)

Abrams' analysis of this change points to the emergence of an aesthetic, as distinct from a utilitarian, attitude toward objects. As he points out, it depends on an institutional setting, which creates and defines that attitude toward many objects. Painting and literature grew as a mass public was educated to appreciate objects "as such" as forms of entertainment or "contemplation" (Mukherji, 1983; Watt, 1957). I have pointed out above that the mass sports public emerged with commercialized sports in urban centers in the late nineteenth century. In the twentieth century, the mass media have expanded that public to a large portion of populations. It is a major point of this paper that such social changes, while significant in many ways, have not changed either the centrality of suspense and uncertainty inherent in the narrative quality of sports, nor have they destroyed the aesthetic character of viewing. These have been only slightly changed since the development of professional athletic events and spectator audiences.

Yet we recognize that the spectators need not uniformly use the same frame in witnessing a sports contest. The frame of achievement in competition and the very rules and assumptions of particular sports have had to be learned as has the very conception of the contest as aesthetic object. The spectator's own participation in some form of play has been one way of socializing the spectator to the sport.[5]

The contests I am discussing are here described through the language of the stage since they are actions performed before an audience. The encounters between contestants or between contestants and some external force, such as weather or natural limits or some standard such as a record, provide the conflict and suspense that heighten the suspense and excitement of the action. From this standpoint, there are "good" games and "bad" ones, dramatic and undramatic ones.

The dramatic encounter is thus the high point of the athletic performance. As Orrin Klapp puts it:

> Of course, drama cannot occur unless images are projected and parts played that an audience can use psychologically, and drama does not become really "dramatic" unless it develops suspense from crisis—from a turning point or unex-

pected outcome that has the audience on the edges of their seats, so to speak. (Klapp, 1964: 24)

The encounters of sports take on additional meanings and dramatic qualities as metaphorical enactments of archetypal experiences. Like Literature, these are repeated recurrently in different guises and forms (Frye, 1957). The audience is able to relate the stories observed to universal experiences of their lives. Even though they may not use archetypal terms, the situations contain the possibilities for analogous resonance. The language of sports in American usage are those of combat, of struggle, of victory and failure, of common themes in literature and life.

This is clearly found in the prevalence of the David and Goliath myth reenacted in sports, sometimes explicitly. David's weapons are makeshift; his physical resources are no match for the giant. He has his cunning and his determination, his will and his bravery. In life, these are usually a poor defense against the Goliaths of this world. The race is to the swift and the game is to those whose natural resources are superior. A basketball game that went always to the strongest and tallest would leave no hope for the weaker and smaller. But in sports, the possibility of upset, of victory or defeat, sustains the audiences. It shows that experience, alertness, intelligence, and cleverness may triumph. Hence the victory of the stronger is earned and merited since their conquest was never assured and the victory of the weaker is always possible.

Archetypal myths pervade athletic events and develop their symbolism. In baseball, it is commonplace to refer to "power pitchers and power hitters" and to "place hitters and place pitchers." The "power hitter" can hit for long distances but is less certain to contact the ball than is the "place hitter," who can contact the ball and direct it but has less distance in his bat. The "power pitcher" has speed but less directional control than the "place pitcher." A Lévi-Strauss of sports might well see in these encounters the clash of Nature versus Culture, the conflict in life between natural endowments of brute force and the skills of intelligence acquired through experience and practice. [6]

To be sure, the impact of such events and the archetypes to which they can be analogized depends upon an audience trained to see such performances as symbolic, to attend to the significance of contest. The narrative embedded in contest, with its beginning, middle and end, may not be the most attended aspect of the performance. Riesman and

Denny, in their account of the history of football in the United States, maintain that the elaboration of the line of scrimmage and the process of "downs" in American football emerged when the game was imported to American college campuses in the early nineteenth century. In the fierceness of intercollegiate competition, heightened by the religious conflicts between Harvard and Yale, the audiences were drawn into concentration on victory or defeat. In the British version, the audiences were the social inferiors of the aristocratic players. Their interest was in how the game is played. Who won was secondary. When winning or losing was fraught with significance, as in the American scene, the concept of "downs" made the contest more equitable through regulating possession of the football (Riesman and Denny, 1954). The emphasis on the narrative does require an audience trained to see the narrative as the way of bringing order out of the chaos of sensations they observe (H. White, 1981; Chatman, 1978).

Heroes, Fools and Victims

Sports events are filled with actions of heroism, of foolishness, of "tough luck." The mighty player, or the record-holder, always presents the possibility that in this particular event, on this day, he may not be "true to form." He or she may stumble, may commit an error of judgment, may become ill.

Contrarywise, the opposite may occur. The weak or insignificant player may rise to the occasion. He or she may perform brilliantly in the particular occasion or may score the winning goal against great odds. The events of the sporting world are the stuff from which heroes arise, fools are generated and *schlimazels* (unfortunate fools) suffer the inequities of evil Fortune.

Two types of archetypal events occur frequently in the annals of spectator sports. They are mimetic in that they mirror the experienced situation of the spectator as Everyman. One is the universal experience of senescence. The other is the occurrence of Luck, what Caillois calls the aleatory element in games (Caillois, 1979).

To grow older is, in some cultures and some activities, to gain in power and influence. In athletics, beyond a certain point, it is the opposite. The aging athlete is faced with the loss of physical power. The contest between the aging hero and the youthful contestant is a repetition of the struggle of the audience with the realities of biological senescence. The battle for physical and sexual power between the young and the old, while shaped by cultural differences, in sports is presented in almost pristine fashion. The experience and sagacity that comes with age is pitted against the force and agility of youth. The will to command the body beyond what is expected is pitted against the ease and stamina that youth possess and which age diminishes. Such contests are deeply dramatic. When the contestant overcomes age in his battle against youth there is a deepened intensity to the drama. Some years ago, at Wimbledon, when Arthur Ashe, then an aging and fading tennis star, managed against the odds to defeat Jimmy Connors, then a youthful and rising star, it was this aspect of the story that occupied the attention of the commentators. It did the same when Connors, then aged thirty-six , lost to Andre Agassi, aged eighteen. The Pelleas and Melisande story is retold again and again.

The element of Fortune, Luck, or Fate is similarly told and retold. The uncertain, the unexpected, the vicissitudes and benefits of Fate and fortune follow all of us and defeat or reward us with little regard for the merits of our talents or industry. Who could have predicted that Mary Decker (Slaney), having prepared so long and so successfully for her 1984 Olympics race, would be accidentally tripped during the running and be forced out. How like Life to trip us up with so little concern for merit! What is the evil star that had kept Ivan Lendl, then the first or second seeded tennis player in the world, from winning Wimbledon when he had so often reached the finals? How like Life to withhold from us the reward we so clearly merit? That element of Fate that we all face is out there to be seen, to be bowed to or defied on every field and in every stadium. In the process of living we are confronted with choices and chances, with risks and opportunities. We make decisions and act in ways that determine our fate from that point on; we take fateful actions. As Goffman puts it, in his brilliant analysis of games and gambling:

> enterprises are undertaken that are perceived to be outside the normal round, avoidable if one chose and full of dramatic risk and opportunity. This is action. The greater the fatefulness, the more serious the action. (Goffman, 1967: 260-61)

From this perspective the athletic contest is also a crystallized encounter with Fate. The sports event is imbued with chance, with uncertainty and unpredictability, as is the life of the audience. An aura of Fatefulness surrounds the possibilities of the contest and the contestants. The more important the event, the more fateful the action. Careers are made and unmade; records set or never reached.

It is the common experience of the audience with the crystallized events of the athletic contest that enable them to perceive the events as dramatic. In this sense, there is a common human element that unites the audience across cultural and historical differences. While such elements of drama, of course, may be distributed differently across the spectrum of human cultures, the closer they come to widely shared elements of life that make for dramatic excitement, the more they draw a diverse audience into a community of attention. The more the audience is "trained" to see the athletic contests within the frame of competition, the more dramatic is the reading.

Symbolic Competitors

In portraying sports competitions as symbolic of archetypal stories, I have been emphasizing the symbolic character of the sports event, the way in which the unique event and the career of the sports contestant takes on a more universal meaning. Meanings can involve other orders of events than the common myths of the culture. In another sense they can, and often do, symbolize aspects of social structure. In an often specific sense, the contestants are the carriers of a class, a race, a nation. Rather than uniting the audience, they play upon the differences that divide them.

From one perspective, a contest is a competition between individuals or individual teams. Yet the social characteristics of the participants can create symbolic meanings for the spectators. In the years shortly after the American game of professional baseball admitted black players, encounters of the common sort, but between a white pitcher and a black batter, contained strong elements of racial competition. This was observable in the talk of spectators, but has now disappeared. In their classic paper on American football, David Riesman and Reuel Denney observe the symbolism of football history (Riesman and Denny, 1954). In the 1920s, the American private universities of the Eastern seaboard, such as Harvard and Yale, began to lose their supremacy to the mid-western state universities and, in a flamboyant fashion, to a Catholic institution, the University of Notre Dame. Here was mirrored the passing of political and social dominance of the Protestant upper-class establishment to the mobile middle classes of the public universities and the *nouveau riche* of the immigrants. Notre Dame beat the prestige schools at their own game and did it by cleverness and accuracy, using the new technique of a passing attack against the old-fashioned methods of brute power at the line of scrimmage (Riesman and Denney, 1954). The game was not "just a game." It reenacted and crystallized the conflicts of social structure. Here were dramas of social division.

Yet there is also a sense in which, akin to rituals, the sports event may transcend the symbolic competition of class with class, of nation with nation, of race with race. The archetypal element of the sports story may conflict with meanings drawn from other identities. In the 1984 Olympics, a young woman running in track was the first from her country, Morocco, ever to win a gold medal. That fact led the 90,000 members of the Coliseum audience, very few of whom were Moroccan or even Islamic, to accord her an especially triumphant response.

Here MacAloon, using Turner's analysis of ritual, seems correct in perceiving the Olympics and other sports events as creating a space and time outside of social and political space and time, a liminal *communitas* in which the common human qualities are highlighted (Turner, 1969; MacAloon, 1984).

One aspect of social structure is glaringly absent: the battle between the sexes. There are very few sports in which women compete against men.[7] Even if we attempt to account for this segregation of the sexes by recognition of differences in biological power, the setting is still capable of providing interesting conflicts between young women and older men as in footracing, basketball and baseball, tennis and a number of other sports, many of which do not involve physical contact.[8]

What I am asserting in this section of the paper is the status of spectator sports as dramatic performances, as the telling of a story. It is the literary quality of sports events that is under consideration here. The content of contests as dramatic performances generates an experience in which the audience is truly a "popular" one, that is, devoid of the social diversities that otherwise separate them. It is this exposure to events that are highly dramatic across such differences as age, class, occupation, region that engenders the identification of persons as part of a common humanity.

But the perception of the individual, or the team, striving toward goals, the drama of skilled peers competing for victory, implies a frame through which the sports event is seen. This is separate from the rules. It implies the terms of order that direct the spectator toward some aspects of what is observed rather than others. Without a cultural frame of categories, purposes and priorities, what Kenneth Burke calls a "grammar of motives" (K. Burke, 1945), the content is an infinitude of sensations. Definition of the situation is made possible by the imposition of frames that establish the kind of significance attributed to actions (Goffman, 1974; Bateson, 1972: 17-193). That is why the form of the contest, its ruled constraints alongside the openness of unpredictability, makes the drama of the event possible. A discussion of the athletic contest as a modern form of sports must keep that in mind.

The absorption of large segments of the population, regardless of class, ethnicity, and age (though not gender) attests to something more universal than is the rule in mass communications. Barth's conception of the American game of baseball strikes an insightful chord in seeing this highly popular game as a contrast to the regulated, predictable, and technological character of modern life (Barth, 1980: Ch. 5). In its uncertainty, its break with the culture of regulated time, in its physical skills and in its transcendent action, athletic sports create a realm where the nature of physical abilities count and where the unexpected is visible and always present. It is a striking contrast to the world of society, where social differences, predictable and programmed organization and utilitarian goals are dominant. Although the events of spectator sports occur within an organizational setting and social framework of rules and teams, the Art they create is an arena where suspense and excitement clash with the structured world of enterprise and routine. Focused on attributes of physical skills and power, they are an anomaly in a world in which the qualities of humans as natural beings are less and less relevant.

The Drama of Sports: Freedom and Organization

Sports, as much of human behavior, has its meanings which, like much of Art, depend upon its form and the perception of that form by audiences. The context is important as the frame, but we cannot dispense with the canvas itself.

This quality of dramatic uncertainty is by no means absent from the stage or the novel. It is, in some sense, a sine qua non of drama the first time the audience experiences it. Will Oedipus avoid his Fate? Will Macbeth get his just punishment? Will Raskolnikov's crime be uncovered? This is story with its suspense, surprise, and excitement.

But even on stage and in novels the ending is known by the author and the actors. It bears a relationship to the beginnings and middles (Kermode, 1966: Ch. 5). In the creation of the literary product, the end becomes known to the creator and can influence the rewriting. Not so in sports. They remain non-reproducible and unplanned. What is more, the spectator is aware that the ending is unknown to the participants or anyone in the game. There is an element of possible surprise in each and every package. In this fashion, it is a species of life.

Significant to the form and content of agonistic sports is the dialectic between organization and disorganization; structure and freedom; expectations and upsets. The occurrence of freedom within constraint enables the spectator to find the story of the race, the match, the game continuously absorbing. It gives it a narrative quality and creates a story rather than a series of discrete events.[9] When it is truly a "foregone conclusion," the story has become intriguing only to the critic and some sociologists.

Considering sports as a form of Art, as telling and acting out stories within its own specific form, enables us to consider the elements that operate in creating meaning. It is not that the sociologist is wrong in seeking for the institutional and structural elements at work. Why we turn to the literary theorist, the aesthetic philosopher, and the art critic is to find the tools to help us understand the activity as an aesthetic, as well as a utilitarian experience. The bridge that has separated the humanities and the social sciences can also be a construction that unites.

Notes

1. This is not to negate the analytical values of both directions. The utility of seeing Art as social behavior is also significantly valuable. I am indebted to the work of Kenneth Burke for realizing the similarities between the two. For a fuller statement, see the introduction to my anthology of Burke's writing (Gusfield, 1989).
2. In his play, *Rosencrantz and Guildenstern Are Dead*, Tom Stoppard has taken immense liberties with the *Hamlet* play. He has rewritten it from the uncomprehending viewpoint of two "bit" characters in the drama. It is not, however, the same play as Shakespeare's, and that is Stoppard's point.
3. It also implies that participation per se is itself a form of equality. The Olympics serves the purpose of defining many member nations as part of the world community just by participation, by appearing in contests even where there is small likelihood of winning any medal. In this, the Olympics is a certifying mechanism, legitimating the claims of nations, especially new nations, to recognition in the world community.
4. DiMaggio, one of American baseball's greatest, hit safely in 56 continuous games in 1941. This record has not been surpassed since nor has any player come closer than 44 games to it.

5. It may be that agonistic games are the exception, rather than the rule, in athletic events. Certainly not all contemporary societies glorify competitive sports. As some suggest, the agonistic character of Greek sports was not the rule for societies in antiquity (Griffin, 1988). This paper, however, takes agonistic sports as its subject because they are dominant in European and American societies. I am not sufficiently knowledgeable of non-agonistic sports to know if my analysis is relevant to them.

6. The symbolism can also operate in the reverse order. Sports become the source of metaphors for life. "The race is to the swift."

7. Rae Blumberg has pointed out to me that where it does occur, as in gunshooting, autoracing, or in horsemanship or horseracing, the contestant operates a machine or animal that supplies the source of power.

8. It is possible, as Wendy Griswold has suggested to me, that women are less drawn to the agonistic elements of athletic events than are men in Western culture. Certainly the aesthetic interests in athletic events is a product of socialization and has been a "man's world" in Western societies. However, it is not exclusively so and as mass media proliferate knowledge, is less and less so.

9. Barthes has made a similar distinction in contrasting boxing with commercial wrestling. The latter, not believed to be a "true" contest, is experienced as a series of specific events rather than with a concern for the outcome, as is the case in boxing. Wrestling, he writes, is not a sport but a spectacle. "Wrestling...demands an immediate reading of the juxtaposed meanings, so that there is no need to connect them. The logical conclusion of the contest does not interest the wrestling fan, while on the contrary a boxing-match always implies a science of the future.(Barthes, 1972: 16).

References

Abrams, M. H. 1985. "Art-as-Such: The Sociology of Modern Aesthetics." *Bulletin of the American Academy of Arts and Science*, 38, 8-33.

Barth, Gunther. 1980. *City People*. New York: Oxford University Press.

Barthes, Roland. 1973. *Mythologies*. London: Paladin.

Bateson, Gregory. 1972. *Steps Toward an Ecology of Mind*. New York: Ballantine Books.

Becker, Howard. 1982. *Art Worlds*. Berkeley and Los Angeles: University of California Press.

Betts, John R. 1969. "The Technological Revolution and the Rise of Sport." In John Loy, Jr. and Gerald Kenyon, eds., *Sport, Culture and Society*. New York: Macmillan.

Burke, Kenneth. 1945. *A Grammar of Motives*. New York: Prentice-Hall, Inc.

Burke, Peter. 1978. *Popular Culture in Early Modern Europe*. London: Temple Church.

Burns, Elizabeth. 1972. *Theatricality*. New York: Harper Torchbooks.

Caillois, Roger. 1979. *Man, Play and Games*. New York: Schocken Books.

Chatman, Seymour. 1978. *Story and Discourse*. Ithaca, NY: Cornell University Press.

Cicourel, Aaron. 1973. *Cognitive Sociology*. London: Penguin Education.

Danto, Arthur. 1981. *The Transfiguration of the Commonplace*. Cambridge, MA: Harvard University Press.

Dunning, Eric. 1986. "The Sociology of Sport in Europe and the United States." In C. Roger Rees and Andrew Miracle, eds., *Sport and Social Theory*. Champaign, IL: Human Kinetics Publishers.

Elias, Norbert. 1978. *The Civilizing Process: The History of Manners*. New York: Oxford University Press.

Fish, Stanley. 1980. *Is There a Text in This Class?* Cambridge, MA: Harvard University Press.

Frye, Northrop. 1957. *Anatomy of Criticism*. Princeton, NJ: Princeton University Press.

Geertz, Clifford. 1973. "Deep Play: Notes on the Balinese Cockfight." In C. Geertz, *The Interpretation of Cultures*. New York: Basis Books.

_____. 1983. "Blurred Genres: The Refiguration of Social Thought." In C. Geertz, *Local Knowledge*. New York: Basic Books.

Gitlin, Todd. 1982. "Prime Time Ideology: The Hegemonic Process in Television Entertainment." In H. Newcomb, ed., *Television: The Critical View*. New York: Oxford University Press

Goffman, Erving. 1956. *The Presentation of the Self in Everyday Life*. Edinburgh: Social Sciences Research Center, University of Edinburgh.

_____. 1967. *Interaction Ritual*. Chicago: Aldine

_____. 1974. *Frame Analysis*. New York: Basic Books.

Gould, Stephen. 1988. *New York Review of Books*. August 18.

Griffin, Jasper. 1988. "Playing To Win." *New York Review of Books*. September 29.

Gusfield, Joseph. 1963. Symbolic Crusade. Urbana: University of Illinois Press.

_____. 1981. *The Culture of Public Problems*. Chicago: University of Chicago Press.

_____, ed. 1989. *The Heritage of Sociology: Kenneth Burke on Symbols and Society*. Chicago: University of Chicago Press.

Huizinga, Johan. 1950. *Homo Ludens*. Boston: Beacon Press.

Iser, Wolfgang. 1978. *The Act of Reading* Baltimore, MD: Johns Hopkins Press.

Klapp, Orrin. 1964. *Symbolic Leaders*. Chicago: Aldine Publishing Co.

Kermode, Frank. 1966. *The Sense of an Ending*. New York: Oxford University Press.

MacAloon, John. 1984. "Olympic Games and the Theory of Spectacle in Modern Societies." In John MacAloon, ed., *Rite, Drama, Festival, Spectacle*. Philadelphia: Institute for the Study of Human Issues.

McHugh, Peter. 1968. *Defining the Situation*. Indianapolis, IN: Bobbs-Merrill, Inc.

Mukherji, Chandra. 1983. *From Graven Images*. New York: Columbia University Press.

Perinbanayagam, R. S. 1985. *Signifying Acts*. Carbondale, IL: Southern University Press.

Real, Michael.1982. "The Super Bowl: Mythic Spectacle." In H. Newcomb, ed. *Television: The Critical View*. New York: Oxford University Press.

Riesman, David, and Reuel Denney. 1954. "Football in America: A Study in Culture Diffusion." In David Riesman, *Individualism Reconsidered and Other Essays*. Glencoe, IL: The Free Press.

Sagan, Françoise. 1984. *Avec Mon Meilleur Souvenir*. Paris: Editions Gallimard.

Turner, Victor. 1969. *The Ritual Process*. Chicago: Aldine.

Watt, Ian. 1957. *The Rise of the Novel*. London: Chatto and Windus.

White, Hayden. 1981. "The Value of Narrativity in the Representation of Reality." In W. J. T. Mitchell, ed., *On Narrativity*. Chicago: University of Chicago Press.

Part 2

Reflexivity

6

The Modernity of Social Movements: Public Roles and Private Parts

The theme of the great transformation to modern life is a major feature of theories of societal growth. In the usage of paired concepts of community and society, tradition and modernity, pre-industrial and industrial, feudal and capitalistic, there is an underlying evolutionary assumption: The past is discarded as the present arises. The present, too, will wither and the future, like a phoenix, will emerge from its ashes. My concern with societal growth in this chapter is with the interplay of the private and the public as minor themes in this narrative. It is a chapter about change, both about some aspects of the mechanisms of change and, reflexively, about how transformation is perceived and acted upon. My focus is on the emergence of public institutions of change in the form of social movements and on their relationship to the transformation of institutions and persons.

The growth that constitutes the subject of this chapter is both societal and personal. It represents some change in what have been my own past views, but also much continuity. Earlier in my own work, I have been sharply critical of evolutionary models of change, especially as embodied in modernization theory (Gusfield, 1967; 1975; 1976). Similarly, I have attacked the utility for political analysis of the concept of modern society as a "mass society" (Gusfield, 1962). In both cases the same message was clear. There is much consistency between seemingly inconsistent social forms, more continuity between the old and the new than is implied in evolutionary models and modernization theory. Traditional relationships and institutions do not die quick deaths as new forms are born. Community is not displaced by Society, tradition defeated by modernity, group life dispersed by mass activities. Social change is not a drama of the chambered nautilus that leaves the old shell behind as it builds a new one. The richest mine for sociological gold is in understanding the interplay of past and present. It lies in seeing how they sometimes conflict, sometimes reinforce, sometimes are indifferent to each other.

While I will continue that perspective in this discussion, I also hope to correct some imbalances, to emphasize some sharp transformations between past and present in advanced, industrial societies. The emergence of aggregates of people conceived as members of a common society and engaged in action in public arenas is the focus of my attention. The development of deliberate attempts to change that society through collective actions, social movements, and shared invocations to change is both a major new civil institution and part of the experience of other civil institutions in modern societies. The paradox of the institution of change is a significant feature of modern as distinguished from traditional or premodern life. Such organizations and associations occupy a large space on the landscape of modernity.

But I am not recanting my emphasis on continuity and duality. The "mass culture" theme calls attention to the new and distinct relation between persons, localities, and provincial groups on the one hand and public events on the other. It does so in this chapter, however, as an interplay between such event and its observers, between public acts as observed events and publics as participants, as spectators, and as audiences. To see public action as theatre is to emphasize the problematic character of the relation between the public level of staged, reported, and observed events and the day-to-day levels of routine and private actions by individuals, groups, and institutions.

It is not significant that modern societies are societies in transformation. Most contemporary societies are. What is unique is both societal and cultural. It is societal in that a structure or organization and association has emerged which is the expected way to produce and define change—forms of collective action and social movements. It is cultural in that people reflect upon and think about change as an aspect of life, that they self-consciously go about deciding in what ways to accept and reject what has become possible. "[T]he dominant culture," writes Zygmunt Bauman, "consists of transforming everything which is not inevitable into the improbable" (1976:123). As public events, theatre, collective actions, and social movements are constantly creating new meanings, new claims to possibility.

The Emergence of Society and the Public

A profound part of the drama of sociology is embedded in the imagery of a lost world of "little communities" and the found world of complex, modern society. It was said of the European peasant of the past centuries that he was oblivious to the wars, the politics, and the grand events that made up historical accounts. Unconcerned and unaware, he tilled the soil no matter who won the battles. This portrait of a world of self-sufficient, autonomous local settlements has been painted over with a vision of centralized national states, interdependent markets, homogeneous cultures, and nationalistic identities that bind large territories into a unity and draw peripheries into contact with and awareness of a center (Tilly, 1975; Shils, 1961; Bendix, 1964: Ch. 2, 3).

Here I call attention to three aspects of that transformation from a world of multiple communities to one of a single centralized society. The first is the expansion of society as a structural fact—the growth of institutions through which disparate people and groups are made interdependent and homogeneous. The second is the expansion of society as a cultural fact—the ability to conceptualize the network of relationships as a society and to identify oneself, one's group, and one's locality as members of a larger society. The third aspect is again cultural. It is the development of society as an object of change—an object understood as a source of change and an object to be thought about, changed, or cherished.

The Expansion of Society

The rise of modern nations is a saga of evolving integration and interdependence. Localisms and primordial identities, while not necessarily disappearing, are no longer the limits of the social world. Markets, communication systems, transportation, and nationalistic ideas are among key factors in expanding the size of the social universe within which people have come to live. Perhaps the most crucial development of the modern period is the growth and importance of the national state, the centralizing of political power over a wider territory and encompassing cultural, economic, and linguistically diverse groups.[1]

Both state and society have expanded in a vertical as well as a horizontal direction. As polity, as state, the modern world has involved the incorporation of classes and groups that have been "outside" society and state. The development of citizenship status that accompanies participation and an ideology of civil and political rights, is one aspect of this (Bendix, 1964; Marshall, 1965). But it also has meant that what happens at the center of the society is a matter of concern and note throughout the territory. "The mass of society has become incorporated *into* society" (Shils, 1960:288). "Society" has ceased to be the exclusive province of elites. This fundamental democratization is a major change which modernization has brought with it (Lerner, 1958; Mannheim, 1940: 44–49).

The Cultural Reality of Society and the Emergence of the Public

"There are no masses," wrote Raymond Williams. "There are only ways of seeing people as masses" (1960: 319). To "see" or imagine events, processes, and people as incorporated into a common unity, a "society" is the cultural side of the expansion of society. "American society," "Western society," are terms that become invested with reality, objects capable of being thought about and acted toward. They imply the emergence of society as an object distinct from this or that specific class or group. It is this universalistic conception of society to which I refer as it forms a basis for modes of acting at societal levels. Bluntschli, writing in 1849, identified the emergence of the concept of society with the rise of the bourgeoisie; it signified parts of societal life outside of the court (quoted in Frankfort Institute for Social Research, 1973: 17, 33).

As most of the late-nineteenth- and early-twentieth-century theorists recognized, the implications of the expansion of society as an object involve imagined interaction rather than the face-to-face relationships of communal groups. The inclusion of strangers, enemies, and celebrated persons into the same society represents a sphere of attention and activity that distinguishes between what is public and what is private in a salient and significant fashion. The discovery of society is an essential requisite to efforts to remake it. It is in the public sphere that such efforts have been most observable.

The emergence of the public is a part of the history of modern societies, a facet in the development of national states and middle-class societies. The word "public" owes its origins to the literary world, where it arose to describe the new and anonymous consumers of literature who came to replace the patronage of wealthy sponsors (Beljame, 1948: 130; Auerbach, 1953: 499–500). It is this quality of accessibility to diverse groups and persons on a formal plane of equality that has been the hallmark of the modern public. As long as politics and society were the "property" of families of notables, the distinction between the private and the public remained blurred. As Alvin Gouldner has put it: "In contrast, however, a public sphere is in its modern sense a sphere open to all, or to all 'men with an *interest*,' and who have a measure of competence in the ordinary language spoken" (1976: 72). The last phrase in Gouldner's concept of the public is important. It suggests the massive significance for social expansion of the revolution in culture that mass education, universal literacy, and mass communication have brought about (Bendix, 1978).

I refer to three dimensions or components of "public" as important to my evolving argument. First, public events, in contrast to private ones, are events visible to audiences of diverse persons and groups. Public acts are "front stage," conducted where they are observable and accessible (Arendt, 1959: 45–53; Gusfield, 1975a). It is in this sense that the "public" has a mass character to it. All can observe it, whether or not they stand in an organized and structured relation to the actors.

The second connotation of "public" is the attribution of collective societal values and interests. Here the word is used in its meaning of "the public interest," as distinguished from private interests. As society is expanded in structure and in thought, the terms of discourse about policy must be those of societal benefit. The assumption is sustained that there is some underlying social agreement about collective ends such that the conflicts of private and special interests and sentiments can be resolved. Thus Rawls' *Theory of Justice* rests upon the logical necessity of a public interest as a criterion for public discourse (1971: Ch. 1). Gouldner (1976) has made a similar argument in asserting that ideology as a modern form of idea system is a product of the development of a public in which rational discourse is essential to justification and argument. Such modes of public discourse further presuppose and grant reality to "society" as an object.

Third, what is public is a common object of attention. Here, once again, the concept of a mass society has relevance. It points to a realm of events and activities that are experienced at a distance but as a common experience among otherwise disparate and diverse people (Blumer, 1939: 241–47; Kornhauser, 1959: 13–38). The public is not only the domain of those who are active in its events; it is also the domain of those who observe it and share it as common spectacle. "To live together in the world means essentially that a world of things is between those who have it in common, as a table is located between those who sit around it" (Arendt, 1959: 48).

The Idea of the Future Society

The participation of the various classes, both as citizens and as spectators, is associated with the development of the idea that the present society is problematic, that it can possibly be other than it is. The English word "reform" once suggested restoration to an original state. It is in the seventeenth and eighteenth centuries that it came to assume a meaning connoting *newness* (Walzer, 1965: 11; Williams, 1976: 221–22). Similarly, the idea of revolution is a product of societies in which a centralized state is both imaginable and possible. The vision of a world transformed through political and social rather than religious conversions is a modern myth of Sorelian form (Walzer, 1965: Ch. 1; Aron, 1962; Gusfield, 1973; Williams, 1976: 229).

Earlier historical periods had, of course, experienced rebellions, revolts, and protest actions. As Rude and Hobsbawm have both pointed out, even the protests of the seventeenth and eighteenth centuries in Europe generally lacked a programmatic focus on changing the rules of society. They were specific responses to specific grievances, more often aimed at restoration of a particular situation than at changing relationships (Rude, 1959; 1964; Hobsbawm, 1959). What the premodern period lacked was a widespread conception of societal change as a constant, pervasive, and tangible possibility.

To speak of social movements as a regularized feature of modern societies is to point out that the widespread imagination of the future society as different and as shapeable by our actions is a unique event in human history. This reflexive awareness of social change and of ourselves as possible authors of it is what is so distinctive to the modern period. William Irwin Thompson, in his study of the impact of literature on the Easter (1916) rebellion in Ireland, described the process eloquently:

> History is, in fact, a process by which a private imagination becomes a public event but any study which restricted itself to the public would have to ignore the fact that history is also the process by which public events become private imaginations. (1967: 235)

The Modernity of Movements

Conscious efforts to design, control, and produce societal change are *not* ubiquitous features of human life. They are historically specific to the modern world of industrialized and industrializing societies. Both interest groups, specifically oriented toward the self-defined interests of members, and "causes," directed toward some principle and action in the interests of others, are products of the modern period (Banks, 1972; Gusfield, 1978; Schlesinger, Sr., 1950). In studying movements, sociologists are studying one way in which social change is instituted in the modern period. The associational character of movements is not universal; it is instead a product of modern life (Tilly, 1969: 4–45).

Organized efforts to promote social change are, in some respects, institutionalized forms of activity in modern society. They constitute a characteristic, widely understood, and anticipated way in which change can be pursued. They are associated with the rise of popular governments, the division of labor, a centralized political nationalism and the growing literacy, education, and standard of living of large segments of populations. Proactive movements, as distinguished from reactive ones, assert new claims not previously asserted, and such collective action, as Tilly (1978: 147) maintains, has been proliferating in the past two centuries in European societies. The political acceptance of movements is also revealed in the substitution of the word "movement" for "mob," a revised way of thinking about collective behavior and social movements (P. Wilkinson, 1971: 11–14; Hovard, 1977).

A digression from the major theme of societal growth and changes is necessary to my argument at this point. Having placed social movements within historical context, I need to discuss the ways in which sociologists study such phenomena. Tilly's analysis of theories and methods for research on collective action is useful. He emphasizes the way in which groups and events are mobilized around interests as the subject matter of the field (Tilly, 1978: Ch. 2, 8–10). In doing so, he specifically turns away from the concept of "social movements" as groups attached to a set of beliefs. "The fact that population, belief and action do not always change together causes serious problems for the student of social movements" (1978: 10).

It is imperative to recognize the difference between studying collective action and studying social movements. In the first case, what is to be studied is the activity of an association of people organized around goals and programs. Much of the study of what is called "social movements" is of this nature. What is studied are the Black Muslims, the Church of Scientology, or the Women's Christian Temperance Union. The second case, closer to what Tilly labels "social movements," is focused on the changes in meanings that occur both inside and outside associations of active partisans. It studies abolitionism, civil rights, temperance, or the movement against the war in Vietnam. The distinction is of course drawn too sharply, yet it is significant. Each draws attention to different corners, defines appropriate areas of study in diverse fashion, and, above all, locates the boundaries of study at different points on the social landscape.

In the remainder of this chapter, I shall argue the importance of perceiving movements as self-consciously understood demands for changes in the meanings of actions at both public and private levels. The emphasis on the study of associations and organizations directs our attention to the public realm of collective goals, to ideologies and discourse, to purposes and activities, membership and followership. My argument is that this perspective concentrates on what happens in the public sphere and, as a result, overstates the importance of the public and understates the significance of the private, local, and routine areas of life and the interplay of the two in developing and directing societal change. Put in terms of an older distinction, it glorifies State at the expense of Society. The cost of this is to overlook crucial processes of cultural changes, especially those probably more emergent in recent chapters of the history of industrial societies. "[I]t is short-sighted," writes Paul Wilkinson, "to focus all our attention on what might be called primary-level politicization among social movements" (1971: 53).

The prominence that sociologists have given to the dramatic—to civil disorder, pressure-group actions, and revolts—is a large part of the politicization of change. The transformation of public agencies, in government and the economy, is the arena of primary conflict in this drama. The transformation of persons and situations plays a secondary part.

Both of these distinctions—between associations and meanings, and between institutional and personal transformation—are hardly unrecognized by sociologists. Most make some distinction between movements or collective actions that seek to transform social institutions and those that gain their significance through transforming persons (Wilson, 1973: Ch. 1). Most make some distinction between movements that affect general and diffuse change, such as humanitarianism, and those seeking specific and bounded changes, such as the child labor movement. Blumer's (1939) distinction between "general" and "specific" movements and Smelser's (1962) between norm-oriented and value-oriented are cases in point.

These typologies of movements can be rephrased as components of movements, aspects that inhere in many transformational processes. The dimension of institutional-personal transformation is what I am referring to in the public and private dichotomy. Here the movement "exists" in its public form as observable, reportable actions. It happens to those who strike public roles—as adherents, enemies, detached analysts. The activity of a civil rights march, the lobbying of the National Organization for Women, the public meetings, parades, and literature of gay rights and opposing organizations—all these are instances of movements in pursuit of fixed goals.

At another level, movements also "exist" in the ways in which transformation is perceived as socially shared, as an aspect of the society in a given historical period. The quality of interpersonal interaction, of decisions in situated moments, in day-to-day actions, is the focus here. The movement is to be found in the housewife considering entry into the labor force, the relations of blacks and whites in ambiguous situations, the response of parent to knowledge of a child's homosexuality, the decision of a Polish- or Italian- or Mexican-American to retain an ethnic name or not.

What distinguishes this component of change from unrecognized, slowly developing social and cultural change (what Sumner called crescive change) is the reflection of participants on the shared nature of transformation, on belief in the existence of the movement. Movement implies momentum, change in process. It signifies that a form of action has become possible, thinkable, a matter at least of conflict in the society. An area of life is in motion, in flux and ambiguity. It has ceased to be either the accepted, unchallenged definition of reality and morality or the unchallenged definition of impossible or idiosyncratic. To be gay in 1978 is not socially the same as in 1948. To expect that an employer recognize union representation was not the same in 1935 as it was in 1900. Movements are not necessarily, nor even entirely, associations. They are also meanings, which construe social behavior as "in motion." They create choices where choices did not exist as possibilities.

Preoccupation with the sense of transformation is the unifying theme in the study of social movements. To talk about the existence of a "movement" is then a way of referring to the quickening of change and its status as a matter of advocacy and rejection in public and/or private arenas. In our time, they run the gamut—general and specific, interest-oriented and cause-oriented, organized and unorganized. What is significant is that new forms of society are imaginable and possible. They are in motion in areas ranging from art, as imagination, to history, as action. When the individual acts in a world of movements, he or she (a phrase I wouldn't have used ten years ago) does so societally, self-consciously as one of a number and not as an isolated person.

The Interplay of the Public and the Private

This reflexivity of movements is at the center of my argumental wheel. Movements are not only objects of attention for members or partisans; they are also objects for nonmembers, the "general public." As such, the existence of a movement is a public fact about the society. It signifies that some aspect of the social environment is in motion, in process of possible change. An alternative arrangement is now available to the structure of thought. What has been unthinkable or impossible can now be thought about and even perceived as possible. The recent tax-relief movement generated in California makes many people and officials in many other states suddenly conscious of possible political responses. It makes the matter of taxation an issue in a different manner than it was prior to the recognition of the movement. The pro-abortion movement signifies not only the effort to achieve certain legislation; its existence now indicates that abortion has become publicly admissible, societally at issue and thus en route to legitimacy. The impact of movements *is* not only in their intended and stated goals. It is also in what they signify by being. In this sense they have audiences as well as adherents.

The belief that social order is a fact, that others neither doubt the legitimacy of institutions nor fail to carry out their roles, is not itself a stable piece of social reality. It, too, has to be constructed and is capable as well of being destroyed. Acts of deviance and alienation, as Durkheim realized, subvert order beyond the immediate effects. Events, processes, and person that disturb belief in the facticity of an orderly society make it apparent that the hold of norms, values, and beliefs on the population is more tenuous than had been imagined. "Creative disturbance" disturbs. It makes the orderly account of events and expectations problematic and no longer taken for granted. The "crazies," the impetuous "left-wing adventurers," the proponents of "revolution for the hell of it" have recognized this by attempts to carry out the absurd and, in this way, to make it possible to imagine the social order as different (Hoffman, 1968).

The Dramatic Character of Public Actions

In the large, diverse, and extended societies of modern-day life, personal experience of a direct kind cannot be depended upon to monitor the society, to convey the most general of generalized others. Much of the object-like character of society, and the sense of social change, emerge in the public arena. The newspaper, the magazine, television, and mass education, including sociology, provide a monitoring of society. Relatively unorganized movements owe much to such media in the construction of belief in a shared demand for change. The Senator Joseph McCarthy movement, as one example, became an object of reality and power in part through the attribution of a powerful movement as a means of explaining fragmented and otherwise unrelated events which might have been construed otherwise (Spinrad, 1970: Ch. 7). As John McCarthy and Mayer Zald (1973) have suggested, the classic pattern of an organized movement with members, leaders, and followers is often an inappropriate model for contemporary societies.

The monitoring of society is a crucial part of the process by which movements are constructed in modern life. The reporting, analysis, and debate over social and cultural changes accentuate attention but also present particular actions as shared over a wide area, publicly statable and adequately described as a "movement." Not only is this the case with relatively organized segments of movements—Right-to-Life, for example—but it is especially pertinent where "movements" are unorganized. The "hippie" movement and the sexual revolution are two cases in point.

I call this process "dramatic" as a way of pointing to several characteristics of how movements emerge in modern societies. The first aspect is that organized and unorganized movements become observable to audiences. They have a presentational as well as a purposive dimension. Secondly, the presentation of movements as spectacles often involves a heightened excitement and interest conveyed by styles that make the actions more interesting, more attention-getting for audiences, more stimulating and engrossing for members. This is what is meant by "dramatizing the news." Thirdly, dramatizing also involves an abstract selecting and filtering process that changes the events through interpretation (Lang and Lang, 1968: 291).

In becoming observable and dramatically interesting, the events and activities construed as movement become signposts of the societal. They convey what is now undergoing change and what is being resisted. The scenarios of conflict, antagonists, and protagonists, of events moving toward climax and resolution are the stuff of the careers of movements. As they symbolize the character of society, they take on symbolic attributes as well as more direct and instrumental purposes. The movement to limit marijuana usage is an instance of an issue containing symbolic conflicts over issues of youth culture and adult power (Gusfield, 1975a). Even the tax revolt in California in 1978 won the votes of many nonproperty owners and suggests actions which symbolize opposition to government and government spending as well as narrower and specifically interest-oriented politics.

Normalization and Social Change

The very concept "movement" indicates that something is in motion, undergoing possible change and transformation. What is occurring through the public arena is that actions, beliefs, and ideas that have been outside the realm of the normal are now portrayed as undergoing the possibility of being transformed into the normal. What has appeared as just, natural, or unquestioned within the public and the society is now posed as an issue, potentially unjust, unnatural, and questioned. A new perspective is offered toward old relations, actions, or ideas. In the past decade homosexuality has been publicly transformed from behavior seen as deviant and abnormal to behavior now in the public realm of conflict. In the view of the society now emerging in public, homosexuality, in the sense that the term was once used, ceases to be "queer."

The implications of this normalization of previously abnormalized beliefs, actions, and ideas is to change the structure of consciousness. The labor movement made unionization less absurd, unthinkable, or "crazy." The women's movement has raised such consciousness-producing implications to deliberate and organized action. The arguments over terminology (*chairman, chairwoman, chairperson, chair*) are dramatized instances in which the unequal position of women is brought to attention and new claims are given support. They are also instances of changing cultural meanings for events, changes that provide new linguistic designations less connoting or supporting of male dominion.

The public character of the normalization process is what I am stressing. The once-dissident act, the previously unexpected alternative, the resolution of tensions through new outcomes are, as they become publicly observable acts or advocacies, no longer individual, idiosyncratic, and bizarre. In one form, the public arena not only reflects the society; it also refracts. It provides definition, explanation, elaboration, and program. It gives value, diffuse, and unspoken thoughts "a local habitation and a name."

The Interplay of the Public and the Private

One of the implications of the growth of centralized states and national societies has been the evolution of the welfare of the citizen as a rightful obligation of the society. Many problems that were once dealt with at the level of the family are in contemporary societies viewed as public woes (Weinberg, 1974).

One of the major areas of interplay between the public and the private is simply the extent and depth with which private issues become public ones. Certainly some of the most poignant sources of human concern are even today outside the realm of public attitudes, discussion, or remedy. No movement or welfare for unrequited love or surcease for parental disappointment has yet emerged. Yet the list of private woes made into public worries is lengthening. Movements of personal identity, of ethnic and racial status, add to the transformations of persons implied in life-style movements and religious transformations. Some are public in that they call for state action, as in the pro- and anti-abortion movements. Some are less state-directed but involve public attitudes and discussion, as in sexual codes. Areas of life left outside of the public realm may move into them or, as in the case of many past religious conflicts, move outside and into the private.

In much of this chapter, I have stressed the way in which public and publicly construed movements impinge upon and affect private areas. In this dimension, "the movement" is to be found in its microsocial arenas, through the realization that areas of life are "in motion." The housewife who decides to enter the labor force or seeks to reformulate her relationship with her husband, insofar as the recognition of male-female relations as undergoing transformation is part of her awareness, does so with a sense that her behavior is shared, her claims are not bizarre. Ibsen's *A Doll's House* is part of a process of recognition that an individual feeling of protest is socially shared. It matters very much whether or not the individual acts alone or with a recognition of being "with history." These transformations are profound and are not registered in the collective goals achieved through organization, in bits of legislation or new institutional regulations. They are deeply implicated in the accommodations by which human beings in modern societies frequently respond to the recognition of a changing society. They make change a more conscious and deliberate act even at individual and situational levels.

In another form, the private interacts with the public in being the source of that which the public arena monitors. I have already called attention to this in discussing how it is that public media, including education, turn private acts into movements by defining and portraying them. Thus a recent study, based on survey research data, found the existence of profeminist attitudes before the advent of women's rights organizations, although the organized movement appears to have accentuated them.

The public, mass character of movements in the modernization of societies should not deceive us into the belief that what occurs in the public arena is either the most significant way or exhausts the ways in which social change happens in a self-conscious fashion. The modernization of society into an object available to the multitude of citizens does not mean the disappearance of continuity, of a separate and semi-autonomous realm of the traditional and the private. In my focus on the evolution of the public I do not mean to turn away from the dualities of community *and* society, tradition *and* modernity, state *and* society, the public *and* the private. The emphasis on social change through organized movement, political goals, and interest-oriented groups hides the cultural sources of change, and, especially, the most recent transformations of contemporary life.

The Overpoliticization of Society in Modern Sociology

A number of years ago, Dennis Wrong (1961) attacked the conformist stereotype of human beings in the sociology of that period. His paper had as its title, "The Over-socialized Conception of Man in Modern Sociology." I have paraphrased that as the title of this final section.

The study of deliberate and self-conscious change has emphasized two aspects of collective action and social movements. One is the role of the state and the importance of political power in defining the goals and impacts of movements. The other is the importance of organized associational forms as the mechanisms for achieving social and cultural change. In both aspects the study of social movements has overstated the degree to which modern societies are unified and centralized entities and exaggerated the extent and significance of political power. In a third failing, the model of social movements as organized efforts to achieve public changes is less adequate for an understanding of transformations occurring in contemporary modernized societies under the impetus of universal education, mass communications, and "middle-class" standards of living. The increase in incomes, the added leisure, and the growth of awareness and imagination have produced a situation in which "all of us have become, simultaneously, workers and aristocrats" (Plath, 1964: 3).

To be sure, there is a spectrum of movements and change-oriented associations. The narrow-interest group, appealing to a specific constituency through a highly organized association, is more likely to find its impact in particular and well-defined purposes which governmental and institutional power can control. Here the interest group, exemplified in the International Longshoremen's Association, the Dairymen's League, and the League of American Wheelmen (Bicyclists), fits the model well. Others appeal to a public morality more directly and "disinterested." Less susceptible to Olsen's "free rider" analysis, organizations like the National Urban League, the American Anti-Slavery Society, the Church Peace Union, and the National Union for Social Justice represent "causes" less than they do interest groups. More diffuse and less organized movements, like the "hippies" or the women's movement, are involved in transformations at levels and arenas outside, in addition to, or alternatively to the public. The spectrum fades into highly general movements almost too amorphous to be represented in any organization or particular event. Here the movement toward narcissism in human relations is an example (Sennett, 1978: 4).[2]

A distinction between state and society is a frequent starting point in the analyses of political sociology (Hintze, 1968: 154–69). The relations between the two, their mutual dependence, their independence, and the dominion of one over the other have been the starting points for controversy. One tradition, deep in orthodox Marxism and in political behaviorism, has been to see the state as largely a creation of society. Political institutions and events are then traceable to the interests and "needs" of major economic and social groups and classes (Lipset, 1960; Mills, 1956; O'Connor, 1973). Other sociological traditions have stressed a "neutral" role for the state, as in pluralist formulations (Rose, 1967; Dharendorf, 1959) or a more significant yet independent role as a source of power in the modern world (Bendix, 1964; 1978).

In many respects, the problems of gaining entry into state power were the crucial issues of conflict and change in the nineteenth century in Europe and America (Tilly, 1969; Bendix, 1964). Acquiring position in state and in institutional life in society were major sources of collective violence. The state, I am asserting, is less vital as the arena of contemporary movements in contemporary modern societies. The Civil Rights Movement may be the last major movement of the nineteenth-century type.

The Failure of State Power

We are today, in my judgment, in a period of retreat from the public arena as the most significant site of social and cultural change. Whether this portends a general shift in modern societies or is a transient, ephemeral trend is not clear. However, in many respects it builds on the structural changes that have made twentieth-century populations in modernized countries more like the middle classes of the nineteenth century. It is accentuated by the educational spread and the public media of mass communications that report the society to itself and turn individual actions into shared ones. The theatrical character of the public arena is also indicative of its weak role as direct and instrumental. Many of the crucial movements of our times have their locus outside of the political and institutional areas of life, at the level of interpersonal encounters, of routine daily life. Although centralized power and legal institutions are utilized to affect them, the power of such agencies is highly limited. In searching for transformation outside of the public realm, in society rather than in state, the contemporary world may be moving away from some of the centralizing trends of the past two centuries into what I have elsewhere called "the privatization of Utopia" (Gusfield, 1973: 31).

One aspect of this is the weakness of government to effectuate its edicts. In the literature of social movements and collective action the story usually ends with "victory" or "defeat" in the halls of the legislatures, the appearance of new agencies, legal decisions, or electoral success. Whether such events are followed by the behavior sought through them is problematic. The capacity of the local area, the organization or industry, or the lone individual to distort and evade public edicts is an old theme in political science and sociology. Murray Edelman (1964) has portrayed much of the drama and language of public, political movements as achieving a "symbolic quiescence" leading the audience of spectators and adherents to believe that a situation has been remedied when, in point of fact, little further effective action occurs. Similarly, studies of the implementation of programs point to the considerable difficulties in making reforms into effective impacts on daily, routine behavior (Pressman and Wildalsky, 1973). The co-optation of regulatory agencies by those they were inaugurated to regulate is a persistent theme.

Sociologists, political scientists, and lawyers have for long discussed the difficulties in using legal decisions as effective means to produce reform behavior. In his forthcoming analyses of thirty-eight cases involving four major social movements, Joel Handler (1978) found it difficult to achieve tangible results from the reforming of the law. The bureaucratic contingencies involved in implementing decisions were particularly impediments. The literature on deterrence and punishment and on deterrence by use of law similarly does not reach sanguine conclusions about attempts to control criminal or other behavior through laws against crimes (Zimring and Hawkins, 1973; Gibbs, 1975).

Nor does the state appear, in many modern societies, to be as effective an agent of repression as hoped or feared. Despite the actions of the CIA and the FBI, the anti-Vietnam war movement was neither extinguished nor greatly weakened. The ability of determined American males to avoid compulsory military service in the 1960s was considerable. Despite the intensive processes of centralization and nationalization in Europe during the past 200 years, the local nationalisms of Spain, the United Kingdom, Belgium, and the Soviet Union remain persistent issues of national integration (Hechter, 1975; Zilborg, 1974). They are not so distant from the linguistic, religious, and tribal schisms of less "advanced" countries such as India and Nigeria.

Like the impact of the public on the private, the effects of the state on the society are problematic eventualities rather than deducible conclusions. It is not that state action has *no* impact on social institutions or human relationships. I am suggesting that the effects of state power and the centralized unity of societies in the modern period are less effective and less significant than has been accepted. My emphasis on the dramatic or symbolic character of political events is also a way of calling attention to the ways in which political conflicts are staging areas for clashes between adherents and enemies that have their significance in the private and routine part of life. The current conflict over government obligations to provide medical expenses for abortions is one such ground on which the public legitimacy of abortion is being tested.

The Privatization of Social Movements

Perhaps the more salient consideration in my theme of the overpoliticization of society in contemporary sociology is the widening areas of change that are less organized than the prevailing models of collective action and social movements encompass; that reflect the growing concern of populations with the transformation of the self in human encounters, in religious experience and in the styles of work and leisure. Although the public arena serves to dramatize and communicate such movements, they represent a turning away from the importance of the public as the focal point of change. They are movements with a locus closer to the private and the self than to the public and the institution. "The insides are where it's at," wrote a student in 1969; "...the current revolution is not an external affair to be determined by political, military and economic means. Primarily it's an internal affair to be engaged in as a learning experience" (quoted in Gusfield, 1973: 30–31).

The retreat from the public and the political is a growing theme in contemporary American intellectual life. Recently several writers— Ralph Turner, Richard Sennett, and Lionel Trilling—have made it, in one way or another, a central point in their work. Turner (1969; 1976) finds the problem of personal alienation, of self- and group-identity, among the major issues of contemporary movements. Sennett (1978), after an examination of European public life in past centuries, asserts the growing privatization of life and the trend away from public interactions and public norms as loci of activity and criteria of behavior. Trilling sums up much of this shifting focus of emphasis on self rather than role in his belief that modern societies are witnessing a transition from glorification of sincerity—the fit between the self and the role— to authenticity—the expression of the self in opposition to role. There is in all three of these writers a supposition that the profoundest problems of modern life are seen as those of expressiveness—of the place that impulse, narcissism, and personal feeling have in the context of social controls and social roles. Not Marx but Freud appears as the patron saint of the twentieth century.

These cultural changes are themselves a movement, a "cultural drift," to use Herbert Blumer's term (1939: 286). They are not without historical analogues in the romantic and youth movements of upper-middle-class European society in the nineteenth and early twentieth centuries (Grana 1964: part 3; Becker, 1946). They bear resemblance to aristocratic attitudes and suggest the nature of social and cultural changes. Populations of "middle-class" character can now focus their attention upon other than material issues.

In the stress on styles of life, on the importance of personal emotions and feelings, in the reassessment of values of ambition and accomplishment, the rationalistic emphasis of an industrial and capitalistic society is undergoing potential deep transformation (Bell, 1976). The major political movements of the nineteenth and twentieth centuries, though often anticapitalistic, were themselves wedded to the same rationalism and scientific culture that characterized the bourgeois society they sought to transform (Gusfield, 1973; Bauman, 1976). The organizational form of movements and their quest for political and economic transformations mirror this as well. Writing in 1969 and commenting on the cultural revolution of the 1960s, Carl Oglesby took issue with the description of the May 1968 Paris uprising by a Marxist theoretician. Andre Glucksmann had written that the student actions were a revolt *of* the forces of production. Wrote Oglesby, "Quite on the contrary....[It] is a revolt *against* the forces of production" (quoted in Gusfield, 1973: 31).

Many of the most strident conflicts of contemporary modern societies are *not* issues of class and material welfare. Social and cultural movements that are transforming society and human life are visible not only in organized demands for new social structure. They appear as well in the perceived and shared questioning of older values and styles of life as they occur in individual and situational areas. Moral and spiritual questions reflect the movements of change that occur at the level of private life but are mirrored in the public reports of societal happenings. The world of public institutions, of politics and economics, of organized associational efforts, is itself a focus of criticism and indifference.

Organized protest and reform have been the institutional mechanisms of change in modernized societies. As a facet of societal growth, social movements and collective action, as we sociologists have defined and depicted them, have represented the accepted, understood, and organized mechanism for social change. Mass collective action, less organized and associational, does not fit easily into our models of change. The shared search for personal salvation and transformation, the generation of new moralities and meanings, is not caught in the nets of understanding that have worked for the nineteenth and early twentieth centuries' obsession with the state. Politicians squirm and wriggle when confronted by issues of abortion, pornography, sexuality, and religion. They lack the institutional ways to treat them as political concerns. Sociologists find mass movements and mass change hard to study. But that is one mark of change—that it catches us unprepared for it. When I was a college freshman, I was impressed by a quotation from John Dewey on the first page of my social science syllabus: "Change is the fundamental fact in the social sciences as motion is in physical science." I have grown more skeptical about any such sweeping statement. Nevertheless, it suggests one important attribute of the modern. We are ourselves both party to change and affected by it in what and how we study change. If history does not package our materials in the containers we have laid out, it becomes necessary to revise our art and construct new ones.

Notes

1. Note how the Federalists defended the new Constitution by arguing for the value of a larger polity, in distinction from the conventional wisdom that democracy required a small society (Federalist Papers, nos. 9, 10). The same process of expanding the sphere within which primordial groups interact appears as well in new nations in the twentieth century (Geertz, 1973).
2. The specific organizations mentioned in this paragraph are taken from the fifty-three used by William Gamson in his study *The Strategy of Social Protest* (Gamson, 1975). Using this description of the groups by Gamson, I classify twenty-four as being directed to a special interest group constituency and twenty-eight toward a more cause-like general constituency. (One is unclassifiable.) Concerned primarily with the public and political arena, Gamson's sample contains no movements that are involved in the transformation of the person. Protest is confined to the public arena.

References

Arendt, Hannah. 1951. *The Origins of Totalitarianism*. New York: Harcourt, Brace.

Aron, Raymond. 1962. *Opium of the Intellectuals*. New York: W. W. Norton.

Auerbach. Erich. 1953. *Mimesis*. Princeton, NJ: Princeton University Press.

Banks, J. A. 1972. *The Sociology of Social Movements*. London: Macmillan Press.

Bateson, Gregory. 1972. "A Theory of Play and Fantasy." In Gregory Bateson, *Steps Toward an Ecology of Mind*. New York: Ballantine Books.

Bauman, Zygmunt. 1976. *Socialism: The Active Utopia*. New York: Holmes and Meier.

Becker, Howard. 1946. *German Youth: Bond or Free*. New York: Oxford University Press.

Beljame, Alexandre. 1948. *Men of Letters and the English Public*. London: Kegan Paul, Trench,Trubner and Company.

Bell, Daniel. 1976. *The Cultural Contradictions of Capitalism*. New York: Basic Books.

Bendix, Reinhard. 1964. *Nation-Building and Citizenship*. New York: John Wiley and Sons.

_____. 1978. *King or People*. Berkeley and Los Angeles: University of California Press.

_____.1966-67. "Tradition and Modernity Reconsidered," *Comparative Studies in Society and History*, IX (1966–67).

Blumer, Herbert. 1939. "Collective Behavior." In R. E. Park, ed., *An Outline of the Principles of Sociology*. New York: Barnes and Noble, Inc.

Cohen, Jean. 1985. "Strategy or Identity: New Theoretical Paradigms and Contemporary Social Movements." *Social Research*, 52 (winter): 663-716.

Dahrendorf, Rolf. 1959. *Class and Class Conflict in Industrial Society*. Stanford, CA: Stanford University Press.

Edelman, Murray. 1964. *The Symbolic Uses of Politics*. Urbana: University of Illinois Press.

Frankfort Institute for Social Research. 1973. *Aspects of Sociology*. London: Heinemann Educational Books.

Gibbs, Jack. 1975. *Crime, Punishment and Deterrence*. New York: Elsevier.

Goffman, Erving. 1974. *Frame Analysis: An Essay on the Organization of Experience*. Cambridge, MA: Harvard University Press.ouldner, Alvin. 1976. *The Dialectic of Ideology and Technology*. New York: Seabury Press.

Grana, Cesar. 1964. *Modernity and Its Discontents* New York: Basic Books.

Gusfield, Joseph, 1968. "Prohibition: The Impact of Political Utopianism." In John Braeman, Robert Bremmer, and David Brody, eds., *Change and Continuity in Twentieth-Century America. The 1920's*. Columbus: Ohio State University Press.

_____. 1973. *Utopian Myths and Movements in Modern Societies*. (Module) Morristown, NJ: General Learning Press.

_____. 1975a. "The (F) Utility of Knowledge: The Relation of Social Science to Public Policy Toward Drugs." *Annals of the American Academy of Political and Social Sciences* (January): 1-15.

_____. 1975b. *Community: A Critical Response*. New York: Harper and Row.

_____. 1976 "Becoming Modern: Review Essay of Inkeles and Smith, Becoming Modern." *American Journal of Sociology* 82 (September): 443-48.

_____.1978 "Historical Problematics and Sociological Fields: American Liberalism and the Study of Social Movements." In Robert A. Jones, ed., *Research in Sociology of Knowledge, Sciences and Art*. Vol. 1. Greenwich, CT: JAI Press Inc.

Handler, Joel. 1980. *Social Movements and the Law*. New York: Academic Press.

Hechter, Michael. 1975. *Internal Colonialism*. Berkeley: University of California Press.

Hintze, Otto. 1968. "The State in Historical Perspective." In R. Bendix, et al, *Education, State and Society*. Boston: Little, Brown.

Hobsbawm, Eric. 1959. *Primitive Rebels*. Manchester: Manchester University Press.

Hoffman, Abbie. 1968 .*Revolution for the Hell of It*. New York: Dial Press.

Hovard, Richard. 1977. "The Interactionist Paradigm: The Collective Behavioral and Pluralist Conceptualization of Politics and Society." American Sociological Association Annual Meetings.

Kornhauser, William. 1959. *The Politics of Mass Society*. Glencoe, IL: The Free Press.

Lang, Kurt, and Gladys Lang. 1968. *Politics and Television*. Chicago: Quadrangle Books.

Lerner, Daniel. 1958. *The Passing of Traditional Society*. Glencoe, IL.: The Free Press.

Lipset, Seymour. 1960. *Political Man*. Garden City, NY: Doubleday.

Mannheim, Karl. 1940. *Man and Society in an Age of Reconstruction*. London: Routledge and Kegan Paul.

Marshall, T. H. 1965. *Class, Citizenship and Social Development*. Garden City, NY: Anchor Books/Doubleday.

McCarthy, John, and Mayer Zald. 1973. *The Trend of Social Movements in America: Professionalization and Resource Mobilization*. Morristown, NJ: General Learning Corp.

Mills, C. Wright. 1956. *The Power Elite*. New York: Oxford University Press.

O'Connor, James. 1973. *The Fiscal Crisis of the State*. New York: St. Martin's Press.

Olson, Mancur. 1971. *The Logic of Collective Action*. Cambridge, MA: Harvard University Press

Plath, David. 1964. *The After Hours: Modern Japan and the Search for Enjoyment*. Berkeley and Los Angeles. University of California Press.

Pressman, Jeffrey, and Aaron Wildavsky. 1973. *Implementation*. Berkeley and Los Angeles: University of California Press.

Rawls, John. 1971. *A Theory of Justice*. Cambridge, MA: Harvard University Press.

Rose, Arnold. 1967. *The Power Structure*. New York: Oxford University Press.

Rude, George. 1959. *The Crowd in the French Revolution*. Oxford: Oxford University Press.

_____. 1964. *The Crowd in History*. New York: John Wiley and Sons.

Schlesinger, Arthur Sr. 1950. *The American as Reformer*. Cambridge, MA: Harvard University Press.

Sennett, Richard. 1978. *The Fall of Public Man*. New York: Vintage Books.

Shils, Edward. 1960. "Mass Society and its Critics." Daedalus 89 (spring).

_____. 1961. "Centre and Periphery." In *The Logic of Personal Knowledge. Essays Presented to Michael Polanyi*. London: Routledge and Kegan Paul.

Shils, Edward. 1972. *The Intellectuals and the Powers & Other Essays*. Chicago: University of Chicago Press.

Smelser, Neil. 1963. *The Theory of Collective Behavior*. New York: The Free Press.

Spinrad, William. 1970. *Civil Liberties*. Chicago: Quadrangle Books.

Thompson, W. I. 1967. *The Imagination of an Insurrection: Dublin, Easter 1916*. New York: Harper Colophon Books.

Tilly, Charles. 1978. *From Mobilization to Revolution*. Reading, MA: Addison-Wesley.

Tilly, Charles, Louise Tilly, and Richard Tilly. 1975. *The Rebellious Century: 1830–1930*. Cambridge, MA: Harvard University Press.

Trilling, Lionel. 1972. *Sincerity and Authenticity*. Cambridge, MA: Harvard University Press.

Turner, Ralph, and Lewis Killian. 1986. *Collective Behavior*. 3rd. ed. Englewood Cliffs, NJ: Prentice-Hall.

Turner, Ralph. 1969. "The Theme of Contemporary Social Movements." *British Journal of Sociology* 20 (December): 390–405.

_____. 1976. "The Real Self: From Institution to Impulse." *American Journal of Sociology* 21 (March): 989–1016.

Walzer, Michael. 1965. *The Revolution of the Saints*. New York: Atheneum.

Weinberg, Ian. 1974. "Social Problems That Are No More." In E. Smigel, ed. *Handbook of Social Problems*. Chicago: Rand McNally.

Wilkinson, Paul. 1971. *Social Movements*. New York: Praeger.

Williams, Raymond. 1976. *Keywords: A Vocabulary of Culture and Society*. New York: Oxford University Press.

_____. 1960. *Culture and Society*. Garden City, NY: Anchor/Doubleday.

Wilson, John. 1973. *Introduction to Social Movements*. New York: Basic Books.

Wrong, Dennis. 1961. "The Over-Socialized Conception of Man in Modern Sociology." *American Sociological Review* 26 (April): 189-193.

Zilborg, Aristide. 1974. "The Making of Flemings and Walloons: Belgium, 1830-1910." *Journal of Interdisciplinary History* 5 (fall): 179-236.

Zimring, Franklin, and Gordon Hawkins. 1973. *Deterrence*. Chicago: University of Chicago Press.

7

Social Movements and Social Change: Perspectives of Linearity and Fluidity

Kenneth Burke once said that every way of seeing is also a way of not seeing. The terms which we construct to provide an orderly understanding of the world arise as well from the problems and concerns of the observers and from the categories for making sense of events that are available to them as they do from the external phenomena themselves. The theories, paradigms, concepts, and assumptions of sociological fields are often, however, couched in a language of Aristotelian science: the explanation of actions and processes whose factual nature bounds and compels the systems of understanding. A beginning to the study of social movements must then be initiated by a definition of what they are and what are their characteristics.

A more Platonist view of the scientific endeavor suggests a Schutzian world of multiple realities in which our language and our perspectives sensitize us to this or that piece of the universe of our interests. A beginning to the study of social movements in this vein avoids definition entirely and attempts to convey why it is that the observer wishes to study this phenomena and what experiences lead him or her to do so in this way. The Aristotelian realist feels safest when furthest from self; when the observer has been exiled from the observed. The Platonist is uncomfortable in such a posture and looks to place the self back in again.

This is a Platonist's paper and a way of seeing the study of social movements from a Platonic perspective. Again Burke, so much the grand Platonist of contemporary social analysis, has put it well:

Reprinted from Louis Kriesberg, ed., *Research in Social Movements, Conflicts and Change: A Research Annual*, Vol. 4, pp. 317–39. With permission of JAI Press Inc., Greenwich, CT., and London, England, 1981. All rights of reproduction in any form reserved.

I do not see why the universe should accommodate itself to a man-made medium of communication....Perhaps because we have come to think of ourselves as listening to the universe, as waiting to see what it will prove to us, we have psychotically made the corresponding readjustment of assuming that the universe itself will abide by our rules of discussion and give us its revelations in a cogent manner. Our notion of causality as a succession of pushes from behind is thus a disguised way of insisting that experience abide by the convention of a good argument. (Burke, 1965: 99)

All this murky philosophizing is a way of introducing a paper about the relation of social movements to social change and about how different frameworks for studying movements have different implications for this topic and this point in history. In describing and analyzing two perspectives—the linear and the fluid—I will argue that the latter has not been sufficiently used in sociology and that its adoption will help in studying some phenomena of change better than the former. Not that one perspective is better than the other, but that one does some things that the other does not and vice-versa. Having done this, I will exemplify some of these issues by a brief examination of three movements.

Social Movements as Collective Action

An effort to characterize a field or subdiscipline must necessarily gloss over many differences, distinctions, and qualifications. In pointing toward certain commonalities in the study of social movements as a field, I am undoubtedly doing injustice to significant nuances. Nevertheless, I do so as a means of highlighting the similarities of many otherwise diverse sociologists.

Characteristically, the field of "social movements" has been seen as a phase of collective behavior. The rationale behind this has stemmed from two considerations, both explicit in the classic and seminal paper by Herbert Blumer (Blumer, 1939). The first is that movements are viewed as attempts to change existing social relationships, processes or institutions. Consequently, they are differentiated from the normal, the status quo, the conventional in belief and action. Collective behavior served as a term of differentiation, dividing such behavior from "social organization," which attended to conventional normalized thought and action.

Secondly, social movements could be conceptualized as a facet of collective behavior because they represented the action of collectivities—aggregates assuming shared goals and interests and acting in the name of group concerns. The ever-present natural history of social movements—from collective protest to social movement organizations to struggle for success to institutionalization is another form of this paradigm.

Even critics of these formulations have shared much of its imagery. Although McCarthy and Zald are highly critical of the "hearts and minds" approach to social movements, nevertheless, they study collectivities in the form of social movement organizations and account for the development of movements by attention to how resources are mobilized toward conscious attempts to bring about change (McCarthy and Zald, 1973).

Tilly is quite wisely sensitive to some differences in what is being studied by diverse frameworks. He distinguishes "collective action" from "social movements" suggesting that the latter attempts to study populations, beliefs, and actions. He defines a social movement as "a group of people identified by their attachment to some particular set of beliefs" (Tilly, 1978: 9). It is clear from his text that it is not any set of beliefs, however, but those directed toward change. "Collective action" studies particular groups and events, such as violence, strikes, protests, etc. Such "collective behavior" has often been the concern of past students of social movements.

The field to which all of these point is, however, one characterized by the two models or frameworks or concepts discussed above:

1. Action is directed in a conscious effort to produce change in the society.

2. The unit of observation is an association organized to achieve change.

The Linear Image of Social Movements and Its Implications

This orientation toward phenomena involves the user in an image I term "linear" because it directs attention to a discrete association of people whose activity is perceived as using means to gain an end. The Labor Movement can be used as an analogy, model or metaphor. The Movement can be studied through the development of a conception of labor goals, a series of actions in strikes and political mobilization to the achievement of goals or their frustration. The focus of attention on empirical events is on how they advance or deter the achievement of goals consciously stated in organizational programs.

For a variety of reasons not all implicit in the logic of its formulations, the linear image has had several characteristics that carry significant implications for the study of social change. These follow below.

1. A preoccupation with the beginnings of movements. A great deal of the social movements literature is intent on understanding how it is that movements have occurred.[1] Because discontent, dissidence or attempted change appear as deviations from a norm of social conformity and convention, movements and their partisans seem to be unusual and hence problematic, something whose occurrence needs explanation. In the theoretical framework of much of sociology, especially in its functional formulations, the absence of conflict occasions less notice than its appearance (Smelser, 1963; also the criticism of Smelser in Currie and Skolnick, 1970).

Once movements are "seen" as directed against some status quo the alienation of partisans from "society" becomes a problem. Focus on origins, however, minimizes the attention to consequences. The current concern for mobilization is again another mode of studying how organization has developed but not what are the outcomes of movements.

2. Focus on organizations and associations. Much of what the literature of sociological studies of movements contains is the study of specific organizations of a population. What is studied is the Hare Krishnas, the Woman's Christian Temperance Union, the Congress for Racial Equality, or the Students for a Democratic Society. "Social movements," as Zald and Ash put it, "manifest themselves, in part, through a wide range of organizations" (Zald and Ash, 1966: 327). The SMO (Social Movement Organization) has become almost synonymous with the Movement.

In part, this is also a function of defining movements as associations of people, as collectivities. In part, it is also a means of studying otherwise elusive phenomena. Fieldwork and other standard sociological methods and techniques make such discrete definition almost an essential.

3. Focus on dissidence, protest, rebellion, deviance. For a variety of reasons, well beyond the scope of this paper, sociologists have been preoccupied with political actions that attempt fundamental reforms and with collective behavior that appears to break with conventional procedures. The events of the 1960s have furthered this and produced

a rash of interest in the genesis and development of violence and protest. Gamson's important work on *The Strategy of Social Protests* is one illustration. Charles Tilly's studies of protest actions is another (Tilly, 1978; C. Tilly, L. Tilly, and R. Tilly, 1975; Shorter and Tilly, 1974).

An implication of this is found in the heightened concern for change directed toward the State. What I have referred to elsewhere as the "overpoliticalization" of sociology has haunted social movements (Gusfield, 1980). Some would even define the field as the study of dissidence (Denisoff, 1974). It has also led to a focus on the value and consequence of specific strategies used by movement organizations or incipient movements (Gamson, 1975).

4. Concern for change as success or failure of movements seen in their own terms. Using an imagery of movements to deliberately achieve change, the movement becomes its own source for defining what happened. Whether success or failure was realized is found in the program or goal of the movement as stated by its proponents and opponents. Thus, Gamson, in a careful discussion of operationalizing the concept of success, uses acceptance by the group's antagonists of the movement organization as legitimate leaders of a legitimate set of interests. In considering the realization of new advantages as a facet of success, Gamson writes: "Did the potential beneficiaries of the challenging group receive what the *group sought* for them?" (Gamson, 1975: 34 [italics mine]). The impact of the movement on social structure or culture is then restricted to programmatic goals.

5. The public area as the focus of movement actions. The imagery of many social movement studies is that of a Romantic ideal of an "underdog" challenging a powerful authority (Gamson uses the term "challenging group"). Victory is wrested from an unwilling foe; defeat comes at the hands of repressing elites. The emphasis of the studies are on the public arena. Legislation, institutional change, policy ended or begun; these are both the measures of success or failure and the points of attention.

A great deal of human life occurs at the day-to-day level of interactions, only dimly affected by public policies (Gusfield, 1980; 1981). A movement such as the anti-Vietnam Movement may be oriented to change in public policy, but a movement such as the Women's Movement or the Gay Rights Movement is, to a large extent, found not only among partisans and antipartisans but in the myriad events of everyday life in which sexual and gender relationships are constructed and evaluated. The same is true even for linear movements. The Prohibition Movement can be studied in its achievement of the 18th Amendment and its enforcement. It can also be studied in the drinking behavior during that period and in the legacy it left, or did not leave, on American drinking habits (Gusfield, 1968; Aaron and Musto, 1981). Attention to political goals overstates the public as an arena of behavior and assumes a greater capacity for centralized social control than is warranted.

A Marx for the Managers; A Michels for the Misbegotten

Whether explicit or implicit, the study of social movements seems pervaded by a practical, political concern about the movements studied. It is not only that political interests emerge in choices of what to study. (Elsewhere I have argued that Liberalism and its vicissitudes have been a major focus of sociological study of movements during the past four decades [Gusfield, 1978].) The image of the movement as directed toward change has made us emphasize the linearity of movements. The form of study appears addressed to those who want to know how to start or how to stop movements from occurring, to those who want to know how to succeed or how to frustrate purposive actions. The "power elite" can read Marx to learn to avoid revolution ("A Marx for the Managers" is a paper by Gerth and Mills, 1942). The "radical left" can study Michels to prevent the "iron law of oligarchy" from deflecting organizations away from their movement goals. Piven and Cloward have done this in their advice to poor people that protest action is more effective than organized movements (Piven and Cloward, 1979: Ch. 1).

The point I am making is that the linear model and its emphasis on the deliberate pursuit of change by an association of partisans is one way of seeing social movements. Other ways are possible and their implications may be useful in other ways and for other interests.

The Fluid Concept of Social Movement

Another model or image of "social movement" has persisted alongside the linear one, although its usage has not been extensive among sociologists. The vocabulary of social movements has included not only the discrete association but also vaguer, more diffuse phenomena such as Abolitionism, Humanitarianism, Feminism and "the egalitarian impulse." Such terms are more often the province of historians than sociologists. For example, in discussing the change in treatment of deviance in America, David Rothman analyzes the rise of the penitentiary as a manifestation of a changed orientation toward institutionalizing criminal offenders. He writes that, "In the 1820s New York and Pennsylvania began a movement that *spread* through the Northwest and then over the next decade to many mid-western states." In the next paragraph he refers to the actions of state legislatures in creating prisons as "all this activity" (Rothman, 1971: 79–80 [italics mine]). These are vague terms and the movement is discovered not in the actions of this or that organization or this or that event but in the quickening of actions, the change in meanings, and the understanding that something new is happening in a wide variety of places and arenas. The movement is seen as a change in the meanings of objects and events rather than the occurrence of associations.

Sociologists have often recognized the large ambits within which particular organized movements occur. Blumer, in his classic paper, distinguished between general and specific movements and referred to "cultural drifts," such as the Labor Movement or the Women's Movement, which constitute the background for general movements. Drifts are "gradual and pervasive changes in the values of people, particularly along the lines of the conceptions that people have of themselves, and of their rights and privileges" (Blumer, 1939: 256). Smelser, in a much different formulation, uses the distinction between norm-oriented and value-oriented movements to encompass a similar recognition of levels and scope of movements (Smelser, 1962: Ch. 9, 10). Recently the French structuralists, notably Michel Foucault, have focused attention on the cognitive frameworks and the pervasive impact of changing cognitive structures on social and cultural transformations (Foucault, 1973; 1975).

Such perspectives operate with a more fluid and diffuse image of "movement" than the linear model encompasses. They blur the line between trend and movement, but they shift attention away from the association and its member-participants to the longer-run and less public areas in which meanings are undergoing transformation. They recognize the less directed aspects of social and cultural change. As Banks has been aware:

Smelser's historical sequence, like that of sociologists who favor a natural history approach to the study of social movements, implies that the undirected phase always precedes the directed in time, or rather, that the directed phase emerges out of a previously inchoate groping toward the collective consciousness of similarities and differences and then in its turn accumulates around it a wider body of partisans. (Banks, 1972: 13)

A more fluid perspective toward the meaning of movement emphasizes the quickening of change and the social sharing of new meanings in a variety of areas and places. It is less confined to the boundaries of organizations and more alive to the larger contexts of change at the same time as it is open to awareness of how the movement has consequences and impacts among nonpartisans and nonmembers as well as participants and devotees. Rather than success or failure of a movement, it is more likely to lead to questions about consequences: What happened?

To continue the liquid metaphor in the imagery of fluidity, we can liken the study of specific and organized movements to a ripple in the water rather than a shot in the dark. The perspective of fluidity emphasizes the cultural side of movements—the transformations of meaning—and the interactive side of consequences—the less public aspects of life. Politically, the focus shifts away from the short-run search for goals and goal realization and toward the less political parts of human life in long-run perspective. Society rather than the State becomes the area of analysis.

In a somewhat different usage, Piven and Cloward also criticize conventional sociological studies of social movements for failure to recognize the significance of collective violence and protest actions in achieving poor people's interests. The focus on organized and directed activity toward articulated goals denies political meaning to much protest:

The stress on conscious intentions in these usages reflects a confusion in the literature between the mass movement on the one hand, and the formalized organizations which tend to emerge on the crest of the movement on the other hand—two intertwined but distinct phenomena. (Piven and Cloward, 1977: 5)

In exploring this distinction between a linear and a fluid conception of movements, I want to stress two considerations: The utility of the fluid conception for (1) understanding both social and cultural change, and (2) for analyzing contemporary movements in particular.

The Consequences of Movements

If we utilize a more fluid, expansive conception of movements, two implications become significant for the study of social change. First, we are led to examine any specific social movement organization in terms of consequences in a wide variety of areas and over a long run.

Given a more fluid image, success or failure and consequences can no longer be gauged in terms intrinsic to the Social Movement Organization. Recent evaluation of the movements of the 1960s have been filled with concerns about realization of movement goals (Perrow, 1979; Oberschall, 1978; Snyder and Kelly, 1979). But they have also indicated a number of ways in which other things occur. Thus Snyder and Kelly make the point that the outcomes of collective violence may vary as between impact on the group's concerns and on the total system. (The implications of racial violence on "white flight," for example.) Joel Handler has shown that achievement of legislation or favorable legal decision by no means implies that the behavior under concern has changed. Much depends on the precise character of the situations covered. Where bureaucratic discretion must be used in applying law to specific causes, there is less homogeneity between law and action than where a general rule can be enunciated and limited discretion is necessary. A law prohibiting construction of a building is far easier to apply than one declaring voting rights (Handler, 1979). A movement may be waning just when its aims are most supported. Hofstadter pointed out that the Anti-Trust Movement had lost much of its public support at the point when anti-trust actions were at their height (Hofstadter, 1965: Ch. 6). The institution of a structure—the Anti-Trust Division of the Department of Justice—made for an autonomous operation, independent of beliefs.

One of the significant consequences of movements and movement organizations is the development of a cadre of movement personnel. Precisely as the movement is a more general concept than the SMO, so too people who participate in one movement or SMO are capable of being carriers to and for others. One of the outcomes of the 1960s was exactly that. Thus the present Anti-Nuclear Movement draws on persons active in earlier movements. In the recent Anti-Nuclear Movement in New England leading roles were played by residents of rural communes organized in the 1960s.[2] A similar cross-fertilization was commented upon at length by several historians of the nineteenth century. A number of leading figures in pre-Civil War movements had origins personally or through earlier generations in a district of Western New York State. Even a generation later in Nebraska there could be seen the working out of the movements that stirred "the burned-over district" of upstate New York (Cross, 1950; Tyler, 1962).

Recognition of such carry-overs and carry-ons between movements has great implications both for assessing the consequences for change of both social movement organizations and movements seen as cultural transformations. Not only values but also cognitive structures are at work. The importance of such cultural implications exist at two levels. At the public level it shifts the nature of public issues. At the private, everyday level it provides a context of new meanings and actions dependent on them.

One of the residues of movements and SMOs is the existence of a vocabulary and an opening of ideas and actions which in the past was either unknown or unthinkable. Compare how the homosexual can be discussed in the contemporary generation with discussion in an earlier one. What was unthinkable in one period has become thinkable and possible. Perrow, writing about his study of the 1960s, observes:

> In every issue we considered, the contrast between the early 1950s and the late 1960s in our data source is extraordinary....No one on the project team has failed to be astounded by the climate of the 1950s and the sharp contrast with the late 1960s. (Perrow, 1979)

Significant also is the way in which major paradigms or structures of public discourse and discussion are generated and retained. In a number of cases, the specific movements of the past twenty years in America can be seen as manifestations or instances of a larger egalitarian impulse at work. Such unstated and yet crucial aspects of social and cultural change are significant aspects of the context within which movements are operative. The struggle over Gay rights, Women's rights and even the rights of handicapped operate differently in the context of presumptions about equality in the 1980s than in the 1950s. Even name changes carry such redefinitions and assume acceptance: Negro—Black; Homosexual—Gay; Feminist—Women's Liberationist.

As some writer's have seen, a longer-run approach to understanding how general movements are formed and developed is necessary in studying social and cultural change. E. P. Thompson studied the development of the English working class as a movement over a long period of time. Carl Taylor studied the specific movements of American farmers over more than a century and substituted for specific studies of particular movements an entity called "the Farmer's Movement" (E. P. Thompson, 1963; Taylor, 1953). It is a matter crying for study that movements remain dormant and reemerge with their rhetoric shining and seemingly unused. This occurs especially with ethnic nationalism (W. I. Thompson, 1967; Hechter, 1975).[3] That old target of American farmer's "Wall Street" disappears and reappears from time to time in American politics. And what happened to the Women's Movement between 1920 and the late 1960s (Green and Melnick, 1953)?

The second level of interest in the cultural changes of specific movements is at the private or everyday level. Here it is necessary to introduce another consideration: the reflexive character of movements.

The Reflexivity of Social Movements

A second implication of fluidity is that social movements, like other phenomena, are also objects of attention and perception. They are matters of interest and evaluation for those who consider themselves members and partisans. They are also objects for the perception and imagination of others. It is this aspect of movements that I refer to as reflexive. The effects of movements on change arises not only from their direct impact on institutions and on members but on those who perceive that a change is taking place, who reflect on the fact of the movement's occurrence.

The movement, specific or general, exists as well in the recognition of many that some matter of interest has now become an object of possible change: something is happening. There is a model implicit in the very sense of "movement"; the "normal" is undergoing movement and change. What was thought to be "taken for granted" has now become an issue. Relations between teachers and students become "problematic." Conceptions of "proper" relations between sexes are being challenged. Race relations are undergoing a new "charter." The existence and perception of a movement signifies that change is now possible.

This perception of a movement is part of the monitoring of "society" in which observers, spectators, and audiences participate. It brings to them a view of the "generalized other" in the form of matters that are now in the realm of conflict and challenge. What was unthinkable is seen as now thinkable. What was taken for granted as an item of consensus can no longer be so taken. An example of this is the way in which cohabitation and marijuana use have moved from the realm of publicly acknowledged deviation to the kingdom of public acceptance.

From this standpoint of fluidity, movements "exist" at the level of the private and the situated, as well as in the linear view of organized and public activities. The perception that a transformation may be happening in the larger society provides a background for the interactive and the micro-level in which people other than members or partisans participate. The Civil Rights Movement has meant more than the achievement of this or that legal or political right. It contributes to ambiguity where once there was norm in black-white interactions, to preferred and demanded equity where there was once dominance and subordination. The Women's Movement happens when the housewife finds a new label for discontents; secretaries decide not to serve coffee and husbands are warier about using past habits of dominance.

The awareness of the movement is thus itself a crucial and significant phenomenon. It is part of the ways in which movements intersect social change; providing the appearance of new meaning in the spectrum of normalization and dissidence. From this perspective, I might even say that a social movement occurs when people are conscious that a movement is occurring. It is a two-step conception of the role of movements in social change. The awareness of change is itself a second step in the production of change.

Contemporary Movements and the Mass Media

The recognition that a movement is occurring is a form of social sharing. Even in a mass form of society, where the members of the audience are not interacting, they are capable of understanding or perceiving that there are others who share their feeling or opinion. They are aware that there are others who make up a demand for transformation. A temperance official I once interviewed supported her stout defense of an old Prohibitionist stance by saying that she wanted it known that there were still some old-fashioned people who stood for Prohibition.

The kind of fluid concept of movement that I am espousing shifts our attention away from the origin of movements in the classical natural history model. It leads us to a concern for how awareness of a movement is constructed. Here McCarthy and Zald have been helpful in their recognition that the movement may emerge without a widespread constituency of partisans (McCarthy and Zald, 1973). So, too, Spinrad's analysis of the Senator Joseph McCarthy Movement demonstrates how a few and specific acts of complaint to agencies were treated as a movement and the emerging snowball impact of such treatment (Spinrad, 1970).

The fluid conception of movements is especially important in understanding the contemporary society and the ways in which change occurs as a consequence of movements. I will discuss two aspects of this; the role of the mass media in the construction of movements and the occurrence of movements of self-transformation and interpersonal relations.

The media of mass communications play a part that is both highly significant and unique to contemporary societies (Gusfield, 1979). It is not that television, movies, newspapers and journals persuade us to this or that set of opinions, this or that candidate. Rather, it arises from the monitoring function of media of communications. They tell us what is happening and, alternately, do not tell us what is happening. In the telling they put together individual acts into general patterns; turn particular acts into movements. A good example of this is the Hippie Movement. Here no organization existed to provide a program; no highly dramatic events occurred to provide demonstrative confirmation of a direction toward change. It takes a generalization of specific events, a form of naming, to produce awareness, even among participants, that a movement is in process. How the movement becomes noticed and depicted bears not only on the general audience but even on the members and conscious partisans of specific movements (Gitlin, 1980).

The almost constant preoccupation of the media with movements brings home to the audience the existence of shared attitudes toward social transformation. Student protest, the Women's Movement, the Anti-Nuclear Movement, the holistic medicine movement, the child abuse movement are examples of how the communication of shared directions in change is made part of the general monitoring system of the spectator. The disposition of commercial and competing forms of communication to dramatize events and movements enhances the awareness of living in a changing environment. The media do more than reflect "society." They refract it and construct it. To that extent, the media may play a significant gate-keeping role.

This is especially important when movements are less organized and more fluid than linear. The very fluidity of such movements may elude their recognition. Perceiving their fluidity enhances them and generalizes them into something with a name and direction. The Women's Movement, seen as something of which the E.R.A. and equal pay are only parts, strengthens the perception of a broader transformation in process that has implications at the micro level as well as at the macro. Putting together a variety of specific responses to changes in abortion, homosexuality, and sexual openness in the form of "the moral majority" provides the spectators with a wider sense of sharing in a more general movement.

Contemporary Movements: Self-Transformation and Interpersonal Improvement

My second point about the contemporaneity of fluid movements heightens the importance of the constructing which mass media (and mass education) do in generating social and cultural change. The kinds of movements that assume importance in this period in American history are more fluid in character, less encompassed by organization and programmatic direction than is true of those movements caught in the net of linear images.

A turn away from public life as a major arena of action is a theme in recent and significant writings. Lionel Trilling, Richard Sennett, and Ralph Turner have all commented on the disposition to blur the distinction between the public and the private and to expend private concerns into public attentions. For Trilling this was inherent in the movement away from the acceptance of public roles as valued and sincere and in the growing glorification of continuity between the private self and the public person in the concept of authenticity (Trilling, 1972). For Sennett it is found in a privatizing trend which sees public life as less significant (Sennett, 1978). For Turner it is manifest in the preoccupation of contemporary movements with problems of alienation and self-identity (Turner, 1969; 1976).

The linear perspective toward social movements fit much of the nineteenth- and early twentieth-century social structure. Specific attempts to remedy social ills were thought of in political and economic terms for which concepts of class and status stratification and political goals encapsulated much of the character of such movements. Tilly's and Gamson's formulations are thus appropriate. They are less so when the movements that occupy attention are more fluid and less public. In a movement like the Women's Movement or the human potential movement or the new fundamentalists, the imagery is even more misleading.

Two changes in American life appear to me to enhance the utility of a fluid conception of movements. One is a tendency toward the break-up of homogeneous classes and status groups and their superimposition on other social categories. The Protestant-Catholic, worker-middle class splits of the past are less salient in American life today. "Social groups" are salient, not only in the older linear fashion in which organization could speak for a social base, but also as emerging and receding clusters of people formed around a specific area of concern. Cultural distinctions, such as "liberal" or "moral majority" or "youthful" may correlate with sociological categories of age or education, but they fail to depict communities of people who share a communal life. The mass basis of such movements as Abortion or human potential rests more on common styles of life than on position in the division of labor or residential commonalities.[4]

The other change is a product of the absorption of leisure as a facet of central life interests. As problems of the division of labor have assumed less salience, issues connected with life-style, with consumption, have achieved greater prominence. Living, as well as livelihood, becomes an object of attention.

What seems to be increasingly the case is that public arenas become the depositories of private worries. Here again the media of mass communication plays a large role in making such areas of life as sex, parenthood, love, and ambition into areas where private feelings are seen as socially shared. The self has become not only an object of transformation but an object whose change can be pursued in concert with others.

In short, the generalizing and normalizing processes by which movements influence change is more and more a process which should not be ignored. Movements are not only linear and directed; they are also fluid and undirected. They build up generalized contexts of cognitive and moral structure in both public and private, transcending and situated actions, at micro and macro levels. As W. I. Thompson put it, "history is also the process by which public events become private imaginations" (W. I. Thompson, 1967: 235).

Problems in Social Movements and Social Change

I bring this paper to a close with an examination of three movements. In each of these the relation between a specific and a more general movement is considered. Each represents a somewhat different problem in analyzing linear and fluid conceptions in the relation between social movements and social change.

1. The Social Security Act. The Problem of Protest and Change

The passage of the Social Security Act of 1935 is seen by many historians of American life as a watershed in the development of a welfare state: from a reliance on voluntary, private activities to assure welfare to a commitment from public, governmental sources (Lubove, 1968: Ch. 1; Schlesinger, 1959: 315). In the light of the general discussion of protest and organized dissent in producing major change, the development of social security cries out for analysis.

Some historians and political scientists give a great deal of weight to the Townsend Movement and see its programs and agitation for pensions of $200 a month as crucial to the emergence and "successful" passage of the Act (Holtzman, 1963; Sanders, 1973). For these observers the Social Movement Organization created a protest movement for which the Act was a response. Piven and Cloward, however, use the Townsend Movement as an example of how organization blunts the effectiveness of opposition which poor people's movements must depend upon for effectiveness. Social Security, they maintain, met the moral demands of the movement without giving the members anything. Seven years would elapse before Townsend members could be eligible and they would have had to have amassed working time to provide adequate pensions (Piven and Cloward, 1979: 31).

A closer look at social security, even though cursory here, suggests another way of seeing the act and its origins, somewhat different from the emphasis of the historians, political scientists, and sociologists above. These focus on the specific movement of the moment and its organized program. In the same fashion, Gamson attributes to the activities of protest organizations the success or failure of their aims. But the Act has a history and a context. Whatever criticisms of the Act at the time for failure to insure a wider segment of the population or for not effecting greater income redistribution, it was, nevertheless, a remarkable break with a dominant operating assumption about the dependence of the aged on the market and on individual resources (Lubove, 1968). It provided old age insurance on a compulsory basis and with government support where this had not occurred in the past. It laid a base for later widening of provisions and coverage, including Medicare. Whether or not it aided the Townsend supporters, it cannot be dismissed lightly as a minor change in American political or social structure

> For all the defects of the Act, it still meant a tremendous break with the inhibitions of the past. The federal government was at last charged with obligation to provide its citizens a measure of protection from the hazards and vicissitudes of life. (Schlesinger, 1959: 315)

What role did social movement and social movement organizations play in producing a social change of such significance? In the absence of a more thorough study, I can only hint at one possible approach which sees the organized efforts as *an* element but only *an* and not *the*.

One significant thread in the cloth of the Social Security legislation came from the circle of advisors and assistants whom Franklin Roosevelt brought with him into power. In such people as Harry Hopkins, assistant to the President, and Frances Perkins, Secretary of Labor, he tapped into groups of people who had been active for many years in various phases of the social insurance movements. For two decades before the New Deal, the social insurance movement had been growing in the United States, manifested in a small corps of people in fields such as social work, labor organizations, and academic life, who had been active in programs for old age assistance, health insurance, pension plans and aid for dependent mothers. The movement in federal and state programs remained relatively subordinate to the dominant American theme of voluntary, private action (Lubove, 1968). Only one prominent American political leader, Franklin Delano Roosevelt (as New York State governor) had been a strong advocate. He named his State Industrial Commissioner, Frances Perkins, to be Secretary of Labor when he assumed the Presidency. In June of 1934, before the Townsend Movement gained momentum, he named a cabinet Committee on Economic Security, with Perkins as chair. They formulated a program for Unemployment Compensation and for Social Security, and in January 1935, the legislation was introduced into the Senate (Schlesinger, 1959: Ch. 18).

The Townsend Movement may have been an important element in getting Congress to accept the legislation, and the Great Depression, of course, a major important context. Even with amendments, it was a change of significant proportions both in effects and in the traditional conceptions of American governmental obligations to the aged. Yet it is hardly attributable to specific protest actions or to the activities of specific movement organizations. The Townsend Movement was not engaged in violent or overt protest. Nor did it make a general Social Security program its major aim. It sought to do something "then and now" for the aged.

The social insurance movement formed a backdrop from which emerged a corps of people, a set of programs (including the influential plan previously adopted by Wisconsin) and a familiarity with ideas. These became more operational in the context of the Depression. I do not mean to imply that specific movements never play a significant role in social change or that protest and mass agitation are necessary. But these need to be seen as problematic and situational and their relation to more fluid, less directed aspects of movements needs to be examined and recognized.

2. The Alcoholism and Prevention Movements: The Nesting of Movements

The relation between specific and general movements, between several specific movements or between "cultural drifts" and both types of movements is an important problem for the delineation of how meanings, associations, and activities interrelated. Such relationships may be structural, in the sense of drawing on similar groups in the social structure, or cultural in the sense of a logical, symbolic or meaningful relation. The movement for the Equal Rights Amendment is clearly both in its relation to the larger and more encompassing Women's Movement. Both, in turn, may have affinities to the generalized equalitarian impulse found in many ethnic, racial, minority, deviant groups. The Gay Rights Movement might be traced to new orientations toward sexual expressiveness as well as the egalitarian impulses. Finding and delineating the nests of movements at differing levels is another avenue along which to investigate how changes are happening.

The analysis of policies and programs connected with alcohol issues since Repeal (1933) provides a good illustration of how such nestings may and may not occur.[5] The Temperance Movement and Prohibition conceived alcohol problems as matters of drinking and drunkenness, as well as chronic inebriety. By 1900, direct controls over the availability of alcohol had come to be the major policy for minimizing and/or eradicating the alcohol problem. With Repeal of the Prohibition Amendment, that policy was discredited. A long period of American history during which church groups had played a dominant role in addressing the public question of alcohol had come to an end. In the wake of that era the problem of alcohol was defined in different fashion by emerging groups espousing new policies.

Chief among the new public opinion leaders and shapers were academic science, in the form of such groups as the Yale School of Alcohol Studies, a corps of self-labeled "alcoholics," especially in Alcoholics Anonymous, and a newly emergent group of professional and quasiprofessional workers drawn from medicine, social work, and clinical psychology. What was common to this otherwise often conflicting association was a focus on the chronic inebriate and the etiology of his problems in a disease called "alcoholism." Removing the stigma against the alcoholic into a definition of his problem as "sickness" and providing for his treatment as a medical problem were the key aims of this movement.

During the period 1933-1970, various associations and programs that were part of what has come to be called "the Alcoholism Movement" were active in gaining a widened commitment of American states for financial support of treatment of alcoholism. In 1970, they played a major role in bringing about the National Institute on Alcohol Abuse and Alcoholism. (Again, as with Social Security, there are several other threads in that cloth.) The NIAAA brought a much-enhanced program of financial support for the treatment of alcoholics.

In attempting to explain the movement toward a redefinition of the alcohol issue into the alcoholism issue and the move to inculcate the disease concept of alcoholism in the American population, it is difficult to relate it clearly to other movements at the same or differing levels in American life during this historical period. The role of psychological counseling and therapy and its growth bears some relation to the development of a corps of professionals and quasiprofessionals committed to treatment as a policy. However, it cannot account for the self-motivated associations of recovered alcoholics and AA nor for the origin and proliferation of the disease concept nor for the absence of a wider definition of alcohol problems or of social control measures. In an era of increasing governmental intervention in the economy, the Alcoholism Movement was going in an opposite direction.

The Alcoholism Movement has been considered in terms of the vacuum created by the sudden discrediting of the dominant religious groups associated with Prohibition and their definition of alcohol questions. It is hard to find a larger movement of ideas or of associations in which the Alcoholism Movement clearly nested. To be sure, the general direction toward medicalization of social and other problems bears some relationship, but this is by no means clear or direct. Medicalization has been under way for a long time in mental "illness."

Currently, however, the nesting of alcohol movements with other medical movements seems clearer. This is especially the case in its relation to the current movement toward Prevention and away from Treatment in medicine.

Since the early 1970s, alcohol studies and alcohol policy has been subject to a new impulse toward prevention of alcohol problems rather than their resolution through treatment and medicalization. Policies aimed at controlling the availability of alcoholic beverages and controlling their use have come to be seriously considered, discussed, and debated in academic, organizational, and governmental circles. Policies of taxation, minimum-age laws, drinking/driving legislation and other environmental changes have gained a corps of adherents as alternatives to alcoholism as the prime problem and to treatment as the major policy. From the dominance of alcoholism and its medicalization, the public issues of alcohol problems now demonstrate a conflict sparked by a new movement critical of the disease concept of alcoholism and oriented toward the prevention of alcohol problems.

The movement toward prevention in the area of alcohol problems coincides with a more general movement away from treatment-oriented medicine and toward public health and prevention as policy models in health in the United States. The general movement has a number of elements in its makeup. The criticism of treatment-oriented medicine is, in part, a response to the growing costs of hospitals and physicians, the commitment of a welfare-committed government to health insurance, and the high proportion of medical expenditures as a part of the gross national product. But it is also more than that. It is also part of the egalitarian wave of distrust of experts and of doctors, itself another piece of the widened conception of citizen rights and egalitarian values. It is also a heightened awareness of environmental elements in health.

At still another level, the increased interest in health as a matter of public policy and private action, independent of professional medical practitioners, represents a redefinition of how health is achievable. An emphasis on appropriate lifestyles shifts the burden of illness responsibility from external agents such as bacteria and constitutional genetic characteristics toward the public provision of information and environment and the citizen's responsibility to live appropriately. It is noteworthy that the model of the effective public prevention program is found, in government prevention papers and in other circles, in the campaign against cigarette smoking and the movement toward exercise and care to avoid heart attacks.

The preventive movement in alcohol problems is thus nested in a general prevention movement in the field of health in which government public health officials have led. That is, in turn, nested in a larger movement toward redefinition of medicine and the responsibility for resolving illness.[6] To study alcohol movements in isolation from such changes is to tell only a piece of the story.

How the nesting occurs and how the specific and general movements relate to each other is a matter of much greater study. In the case of the "new Temperance Movement" (as I call it), the linkage would appear to have much to do with the inclusion of alcohol issues in the Federal government with the establishment of the National Institute on Alcohol Abuse and Alcoholism in 1970. As a part of the National Institutes of Health and the Public Health Service, it became more open to general movements in health.

3. The Natural Foods Movement: The "Deep Structure" of Movements

An emphasis on the fluidity of movements leads also to the recognition that a change in meaning on one level can also be viewed as change in meaning at other levels. Foods, being an aspect of everyday life in its most mundane fashion, offer a clue to the general paradigms of existence. They can serve as instances in which is revealed the underlying, "deep structure" by which events are given order and made understandable. Levi-Strauss has made the distinction between the raw and the cooked a basic device by which to make sense of a wide variety of primitive myths (Levi-Strauss, 1969). Others, such as Mary Douglas and Roland Barthes, also call attention to the significa- tion used in the consumption of foods (Douglas, 1971; Barthes, 1979). Thus Barthes writes:

> Sugar is not just a foodstuff, even when it is used in conjunction with other foods; it is, if you will, an "attitude"....I remember an American hit song Sugar Time. Sugar is a time, a category of the world. (Barthes, 1979: 166–67)

The shifts in food usages and the movements for and against the use of certain foods or drink may then be clues to wider changes in thought and meaning. The symbolic properties projected onto foods constitutes part of a system for understanding and evaluating that may be found in other areas and in other movements.

The concept of "natural foods" contains in its very naming a con- trast with artificial, human-made food. The alternative term "health food" carries with it the conception that nonnatural forms of food are unhealthy. Processed foods, foods using preservatives, foods to which chemicals have been added—all qualify as other than food as found in nature. The products of food technology are thus derogated and placed in the category of harmful. The standardized, the mass-produced and mass-consumed items are, by virtue of their departure from the natu- ral, ipso facto unhealthy and unaesthetic. Perhaps no food is as sym- bolic of the unnatural as processed and presliced white bread.

The opposite has, of course, also been the case. The quest for the new and the modern has taken supremacy over traditional food. The rise of middle classes in many underdeveloped countries has been accompa- nied by shifting food habits away from the native, the peasant, the traditional foods toward those of Western origins. The products of mod- ern technology take on social status from their users but they also carry meanings about the virtues of the artificial and the vices of the natural. Even the shift from breast feeding to formula milk for babies in parts of Africa has had this set of meanings (Uchendu, 1970).

I am just beginning the study of natural food movements but they are by no means confined to the present period in history. Certainly in the late nineteenth century in the United States such a movement was rife. It lives on in the legacy of corn flakes. The humble morning cereal had its origins in health food missionaries, Kellogg and Post, who invented the common flake as a natural food to replace meat (Carson, 1957).

The movement toward the use of natural foods may then be seen in the context of paradigms concerning the values of nature vs. culture; of the natural against the artificial; human nature against civilization. It is an old theme, but one that all cultures have developed some meaning about. Henry Nasby Smith, in his analysis of American literature about the frontier, suggests that American writers saw the frontier as overcoming the natural side of human beings—their impulsive, destructive, and antisocial humanness. It was civilization—the artificial control of the human—that made the frontier livable (Smith, 1956; also see Wright, 1975). The transformation was to be appreciated, not lamented. Against this Hobbesian and Freudian theme, there has also been the Rousseauistic glorification of the noble savage and the regret that culture and civilization create an artificial and desiccated human being, devoid of the innocent virtues that are inherent but covered over by society.

While the theme of nature and culture and the resulting tension between the two is by no means new, just how and when one or the other side of the conflict becomes dominant and in what parts of the society is a theme which the study of social movements can find significant. The paradigms of thought is linked to the antimodern, the antitechnological, the antiscience movements which appear and disappear and reappear. These cannot easily be explained as responses to industrialism since they occurred again well after industrialism was enthroned. The communes movements of the 1960s contained a glorification of the simple, the natural and nontechnological, preferring natural food to artificial, human energy to motors, feelings to reasons (Berger, 1981).

An analysis of natural foods movements, from this fluid perspective, would attempt to find the "deep structure" that makes the symbolism of natural and artificial food convincing and understandable. It would be a cultural search, in its efforts to construct the categories of logical understanding in use in the symbolism of foods. It would be social structural in attempting to find which parts of the social structure were carriers of the movement and the congruent mental structures.

For each of these movements discussed above, I posit the hypothesis of dual action and reaction; the specific influences the general by providing the reflective realization that change is happening at several levels. The more general movements in turn strengthen and support the specific ones, make them more understandable and acceptable.

What this programmatic paper calls for is less attention to change as defined in the program of the movement and less attention to movements as organized demands for change. What I have in mind is a greater role for the observer, the sociologist, in finding and naming the presence of a movement and in telling the reader or the listener what is happening from as wide a perspective as he or she, the observer, concludes is relevant.

Notes

1. Two outstanding exceptions to this generalization are Ash (1972) and Gamson (1975). Both of these are greatly concerned with effects of movements, although within a linear model (especially Gamson).
2. I am indebted to Jerzy Michalowicz for my knowledge of the movement and its leadership composition.
3. Henry Johnston is currently studying this problem in analyzing the waxing and waning of Catalan Regional Nationalism in Spain.
4. I have presented this theory before in *Symbolic Crusade* (1963), Ch. 6. The Civil Rights movement and ethnic renaissance of recent years represents an important qualification. Yet, as Wilson's study indicates, even race is receding as a superimposed category (Wilson, 1978).
5. I have examined the alcohol movements discussed here more carefully in a forthcoming paper. Biographical references are contained here (Gusfield, forthcoming).
6. In a personal communication, Jerzy Michalowicz has suggested that the movement toward greater concern for health has roots in a new glorification of the body as an object.

References

Aaron, Paul, and David Musto. 1981 "Temperance and Prohibition in America: A Historical Overview." In Mark Moore and Dean Gerstein, eds., *Alcohol and Public Policy: Beyond the Shadow of Prohibition*. Washington, DC: National Academy Press.

Ash, Roberta. 1972. *Social Movements in America*. Chicago: Markham Publishing Co.

Banks, J. A. 1972. *The Sociology of Social Movements*. London: Macmillan.

Barthes, Roland. 1979. "Toward a Psychosociology of Contemporary Food Consumption." In R. Forster and O. Ranum, eds., *Food and Drink in History*. Baltimore, MD: The Johns Hopkins University Press.

Berger, Bennett. 1981. *The Survival of a Counter-Culture*. Berkeley: University of California Press.

Blumer, Herbert. 1939. "Collective Behavior." In Robert Park, ed., *An Outline of the Principles of Sociology*. New York: Barnes and Noble, Inc.

Burke, Kenneth. 1965. *Permanence and Change*. Indianapolis, IN: The Bobbs-Merrill Co., Inc.

Carson, Gerald. 1957. *Cornflake Crusade*. New York: Rinehart.

Cross, Whitney. 1950. *The Burned-Over District*. Ithaca, NY: Cornell University Press.

Currie, Eliot, and Jerome Skolnick. 1970. "A Critical Note on Conceptions of Collective Behavior." *Annals of the American Academy of Political and Social Science* 391 (September): 34–45.

Denisoff, R. S. 1974. *The Sociology of Dissent*. New York Harcourt Brace Jovanovich.

Douglas, Mary. 1971. "Deciphering a Meal." In C. Geertz, ed. *Myths, Symbols and Culture*. New York: W. W. Norton and Co.

Foucault, Michel. 1973. *The Order of Things*. New York: Vintage Books.

_____. 1975. *The Birth of the Clinic*. New York: Vintage Books.

Gamson, William. 1975. *The Strategy of Social Protest*. Homewood, IL: Dorsey Press.

Gerth, Hans, and C. Wright Mills. 1942. "A Marx for the Managers." Ethics 52 (January).

Gitlin, Todd. 1980. *The Whole World Is Watching*. Berkeley: University of California Press.

Green, Arnold, and Eleanor Melnick. 1950. "What Has Happened to the Feminist Movement?" In A. W. Gouldner, ed. *Studies in Leadership*. New York: Harper and Row.

Gusfield, Joseph. 1963. *Symbolic Crusade*. Urbana: University of Illinois Press.

_____. 1968. "Prohibition: The Impact of Political Utopianism." In John Braeman, Robert Bremmer, and David Brody, eds., *Change and Continuity in Twentieth-Century America. The 1920's*. Columbus: Ohio State University Press.

_____. 1978a. "Historical Problematics and Sociological Fields: American Liberalism and the Study of Social Movements." In Robert A. Jones, ed., *Research in Sociology of Knowledge, Sciences and Art*. Vol. 1. Greenwich, CT: JAI Press Inc.

_____. 1978b. "The Sociological Reality of America: An Essay on Mass Culture." In H. Gans, N. Glazer, J. Gusfield, and C. Jencks, eds., *On the Making of Americans*. Philadelphia: University of Pennsylvania Press.

_____. 1980. "The Modernity of Social Movements: Public Roles and Private Parts." In A. Hawley, ed., *Societal Growth*. New York: The Free Press.

_____. 1981. *The Culture of Public Problems: Drinking-Driving and the Symbolic Order*. Chicago: University of Chicago Press.

_____. 1982. "Prevention: Rise, Decline and Renaissance." In T. Coffey and E. , eds., *Alcohol, Science and Society Revisited*. New Brunswick, NJ: Rutgers University Center of Alcohol Studies.

Handler, Joel. 1980. *Social Movements and the Law*. New York: Academic Press.

Hechter, Michael. 1975. *Internal Colonialism*. Berkeley: University of California Press.

Hofstadter, Richard. 1965. *The Paranoid Style in American Politics and Other Essays*. New York: Alfred A. Knopf.

Holtzman, Abraham. 1963. *The Townsend Movement: A Political Study*. New York: Bookman Associates, Inc.

Lévi-Strauss, Claude. 1968. *The Raw and the Cooked*. New York: Harper Torchbooks.

Lubove, Roy. 1968. *The Struggle for Social Security, 1900–1935*. Cambridge, MA: Harvard University Press.

McCarthy, John, and Mayer Zald. 1973. *The Trend of Social Movements in America: Professionalization and Resource Mobilization*. Morristown, NJ: General Learning Corp.

Oberschall, Anthony. 1978. "The Decline of the 1960s Social Movements." In Louis Kriesberg, ed., *Research in Social Movements, Conflicts and Change*. Vol. 1. Greenwich, CT: JAI Press Inc.

Perrow, Charles. 1978. "The Sixties Observed." In Mayer Zald and John McCarthy, eds., *The Dynamics of Social Movements*. Cambridge, MA: Winthrop Publishers.

Piven, Frances Fox, and Richard Cloward. 1979. *Poor People's Movements*. New York: Vintage Books.

Rothman, David. 1971. *The Discovery of the Asylum*. Boston: Little, Brown and Company.

Sanders, Daniel. 1973. *The Impact of Reform Movements on Social Policy Change: The Case of Social Insurance*. Fair Lawn, NJ: R. E. Burdick, Inc.

Schlesinger, Arthur M., Jr. 1959. *The Coming of the New Deal*. Boston: Houghton Mifflin Co.

Sennett, Richard. 1978. *The Fall of Public Man*. New York: Vintage Books.

Shorter, Edward, and Charles Tilly. 1974. *Strikes in France, 1830–1968*. Cambridge: Cambridge University Press.

Smelser, Neil. 1963. *The Theory of Collective Behavior*. New York: The Free Press.

Smith, Henry Nash. 1950. *Virgin Land: The American West as Symbol and Myth*. Cambridge, MA: Harvard University Press.

Snyder, David, and William Kelly. 1979. "Strategies for Investigating Violence and Social Change." In Mayer Zald and John McCarthy, eds., *The Dynamics of Social Movements*. Cambridge, MA: Winthrop Publishers.

Spinrad, William. 1970. *Civil Liberties*. Chicago: Quadrangle Books.

Taylor, Carl. 1953. *The Farmers Movement 1620–1920*. New York: American Book Co.

Thompson, E. P. 1963. *The Making of the English Working Class*. New York: Vintage Books.

Thompson, W. I. 1967. *The Imagination of an Insurrection: Dublin, Easter 1916*. New York: Harper Colophon Books

Tilly, Charles. 1978. *From Mobilization to Revolution*. Reading, MA: Addison-Wesley.

Tilly, Charles, Louise Tilly, and Richard Tilly. 1975. *The Rebellious Century: 1830–1930*. Cambridge, MA: Harvard University Press.

Trilling, Lionel. 1972. *Sincerity and Authenticity*. Cambridge, MA: Harvard University Press.

Turner, Ralph. 1969. "The Theme of Contemporary Social Movements." *British Journal of Sociology* 20 (December): 390–405.

_____. 1976. "The Real Self: From Institution to Impulse." *American Journal of Sociology* 21 (March): 989–1016.

Tyler, Alice. 1962. *Freedom's Ferment*. New York: Harper Torchbooks.

Uchendu, Victor. 1970. "Cultural and Economic Factors Influencing Food Habit Patterns in Sub-Saharan Africa." *3rd International Congress of Food and Science Technology* (August 9–14): 160–168. Washington, DC.

Wilson, William J. 1978. *The Declining Significance of Race*. Chicago: University of Chicago Press.

Wright, Will. 1975. *Six Guns and Society*. Berkeley: University of California Press.

Zald, Mayer, and Roberta Ash. 1966. "Social Movement Organizations: Growth, Decay and Change." *Social Forces* 44 (March): 327–41.

8

The Reflexivity of Social Movements:
Collective Behavior and Mass Society
Theory Revisited

Concepts and theories in the Social Sciences are marked by a distinctive thriftiness. Few are wasted. Fashionable for a while they are criticized, discarded and then, sometime later, salvaged from the ash can of ideas and revived, often in new contexts and with new polish on them. In this paper, I shall examine some characteristics of contemporary social movements. It is my assertion that collective behavior and mass society theories, partially discredited in current thinking about social movements, can be very useful in examining certain movements and some aspects of many others. In the context of recent thinking about the "new social movements," this is especially the case.

My intention in this paper is not to suggest yet another totalizing paradigm that seeks to destroy the usefulness of all existing perspectives in the eager effort to enter a claim to a monopolistic ownership of the entire turf of "social movements." I have no theory for all seasons.

Definitions of social movements and theories about them abound in sociology. The textbooks are filled with the names of theories and theorists, each purporting to provide the definitive way of thinking about and of studying the subject matter of the field. But definitions and theories, especially in this area, bear a relation to the objects and

Reprinted from Enrique Larana, Hank Johnston, and Joseph Gusfield, eds., *New Social Movements*. With the permission of Temple University Press.

historical contexts that elicit curiosity and attention (Gusfield, 1978). In part, arguments about differing perspectives are reactions to the different questions which analysts are asking about different phenomena.

In many respects, all of us are a little like the famed six blind Asian Indians in the classic parable. Each places his hand on a different part of the elephant and each, as a consequence, describes a different kind of animal. Part of our arguments about theories are as much arguments about what is worth studying and in reference to what intellectual, social, or political problem as about the behavior of that which we study.

The interest in social movements in sociology has been occasioned in great degree by attention to reformist and dissident mobilization of partisans into organized attempts to change the institutional and political structure of a society. Studies of labor movements, of political movements and ideologies, of religious dissidence and sectarian development have abounded in the studies of sociologists, both in Europe and the United States. Much attention has been given to major ideological partisanship, such as communism, fascism, liberalism and socialism. Research has been fueled by the emergence of current events. Thus the emergence of German fascism led to a generation occupied with the problem of the requisites for democracy and the decline of liberalism. The rise of student protest and civil violence in the 1960s prompted a concern for the problem of the conditions of protest and riot (Gusfield, 1978).

It is not that social studies mirror historical events or that they are directed towards one or another resolution of political issues. Rather the development of historical actions poses problems of scholarly attention. Concern for understanding the roots of social violence became a major scholarly pursuit in the wake of the riots and demonstrations of the 1960s in the United States.

The emergence in the 1970s and 1980s of movements concerned with such matters as the ecology of the planet, nuclear protest, gender equality, Gay rights, animal rights, and new religions has seemed perplexing to older schemes of understanding which have been directed toward relatively organized collectivities. In the current stage of thinking about movements, such movements have taken the foreground in efforts to understand the conditions of emergence, development, and disappearance of social movements. They have constituted an anomaly, a puzzle for earlier formulations and paradigms. In this sense, there has been a Kuhnian motion in which a normal science has found it difficult to encompass new data in old theories (Kuhn, 1962).

Social Movements as Associations and as Meanings

The history of the sociology of social movements characteristically recounts the criticism of collective behavior and mass society theories for their failure to consider the importance of the mobilization of partisans into organized, collective action. Such action is posited as essential to the emergence and effectiveness of movements. (Oberschall, 1973; Tilly, 1978; McAdam, 1982; Morris, 1984). This criticism has been especially striking in the development of rational choice and resource mobilization approaches (Tilly, 1978; McCarthy and Zald, 1973). It has also been central to my own criticism of mass society perspectives (Gusfield, 1962).

Collective behavior and mass society theories on the one hand and resource mobilization theories on the other reflect two diverse images of the elephant we call social movements. The distinction has been nicely put by Alberto Melucci in a recent book (Melucci, 1989: 17-20). The first, collective behavior theories, he refers to as "actors without action." The second—resource mobilization—he refers to as "actions without actors." I shall discuss these differences as those which emphasize movements as the emergence of new meanings and those that emphasize movements as collectively organized actions. The first places an emphasis on ideas, the second on organizations.

A great deal of the study of social movements has been the study of people organized into associations. In American sociology, the National Organization of Women; the American Federation of Labor; the Hare Krishnas; or the Southern Christian Leadership Conference have been the stuff of social movement analysis. So conceived, the study of movements is preeminently the study of the actions and reactions of associations, of people organized into a coordinated structure. The resources mobilization theory has emphasized this image and focused analysis on the strategy of mobilization and action as rational means for attaining fixed goals (McCarthy and Zald, 1973;1977; Tilly, 1978; Olson, 1971).

The collective behavior approach, as developed by Blumer and later by Turner and Killian, took as its focus the emergence and construction of new norms of social relationships and new meanings of social life (Blumer, 1939; Turner and Killian, 1986; Turner, 1981). Such meanings emerged from processes in which people, in interaction with each other, develop new conceptions of justice and injustice; morality and immorality; the real and the fictitious. So conceived, the subject matter of social movements is the appearance of new constructions of rights, of procedures, of norms, of beliefs. To speak of Feminism or the "New Age" as movements is to place the stress of analysis on the growing adoption of an idea, an identity, a way of conceiving a situation. Association and organizations are then instances and embodiments of meanings.

What the critique of this imagery by resource mobilization theorists did was to bring the image of association from the background into the light of the foreground. They emphasized the importance of the mobilization of partisans or others into the associational contexts without which the ideas would remain ineffective and unrealized. In the imagery of collective behavior, what was important about a movement was its consequences for change. For the image of resource mobilization the movement had to be studied as a form of organizational behavior, gathering and utilizing resources (McCarthy and Zald, 1973; 1977; Jenkins, 1983).

Complementing the approach of the resource mobilization paradigm, the economic analysis of Mancur Olson and the delineation of the "free rider" problem has had a major influence on thinking about social movements (Olson, 1971). Whether analysts agreed with it or not, Olson's work focused attention on individual goals and rational considerations. It brought utilitarian considerations of costs and benefits into the picture (Handler, 1978). In throwing the light of deductive economic logic on the inductive analyses of sociologists it made the question of how and where movements obtain resources a major question (Tilly, 1978).

These highly warranted criticisms of collective behavior theory have led to an implicit deemphasis on ideas and changing meanings as pivotal to the understanding of many movements. Yet the diffuse and often apolitical character of many current movements gives us considerable pause in the focus on organizational and associational elements as sufficient tools of understanding in this area of knowledge. The recent movements that have piqued the interest and attention of many sociologists have often not displayed a clear relationship to utilitarian interests, formed organizational agents, created communal sects or emerged as attempts to alter existing institutions. What have come to be known as "new social movements" are, in one or another of these features, distinguished from the model of the social movement as sociologists have portrayed them in the past (Cohen, 1985; Eder, 1985; Melucci, 1985; Offe, 1985). Others, using different designations, have presented similar conceptualizations stressing the class or other structural and cultural characteristics of contemporary movements (Gusfield, 1979a; Turner, 1969).

It is important to this paper to clarify the distinction between movements seen as associations and movements seen as ideas or meanings. The Labor Movement and its specific organizations are models of associational units that comprise a movement. There are members and non-members; programmatically stated goals, and an internal organization that constitutes a hierarchy of office-holding leaders and a rank and file of members. In contrast, while there are organizations that are part of the Woman's Movement, they are in the current movement only a part of the diffuse goals, the process of mobilizing partisans, the locus of partisanship. Being a member or non-member is not constituted by a specific act but refers to types of ideational commitment. The action of the movement has its locus in a multiplicity of events, often that of individuals, in everyday interaction as well as in the context of collective action in institutions and toward the State.

This typology of images like most, is too definitive. Most movements do both: take an associational form and a form in the spread of new meanings. Some movements involve one form to a greater extent than the other. The Civil Rights movement, while emphasizing collective action of organizations, was also a movement that changed both white and black conceptions of what is just and what rights are both legitimate and possible. Its major thrust was toward the reform of institutions, but it has had significant impacts on racial identities and self-conceptions. The Woman's movement has its organizational side, but is even more saliently a movement toward a change in conceptions of females and female rights vis-à-vis men. As such, it exists both inside and outside associational or organizational phases. Some movements, notably the "hippie" movement or the physical fitness movement have no associational or organizational existence at all. Yet they manifest a shared direction, a set of goals, and a shared conception of what is right and just and a procedure to obtain such goals.

Utopianism of Social Movements: Back to the Future

Am I putting irreconcilables together? Why place the "hippie" movement, an unorganized phenomena with little overt social conflict, in
the same sociological bin as the abortion or anti-abortion movement
or the Civil Rights movement? Certainly, for many purposes they are
radically different. Yet all three are perceived and talked about as
"movements." (That they are so perceived will become very important
for my analysis below.) Two considerations prompt my procedure.

First, the quality of deliberateness, of a socially shared and conscious search for change has been the hallmark of phenomena labeled
"social movement"(Gusfield, 1970). The imagination of a future as a
new way of behaving is common to both movements. It has distinguished the social movement, as an instrument for producing change,
from those changes that occur without specific direction or plan. A
changing birth rate is an example of unplanned, non-deliberative
change, arising from the consequences of multiple acts without mutual awareness of others. The sources of change through movements
imply the imagination of the future and the attempt to realize imagined states. It is an imagination that is perceived as shared, as developing a solidarity of partisans and a sense of opposition. Even without
organizational affiliations, people can be "feminists," "woman's
libbers," "hippies," or "New Age freaks."

Imagining an alternative to the present is the Utopian element in all
social movements. Social movements become issues about change or the
repelling of change in ways that prescribe changes more general than
individual, idiosyncratic choices. The movement produces a state of choice,
of decision between what has been accepted and even enforced and what
is now conceived as unacceptable. What may have been unthinkable is
now thinkable and possible. Once set in motion, the "hippie" movement
provided a socially shared and supported choice of life style where such
social support had not existed (Berger, 1982). It is further distinguished
from an individually chosen life-style where the knowledge and support-
ive example of others is absent or not influential. Even where action is not
collective in the sense of organized and interactive, it nevertheless occurs
with the knowledge that others are similarly acting. The "hippie" movement became such as individuals became aware, through reading and
through personal accounts of others, that new styles of living and new
opportunities for action were emerging.

Secondly, while associational structure and cultural meanings are typological distinctions, in practice few movements are entirely one or the other. Even if a movement lacks overt conflict, it engenders contention about possibilities and choice between alternatives. It represents social relations and culture in possible transition. The Gay rights movement, which has its organizational manifestation, also exists in daily judgments that pose new issues for homosexuals and heterosexuals as to how they are to identify themselves and others. Self-conscious and deliberate choice being made against a background of awareness of movements is in process. In this way, they affect and influence more than their members and opponents (Greenberg, 1988; D'Emilio, 1983).

Social Movements: Linear and Fluid

With the above in mind, it is useful to make a distinction I have made in a previous publication-between linear and fluid movements (Gusfield, 1981). Linear movements present the image of a straight-line narrative. The movement is a means toward an end: a goal, a new state of affairs. The Labor Movement and its individual labor unions is the model of such phenomena. The movement is perceived as associational. What is studied are the careers. The effort to change brings the movement into overt conflict and extra-institutionalized action. Being goal-directed it is assessed in terms of achievement—of success or failure, of new patterns of labor-management relations or continuance of the old. Most significantly for this paper, the arena of action is public. It seeks institutional and/or political change. The goals of the movement are fixed and crafted into programmatic action.

Fluid movements are much more difficult to specify. Since they imply changes in how values and realities are conceived, they occur outside or in addition to organized and directed action. They may involve contention with others and with alternative meanings and constructions. However they are less likely to be drawn into collective action on the model or image of strikes, boycotts, pickets, or demonstrations. They occur in the myriad actions of everyday life, in micro and less public acts. As such, to specify success or failure is more problematic than in goal-directed organizations. The Woman's Movement and Feminism occur in more than the organized efforts at constitutional amendment, equal rights legislation, and affirmative action.

They also involve relationships and interactions between men and women in micro and even intimate relations. The movement occurs in the multiplicity of events where a conception of women's rights and gender justice have become issues.

The distinction is important and has been conceptualized in different ways by different writers. There is much that is akin to, as well as different from, Flacks' distinction between history and everyday life. "History is constituted by activity which influences the conditions and terms of everyday life of a collectivity" (Flacks, 1988: 3). Yet by no means is all of everyday life in history. Much of it also creates and is History. My image here is rather that of the locus of action than the content of ideas or institutions. The institutional level of a movement is found in the efforts to change the rules, the procedures, of organizations and institutions. Often the State is either the target of change or the instrument through which the linear movement hopes to gain change. The animal rights movement and the anti-nuclear movement are illustrations of linear movements where the effort is toward protest of current procedures at the levels of the State and such organizations as research laboratories. Goals are defined as those of changes in the institutional rules. The animal rights movement, for example, is an attempt to change procedures of medical research so that animals are no longer used for research purposes (Jasper and Nelkin, 1989).

The everyday or interactive level is more fluid. It may not even have an organizational base. The "hippie" movement is, perhaps, a model. Many health movements, such as holistic health care, are illustrative (Lowenberg, 1989). Here there is no organizational base at all. The dissidence is not directed at changing the State or an institution. Rather it is concerned with developing alternative styles of medicine. The movement is found in the set of ideas and the individual responses to those ideas as they affect life styles. Such ideas are promoted through journals and through interaction. Health movements, such as holistic health, have little impact on the State, nor do they seek it. They are dissenting movements within medicine but they do little to change professional medicine, develop new State laws or protest current medical or hospital practices. They become arenas of action with little direct conflict with institutions. They are alternatives to professional medicine but not movements to change the medical institutions. In a sense, they bypass rather than change institutions.

In what sense are fluid movements socially shared? I will examine this aspect of analysis more carefully below in relation to mass society theories. For the present, what is involved is action taken with the recognition that it is not isolated and individualistic. "[T]he train of thought and action in each individual is influenced more or less by the action of every other" (Park and Burgess, 1967: 225). If we imagine the interaction between homosexual and heterosexual persons prior to the emergence of the Gay rights movement, we posit a conventionalized set of norms to which people adhere or behave in idiosyncratic, individualistic forms. Once set in motion, the behavior is no longer so conventionalized. It becomes problematic, undertaken with a recognition that alternatives are both possible and socially legitimated at some level. Homosexuals attempt to change discriminatory laws, but also become open about their identity. Interaction between homosexuals and heterosexuals takes on a new tone. That interaction need not be direct or face-to-face. It may exist in the imaginative rehearsals of action, which are fostered by vicarious experience, such as reading or watching news or dramatic presentations. What is happening is that the conventional norms of deviance that have guided both homosexuals and heterosexuals have come to be doubted and their acceptance made problematic. What was "taken for granted" has become an issue.

Micro- and Macro-arenas: Collective Behavior Theory Revisited

The distinction between public and everyday arenas is significant in two senses. First, it indicates the importance of the linear-fluid distinction. Second, it indicates aspects of contemporary society which accentuate the fluid elements of social movements. Here aspects of collective behavior theory point to a more important characteristic of modern societies that social movement analysis needs seriously to consider.

Both in Park and Burgess and in Blumer, the concept of collective behavior was used as a contrast to social organization (Park, 1967: Ch. 15; Blumer, 1939). Social organization is conventionalized, recurrent, and provides institutionalized definitions of situations and expected behavior. Collective behavior was postulated as elementary social behavior—what occurs when social organization breaks down:

> those phenomena which exhibit in the most obvious and elementary ways the processes by which societies are disintegrated into their constituent elements and the processes by which these elements are brought together again into new rela-

tions to form new organizations and new societies. (Park and Burgess, 1970:440-41, quoted in Turner, 1981: 3)

Where the Chicago school differed from the French sociologists, such as LeBon, was in their assessment of the potentialities of collective behavior for social organization. The French saw crowds through the model of irrational, blind, and savage actors (Barrows, 1988). The Chicago school saw them as the source of new ideas and new social organization—as the basis for the emergence of new norms (Turner and Killian, 1986). Rather than viewing collective behavior as deviant, fearful, and anomalous, the Chicago school saw it as the seedbed of new institutions. Thus they could conceive of social movements and fashion as part of the same area called "collective behavior."

The image of society that the collective behaviorists shared with other sociologists was the classical contrast conception of the integrated community versus the institutionalized society. It was in disorganization, "social unrest"(what today we might call "alienation") that movements emerged. Movements and the emergence of new constructions of reality were contrasts to everyday, recurrent, and organized social life. Hence the appearance of collective behavior was something to be explained. How new patterns of thought and new institutions emerged from elementary non-organized actions was what the sociologist had to study.

It is at this point that the collective behavior theorists need revision. That contrast between a normal, established pattern of routine and one of the creation or construction of new meanings and institutions is not adequate to the understanding of contemporary societies. As a number of sociologists (Gusfield, 1979; Touraine, 1977; Melucci, 1989) have indicated, social movements, heterogeneity, and the presence of alternatives and choices is as much a pattern of contemporary life as is the model of social organization. Collective behavior is not an abnormal aspect of social life. It is a part of modern life. The general increases in income, of discretionary time, the technology of communication, and transport—all these effectuate large areas of life which are open to choice and where the interactive order of everyday life operates with varying degrees of freedom from the constraints of institutional organization. Richard Flacks suggests that in the United States political parties are less and less centers of political power and innovation. Increasingly, he argues, social movements are supplanting established political parties as the focus of political activity (Flacks, 1988).

A rigid view of social organization as "social fact" is giving way to a view of social order as a product and subject of deliberate action by members in what Touraine calls "the self-production of society":

> The sociology of social movements cannot be separated from a representation of society as a system of social forces competing for control of a cultural field...this sociology of action ceases to believe that conduct must be a response to a situation, and claims rather that the situation is merely the changing and unstable result of relations between the actors who, through their social conflicts and via their cultural orientations, produce society. (Touraine, 1981: 30)

Social Movements as Sign and Symbol: The Reflexivity of Social Movements

Such considerations imply a revision of the collective behavior approach. Such behavior is not an island in a sea of organized, conventional, and static human behavior. Social choices and social movements are deeply embedded in daily interaction. Change, conflict, and reassessment are constant aspects of human societies.

The collective behavior image of movements has reappeared in recent years in the attention given to movements as forms of framing (Snow and Benford, 1988; 1992; Gamson, 1992). Here attention is given to the cognitive force of movements in defining events and in the social construction of objects toward which the movement is oriented.

"Frame" is a vernacular term generally associated with paintings and photographs. "Frame" applied to everyday conduct is a means of defining situations and objects. Except in Hindu meditation, experience is never "pure"; it is an experience of something. That something involves a definition or meaning given to phenomena.

> [D]efinitions of a situation are built up in accordance with principles of organization which govern events—at least social ones—and our subjective involvement in them: frame is the word I use to refer to such of these basic elements as I am able to identify. (Goffman, 1974: 10-11; also see Bateson, 1972)

The concept of framing is a recognition that meaning of events may make for differing experiences of the "same" data. What is centrally attended to by one kind of interest or audience may not be attended to at all by another. As Goffman wrote, "There is a sense in which what is play for the golfer is work for the caddy" (Goffman, 1974: 8).

Social movements are then involved in constructing the experience
of partisans and would-be partisans through the ways in which they
define and describe the arena of their interest. The current abortion
and anti-abortion movements are examples of how the "same " actions are differently framed. The terms "pro-life" and "pro-choice"
bring into play very different images of the abortion issue and relate it
to very different clusters of other issues and movements (Luker,
1984).In this form, change has a significant ideational component.

Awareness that norms and meanings are at issue and in contention
is itself a step in the development of change. From this standpoint
social movements have a reflexive character. They are something members of a society reflect upon, think about, and are aware of. In attending to movements, members of a society recognize that social rules
are at issue (Gusfield, 1981). Even where no association exists, as in
the "hippie movement," the recognition that a similarity of actions is
occurring creates the movement; the belief that aspects of the society
are in motion. The very existence of a movement is itself a mode of
framing: it presents an area of life as at issue where it had previously
been accepted as the norm. Alternatives now exist where choice and
contention were absent.

In one sense the social movement exists when members of a society share the recognition that specific social rules are no longer taken
for granted. In the United States, the movement connected with laws
against child abuse, both sexual and physical, has made the treatment
of children by parents or other family members a matter of issue.
What constitutes the "proper" behavior of parents to children has
taken on a variety of new meanings. Attention and notice is taken of
behavior which, in the past, was either unnoticed or unmentioned.
Degrees and content of affection and of physical discipline have become matters to think about and to calculate. The relations between
parent and child, which were less open to State intervention are now
legitimately regulated by law as well as community opinion.

What takes place in the organized activities of many movements
has significance not alone in its stated goals but as symbolic of what
has become public acceptance or rejection of alternative possibilities.
It is not only that the program of the movement has achieved victory
or defeat in legislative, bargaining, or legal arenas. It serves also to
establish the public order, the rules that are admissible in public arenas. As such, it may support or undermine action at the interactional

level, at the level of everyday life (Gusfield, 1981). The struggle over abortion in the United States is symbolically a struggle about the place of women vis-à-vis men (Luker, 1984). Even local movements to change, as in the proposed changes of streets in some cities from an existing name to one honoring Martin Luther King, comes to symbolize the relative place of blacks in the American social order. In a paradoxical sense, *social movements occur when they are perceived to be occurring.* The existence of organized movements or the monitoring of events to suggest a movement in action can create the recognition that some accepted pattern of social life is now in contention, has become an issue.

Insofar as movements possess a fluid rather than a linear quality the question of membership is also fluid. Movements can have consequences and influence behavior without the kind of commitment or ideological agreement that is often posited for them. Frequently, we develop a language of social types to identify many, such as "woman's libbers" or "peaceniks." Movements may achieve stated, formal goals with little effect on the everyday behavior they seek to transform (Handler, 1978) and, of course, vice versa. They may fail in achieving major political goals while deeply affecting everyday behavior.

The Communication of Social Movements: Monitoring the Society

Movements thus exist along at least two dimensions. On one level they are events and processes seeking, in a more or less deliberate fashion, to produce change in the political or institutional character of the society. On another level they are signs that a segment of social life is potentially under challenge and alternatives possible(Melucci, 1989). Something that may have been unthinkable is now thinkable. They have significance for those who engage in their activities. But they may have significance for those who become aware of them, to whom they are communicated. They symbolize the transformation of a fixed social organization into an issue. Whether or not they are perceived as "right" or "wrong," they are perceived as in flux and in contention.

"Society" is not only the result of face-to-face interaction or of institutionally organized rules. It also exists as an object of observation and reflection (Gusfield, 1979b). In this fashion it exists at a distance from most observers. To perceive it requires organization and specialized institutions and their functionaries. It has to be monitored and constructed in the process of being monitored

In understanding contemporary movements, the rise of major communications industries and widespread formal education is difficult to over-estimate in its influence. While they monitor events they also construct a more general sense of how events coalesce. The "hippie" movement, for example, could not be perceived as a movement without an agency that framed a set of individual events as a movement. Mass media are major sources of the process of framing movements, of interpreting individual events as movements of change (Snow, et al., 1986). Such an agency, the TV news for example, puts together the separately occurring events and frames them as a unity, as a movement of a particular kind. Whether movements are relatively organized or not, their depiction by the mass media influence both their understandings and those of less partisan observers in the audiences.

In the process of constructing the reality of the society, mass media do more than monitor. They dramatize. They create vivid images, impute leadership, and heighten the sense of conflict between movements and the institutions of society (Gitlin, 1980; Ericson, Baranek, and Chan, 1987). They project a vocabulary with which to discuss the movement. Consider some of the social types that are conveyed by terms such as "woman's libber," "peacenik," "Gay rights." The framing process is deeply influenced by the ways in which vehicles of news and entertainment frame the movements and their objects.

Mass Society Theory Revisited: Social Movements as Theatre

Despite its considerable drawbacks as a theory of modern politics, mass society theory contains a perception of significant aspects of modern societies that needs restatement and was developed in the effort to explain the emergence and character of totalitarian and other extremist movements. Mass society theorists stressed the breakdown of class and interest-oriented groups and the importance of groups alienated from social institutions, uncontrolled by elites and open to leadership that projected emotive, expressive elements into public life (Mannheim, 1940; Arendt, 1951; Selznick, 1952: Ch. 7; Kornhauser, 1959).

The mass society theory emerged in an effort to understand totalitarian, nondemocratic movements in Western, industrialized societies. As Kornhauser points out, aristocratic theorists focused their attention on the decline of the authority of established elites and institutional controls. Democratic theorists focused attention on the ways in which rank and file members of bureaucratized organizations were unable to effectuate participation and influence decisions and policies. Both, however, projected a view of modern societies as ones in which great distances now prevailed between the institutions of social control and influence—church, school, government, class, ethnicity, even family and the individual at the level of his or her everyday life. The social and cultural diversities through which social commitment and control were conducted were no longer operative. The result was an alienated and homogeneous mass available to project raw, unmediated, unsocialized feelings into public policies.

Karl Mannheim, in *Man and Society in an Age of Reconstruction*, was perhaps especially prescient (Mannheim, 1940). In an era of fundamental democratization, he argued, social and economic organization were increasingly rationalized on a functional basis. The control and influence of cultural elites diminished and the mass were unable to achieve the kind of substantive rationality essential to the complex technology and political participation of modern social organization.

The average person surrenders part of his own cultural individuality with every new act of integration into a functionally rationalized complex of activities...gradually gives up his own interpretation of events for those others have given him. When the rationalized mechanism of social life collapses in times of crisis, the individual cannot repair it by his own insight. (p. 59)

In a society in which the masses tend to dominate, irrationalities that have not been integrated into the social structure may force their way into political life. (p. 63)

Akin to collective behavior theory, mass society theory was vulnerable to the criticism that alienated, unorganized people were unable to mobilize for collective action (Gusfield, 1962).Further, it became obvious that modern life was by no means so devoid of social organization or so alienated and anarchic as mass society theorists described (Shils, 1972: Ch. 11, 12).

Nevertheless, the insights of mass society theorists have relevance for the kinds of fluid movements, which I have been describing. It is not necessary to a sociology of social movements that all movements be studied through the same theory or that contrasting images of modern life may not both be applicable, sometimes to the same movement.

Three aspects of mass society theory retain importance. They catch the nature of "interaction" in a significant area. First, a great deal of human "interaction" takes place at a distance, apart from face-to-face interaction, in a form of "para-social interaction" (Horton and Wohl, 1956). I have stressed this in discussing the role of mass media above. In this sense, the image of society as an audience, which is implicit in mass society studies, is still viable. Secondly, such interaction is, at least to an important extent, unmediated by socially organized institutions and groups. In that sense, the mass is useful as a concept, not so much as a collectivity but as an area of action. Thirdly, the mass audience is thus more standardized and homogenized than given by concepts of class, status, and ethnicity. This is not to negate the importance of these concepts but to attempt to specify where and when they may be most useful as analytical instruments. The same aggregate of people may be divided into classes, ethnic groups, and the usual sociological distinctions, yet, at other times and in other arenas, operate as masses where a differentiated identity is absent.

The conception of the mass audience as the observers of the monitoring of movements underlines the view taken here of social movements as theatre. The theatrical component of movements is a central way in which new meanings are disseminated (Edelman, 1989). This is especially the case where the movement is oriented toward changing behavior of everyday life rather than the rules of institutions. Here again the Labor movement or Suffrage movements are not useful models for more fluid movements while the "hippie" movement or the Woman's movement are. The insistence of many women on redirecting conventional language to erase the dominance of male imagery is an effective form of theatre, of dramatizing changed conceptions now brought into consciousness.

This dramaturgical character of modern movements is of crucial importance (Snow, 1983). Both the interpretive work of the monitors and the actions of organized movements toward those interpretations become significant. They form the essential linkage between public arenas and everyday life. The disposition of movements to undertake actions in order to dramatize the movement is a facet well caught in the title of Todd Gitlin's account of the interaction between the world of news coverage and student movements of the 1960s: *The Whole World is Watching* (Gitlin, 1980). As others have pointed out, it often leads the monitors to depict movements by concentrating on images of extremes of greater dramatic content. This has been recently observed in accounts of the news coverage of the anti-abortion movement in the United *States (Los Angeles Times,* July 2, 1990: p. 1).

It is such monitoring and dramatic framing of events that makes alternative modes of behavior accessible to wide audiences. Movements can be transmitted in short time and people made aware that what might be individual thoughts and individual actions are shared and acted on by others, even though outside the orbit of personal acquaintance. The movement becomes a "sign of the times."

The revision of mass society theory that I assert as useful is found in distinguishing the alienation thesis from the understanding of mass communications as imagining society as a homogeneous, mass audience. The former, the alienating character of mass society, is far less viable than the latter, the image of the mass as an audience.

Both collective behavior and mass society theories focus attention on the less organized aspects of social life. As perspectives toward social movements they face in opposite directions. Collective behavior restores the importance of the interactive order as a significant locus of movements, especially many of the new movements oriented toward personal change. Mass society theories heighten our sensitivity toward the homogenizing, standardizing aspects of modern life. Here the impact of mass communications media provides monitoring and framing functions that enable audiences to share experiences despite large diversities in class, culture, gender, and nation.

Conclusion

The plenitude of social movements that exist and persist in modern societies makes any single scheme of analysis too partial for expansion to all or even most movements (Gamson, 1992). The more abstract the perspective, the less it becomes usable for empirical study. In this paper, I have been emphasizing the more fluid quality of many contemporary movements. In this regard, my conclusion has been well presented in a paper by David Snow. He points out that new or differing theoretical perspectives have the virtue of calling attention to otherwise unnoticed phenomena. As he puts it:

> theoretical perspectives, functioning much like metaphors, not only highlight; they also hide. By focusing attention on some phenomena, other equally relevant things may be hidden or glossed over. Thus, just as it is useful and illuminating to

approach the world with a range of metaphors, so it is useful to explain with a range of theoretical perspectives. And this is especially the case of phenomena which are not well bounded and about which there is much taxonomic debate and confusion, as is the case with collective behavior. (Snow, 1983: 9)

It might be objected that many of the movements to which I have alluded in this paper are either trivial or do not involve dissent and great conflict. I have argued elsewhere (Gusfield, 1979a) that social movements studies have shown an undue emphasis on the political and have understated the importance of movements that create changes in everyday living outside the institutional structures of modern life. As social historians have been telling us in recent years, these, too, are very much part of history.

References

Arendt, Hannah, 1951. *The Origins of Totalitarianism*. New York: Harcourt, Brace.

Barrows, Susanna. 1988. *Distorting Mirrors*. New Haven, CT: Yale University Press.

Bateson, Gregory. 1972. "A Theory of Play and Fantasy." In Gregory Bateson, *Steps Toward an Ecology of Mind*. New York: Ballantine Books.

Beauchamp, Dan. 1980. *Beyond Alcoholism*. Philadelphia: Temple University Press.

Berger, Bennett. 1982. *Survival of a Counter-Culture*. Berkeley and Los Angeles: University of California Press.

Blocker, Jack. 1989. *American Temperance Movements: Cycles of Reform*. Boston: Twayne Publishers.

Blumer, Herbert. 1939. "Collective Behavior." In R. E. Park, ed., *An Outline of the Principles of Sociology*. New York: Barnes and Noble, Inc.

Castells, Manuel. 1983. *The City and the Grass Roots*. Berkeley and Los Angeles: University of California Press.

Cohen, Jean. 1985. "Strategy or Identity: New Theoretical Paradigms and Contemporary Social Movements." *Social Research* 5, 2 (winter): 663-716.

Cornell, Steven. 1988. *The Return of the Native*: American Indian Political Resurgence. New York: Oxford University Press.

Edelman, Murray. 1988. *Constructing the Public Spectacle*. Chicago: University of Chicago Press.

Eder, Klaus. 1985. "The 'New Social Movements': Moral Crusades, Political Protest Groups or Social Movements?" *Social Research* 52 (winter): 869-901.

Ericson, Richard, Patricia Baranek, and Janet Chan. 1987. *Visualizing Deviance: A Study of News Organization*. Toronto: University of Toronto Press.

Flacks, Richard. 1988. *Making History*. New York: Columbia University Press.

——————. 1994. "The Party's Over—So What Is to Be Done?" In E. Larana, H. Johnston, and J. Gusfield, eds., *New Social Movements: From Ideology to Identity*. Philadelphia: Temple University Press.

Friedman, Lawrence. 1985. *Total Justice*. New York: The Russell Sage Foundation.

Gamson, William. 1992. "The Social Psychology of Collective Action." In Aldon Morris and Carol M. Mueller, eds., *Frontiers in Social Movement Theory*. New Haven and London: Yale University Press.

Gitlin, Todd. 1980. *The Whole World Is Watching*. Berkeley and Los Angeles: University of California Press.

Goffman, Erving. 1974. *Frame Analysis: An Essay on the Organization of Experience*. Cambridge, MA: Harvard University Press.

Greenberg, David. 1988 . *The Construction of Homosexuality*. Chicago: University of Chicago Press.

Gusfield, Joseph. 1962. "Mass Society and Extremist Politics," *American Sociological Review* 27: 19-30.

_____. 1970. *Protest, Reform and Revolt*. New York: John Wiley and Sons.

_____. 1978. "Historical Problematics and Sociological Fields: American Liberalism and the Study of Social Movements." In R. Jones, ed. *Research in Sociology of Knowledge, Sciences and Art*, Vol. 1. Greenwich, CT: JAI Press.

_____. 1979a "The Modernity of Social Movements." In A. Hawley, ed. *Societal Growth*. New York: The Free Press.

_____. 1981. "Prevention: Rise, Decline and Renaissance." In T. Coffey, ed., *Alcohol, Science and Society Revisited*. New Brunswick, NJ: Rutgers School of Alcohol Studies.

_____. 1981. "Social Movements and Social Change: Perspectives of Linearity and Fluidity." In L. Kriesberg, ed., *Research in Social Movements, Conflict and Change*, Vol. .4. Greenwich, CT: JAI Press.

_____. 1988. "The Control of Drinking-Driving in the United States: A Period in Transition?" In M. Lawrence, J. Snortum, and F. Zimring, *Social Control of the Drinking Driver*. Chicago: University of Chicago Press.

_____. 1989. "Constructing the Ownership of Public Problems." *Social Problems* 36 (December): 431-41.

_____. 1979b. "The Sociological Reality of America." In H. Gans, N. Glazer, J. Gusfield, and C. Jencks, eds., *On the Making of Americans: Essays in Honor of David Riesman*. Philadelphia: University of Pennsylvania Press.

Handler, Joel. 1978. *Social Movements and the Legal System*. New York: Academic Press.

Horton, Donald, and Richard Wohl. 1956. "Observations on Intimacy at a Distance." *Psychiatry* 19: 215-29.

Jasper, James, and Dorothy Nelkin. 1992. *The Animal Rights Crusade: The Growth of a Moral Protest*. New York: The Free Press.

Jenkins, J. Craig. 1983. "Resource Mobilization Theory." In R. Turner and J. Short, Jr., eds., *Annual Review of Sociology*, Vol. 9. Palo Alto, CA: Annual Reviews, Inc.

Kornhauser, William. 1959. *The Politics of Mass Society*. Glencoe, IL: The Free Press.

Kuhn, Thomas. 1962. *The Structure of Scientific Revolutions*. Chicago: University of Chicago Press.

Los Angeles Times. 1990. "News Coverage of Abortion Conflicts: Are They Biased?" July 2, Section A, p.1.

Lowenberg, June. 1989. *Caring and Responsibility: The Crossroads Between Holistic Practice and   Traditional Medicine*. Philadelphia: University of Pennsylvania Press.

Luker, Kristin. 1984. *Abortion and the Politics of Motherhood*. Berkeley and Los Angeles: University of California Press.

Mannheim, Karl. 1940. *Man and Society in an Age of Reconstruction*. London: Routledge and Kegan Paul.

McAdam, Doug. 1982. *Political Process and the Development of Black Insurgency, 1930-1970*. Chicago: University of Chicago Press.

McCarthy, John, and Meyer Zald. 1973. *The Trend of Social Movements in America*. Morristown, NJ: General Learning.

_____. 1977, "Resource Mobilization and Social Movements." *American Journal of Sociology* 82: 1212-1241.

McCarthy, John. n.d. "A Media Framing Contest: Its Shape, Newspaper Coverage Outcomes and Impact upon the Citizen's Movement Against Drunken Driving." (Unpublished manuscript).

Melucci, Alberto. 1985. "The Symbolic Challenge of Contemporary Movements." *Social Research* 52 (winter): 789-816.

_____. 1989. *Nomads of the Present*. Philadelphia: Temple University Press.

Morris, Aldon. 1984. *The Origins of the Civil Rights Movement*. New York: The Free Press.

Nelson, Barbara. 1984. *Making an Issue of Child Abuse*. Chicago: University of Chicago Press.

Oberschall, Anthony. 1973. *Social Conflict and Social Movements*. Englewood Cliffs, NJ: Prentice-Hall.

Offe, Claus. 1985. "New Social Movements: Challenging the Boundaries of Institutional Politics." *Social Research* 52 (winter): 817-68.

Olson, Mancur. 1971. *The Logic of Collective Action*. Cambridge, MA: Harvard University Press.

Park, Robert, and Ernest Burgess. 1967. "Collective Behavior." In R. Turner, ed., *Robert Park on Social Control and Collective Behavior*. Chicago: University of Chicago Press.

Pfohl, Stephen. 1977. "The Discovery of Child Abuse." *Social Problems* 24: 310-323.

Ross, H. Laurence, and R. B. Voas. 1989. *The New Philadelphia Story: The Effects of Severe Punishment for Drunk Driving*. Washington, DC: AAA Foundation for Traffic Safety.

Selznick, Philip. 1952. *The Organizational Weapon*. New York: McGraw-Hill.

Shils, Edward. 1972. *The Intellectuals and the Powers & Other Essays*. Chicago: University of Chicago Press.

Snow, David. 1983. "A Dramaturgical Approach to Collective Behavior." (Unpublished manuscript) Paper presented to the American Sociological Association, Detroit, MI.

Snow, David, E. Burke Rochford, Steven Worden, and Robert Benford. 1986 "Frame Alignment Processes, Micromobilization, and Movement Participation." *American Sociological Review* 51: 464-81.

Snow, David, and Robert Benford. 1988. "Ideology, Frame Resonance and Participant Mobilization." *International Social Movement Research* 1: 197-217.

Snow, David, and Robert Benford. 1992. "Master Frames and Cycles of Protest." In Aldon Morris and Carol M. Mueller, eds., *Frontiers in Social Movement Theory*. New Haven, CT: Yale University Press.

Tilly, Charles. 1978. *From Mobilization to Revolution*. Reading, MA: Addison-Wesley Publishing Co.

Touraine, Alain. 1977. *The Self-Production of Society*. Chicago: University of Chicago Press.

Turner, Ralph, and Lewis Killian. 1986. *Collective Behavior*. 3rd. ed. Englewood Cliffs, NJ: Prentice-Hall.

Turner, Ralph. 1969. "Themes in Contemporary Social Movements." *British Journal of Sociology* 20 (December).

_____. 1981. "Collective Behavior and Resource Mobilization as Approaches to Social Movements: Issues and Continuities." In L. Kriesberg, ed. *Research in Social Movements, Conflict and Change*, Vol. 4. Greenwich, CT: JAI Press.

9

The Social Construction of Tradition:
An Interactionist View of Social Change

I

The recent discussion of modernization theory by critics of functional and evolutionary concepts carries with it implications for the imagery and perspectives with which social scientists conceive of social change as a process. Recent criticisms have been directed at the use of concepts that utilize polar opposites, as beginning and end points in social and cultural change.[1] In conventional views of social change, the encounter between the colonial and colonizing people, between the West and the non-West and between the industrial and the peasant societies of the world is depicted as having brought about a series of conflicts and transitions from a static society to a moving one. In this encounter, old and fixed traditions are assumed to be poorly adapted to new situations. Men must make choices between the old and the new. New forms replace the old or are successfully resisted.[2] In this information, what is "old" and traditional is assumed to be comparatively uniform, persistent, and clear. What is past is clear and has only to be discovered, like pebbles on a beach.

More complex and sophisticated views of tradition are also found among social scientists. The work of Robert Redfield and of other students of India has replaced a homogeneous view of a single tradition with a perspective that stresses sharp differences between the

Reprinted from A. R. Davis, ed., *Traditional Attitudes and Modern Styles in Political Leadership*, pp. 83-104, Sydney: Angus Robertson, 1973. With the permission of Harper Collins Publishers (Australia).

literate and the popular, between the "great tradition" and the "little tradition" (Redfield, 1960; Marriott, 1955). Here processes of modernization, including literacy and increasing channels of communication, have operated to reinforce and spread the classic Hindu civilization of the urban literati through village, town, and city.

Another significant departure from the view that "tradition" is unproblematically given is found in the description and analysis of cultural revivals. The study of national movements in Asia and Africa has given attention to the ways in which attacks on colonial domination have often been accompanied by movements to revive, extend, and defend customs associated with less cosmopolitan and more "folk-like" sectors of the population (Heimsath, 1964: Ch. 6, 12; Geertz, 1963; Wallerstein, 1961: Ch. 7; Emerson, 1960: Pt. 2). Here, as in the concepts of great and little tradition, the assumption is retained that these aspects of culture were once dominant but have now become dormant. The movement attempts to revive the dormant:

> Blyden urged Africans to emancipate themselves from the mental slavery imposed by European cultures and to *rediscover* themselves [italics mine]. He urged them to establish their own independent churches and a West African university where African studies would be welcomed and respected. (Ayai, 1966: 608)

Such views have formed the stock of structural anthropology and sociology. They have taken their basic units in the form of "cultures" and "societies" as given and have tended to see changes in culture or tradition as reflecting a transition from one state of being to another. The problems of achieving cultural identity, as in nationalist and independence movements, are thus viewed as problems of recovering or expressing existing or past cultures rather than as creation of new ones.

"Culture," however, is not alone a descriptive term, indicating to the observer the unique content of a group's way of life. It also has a reflexive dimension. The actor can perceive of himself and his behavior as cultural, as signifying the unique character of his group, community or "subculture." It is as an aspect of a present situation that a group shares a definition of itself as possessing a culture or a tradition with a particular content. Conceptions of past and future, of tradition and modernity, of culture itself are all phenomena about which people can think and toward which they can be self-conscious.

This reflexive character of tradition is the inciting point for the present paper. In analyzing "traditional culture" as an idea we will describe and analyze movements that have played significant roles in identifying the uniqueness of social groups and the content of their own culture. The materials will be drawn mostly from Japan, India, and the United States. In treating movements for self-identification and cultural change as reflexive, we emphasize that these are movements of both self-discovery and of self-definition and redefinition. Rather than solely discovered, tradition is also created and constructed out of alternative forms. As Kim Marriott has put it, "the 'national' culture of every new state is a product of modern manufacture" (Marriott, 1963: 56; also see Shibutani and Kwan, 1965: Ch. 2). It is more than that, however; it is also a belief and a statement about what is now perceived as having been typical in the past.

Monographs on primitive societies seldom contain material about such reflexive concerns as we find in peasant and industrial societies. They do not reveal a folk anthropology showing that the members of the tribe are self-conscious of their culture. Herodotus distinguished between "Greeks" and "barbarians," but this is a long way from the quest for identity that marks the phenomena of national, regional, and other communal movements. This suggests that consciousness of culture, as defining the uniqueness of a group or people, is itself a product of particular experiences. Ethnic identity is enhanced in the interaction between peoples, even those previously unaware of themselves as similar. In his study of the Chinese in Hawaii, Glick points out that the migrants from the Cantonese area, from the Peking area, from northern, central, and southern China did not perceive of themselves as at all part of a common people or culture until they found this to be the case in the eyes of the residents of Hawaii (Glick, 1942).

One would need to search in a history not yet written for the development of the reflexive idea of culture. Kroeber and Kluckhohn found the origins of the term "culture" in the universal histories of German philosophers and historians appearing toward the end of the eighteenth century (Kroeber and Kluckhohn, 1952: Pt. 1). But there its usage remains fairly close to the concept of "civilization" rather than "culture" as we use it here. It also suggests that as a term, "culture" appears earlier and more popularly in Germany as a synonym for "society" than it does in France or England. Kroeber and Kluckhohn interpret this as a result of greater differentiation between areas in the prenational German area than in the other two countries. This interpretation is for them also enhanced by what they feel to be the greater popularity of the term in the United States than in the more culturally homogeneous societies of France and England (Kroeber and Kluckhohn, 1952: 68).

In his analysis of nineteenth-century English literature, the critic Raymond Williams finds the concept of culture emergent with the advent of industrialization and the growing separation of classes (Williams, 1959). The working-class conception of a "working-class culture" required specific conditions of class differentiation. Culture in the conventional anthropologist's sense of a "localized more or less different and unique system of behavior, e.g., Eskimo culture, Cherokee Indian culture" is itself problematic. It would take the much-needed work of a good cultural historian to do for the idea and consciousness of culture what recently some of the British historians of industrialization or of the French Revolution have attempted to do for concepts of "class"(Cobban, 1964).

In this paper we are not concerned with how traditions change but rather with how a given content is itself defined as traditional. How is it that groups designate themselves and define the content of their histories and characteristics? How do such definitions change? How is the "traditional" itself constructed?

In analyzing the uses of tradition, we are investigating how and why groups define events, structures or values as being part of the past. To confer this meaning of "pastness" is not a neutral matter. For many it gives a special legitimacy to that which is defined as traditional or derived from it. The past has a sacred aura about it and in the publicly defined conflicts between the traditional and the modern it often matters very much what a particular set of ideas can be labeled.[3]

II

We begin with Japanese society. The success story of Japanese industrialization is too well known to be recounted again here. For our purposes what is so intriguing is the impact of that story on conceptions of social change that social scientists had held in the past. Japan has appeared as a contradiction to the theories of the linear evolution of Western societies from feudalism to capitalism, from tradition to modernity, and from folk to urban societies. The Japanese have presented us with a seeming amalgam of the feudal and the capitalist in which communal identities and loyalties reinforced and supported new modes of economic and technological activity (Saniel, 1965; T. Smith, 1960-61).

In the process of change, Japanese intellectuals and academics have themselves been engaged in characterizing Japanese culture. John Bennett has recently pointed out that Japanese scholars, as well as foreign scholars, have wavered in their characterizations. At several times, the communal characteristics of a high level of solidarity and a functioning hierarchy were seen as continuing to be characteristic of the Japanese. At other times, they were viewed as disappearing with Western influences (Bennett, 1968). Consensus has shifted back and forth. The Japanese have been concerned with modernization and tradition, sometimes seeing in the latter a barrier to the former and sometimes stressing the detrimental effects of modernization in displacing traditional Japanese ways. Whatever the ideology, there has often been an agreement that Japanese culture has had a traditional set of customs and ways of behaving which can be specified and which constitute that which is changing or which resists further change.

What is now clear is that conceptions of the communal character of Japan have themselves been responses to immediate situations. In this sense they have been part of the process by which Japanese, operating through intellectualized versions of culture, have created their culture in the process of perceiving it. At each stage, the observers and analysts have defined the traditional past for that point in historical time.

An interesting form of such concerns can be seen in what is often hailed as a typical illustration of traditional Japanese communalism, the *nenko* system—the pattern of lifetime employment and of a wage structure geared to age and seniority rather than productivity. The nenko system was brought to attention in American scholarship with the publication of James Abegglen's book, *The Japanese Factory* (Abegglen, 1958). In his description of the system, Abegglen described a dual pattern of loyalty of the worker to the firm and of the firm to the worker. Here again was another illustration of the way in which a feudal culture not only continued to exist in capitalist Japan but even became the basis for industrial relations in the citadel of Westernized technology and economics—large-scale manufacturing. On the basis of this, Abegglen insisted that economic mobility was nonexistent in Japan, that the market of classical economics was sharply limited by the continuation of Japanese traditions of communalism.

The view of the nenko system as a continuation of Japanese labor relations on a feudal basis is among many myths of cultural traditions. A closer look indicates that this unique system of industrial relations developed in relationship to intensive problems of labor turnover in the twentieth century. Rather than being a continuation of an old tradition, the nenko system is itself relatively recent and its origins go back not much further than the 1920s.[4] Even today it is far less characteristic of the smaller establishments where communal ties might seem to be most persistent. The idea that labor mobility has been or is nonexistent in Japan is also quite erroneous. Both present and previous generations displayed relatively high rates of job change.[5]

Significant in this history of ideas about Japanese mobility is the extent to which recent change so quickly becomes viewed as tradition.[6] Abegglen's view has not seemed to the Japanese critics of it simply an anomaly of Western ignorance. It has also been a view utilized by Japanese scholars until recently (Matsumoto, 1960; Nakane, 1970; Cole, 1971, esp. pp. 7-11). It has taken considerable pains of research to develop alternate findings that altered the view of Japanese "tradition" and showed its complexity.

We are not trying to prejudge the issue of the relationship between Japanese communalism and the nenko system by pointing to its recency but merely to indicate that tradition has a phenomenological characteristic. People define their cultures and their traditions. They are not necessarily metaphysical entities given in the nature of things; they are not Durkheimian "social facts," but are instead cut and ordered and chosen, products of a social process. Whether or not earlier "feudal" Japanese institutions, such as the *oyabun-kobun* (patron-worker) relationship, were precursors of the nenko system is a matter debated by scholars.[7] What is evident, however, is that the "real" situation is itself ambiguous and that self-definitions of "traditional" Japanese communalism using the nenko system are constructions of that tradition rather than continuances, rediscoveries, or revivals.

Still another instance from the Japanese case will show us how ambiguities involved in understanding the past can be resolved and "traditional culture" determined and defined as a political act. Here the example is drawn from the Meiji Restoration and the characteristic loyalty to the emperor, which so many foreigners have seen as deeply embedded in Japanese traditional conceptions of the relation between the self and the state.

In a fascinating bit of exposition, the author of a textbook on Japanese politics introduces a chapter on "The Emperor: The Nation's Symbol and Rallying Point" by saying, "The emperor has been and still is the living symbol of the nation's history, heritage, and achievements, of all that is glorious in the nation's past and present, of its continuity and durability" (Yanaga, 1956). In a footnote to the paragraph he writes, however, "this has not always been so for it is a relatively recent development which accompanied Japan's emergence as a modern power in the nineteenth century" (Yanaga, 1956, note 1). The scholar giveth and the scholar taketh away.

Belief in the dominant role of the emperor in the Japanese state has seemed a traditional part of Japan continued into its modern phase and therefore a great source of continuity with feudal Japan. Nevertheless, it is the case that both Japanese and Western students of Japanese history recognize that the actual status of the emperor in pre-Meiji Japan has often been inconsistent with the position given to him by the Meiji constitution (Webb, 1965). The position of the emperor vis-à-vis the government and the people of Japan has fluctuated through its history. No matter how one interprets the varying status of the emperor, what is implied by the phrase, "the Meiji Restoration" involves but a decided break with what had existed through the Tokugawa period and not a continuity with tradition. In this sense, the present form of loyalty of the individual citizen to the emperor and the importance of the emperor in the state system dates from 1868. Giving it the status of the traditional heightens its legitimacy.

The philosophy that gave the emperor so central a role in the life of the citizen and the state as implied by the Imperial Rescript of 1890 on education was not a reiteration of a clearly defined culture. It was instead the almost deliberate development by an élite of a myth of loyalty as part of past cultural tradition. It served to provide a cohesion and consensus that was stressed in the effort to centralize and nationalize Japan.

> The state improved the material condition of the court and invested it with new glamour and aura. Criticism of the throne was silenced and a system went into effect which made it difficult, if not impossible, for there to be open disagreements between the Imperial Court and the government. (Webb, pp. 184-85)[8]

The Meiji elite thus became the definers of the tradition and its change. In "restoring" the emperor they were defining a pre-Tokugawa Japan whose characteristics of imperial power are by no means clear. In this fashion, Japanese culture was not only being found or revived; it was being formed.

The Japanese situation has provided us with two examples of the ambiguity in the concept of a traditional culture. What appeared to have been continuations of phenomena existing for centuries—the nenko system of industrial relations and the dominance of the emperor in the Japanese system—are not unambiguously "traditional." In both cases, the designation of these behavior patterns as an ongoing part of continuing Japanese culture was constructed. The latter case, that of the emperor, is illustrative of the role that political authority can play in determining and defining the group culture.

III

Unlike Japan, India represents a society of immense diversities where region, caste, and religion all constitute important sources for primordial identification. The question is often asked: Is India a nation? The development of the nationalist movement stirred into being an all-India identification, but the process of increasing communications and political hegemony has also accentuated regional unities. In the development of national and subnational groupings, Indian social structure today presents a remarkable process of group formation and self-designation through cultural revival. In Africa, Westernized intellectuals accentuated supposed African styles of life into a philosophy of "negritude." Similarly, the Indian nationalist movement produced efforts to reinstate the styles of life and forms of culture identified with the non-Western and the traditional in India.

This process, which Georges Balandier calls "rehabilitation of culture" (Balandier, 1968: 475-84), is by no means simply a reaching out and grabbing of a well-defined conception and then putting it on like an old overcoat. In the process, the tradition itself is as much formed as it is discovered. The nationalist movement gave considerable impetus to an all-India culture. It stressed those symbols of "great tradition" that could be accepted at popular levels. Since Independence, the quest for symbols of India, as distinct from that of specific subcommunities, has made it necessary to expand and reinforce symbols and legends which have been little used in the past. Kim Marriott has shown how Asoka and the symbol of the lions, little-known aspects of the Indian past, were "rescued" from history because they represented Indian symbols which, in a period of communal conflict, would not be offensive to any group (Marriott, 1963: 35-36). Thus the traditional culture is itself defined by new myths of the past. In similar fashion, Milton Singer has shown how the role of the Brahmin in the Bhakti movements in contemporary Madras involves a reformulation of classic, Sanskritized elements into new modes of cultural performance and into new forms such as movies and music (Singer, 1968;1960). Sanskritization therefore involves more than imitation. It also involves an imputation or judgment about the content of that tradition. What is perceived as Sanskritic and ancient may actually be new mint.

Those forces that act to expand the arena of political and economic association in India deeply affect the construction of tradition. They provide the conditions, the occasions, and the rewards for elaborating a consciousness of group membership and identity. One result of electoral politics and independence has been the intensification of movements for change in caste position. Frequently, these involve new cultural content now defined as being old and preexisting patterns. In this smelting process new group identities are forged.

These demands for reformulation must be seen in the context of Indian caste competition and conflict intensified by the political process of electoral democracy. The political importance of numbers and the economic concerns emergent on regional and national bases make for the development of new associations in which caste and other communal identities are sources for new groupings. The rise of caste associations appears to be an important part of a tendency for Indian society to develop new and extra-local groups.[9] Castes are also now formed by uniting local "castes" in wider ones. These emerge when common interests, cultural similarities and similar general caste category make it possible for local groups to pull together with groups from other localities to pursue aims and goals which exist at the state and national levels. In this process the caste uses whatever is available in the "culture" and develops the presupposition of its own common culture.[10] It proceeds to act "as if" the status now sought is the reality of old.

In one common pattern of mobility, the classic form of Indian social change is used and heightened. Here the caste proceeds to take on styles of life associated with Brahmins.[11] Such Sanskritization involves the redefinition of tradition through leadership. The caste panchayat has provided a model of central control that has made it possible to state and reinforce demands for greater Sanskritizing of the caste culture. In this fashion, whole styles of life shifts can and have been developed quickly. These have involved changes in such culture contents as eating habits, clothing style, and marriage customs. This has been described in a number of cases when previously lower castes have used their political power to enable them to "make good" their claims to new styles and thus legitimate their new positions.[12]

In these cases, the quest for social mobility has frequently carried with it "rediscovery of the past." The new status is bolstered by efforts to prove that myths that reinforced a lower position in the society are false, that in truth the history of the caste has not been recognized correctly in the past. Having developed new aspirations and often new economic capabilities, members of the caste find it essential for their own personal mobility that the mobility of the caste also be raised. The new mythologies are therefore the development of wholly new "traditions" by which the caste or regional group seeks its new level and expresses its new self-confidence.[13]

The movement for a traditional identity also exists where new groups come into being. The impact of a common Westernized style of life and associations has cut across previously exclusive castes and subcastes. Common life styles are generating the development of totally new groups, especially among Indian élites. These define themselves as new subcastes in a similar process to that which we have just described above for preexistent ones. As André Béteille has shown, the development of mythology and tradition helps to cloak the changes which are occurring and which would be very difficult to define in older terms (Béteille, 1967; also Bottomore, 1967; Srinivas, 1968).

It is not that caste as a system of human relationships is either disappearing or continuing in India that is significant for our argument. What we are stressing is that the caste idiom and the normative structure of caste loyalty and interest are used as a part of the available materials out of which to fashion new mechanisms of group formation and action. In its use, structures and "cultures" come into being which are legitimated as if they were part of an existing culture.

The conventionally understood forms of cultural identity of course also go on. Here the group reinforces and reestablishes what they have been doing in the past. Now, however, they are self-conscious about it. The conflicts and opportunities attendant in the political process and in the contact between a variety of local groups make it necessary to define and defend styles of life and group memberships as bases for political trust and obligation. How deeply the process of identity is also the process of new identity is revealed in the extensiveness to which castes undergo changes in name as well as changes in behavior. A saying among Indian Muslims expresses the process: "Last year we were weavers, this year we are Shaikhs and next year if the harvest is good we shall be Sayyids" (Mandelbaum, 1970: 434; also see Rudolph and Rudolph, 1967).

One of the clearest examples of the process of culture change as culture invention can be seen in the development of linguistic movements in India and in their impact on language, especially in the period since Independence. There is no element of culture seemingly as deeply part of a people as its language. Yet this, too, involves both the process of self-designation of a language as "ours" and the similar process of reinforcement or rejection of prevalent or suggested linguistic habits and styles. Once again our reference is not to the general sense in which language changes under shifting conditions such as migration and education. We are rather calling attention here to those aspects that are political in that they involve mobilizations of people in explicit fashions and in conflict with others concerning control and use of state power.[14] What does a group perceive as "its" language? What aspects of its language are reinforced and rejected by considerations of identity? How do these rejections and acceptances affect the existing state of the language?

In the development of the Indian nationalist movement and in the Independence period, English has often seemed a paradoxical anomaly. In rejecting the colonizer the nationalist's use of the English language presented a problem, especially in the quest for an all-India and non-British style of life. Even those who favor the retention of English as an official language in India and reject the uses of Hindi have recognized the inconsistent position in which this places the Indian nationalist.

It is in this context that the move toward the development of the Hindi language has itself to be seen. Linguists may argue about whether or not there "is" such a language as Hindi, given the diversities in dialect that exist across North India and the so-called Hindi plains. Certainly the language of areas which had been under the domination of the Muslims or which contained large Muslim populations included far more Urdu than did the non-Muslim sections of North India. Arguments over the content of the North Indian language were destined to reflect the political, cultural, and religious conflicts that have divided groups in North India.

As national and regional and religious conflicts were sharpened, differentiation occurred precisely along these lines. A greater importation of Sanskrit occurred into Hinduized areas and a greater retention of Urdu in more Islamic sections. Words fell into disfavor because they came to be associated with one or another group. Gandhi, recognizing the implications of this for conflict, championed Hindustani, a less-Sanskritized version of a language which he felt would be mutually acceptable to the Hindus and Muslims (Taboret-Keller, 1970, Ch.4, 5).

The development of Hindi imperialism would be far more difficult were the various states on the Gangetic plain to attempt to retain their specific languages as official public ones. An example of this is seen in the fear among the inhabitants of North Bihar that their regional importance within the state will be diminished by the usage of Hindi rather than their own Maithili. Here the argument about whether Maithili is a separate language or only a dialect of Hindi is more than just the linguist's scholarly problem (Brass, n.d.). The movement for retention of Maithili and its identification as a language distinct from Hindi has roots in political realities as well as regional pride.

The accompanying cultural revival, the discovery of the importance of older texts, and the quest for translating and publishing materials in the now-reinforced language supplies the facilities and impetus for fulfilling the prophecy that the language is indeed a common one and is essential to enable a given group to practice its culture. The political reinforcement of this through requirements for jobs and through the school system in turn now make the culture, in a sense of existing practices, square with the view by which it has been justified. Paul Brass has summed this up very well in referring to regional and national movements in India by saying:

> It appears, in fact, that such movements benefit more from the full freedom to select the desired symbols from the past than from the living embodiment of an historical-political tradition in the present. (Brass, n.d.: 10)

Both political and "cultural" leadership are responsible for a new language content. The Indian government has subsidized the publication of Hindi materials, its use in broadcasting and translations of scientific and other materials from foreign languages into Hindi. New encyclopedias and dictionaries and the development of literary prizes have produced a seeming renaissance of Hindi in both written and verbal forms (Das Gupta, 1970: Ch. 6).

This "renaissance" is deceptive. Much of the leadership in the work of disseminating Hindi has come from the literati of writers, artists, and humanistic academics. They are introducing a "pure" or highly Sanskritized Hindi, which is not a reflection of common elements in the Hindi used in the past in Northern India. The use of these forms of Hindi has been defended as efforts to produce a more standardized language, capable of being used in a wide area across local variations. Introduction of this "pure" Hindi on All-India Radio was met by protests of nonunderstandability (Das Gupta, 1970: 176-77). Whatever the merit of the argument, the Hindi urged and institutionally supported as Indian neither represents the "great tradition" nor a folk culture:

> The guiding norm of going back to "Mother Sanskrit" and the unremitting zeal in purifying Hindi from all "alien" influences have created a language which may satisfy the regional pride of the Hindi leaders, but...the artificial product has tended to erect barriers between literary communication and mass communication. (Das Gupta, 1970: 187-88)

Such movements to define the culture of a given group succeed also in developing the groups. Language, by being now connected with a set of political and social loyalties and facilities, is now a source of group definition. The Hindi-speaking North is now a linguistic and political area. So, too, other groups, such as the Punjabi-speakers or the Dravidians, are mobilized in self-defense. The hauteur with which the Bengali talks about Hindi as an "upstart language" testifies to the ways in which tradition is invented as much as it is discovered and to the political importance which the process possesses.

The material from India is further illustration of socially constructed traditions. It reinforces the analysis drawn from Japan. It adds to it, however, an understanding of the role such constructions play in the context of group diversities and political conflict. In modern India, new castes, communal groups, and linguistic associations are formed through amalgams, alliances, and revisions of old ones. National and regional consciousness are emergent new phenomena. "Tradition" and "culture" are constructed in the process of defining the group to itself through associations, intellectual products, political leadership, and governmental sponsorship.

Conceptualizing such change as transitional points between "traditional" and "modern" society begs the question. First, the points of cultural emphasis around which loyalties of tradition congeal are often, as we have seen, products of present or recent occurrence. They

are often constricted in a context of political conflict and/or government policy. Seeing them as vestiges of a past both falsifies the content and obscures the process. Secondly, the cultural revival and the
renaissance of tradition are not only found in the nationalism and
regionalism of new nations. They are also discoverable within old
nations and affluent societies. Ethnic communalism does not disappear and its assertion can and does occur even generations after migration and "assimilation." Recent developments in the United States
will illustrate this.

IV

That such movements can and do occur in highly industrialized
societies is seen in the movement connected with cultural identity
among black people in the United States. The developing movement
towards a greater political separation of the black community from
the white is part of the present ideology of one wing of the black
movement. It is not new. From time to time it has appeared in the
general history of the movement, especially among the Garveyites in
the 1920s and of course with the growth of the Black Muslim movement in the 1950s and 1960s.[15] Whatever may be the ultimate fate of
the political ideology of black nationalism, certainly the development of black culture as part of the process of new identification of
who "we are" and what are the unique aspects of being black is at
present a very salient part of the movement in most black communities and in many political wings. Cultural nationalism has had an
appreciative response.

So many scholars and intellectuals have commented on the problems of self-confidence and identity among the American Negro that
it is by now an aspect of popular as well as literary perceptions (Erikson,
1967; Isaacs, 1965). Here the need to reformulate the past is connected not only with political reasons for maintaining separateness but
as a means of developing a sense of self-confidence. It is both intrinsi-
cally meritorious and essential as well for a movement that is in
conflict with other aspects of the society.

The demand for courses and programs of study at secondary and
higher educational levels in areas of ethnic or black studies is again
the concept of "reestablishing" traditions; here it is that of "rediscov-
ering" Afro-American roots and revising the errors of past "white

history." It is coupled also with a strong assertion that the black was robbed of his culture by slavery and by his treatment during the slave period. Thus new history is being written, as revisionist history frequently is (Higham, 1962; Monteil, 1966). As we have seen in Japan and in India, it is an open·question as to whether past "false" history is now corrected or whether history, as often happens, is being revised or reformulated in accordance with new needs for identity (Monteil, 1966; Genovese, 1970). The question of the "truth" of history is separate from its import as myth and justification.

The rediscovery also takes the form of importation into present styles of living of Africanisms and of other styles associated with "the black folk." Thus the growing use of African dress, of "soul food," the extolling of the jazz and blues music, and the shifting perception of black dialects as "mother tongue" is part of the impact of the movement on styles of living. Middle-class black families now find there are internal as well as external pressures to adopt the modes of living which may be strange to them but which are set forth as the culture that has been lost. This "going home" is now defined as "being natural."

Even the very name is part of this process. Thus the black has gone through a variety of different names by which he has designated himself to himself (Bennett, Jr., 1970). For much of the last half of the nineteenth century, the term "colored people" was the dominant term and the development in 1905 of the National Association for the Advancement of Colored People is indicative of its wide acceptance. A number of leaders during the first half of the twentieth century made strong efforts to get rid of this as the term of self-designation. Thus Garvey called his secessionist group the Universal Negro Improvement Association. At present, the term Negro has become associated with an earlier stage in history and the terms black or Afro-American are now more widely used. The use of the word "black" is itself enormously revealing of a strong effort to transvalue aspects associated heretofore with derogatory white designations and thus to change a negative self-conception into a positive one. Here again the theme of cultural nationalism implies an identity with "folk" themes and low-status sectors of the population.

In his defense of the use of the concept of black culture, Robert Blauner has in many ways summarized this paper. Referring to criticisms of the use of black culture as either describing what does not exist or as describing a general American or southern lower-class culture, Blauner suggests that these are:

> based on a static, deterministic approach to cultural development, an approach which minimizes its open-ended quality and therefore underplays the role of consciousness and culture-building in effecting that development. (Blauner, 1970: 349)

The conventional approach to social change in many parts of the world has similarly been at fault in its static model of human behavior. In viewing people as possessing fixed cultures that come into conflict with new situations, it ignores the reflexive character of human behaviors, it redefines culture and tradition as social facts that are more stubborn than our materials and perspectives would indicate.

The difficulty with this model is that it ignores both the ways in which new structures, new values, and new self-perceptions emerge without clear-cut affiliation to either end of the polar opposites of tradition and modernity. The processes of social change involve interpretation and interaction between persons and situations that are both more complex and less fixed than that.

Notes

1. For some of these criticisms, see Bendix, 1966-67 and my paper, 1967. For a "rejoinder," see Eisenstadt, 1968.
2. A major statement of this view is contained in the influential study by Daniel Lerner and Lucille Pevsner, *The Passing of Traditional Society*, 1958.
3. See the general analyses of tradition in Edward Shils, "Tradition," Comparative Studies in Society and History, XIII (April 1971): 122–59, esp. 138–44.
4. For discussion of the sources of *nenko*, see Taira, 1962 and Levine, 1965. For a recent field study, see Cole, 1971.
5. Tominaga, 1962; Taira, op. cit. The findings concerning small and large establishments in Japan are based on an unpublished study by Gusfield and Tominaga.
6. This is by no means confined to Japan. For other examples, see my "Tradition and Modernity," op. cit. For an American example that documents the relative "recency" of a "tradition," see Woodward, 1955.
7. See the differences between the Taira and Levine papers cited above and the view of John Bennett and Iwo Ishino, 1963.
8. Webb, pp. 184–85. For the importance of the emperor in establishing Japanese identity during modernization, see Kenneth Pyle, 1969.
9. The rise of caste associations and consequent shifting character of caste as a unit of social structure is a dominant theme in the sociology of post-Independence India. From a large literature of empirical studies and analyses the following are among leading statements: M. N. Srinivas, 1966; L. and S. Rudolph, 1967: Part 1; Béteille, 1967: 223–43); articles by M. N. Srinivas, William Rowe and Owen Lynch, in M. Singer and B. S. Cohn, eds., 1968.

10. See the case of the Shanans who became Nadars and the Pallis who became Vanniyars and the legitimation of their mobility through political exchange in Rudolph and Rudolph, op. cit., pp. 36–64.
11. The concept of Sanskritization has been developed in describing and explaining this process. The seminal statement is M. N. Srinivas, "A Note on Sanskritization and Westernization," reprinted in Srinivas, 1962: 42–62.
12. In addition to the work of M. N. Srinivas and the Rudolphs cited above, see also Hardgrave, Jr., 1969; Lynch, 1969; Béteille, 1965. For a general account of these mobility processes, with many examples of castes, see Mandelbaum, 1970: Chs. 23–27.
13. See the account of caste mythologies in Hardgrave, op. cit., Ch. 3; and in Lynch, op. cit., Ch. 4. The process is similar to that found in Leach, 1964: Ch. 9, "Myth as a Justification for Faction and Social Change." Irschick finds the same process in the use of the myth of Dravidian origin. See Irschick, 1969: 278ff. and 354ff.
14. For a clear statement embodying this conventional approach, see A. Taboret-Keller, 1970.
15. For a historical survey of black nationalist movements in the United States, see the introduction and materials in John Bracey, Jr., August Meier, and Elliott Rudwick, 1970.
16. In addition to Monteil op. cit., see the criticism of revisionist black history in Eugene Genovese, 1970: 31–52.

References

Abegglen, James. 1958. *The Japanese Factory* (Glencoe, IL: The Free Press, 1958).

Ayai, J. F. 1966. "The Place of African History and Culture in the Process of Nation-Building in Africa South of the Sahara." In I. Wallerstein, ed., *Social Change: The Colonial Situation.* (New York: John Wiley).

Balandier, Georges. 1968. "Political Myths of Colonization and Decolonization in Africa," trans. by Jean-Guy Vaillancourt. In Reinhard Bendix, et al., eds., *State and Society* (New York: Little, Brown).

Bendix, Reinhard. 1966-67. "Tradition and Modernity Reconsidered." *Comparative Studies in Society and History* IX (1966–67): 292–346

Bennett, John and Iwo Ishino. 1963. *Paternalism in the Japanese Economy* (Minneapolis: University of Minnesota Press).

Bennett, John. 1968. "Tradition, Modernity and Communalism in Japan's Modernization." *Journal of Social Issues*, XXIV (October 1968): 25–44.

Bennett, Lerone Jr. 1970. "What's in a Name?" In Peter Rose, ed., *Old Memories, New Moods.* (New York: Atherton Press).

Béteille, Andre. 1965. *Caste, Class and Power.* Berkeley: University of California Press.

_____. 1967. "Elites, Status Groups, and Caste in Modern India." In Philip Mason, ed., *India and Ceylon: Unity and Diversity* London: Oxford University Press.

Blauner, Robert. 1970. "Black Culture: Myth or Reality?" In N. Whitten, Jr., and John Szwed, eds., *Afro-American Anthropology* (New York: The Free Press).

Bracey, John Jr., August Meier, and Elliott Rudwick, eds. 1970. *Black Nationalism in America* (Indianapolis, IN: Bobbs-Merrill).

Brass, Paul. "The Politics of Language: The Maithili Movement in North Bihar" (Unpublished manuscript).

Cobban, Alfred. 1964. *The Social Interpretation of the French Revolution.* Cambridge: Cambridge University Press.

Cole, Robert 1971. *Japanese Blue Collar* Berkeley: University of California Press.

Eisenstadt, S.N. 1968. "Reflections on a Theory of Modernization." In Arnold Rifkin, ed., *Nations by Design* New York: Doubleday, Anchor Books.

Erikson, Erik H. 1967. "The Concept of Identity in Race Relations." In T. Parsons and K. Clark, eds., *The Negro American* (Boston: Houghton-Mifflin).

Geertz, Clifford, 1963. "The Integrative Revolution." In idem (ed.), *Old Societies and New States* Glencoe, IL: The Free Press.

Genovese, Eugene. 1970. "The Roots of Black Nationalism." In Peter Rose, ed., *Old Memories, New Moods* New York: Atherton Press.

Glick, Clarence. 1942. "The Relation Between Position and Status in the Assimilation of Chinese in Hawaii." *American Journal of Sociology* XLVII: 667-79.

Gusfield, Joseph. 1967. "Tradition and Modernity: Misplaced Polarities in the Study of Social Change." *American Journal of Sociology* LXXII: 351–62.

Hardgrave, Robert L. Jr. 1969. *The Nadars of Tamilnad: Culture of a Community in Change* Berkeley: University of California Press.

Heimsath, Charles. 1964. *Indian Nationalism and Hindu Social Reform* Princeton, NJ: Princeton University Press.

Higham, John, ed. 1962. *The Reconstruction of American History* New York: Harper, Torchbooks.

Irschick, Eugene. 1969. *Politics and Social Conflict in South India: The Non-Brahman Movement and Tamil Separatism, 1916–1929* Berkeley: University of California Press.

Isaacs, Harold. 1965. "Group Identity and Political Change: The Role of History and Origins." (Paper presented at the American Association for Asian Studies, San Francisco, April 3, 1965.)

Kroeber, A. L., and Clyde Kluckhohn. 1952. *Culture.* New York: Vintage Books.

Leach, Edmund. 1965. *Political Systems of Highland Burma* Boston: Beacon Press.

Lerner, Daniel, and Lucille Pevsner. 1958. *The Passing of Traditional Society* Glencoe, IL: The Free Press.

Levine, Solomon. 1965. "Labor Relations in Japan." In William Lockwood, ed. *State and Economic Development in Japan* Princeton, NJ: Princeton University Press.

Lynch, Owen. 1969. *The Politics of Untouchability* New York: Columbia University Press.

Mandelbaum, David. 1970. *Society in India.* Vol. II Berkeley: University of California Press.

Marriott, Kim. 1955. "Little Communities in an Indigenous Civilization." In idem (ed.), *Village India* New Delhi: Asia Publishing House.

_____. 1963. "Cultural Policy in the New States." In C. Geertz, ed., *Old Societies and New States.* Glencoe, IL: The Free Press.

Matsumoto, Y. Scott. 1960. *Contemporary Japan.* Transactions of the American Philosophical Society, new series, L, part 1. Philadelphia: American Philosophical Society.

Monteil, V. 1958. "The Colonization of the Writing of History." In I. Wallerstein, ed. *Social Change: The Colonial Situation.* New York: John Wiley.

Nakane, Chie. 1970. *Japanese Society* Berkeley: University of California Press.

Pyle, Kenneth. 1969. *The New Generation in Meiji Japan* Stanford: Stanford University Press.

Redfield, Robert. 1960. *Peasant Society.* Chicago: University of Chicago Press, Phoenix Books.

Rudolph, Lloyd I., and Susanne Hoeber Rudolph. 1967. *The Modernity of Tradition: Political Development in India.* Chicago: University of Chicago Press.

Rupert Emerson. 1960. *From Empire to Nation.* Cambridge: Harvard University Press.

Saniel, Josefa. 1965. "The Mobilization of Traditional Values in the Modernization of Japan." In Robert Bellah, ed., *Religion and Progress in Modern Asia.* New York: The Free Press.

Shibutani, Tamotsu, and Kian Kwan. 1965. *Ethnic Stratification.* New York: Macmillan.

Shils, Edward. 1971. "Tradition." *Comparative Studies in Society and History* XIII (April): 122–59.

Singer, Milton, and Bernard Cohn, eds. 1968. *Structure and Change in Indian Society.* Chicago: Aldine.

Singer, Milton. 1960. "The Great Tradition of Hinduism in the City of Madras." In Charles Leslie, ed., *Anthropology of Folk Religion.* New York: Vintage Books.

_____. 1968. "The Radha Krishna Bhajanas of Madras City." In idem (ed.) *Krishna: Myths, Rites and Attitudes.* Chicago: University of Chicago Press.

Smith, Thomas C. 1960-61. "Japan's Aristocratic Revolution." *Yale Review* V: 370–83.

Srinivas, M. N. 1962. "A Note on Sanskritization and Westernization." Reprinted in idem, *Caste in Modern India.* New Delhi: Asia Publishing House.

_____. 1966. *Social Change in Modern India.* Berkeley: University of California Press.

Taboret-Keller, A. 1970. "Sociological Factors of Language Maintenance and Language Shift." In Joshua A. Fishman, Charles A. Ferguson, and Jyotirindra Das Gupta, eds., *Language Conflict and National Development: Group Politics and National Language Policy in India.* Berkeley: University of California Press.

Taira, Koji. 1962. "The Characteristics of Japanese Labor Markets." *Economic Development and Cultural Change* X, 1 (January): 150–68.

Tominaga, Ken'ichi. 1962. "Occupation Mobility in Japanese Society." *The Journal of Economic Behaviour* II (April): 1–37.

Wallerstein, Immanuel. 1961. *Africa: The Politics of Independence.* New York: Vintage Books.

Webb, Herschel. 1965. "The Development of an Orthodox Attitude toward the Imperial Institution in the Nineteenth Century." In Marius Jansen, ed., *Changing Japanese Attitudes toward Modernization.* Princeton, NJ: Princeton University Press.

Williams, Raymond. 1959. *Culture and Society: 1780-1930.* New York: Anchor Books.

Woodward, C. Van. 1955. *The Strange Career of Jim Crow.* New York: Oxford University Press.

Yanaga, Chitoshi. 1956. *Japanese People and Politics.* New York: John Wiley.

Part 3

Symbolism

10

Secular Symbolism:
Studies of Ritual, Ceremony, and
the Symbolic Order in Modern Life

Introduction

Among anthropologists, words like ritual, myth, ceremony, and symbolism are central to the study of social life in primitive societies. In contemporary sociology they have been, at best, peripheral and exotic terms, and the activities they denote have not usually been studied in modern societies. While major anthropologists figured prominently in studies of such phenomena in the past, in recent years a special field of symbolic anthropology has emerged especially oriented to the analysis of symbols and meanings in many areas of social life (Firth, 1973; Dolgin, et al., 1977). In the past two decades, and especially in the last few years, some sociologists and anthropologists have begun to examine a number of areas and activities in modern societies using approaches drawn from analyses of ritual, ceremony, and symbolism. In this paper, we review these kind of sociological studies in the hope of achieving a clearer understanding and some sense of direction to the use of symbolic analysis in contemporary sociology.

Reprinted from *Annual Review of Sociology* 10 (1984):417–35. Copyright © 1984 by Annual Reviews Inc. All rights reserved. With permission of JAI Press, Inc., Greenwich, CT., and London, England. Jerry Michalowicz assisted in gathering material and in the writing.

Analyzing Symbols

Symbolism in Modern Societies

Although a distinction between symbolic and nonsymbolic forms of thought and action lies at the center of our discussion, it must be approached from the perspective of the perceived difference between modern and primitive societies. The absence of a significant place for ritual, ceremony, and myth in modern sociology and their honored positions in anthropology reflect underlying sociological conceptions. Modern life is viewed as being dominated by a secular, matter-of-fact, rational culture and social organization in which human responses are governed by attention to means and ends. In other words, Max Weber's view of a disenchanted, nonmagical, rationalized world has dominated sociologists' conceptions (Weber, 1946). For the past 100 years, anthropologists have vigorously debated the issue of the similarities of thought between primitive and modern cultures (Malinowski, 1954; Lévi-Strauss, 1966; Levy-Bruhl, 1966 [1923]; Goody, 1977). With some notable exceptions, sociologists have accepted the significance of symbolic analyses in the study of religious ritual and myth and in art, but they have not recognized the validity of anthropological methods of analysis in other contexts (Nagendra, 1971; Bocock, 1974: Ch. 1; Duncan, 1968, 1969).

What is striking and important about the recent sociological interest in secular symbolism is the appearance of a viewpoint that runs counter to the traditional emphasis on utilitarian behavior. The discovery of symbolic levels of meaning in areas where peoples' interest in power, economic values, and organizational goals are conventionally at work is a major development. The anthropologists J. L. Dolgin, D. S. Kemnitzer, and D. M. Schneider have clearly stated our point of view:

> But meaning and symbol are not dependent as things on context; *they are relations*, not objects. Ignoring this point, seeing meanings and symbols as things, has allowed cultural analysts to erect a distinction between symbolic structures and concrete structures; to differentiate religion, myth, art—held to be "essentially" symbolic forms—from economics, politics, kinship, or everyday living. This is a position we reject. (Dolgin, et al., 1977:22)

The relationship between the symbolic and the nonsymbolic is a, if not the, major sociological problem in this area, and much of what follows will concentrate on that issue.

What Does Symbolic Mean?

Sociological interest in symbolic forms is part of the renewed concern about problems of meaning stimulated by linguistic, philosophical, and anthropological studies over the past twenty-five years (Giddens, 1976). Prior to any analysis of experience, one must answer the question: What is happening here? Recognizing the potentially multiple responses to this question illuminates the way in which meaning is mediated by cultural categories and structures of thought. This awareness of the social construction of reality, which Richard Brown calls symbolic realism (Brown, 1977), implies that any segment of human, social activity can be experienced in different and in multiple ways by diverse actors and observers.

In most discussions of symbolic forms, a distinction is made between kinds of meanings. Such discussions, in keeping with our topic, do not use the term to include the general analysis of language. Words are not, of course, the same as their referents. The word tree cannot yield shade. The denotation of symbolism is rather that in which something stands for something else (Firth, 1973:26), as the poet or the Freudian analyst uses symbols—e.g., the sense in which a lion is a symbol of strength or a banana is a phallus.

What persists in the many uses of the term symbolism is a distinction between levels or kinds of meanings. Thus, there is "a gap between the overt superficial statement of action and its underlying meaning" (Firth, 1973:26); and it is "significant not for its ostensible meaning but [because of] that (which) it stands for and has to be interpreted by reference to, a transcendent principle outside the means-goal relationship" (Lane, 1981:11). Other distinctions have been made between the symbolic and the rational, the symbolic and the instrumental, and the symbolic and utilitarian. All suggest that to see what is happening with a symbolic is to distinguish that experience as other than a more common meaning—usually one of means and ends; of reason rather than emotion; of universal terms rather than particular images (Bocock, 1974:31). The nub of the distinction then, is, between manifest meanings that are immediately apparent and latent meanings, not immediately apparent but perceptible.

This conception of a hidden or latent meaning that contradicts or differs from the manifest is exemplified in Clifford Geertz's classic analysis of Balinese cockfights entitled "Deep Play" (Geertz, 1973:

Ch. 15). At one level, cockfighting is a gambling and a sports event; what is happening is a fight between animals. At another level, Geertz perceives it as an enactment—a presentation in which the cocks are the men who own them, who bet on them, and whose fortunes will be affected by victory or defeat.

At still another level, Geertz interprets the cockfight as a commentary on Balinese society, contrasting the murderous aggression of the fight with the gentle formalism of Balinese behavior. He differentiates this mode of understanding from the scientific analysis of causes and likens it to the analysis of a literary text:

> If one takes the cockfight, or any other collectively sustained symbolic structure, as a means of "saying something of something" (to invoke a famous Aristotelian tag) then one is faced with a problem not in social meanings but in social semantics. (Geertz, 1973:448)

While some aspects of Geertz's formulation are a product of his own specific viewpoint (and will be discussed below), like all symbolic analysis it identifies different levels of meanings, so that the activities are not understood only at the ostensible, conventional, and manifest level. Symbolic action is a level of meaning in which the nonsymbolic and manifest stand for something else. Lions stand for strength; flags, for the nation; the wine of the Eucharist, for the blood of Christ.

Where is Symbolism Located?

For whom does "something stand for something else?" Answers to this question are at the heart of our review, since the conclusions of symbolic analyses, we assert, depend considerably on the anticipated meanings of events that are contradicted by symbolic understandings.

There are two basic approaches to the symbolism of human actions. In one, which we label the *metaphysical* approach, there is a great effort to delineate the character of the object or term used. Symbolism is located in the nature of the language used and in the objects or events to which it refers. Such locational concerns lead to a discussion of how symbols differ from nonsymbols (Firth, 1973; Leach, 1976). The work of the nineteenth-century American philosopher Charles Peirce has been most influential in this area. Peirce considered a symbol one of three kinds of signs (Peirce, 1931: Ch. 3): Icons resemble their referents as a painting of a tiger resembles a tiger; an index of a tiger points to a tiger as a tiger's tracks do; a symbol of a tiger has no inherent relation to the tiger but is dependent on convention, as the word tiger is a symbol of a tiger and the energy of an automobile may be related to the energy of a tiger as a symbolic meaning.

A second formulation of symbolism is what we call *contextual*. Its proponents are less concerned about the relation between the subject and the object than about that between the observer and his audience of readers. The primary emphasis is on the distinction between symbolic and nonsymbolic meaning. What is symbolic for some may be nonsymbolic for others. Sperber defines the symbolic as follows:

> I note then as symbolic all activity where the means put into play seem to be clearly disproportionate to the explicit or implicit end...that is all *activity whose rationale escapes me*." (Sperber, 1974: 4 [italics added])

As we will show, this manner of defining symbol is much closer to what sociologists, as contrasted with anthropologists, do when they engage in "symbolic analysis." The meaning and import of describing activity as symbolic in studies of contemporary social life is derived from contrasting it with the nonsymbolic. The symbolism is located in the set of contrasting expectancies in the observer and his audience. It is to be seen less as a linguistic than as a literary or theoretical designation.

These formulations are not mutually exclusive, and both are used by sociologists but, we assert, for different kinds of materials and with distinct consequences. These differences are especially evident when the sociologist studies power, organizations, and social control, where symbolism has traditionally been left out of sociological analyses.

When Are Meanings Symbolic? Nonsymbolic?

The preceding section dealt with a "where" question. Much can be gained by turning it into a "when" question. Doing this shifts the focus from the relationship between participants and objects to the historical moment. Both questions will be our concern in this section.

Sperber suggests that the symbolic mechanism operates by evoking meanings existent in one's memory (Sperber, 1974: Ch. 3). Burke refers to symbolic action as "the dancing of an attitude" (Burke, 1957: 9), emphasizing its presentational form. But to whom is the meaning latent or manifest? The American flag symbolizes national feeling or the "presence of the nation," but that meaning is quite manifest to socialized members of American society. It is not interesting or surprising to describe it as symbolic to American audiences. For an anthropologist from the Trobriand Islands, it could be a hidden meaning of considerable interest to the Trobriand Anthropological Association. What is symbolic and metaphorical in one context and for one audience may be literal and mundane for another group in a different context.

The analyses of symbolism by the anthropologist Victor Turner and the discussion of metaphors by the philosopher Paul Ricoeur provide a way out of these difficulties. For Turner, whose work has been pre-eminently influential, the anthropologist is by no means limited to the actor's understanding of meanings. Indeed, the values and norms of ritual actions may be so axiomatic as to preclude the actor from seeing it in relation to either part or all of society.

In examining the symbolic structure of Ndembu rituals, Turner describes three different levels or procedures for arriving at meanings that go beyond the description of activity (Turner, 1967): (a) Exegetical, where meaning is obtained from the layman or from the ritual specialist. Thus, the meaning of the flag is derived from individuals' accounts. (b) Operational, where meaning is equated with use and inferences are drawn. Thus, where the flag is displayed, by whom, and the times of display would be considered. (c) Positional, where meaning is derived by observing the relation of one symbol to others in a totality. In relation to the flag, its sacred character can be seen in comparison to other decorative items. An example of Turner's method can be seen in the following discussion of the use of colors in Ndembu rituals:

> Whiteness differs from redness in that it stresses harmony, cohesion and continuity, while redness, associated with blood spilling as well as blood kinship, tends to denote discontinuity, strength acquired through breach of certain rules, and male aggressiveness. (1967:57–58)

A further aspect of Turner's method, exemplified in the above quote, is an emphasis on the polysemic and multivocal character of symbolic structure. That is, there may be more than one meaning attached to any activity or object, at the same moment in time and for the same audience.

For Paul Ricoeur, the capacity to create metaphors is a renewing aspect of language (1977, 1978). The difference between the poetic (metaphorical) function of language and the referential (metonymic) is the difference between referring to the nonlinguistic context, as metaphors and symbolism do, and to the linguistic context by itself, as referential language does. The metaphor surprises: It redefines reality by creating points of resemblance between actions and objects normally understood as unrelated or contradictory. "A significant trait of living language...is the power always to push the frontier of nonsense further back" (Ricoeur, 1977: 95).

Both Turner and Ricoeur emphasize the integrating character of the act of discovering symbolism and creating metaphoric reality. These insights are helpful clues to unraveling our puzzle. The symbolic process involves the observer as well as the actor and the activity or object. The act of attributing symbolic properties to action or speech is first that of the observer, but it may in turn be attributed directly and exegetically to the actor, as in the symbolism of the flag. It may also, however, be the inference of the observer making "sense" (i.e., reality) out of actions otherwise not understandable to him- or herself and/or his or her audience.

This emphasis on the observer's role also indicates the importance of the implied contrast between literal meaning and symbolic meaning. First, it suggests that meaning may be literal to one audience but symbolic to another. Much depends on the conventional, "normal," and "proper" meanings existent in the culture of the observer or audience. The thrust of symbolic analysis lies in the distinction between a literal and a symbolic reading. Literalness, however, cannot be defined apart from a norm of conventional expectations for the observer. "Literalness is a quality which some words have achieved in the course of their history; it is not a quality with which the first words were born" (Barfield, 1960: 55).

It should be recognized that a concern for symbolic elements does not necessarily diminish conventional referential and functional interests. The same activity may possess a variety of meanings and consequences. Shoes protect the feet, but in American society they also signify taste and income.

We have divided our review of contemporary studies into three groups. The first is comprised of studies in traditional sociological areas where other perspectives have conventionally been used. We refer to them as studies of the institutional order. They are broken up further into those that focus on politics, political ceremony and ritual, and the law and social control. The second includes analyses of special events—life-cycle rituals and festivals. The third encompasses studies of everyday life that employ less conventional perspectives.

Studies of the Institutional Order

Politics

The authors of these studies examine political actions as events whose meaning is unrelated to the ostensible instrumental behavior suggested by nonsymbolic interpretations. In his studies of symbolic politics and its language, for example, Edelman describes such political programs as labor legislation, poverty programs, and international relations as forms of "symbolic quiescence" (Edelman, 1964; 1971; 1977). These acts provide the spectator with reassurance that his or her values are respected and that his or her goals are being pursued. Such acts have little relation to the "actual" world of political events. Thus, elections may represent a political system in which citizen participation is powerful, but its significance is mainly symbolic. Labor relations take the form of conflict between management and labor, but that form belies the reality of limited opportunities and existing constraints. The public events symbolize a participatory democracy that instrumental reality contradicts.

In his study of the American Temperance Movement, Gusfield (1963) found that temperance and prohibition legislation served as a means of dramatizing the status gains and losses of conflicting groups in American life. Since drinking occupied a different value in Protestant, "native," and rural groups than in Catholic, immigrant, and urban groups, the alcohol issue formed a public arena in which struggles over relative prestige and power in American society were conducted. The significance of the legislation cannot be understood solely in terms of its instrumental effects on drinking behavior.

Several other studies of legislative movements have used similar conceptions of the symbolic status of legislative acts. Carson has studied the early factory acts in nineteenth-century England, arguing that they provided a mechanism for an older agricultural elite to protect its status against commercial and manufacturing classes by presenting a symbolic villainy (Carson, 1976). Zurcher & Kirkpatrick (1976) have studied local laws against pornography with the same emphasis on their symbolic importance rather than on their instrumental value. Chandler and Rothman have each done the same for capital punishment laws and First Amendment guarantees (Chandler, 1976; Rothman, 1978).

Political Ceremony and Ritual

Many of the studies of secular symbolism build on Durkheimian theory (Durkheim, 1947) and on W. Lloyd Warner's (Warner, 1959) seminal studies, especially of political ritual. Shils & Young have examined the British coronation as a symbol of the moral values that unite the British people and provide a consensus underlying political differences (Shils & Young, 1953). This view was first criticized by Birnbaum (1955), who argues that there is no evidence that the entire public interprets the coronation this way. Furthermore, Birnbaum maintains, the coronation articulates upper- and middle-class values and glosses over class conflicts. In a later critique and analysis of political ritual studies, Lukes similarly suggests that rituals such as the coronation represent official interpretations of the society and thus "help to define as authoritative certain ways of seeing society" (Lukes, 1975: 306). Thus, they may represent one strategy by which groups attempt to gain or maintain power.

Christel Lane's study of political rituals in the Soviet Union is similar to Birnbaum's and Lukes' in emphasizing the importance of rituals in maintaining allegiance to the elite's authority (Lane, 1981). Thus, she finds that a wide spectrum of rituals has been politicized and given symbolic import that fosters a collective identification. They include life-cycle events, such as births and weddings; institutional events, such as graduations and labor rituals; and political holidays. Old rituals have been given new symbolic meanings, and new rituals have been added. Lane concludes that the existence of a professional corps of ritual specialists and their control by powerful elites show that a ritual system can take hold and grow in modern industrialized societies.

The Law and Social Control

In the 1930s, the legal scholars J. Frank and T. Arnold interpreted appellate court decisions less as utilitarian directives describing the consequences derived from established doctrines than as expressive, ritual-creating reassurance about the legal and social order (Frank, 1936; Arnold, 1935). In an influential paper in 1956, H. Garfinkel presented a view of trials, hearings, and other events as degradation ceremonies (Garfinkel, 1956). In recent years, there have been several studies of law, legislation, and law enforcement that focus on the symbolic meanings of acts formerly understood solely as utilitarian and instrumental.

Manning's field study of British and American police emphasizes the public's perception of police as "crime fighters." He found a sharp discrepancy between policemen's daily activities and the dramatic presentation of that work to the public. In their daily work, the police serve many functions and have relatively little control over the occurrence of crimes. In presenting themselves to the public, however, they dramatize a "police myth" that they possess the power to prevent crime and apprehend most criminals—a myth that is contradicted by the facts. Such strategies increase both public understanding of and support for police practices (Manning, 1977).

In a study of the drinking-driving problem, Gusfield analyzes the process by which scientific research has created a cognitive order about auto accidents and legislation and by which legal decisions have created a moral order about drinking and driving. Together, they produced the perception of drinking and driving as a criminal act (Gusfield, 1981). Both functioned to symbolize the drinking driver in the dramatic model of the "killer drunk." The development of this myth about drinking and driving has produced a belief in an empirical order of reality and a legal order of criminal act and punishment. Both are contradicted by the limited character and selectivity of the scientific data and by the negotiated character of the law enforcement process in practice. What is a criminal offense based on concrete fact at the level of the public arena is a traffic offense and an ambiguous fact at the more routine and private levels. Public awareness of the drinking-driving phenomenon represents the construction of a symbolic world in which factual and moral attributes are orderly and consistent.

Several other noteworthy studies have examined law enforcement from the perspective of its symbolic and ceremonial content. Skolnick found that police respond less to suspects' actual behavior than to their imagined behavior, which is determined by a model of the "symbolic assailant" to whom they are compared (Skolnick, 1966). Foucault's seminal study of punishment contrasted the physical punishment meted out by the French authorities in the past with the discipline and bureaucratic controls of modern society (Foucault, 1977). In the earlier period, the physical nature of punishment symbolized the absolute control of the state over a subject's body. In the modern period, the symbolism is one of control over the mind and the self through reshaping those who are disciplined. In this fashion, the deviant character of the criminal is constructed through the symbolic meaning of discipline. Lofland's study of state executions is somewhat similar in contrasting the public character of executions in eighteenth-century England with their impersonal, bureaucratic, and secretive nature in contemporary life. He maintains, however, that while executions in the earlier period symbolized the power of the state, today they are more bureaucratic and less dramaturgical and symbolic (Lofland, 1977).

These studies of politics and law have reconstructed the meanings of institutional procedures. They reject previous explanations of actions as solely instrumental or insignificant and underline significant aspects of the actions that are not oriented toward ostensible goals. They point to a presentational element in human behavior in which drama, symbol, and ritual are significant factors in the consciousness of social life.

The authors of these studies strongly imply that ritual and ceremony promote the authoritative, official, and public images of the society. In Lukes' words, "the symbolism of political ritual represents particular models or political paradigms of society and how it functions...it helps to define as authoritative certain ways of seeing society" (Lukes, 1975: 305). Verba makes the same point in his study of the Kennedy assassination (Verba, 1965). The nonpartisan character of the reaction to it and the familial, religious, and civic grieving ceremonies point to the role of the presidency in portraying the transcendent nature of the political community. The president's dual role—both partisan and communal—contrasts with the separation of these roles in the British institutions of prime minister and monarch. In similar fashion, Bellah has seen in these communal-political events the emergence of a secular yet civic religion (Bellah, 1980). Bocock has pointed to such events as part of a wide variety of ritual actions that he finds significant in modern life (Bocock, 1974).

Issues in Institutional Studies

Two sets of issues associated with how symbolism and ritual relate
to social structure and instrumental behavior divide many of the studies
described above. The first set raises the question of the interests and
goals of rituals, as well as the forms of symbolism; the second, the
question of whether social structure is implicated at all in ritual action.

Functional and Manipulative Theories.

The Durkheimian idea that rituals and myths are activities that
solidify and unite primitive societies has had a significant influence
in anthropology. This functionalist position has led to an emphasis
on the consensual basis and unifying effects of institutional ritual
and symbolism. Shils & Young's analysis of the British coronation
is exemplary of this approach, as is Bellah's discussion of civic
religion (Shils & Young, 1953; Bellah, 1980). Symbolic meanings
are viewed as producing harmony through the resolution of conflicts
or the reinforcement of existing sources of consensus. Others, e.g.,
Gusfield in his earlier work, have interpreted the polysemic character of political symbols as providing unity for one group in conflict
with others, thus creating more general "emblems of identity"
[Singer's phrase (1982)] in a diverse society (Gusfield, 1963).

A frequent criticism of these approaches has come from scholars
who stress power and class differences in modern societies and the
conflicting interests resulting from them. The symbolized consensus is then viewed either as an effort to hide and weaken sources of
conflict or as a mistaken attribution of greater and more widespread consensual beliefs than actually exist (Edelman, 1964; Lukes,
1975). The political symbolism described is thus held to be manipulative, a means by which one group advances or defends its
interests by exaggerating the degree of consensus and hiding the
realistic interests of other groups. Thus, potential conflicts in the
public arena are hidden from consciousness. From this standpoint,
the power differences in the society must form part of any analysis
of symbolic actions and political or legal rituals.

Expressive and Dramaturgical Perspectives.

Both the functional and manipulative perspectives are functionalist
in that they assess symbols and rituals from the standpoint of the
interests and values of instrumental behavior affected by such actions.
An emphasis on culture rather than social structure leads in another

direction. From a cultural standpoint, symbolic activities represent performances and presentations expressing perceptions of social life but not necessarily affecting behavior. In Geertz's phrasing, they are "models of" rather than "models for" (Geertz, 1973: 89–123). They provide basic categories and concepts for recognizing, expressing, and understanding society. In a famous critique of functional theories of totemism, Lévi-Strauss has remarked: "natural species are chosen not because they are 'good to eat' but because they are 'good to think'" (Lévi-Strauss, 1963: 89).

Both Gusfield (in his later work) and Manning emphasize the presentational or dramatic nature of the ritualization of myth in law enforcement (Gusfield, 1981; Manning, 1977). Such acts are viewed as communication rather than as a means to achieve goals. Their relationship to behavior is problematic, and they cannot be judged in instrumental, utilitarian terms. The consensual or conflicting elements represented provide a public or official set of categories, but they need not be assessed in relation to the social structure or to institutional functioning.

Studies of Secular Ritual

The studies reviewed above describe and analyze areas that sociologists have generally treated as characterized by instrumental behavior—where power and utilitarian interests allegedly provide one-dimensional meanings. In this section, we analyze two forms of ritual and symbolic action. In one, life-cycle ritual, the events are perceived as ritualistic, not as instrumental, behavior. The second, sports festivals, represents other activities where symbolism has been an object of analysis in the context of large, crowd-like interaction.

Life-Cycle Rituals

Van Gennep's early work on rites of passage in primitive societies has been the major influence on studies of the rituals and symbolism attending events such as weddings, graduations, and even funerals (Gennep, 1960 [1909]). V. Turner's work has also been important with its new orientation toward the ritual process (Turner, 1969; 1974). Turner views transition points as situations where the person is in limbo—with ambiguous, unstructured statuses. Such liminal states are threatening both to the self and to the social group at points at which the social structure is less compelling. In these situations, the antistructural elements of common human ties, which Turner labels *communitas*, gain importance.

The role of ritual in easing the transition from one place in the social structure to another occupies a central position in analyses of those transition points connected to biological processes—i.e., birth, puberty, procreation, aging, and death. In his study of rites of passage in primitive and modern societies, Young asserts that the dramatizing and symbolizing aspects of such rituals produce more intense emotions. This intensification, in turn, helps alleviate tension and incorporate the person into a new role. The ritual both symbolizes the anomalies of the liminal state and resolves them in new roles (Young, 1965).

In his general analysis of ritual in industrial societies, Bocock analyzes baptisms, weddings, and funerals (Bocock, 1974). He concludes that such crisis points lead to ritualization, often through religion. There is a general trend away from religious ritual and toward secular forms, however, especially in weddings and funerals.

The conception of rites of passage is transferable, however, to other parts of social existence. Barbara Meyerhoff has analyzed a graduation ceremony at a Jewish Senior Citizen's Center in Los Angeles (Meyerhoff, 1977). These ceremonies, which follow a course of study, unite aspects of the sense of individuality and of collective membership. Through the sequencing of diverse symbols, a unity of secular and religious, of individual and of group membership is achieved. Zerubavel's study of time rhythms in modern life emphasizes the segregation and segmentation of areas of life by time (Zerubavel, 1981). In his analysis of sacred and profane time, he suggests that rituals emerge to express and symbolize the liminal states at the margins of time, such as twilight in the passage from profane time to sacred time in the Jewish Sabbath. Gusfield has applied a similar idea in his analysis of how drinking alcohol is a symbol of the passage from day to night and from daily rounds to the weekend, i.e., from serious work attitudes to a period of play and leisure (Gusfield, 1984). McAndrews & Edgerton (1969) and Cavan (1966) have analyzed time and space in drinking behavior and use a complementary concept of "time out." They explain drunkenness and drinking less as responses to the chemical attributes of alcohol than as a product of the meaning symbolized by the use of alcohol and the space or time of its consumption.

Sports and Festivals

Sports and festivals both involve the gathering of large crowds around relatively fixed and recurrent events. It is crowd behavior that differentiates these events from life-cycle rituals. MacAloon's unique analysis of the elements of spectacle, game, ritual, and festivity present at the modern Olympic games can be applied to other sports events as well (MacAloon, 1981).

Sports and festivals are also alike in being framed events of limited time and space. Within the frame, they can assume properties laden with polysemic meanings. In his study of the Olympic games, for example, MacAloon analyzes the symbols of both nation and individual, of separateness and commonality—themes symbolized both by the sports events as a whole and in the specific rites and spectacles of the Olympics (MacAloon, 1981; 1982).

This theme of the dialectical unity and simultaneous coexistence of opposites is salient in the studies of festivals. Turner's concept of *communitas* as antistructure is found in several of the articles in the recent volume on celebrations, especially those by Grimes and Wiggins (Wiggins, 1982; Grimes, 1982). The Saturnalia element is an enactment of the unity that cuts across the hierarchies of structure, reversing social structure or erasing status differences by building a common mood, a common experience. As MacAloon maintains—both for the Olympics and for festivities in general—"international sport is politics conducted as sociability" (MacAloon, 1982: 269). In these analyses, solidarity is fostered both by the character of the symbols carried by objects, performances, and costumes and also by the common experiences of communality. As Turner says, "much that has been bound is liberated, notably the sense of comradeship and communion" (Turner, 1982: 29).

Another theme discussed in this literature is the unique way in which the framed event can take ordinary actions from diverse settings and put them together to heighten and transfigure the festive experiences (DaMatta, 1977). Grimes analyzed the Fiesta of Santa Fe, New Mexico, and a drama group's Public Exploration Projects in Toronto (Grimes, 1976, 1982). In the Santa Fe study, he found a "super-structuring" theme, ritually symbolizing the benefits of authority and solemnly accounting for the resultant festive atmosphere. In Toronto, in contrast, he discovered a ritual "deconstruction." The goal there was not a solemn support of social structure but rather a taking apart of that structure, i.e., of provoking new and outrageous actions. Both events had a festive atmosphere, however.

Symbolism and Everyday Life

There is another group of studies that exemplify the importance of symbolic meanings in sociological analysis, but neither is related to the institutional order nor examines highly public events. They include studies of consumer goods, especially food. The theoretical significance of several of these studies lies in the cognitive approach used. In addition to the functionalist and dramaturgical theories already discussed, we thus add the category of structuralist perspectives, exemplified especially by the work of Mary Douglas.

Consumer Goods

Thorstein Veblen's early study of status symbols has had a profound impact on much of the contemporary analysis of symbolism as well as of consumership (Veblen, 1931 [1899]). Despite his influence, however, there have been few direct studies of the symbolic process in the development or use of goods as status symbols.

Recently, however, sociologists and anthropologists have begun to look at economic behavior from a more cultural standpoint. In a major theoretical statement, Sahlins maintains that material objects cannot be understood, either in modern or in primitive societies, solely by reference to instrumental utilities (Sahlins, 1976). His analysis of food and clothing in America stresses the latent meanings of goods. For example, the exclusion of dogs and horses from categories of edibles in American culture cannot be understood apart from their meanings as "human objects" (Sahlins, 1976: Ch. 4).

Consumption, a basic economic category, is thus reconstituted as a system of information and as a relationship between consumer and object. An understanding of the latent meanings of each good is needed in order to make the economist's consumption function a usable concept. In their study of that function, Douglas & Isherwood (1979) stress the primacy of such cultural codes for the study of economic behavior. Goods stabilize and dramatize basic cultural categories. In their discussion of different modes of grinding coffee—by machine or by mortar and pestle—they point out (relying on Barthes' treatment) that one stems from an impersonal world in which metal and machine produce an impersonal dust, while the other is a human process producing a gritty powder and seeming analogous to ancient alchemy. Choosing one over the other is not a utilitarian matter, as Barthes also pointed out (1979). The choice is "between two different views of the human condition and between metaphysical judgments lying just below the surface of the question" (Douglas & Isherwood, 1979: 74). Goods should thus be seen as marking devices, i.e., as modes of classifying persons and events.

A less structuralist account that is more similar to Veblen's work is found in Csikszentmihalyi & Rochberg-Halton's analysis of the survey they conducted in 1974 (Csikszentmihalyi & Rochberg-Halton, 1981). They asked a sample of families about the meanings of various objects in the home and of the home itself. They discovered the importance of the latent rather than the manifest characteristic of objects. They found that there is a close relationship between objects, the home, and the development of self. There were sharp differences between age and sex groups, for example. Objects were much more repositories of memories for older than for younger family members.

Food

The symbolic study of food has been the central concern of several major analyses. We have described Sahlins' discussion of the status of dogs and horses in American life as reflective of the cultural definition of their quasihuman character. Lévi-Strauss has built an elaborate model of cultural understanding based on the linguistic structures distinguishing the raw and the cooked (Lévi-Strauss, 1969). He uses these distinctions in cooking as examples of general elements discoverable in other aspects of cultures that illustrate the contrast and conflict between nature and culture.

This same search for homologous elements is also found in the now classic paper by M. Douglas, "Deciphering a Meal," as well as in her analysis of British meals. Unlike Lévi-Strauss, Douglas uses cultural categories rather than linguistic structures (Douglas, 1975; Douglas & Nicod, 1974). In her analysis of Hebraic dietary laws, she finds a similarity between the bounded character of foods (clean/unclean; clear/ambiguous) and the ancient Hebrews' social concern with retaining the boundaries between themselves and others. In both, there is an interdiction of ambiguous states; animals not easily classified are tabooed, for example (Douglas, 1966). In this fashion, the meal, in contemporary as well as other societies, both reflects and reinforces fundamental cultural categories. Thus food, as a matter of cognition, symbolizes social relationships and institutions. R. Barthes has analyzed modern food habits from the perspective of semiology, treating foods as systems of signs. For example, sugar can be seen as a product of indulgence, of sweetness, as exemplified in the American popular song, "Sugar Time" (Barthes, 1979).

These studies of consumership and food are indicative of the importance—derived from symbolic and structuralist anthropology—of a cognitive approach to symbolism. Unlike the functional or dramaturgical orientations, the cognitive approach emphasizes the cultural categories that give meanings to objects and events beyond their manifest or instrumental ones. These meanings emerge through the nature of the cultural or linguistic categories by which members of a society perceive and think about their experiences. In a study of social stratification, B. Schwartz has examined the categories of up and down high and low, as terms for describing and experiencing class and status hierarchies. He believes that they originate in the biological relationship between a dependent infant and an overpowering parent (Schwartz, 1981).

Interaction

Despite the seminal importance and great influence of Erving Goffman's dramaturgical studies of face-to-face interaction, we have not discussed his work in depth. It has been reviewed extensively elsewhere, and his concerns with symbolism have been peripheral. Although deeply concerned with how meanings are created and managed, Goffman deals largely with manifest, literal meanings that are often instrumentally patterned. In the famous essay on role-distance, for example, the posture and visage of the adults riding the carousel are calculated to present themselves as people not "seriously" riding a merry-go-round, not "really" childish (Goffman, 1961:97–99). Such analyses, like M. Davis' (1983) phenomenological study of sexuality, are marginal to the symbolic studies reviewed here.

Mass Communications and Popular Culture

We have not included this area in our review because scholars in this field, as well as in the sociologies of religion and art, have long accepted symbolic and ritual analyses. The work of Orrin Klapp, however, is both difficult to classify and important. In an early work, Klapp studied celebrities, including movie stars, sport figures, and politicians, as well as TV personalities. He found that the emergence of such "symbolic leaders" is one aspect of the public dramas a mass society observes, in contrast to the conventional, communal interactions of earlier societies. These leaders become symbols of abstract roles and orientations and serve as points of identity in modern life (Klapp, 1964). In a later work, he assesses a range of social movements and collective behavior, including fads, fashions, and cults (Klapp, 1969). He interprets many aspects of these behaviors as resulting from the disappearance of ritual and symbolic elements in modern life. Thus, he argues, the mobility of persons and physical environments destroys the symbolic significance of a space that was suffused with memories. The standardization of goods weakens the ritualistic and symbolic attributes of class, age, etc. In this situation, people resort to highly individualistic modes of gaining and presenting identities, including forms of "ego screaming" and "style rebellion," by which they symbolize and ritualize themselves and their positions in the social structure.

Methodological Issues

Issues of Location

Manning's study, *Police Work* (1977), illustrates the general problems of determining the people for whom the meanings are symbolic. Manning concludes that the presentation of police work as a "cops and robbers story," which is buttressed by an emphasis on crime statistics, conveys an image of police that symbolizes their activities and capacities in ways that are not accurate. The public is led to believe that police have greater control over crime than they actually do.

But who believes the "police myth?" The police, the police management, or only the general public? Is Manning, as the scientific observer, occupying a privileged position as the "true" observer of the symbolic and ritual character of the myth? Does the police myth lie on a spectrum with cynical manipulation at one end and naïve belief at the other? The observer's role in locating the source of symbolic meanings is, as Spiro (1969) has pointed out, a central problem and one seldom addressed in symbolic analysis.

Dimensionality

In several of the studies reviewed here, it is uncertain just what the discovery of symbolic meanings is meant to explain. The relationships among other elements, such as social structure or biological factors, are often vague. Especially in studies emphasizing the cognitive role of culture, there seems to be an either/or implication: culture or social structure, symbolic or instrumental meaning. This ambiguity is a major part of J. Goody's criticism of the studies of food by Lévi-Strauss, Sahlins, and Douglas:

> there is little evidence, except of a purely *post hoc* kind, on which to base the claim that the decisive element in the selection of alternative possibilities…is solely, or even mainly, the voice of this abstract structure. (Goody, 1982: 35)

References

Arnold, T. 1935. *The Symbols of Government*. New Haven, CT: Yale University Press.

Barfield, O. 1960. The Meaning of the Word "Literal." In L. C. Knights and B. Cottle (eds.) *Metaphor & Symbol* London: Butterworth.

Barthes, R. 1979. Towards a Psychosociology of Food and Consumption. In R. Forster and O. Rawum (eds.) *Food and Drink in History*. Baltimore: Johns Hopkins University Press.

Bellah, R. N. 1980. Civil Religion in America In R. N. Bellah *Beyond Belief: Essays on Religion in a Post-Traditional World*. New York: Harper & Row.

Birnbaum, N. 1955. "Monarchs and Sociologists: A Reply to Mr. Shils and Mr. Young." *Sociological Review* (NS) 3: 5–23.

Bocock, R. 1974. *Ritual in Industrial Society*. London: Allen & Unwin.

Brown, R. H. 1977. *A Poetic for Sociology*. Cambridge: Cambridge University Press.

Burke, K. 1957. *The Philosophy of Literary Form*. New York: Vintage.

Carson, W. G. 1976. "Symbolic and Instrumental Dimensions of Early Factory Legislation." In R. Hood (ed.) *Crime, Criminology and Public Policy: Essays in Honor of Sir Leon Radzinowicz*. New York: The Free Press.

Cavan, S. 1966. *Liquor License: An Ethnography of Bar Behavior*. Chicago: Aldine.

Chandler, D. B. 1976. *Capital Punishment: A Social Study of Repressive Law*. Toronto: McClelland & Steward.

Csikszentmihalyi, M., and E. Rochberg-Halton. 1981. *The Meaning of Things: Domestic Symbols and the Self*. Cambridge: Cambridge University Press.

DaMatta, R. 1977. "Constraint and License: A Preliminary Study of Two Brazilian Rituals." In S. Moore and B. Meyerhoff (eds.) *Secular Ritual*. Amsterdam: Van Gorcum.

Davis, F. 1982. "On the 'Symbolic' in Symbolic Interactions." *Symbolic Interaction* 5:111–26.

Davis, M. 1983. *Smut: Erotic Reality/Obscene Ideology*. Chicago: University of Chicago Press.

Dolgin, J. L., D. S. Kemnitzer, and D. M. Schneider. 1977. *Symbolic Anthropology*. New York: Columbia University Press.

Douglas, M. 1966. *Purity and Danger: An Analysis of the Concepts of Pollution and Taboo*. London: Routledge and Kegan Paul.

_____. 1975. "Deciphering a Meal." In M. Douglas (ed.) *Implicit Meanings: Essays in Anthropology*. London: Routledge and Kegan Paul.

Douglas, M., and B. Isherwood. 1979. *The World of Goods*. New York: Basic Books.

Douglas, M., and M. Nicod. 1974. "Taking the Biscuit: The Structure of British Meals." *New Sociology*, (December 19): 744–47.

Duncan, H. D. 1968. *Symbols in Society*. New York: Oxford University Press.

_____. 1969. *Symbols and Social Theory*. New York: Oxford University Press.

Durkheim, E. 1947. *The Elementary Forms of the Religious Life*. Glencoe, IL: Free Press.

Edelman, M. 1964. *The Symbolic Uses of Politics*. Urbana, IL: University of Illinois Press.

_____. 1971. *Politics as Symbolic Action*. New York: Academic Press.

_____. 1977. *Political Language*. New York: Academic Press.

Firth, R. 1973. *Symbols: Public and Private*. Ithaca, NY: Cornell University Press.

Foucault, M. 1977. *Discipline and Punish: The Birth of the Prison*. New York: Pantheon.

Frank, J. 1936. *Law and the Modern Mind*. New York: Tudor Press.

Garfinkel, H. 1956. "Conditions of Successful Degradation Ceremonies." *American Journal of Sociology* 61:420–424.

Geertz, C. 1973. *The Interpretation of Cultures*. New York: Basic Books.

Gennep, Van A. 1960 [1909]. *The Rites of Passage*. Chicago: University of Chicago Press.

Giddens, A. 1976. *New Rules of Sociological Method*. New York: Basic Books.

Goffman, E. 1961. *Encounters: Two Studies in the Sociology of Interaction*. Indianapolis, IN: Bobbs-Merrill.

Goody, J. 1977. *The Domestication of the Savage Mind*. Cambridge: Cambridge University Press.

_____. 1982. *Cooking, Cuisine and Class*. Cambridge: Cambridge University Press.

Grimes, R. L. 1976. *Symbol and Conquest: Public Ritual and Drama in Santa Fe*. Ithaca, NY: Cornell University Press.

_____. 1982. "The Lifeblood of Public Ritual: Fiestas and Public Exploration Projects." In V. Turner (ed.) *Celebration*. Washington, DC: Smithsonian Institution Press.

Gusfield, J. 1963. *Symbolic Crusade: Status Politics and the American Temperance Movement*. Urbana: University of Illinois Press.

_____. 1981. *The Culture of Public Problems: Drinking-Driving and the Symbolic Order*. Chicago: University of Chicago Press.

_____. 1984. "Passage to Play: The Ritual of Drink in Industrial Society." In M. Douglas (ed.) *The Anthropology of Drink,: Hospitality and Competition*. Cambridge: Cambridge University Press.

238   Performing Action

Klapp, O. E. 1964. *Symbolic Leaders: Public Dramas and Public Men*. Chicago: Aldine.

_____. 1969. *Collective Search for Identity*. New York: Holt, Rinehart & Winston.

Lane, C. 1981. *The Rites of Rulers*. New York: Columbia University Press.

Leach, E. 1976. *Culture and Communication*. Cambridge: Cambridge University Press.

Lévi-Strauss, C. 1963. *Totemism*. Boston: Beacon Press.

_____. 1966. *The Savage Mind*. Chicago: University of Chicago Press.

_____. 1969. *The Raw and the Cooked: Introduction to a Science of Mythology*. New York: Harper Torchbooks.

Levy-Bruhl, L. 1966 [1923]. *How Natives Think*. New York: Washington Square.

Lofland, J. 1977. "The Dramaturgy of State Executions." In H. Bleackley and J. Lofland (eds.) *State Executions Viewed Historically and Sociologically*. Montclair, NJ: Patterson Smith.

Lukes, S. 1975. "Political Ritual and Social Integration." *Sociology* 9: 289–308.

MacAloon, J. J. 1981. *This Great Symbol: Pierre Coubertin and the Origins of the Modern Olympic Games*. Chicago: University of Chicago Press.

_____. 1982. "Sociation and Sociability in Political Celebrations." In V. Turner, (ed.) *Celebration*. Washington, DC: Smithsonian Institution Press.

Malinowski, B. 1954. *Magic, Science and Religion*. Garden City, NJ: Doubleday Anchor.

Manning, P. 1977. Police Work: *The Social Organization of Policing*. Cambridge, MA: The MIT Press.

McAndrews, C., and R. B. Edgerton. 1969. *Drunken Comportment: A Social Explanation*. Chicago: Aldine.

Meyerhoff, B. 1977. "We Don't Wrap Herring in a Printed Paper." In S, Moore and B. Meyerhoff, *Secular Ritual*. Amsterdam: Van Gorcum.

Nagendra, S. P. 1971. *The Concept of Ritual in Modern Sociological Theory*. New Delhi: Acad. J. India.

Peirce, C. S. 1931. *Collected Papers*, Vol. 2. Cambridge, MA: Harvard University Press.

Ricoeur, P. 1978. "Metaphor and the Main Problem of Hermeneutics." In C. S. Reagan and D. Stewart (eds.) *The Philosophy of Paul Ricoeur*. Boston: Beacon Press.

Rothman, R. 1978. "The First Amendment: Symbolic Import—Ambiguous Prescription." *Res. Law Sociol.* 1:26–40.

Sahlins, M. 1976. *Culture and Practical Reason*. Chicago: University of Chicago Press.

Schwartz, B. 1981. *Vertical Classification: A Study in Structuralism and the Sociology of Knowledge*. Chicago: University of Chicago Press.

Shils, E., and M. Young. 1953. "The Meaning of the Coronation." *Sociological Review* (NS) 1: 63–81.

Singer, M. 1982. Emblems of Identity: A Semiotic Exploration. In J. Maquest (ed.) *On Symbols in Anthropology: Essays in Honor of Harry Hojer*. Malibu, CA: Undena.

Skolnick, J. 1966. *Justice without Trial*. New York: John Wiley.

Sperber, D. 1974. *Rethinking Symbolism*. Cambridge: Cambridge University Press.

Spiro, M. E. 1969. "Discussion." In R. F. Spencer (ed.) *Forms of Symbolic Action*. Seattle: University of Washington Press.

Turner, V. W. 1967. *The Forest of Symbols: Aspects of Ndembu Ritual*. Ithaca, NY: Cornell University Press.

_____. 1969. *The Ritual Process*. Chicago: Aldine.

_____. 1974. *Dramas, Fields and Metaphors: Symbolic Action in Human Society.* Ithaca, NY: Cornell University Press.

Turner, V. W. (ed.) 1982. *Celebration: Studies in Festivity and Ritual.* Washington, DC: Smithsonian Institution Press.

Veblen, T. 1931 [1899]. *The Theory of the Leisure Class.* New York: Modern Press.

Verba, S. 1965. "The Kennedy Assassination and the Nature of Political Commitment." In B. S. Greenberg and E. B. Parker (eds.) *The Kennedy Assassination and the American Public.* Stanford, CA: Stanford University Press.

Weber, M. 1946. From Max Weber: *Essays in Sociology.* New York: Oxford University Press.

Wiggins, W. H. 1982. "They Closed the Town Up, Man! Reflections on the Civic and Political Dimensions of Juneteenth." In V. Turner (ed.) *Celebration.* Washington: DC: Smithsonian Institution Press.

Young, F. 1965. *Initiation Ceremonies.* Indianapolis, IN: Bobbs-Merrill.

Zerubavel, E. 1981. *Hidden Rhythms.* Chicago: University of Chicago Press.

Zurcher, L., and G. R. Kirkpatrick. 1976. *Citizens for Decency.* Austin: University of Texas Press.

11

Nature's Body and the Metaphors of Food and Health

> *"No diet comes without a larger social agenda"*
>
> —*Hillel Schwartz, p.37*

"The doctrines which men ostensibly hold" wrote the British historian Leslie Stephen, "do not become operative upon their conduct until they have generated an imaginative symbolism". (Stephens, 1927: II, p.329. Quoted in Schorer, 1959: 25) "Imaginative symbolism" pervades the cultural frames by which human beings constitute their experience and provides the sense of order and understanding through which sense is made of events and objects. A study of symbols and their meanings is an essential part of sociological analysis and inherent in the study of cultures.

The human body is a perpetual source of meaning and an object of historical variation. It is an instrument of purpose and a goal of aesthetic perfection. It can be attractive or repulsive; glorified or transcended; covered with adornment or exposed and revealed. How the body is conceived and how human beings act toward it is as much a matter of culture and history as are the manners and morals of food habits and the canons of sexual behavior. The human body is at once both a physiological and anatomical entity and a cultural object.

From M. Lamont and M. Fournier, eds., *Cultivating Differences: Symbolic Boundaries and the Making of Inequality,* Chicago: University of Chicago Press, 1992. Reprinted by permission of the publisher. All rights reserved.

An inquiry into the meaning of body is both a descriptive account of how men and women act toward their bodies and an analytic exploration of how such actions are linked to other aspects of life. "The body," wrote Jayme Sokolow, "symbolizes the struggle between order and disorder in all societies." (Sokolow, 1983: 92) An analysis of the meanings of health and food is a search for such symbolisms and a hunt for possible social and political orders to which they might be related. This chapter is such a search, using the symbolism of Nature and Culture in a discourse on the natural foods movements of the nineteenth and twentieth centuries as a means for conducting that search.[1]

Culture can be thought of a set of possible meanings that can be drawn upon to constitute experienced realities (Schutz, 1967; Swidler, 1986). There are many examples of how objects are differently constituted in differing historical contexts. How the object "child" is perceived has varied in Western history. At times, children have been experienced as small adults and have had attributed to them the same motivations, understandings, and moral responsibilities as adults (Aries, 1962). Another example of how culture constitutes the experience of objects and events is given in the very conception of art. To "see" artistic products as creative "for their own sake," to be contemplated rather than for some other end such as religious, instructive, or decorative is not given in the nature of artistic production. It did not emerge until the eighteenth century (Abrams, 1985). Conversely, symbols and myths may appear as continuous archetypes, appearing again and again in history. Such is the "myth of the eternal return," of a golden age to which humans dream of returning (Eliade, Frye, 1957). Symbols such as Nature or Primitive can occur frequently in history. They exist as part of the stock of symbols, ideas, myths, images, and legends capable of being drawn upon in particular periods (G. Boas and Lovejoy, 1935; H. White, 1972; Stocking, 1989).

The conception of culture as the a priori categories constituting the possibility of experience has presented a methodological problem for the sociological analysis of ideas. The key concepts of the sociologist have been, and I assert still are, those of social structure, hierarchy, and social group. The Marxian principle that existence determines consciousness has summed up a major part of sociological weaponry. In the general intellectual movement of the social sciences in the past two decades that dogma has seemed less and less viable and its reverse increasingly relevant.

The relation between culture and social structure remains a major intellectual problem of sociological method. This paper is one effort in reconciling concepts that are on the verge of divorce. In it, I examine the concept of "Nature" as it takes on divergent meanings in differing social contexts, with differing consequences and understandings in relation to the social structure and to the perception of the body. While "the body" is a common object, its symbolic properties, its meanings, may be distinctly different in different contexts.

The cultural symbols and meanings that order experience do not exist in an abstract vacuum. They possess implications for living that operate for and against groups and institutions. In most societies such symbols and meanings do not exist homogeneously, shared by everyone. Concepts of health and of food, which will be analyzed here, are symbols of who and what we are and of who and what we are not. Such symbols take on meanings that, implicitly or explicitly, have a structural as well as a cultural meaning. They not only order experience but they order it in distinction from other meanings and from others who manifest counter-meanings. In this paper, my theme is not only the meanings and symbols through which health and eating are espoused. It is also the structural contexts that provide meanings that are more temporal and spatial than the cultural meanings and symbols. The contrasts between "folk medicine" and professional medicine and between natural foods and commercial foods provide different contexts of understanding. They create and maintain boundaries that define loyalties and provide distinctions that draw upon and accentuate social conflicts and aspirations rooted in social structure. Eating is not only a physiological process. It is also a form of self-production through communication. We ingest symbolic forms.

Contrasts and conflicts between differing cultural and structural forms set the framework for this analysis of the natural foods movements of the nineteenth and twentieth centuries. A basic struggle between the hedonistic tenets of a market economy and the abstemiousness of philosophies and religions of self-control, between the needs for social order and the fears of social control, lie deep within American individualism. These form a context within which diet and health become differently interlocked in the movements of the 1830s and the 1950s.

The Counter-Culture of Popular Medicine

American movements to reform how we eat have always been set in the context of health. Historians and social critics interested in the forms of recreation, leisure, and play have discussed at length the similarities and differences in play within social structures. Varieties of entertainment, activities of play, and rules of morality between classes have been the focus of studies and critical essays (Burke, 1970; Gans, 1974; E. P. Thompson, 1974). The customary terms used to describe such divisions have been those of a "popular" or "folk" culture and those of an "elite" or "high" culture. These contrasts have been drawn from a class or other hierarchical order in which a more powerful group or institution, such as church officials or a social elite, attempt to control or change the behavior of those lower on the ladder of power and prestige (Rosenzweig, 1983; Burke, 1970).

The distinction is drawn in another fashion when scholars of medicine and health discuss the practice of medicine and the idea of health as it is pursued within and without the institutions of medical care embodied in doctors, nurses, clinics, hospitals, and patients. The distinctions are less those of class and more those of formal training and informal, untrained "folk belief." The terms become those of "professional" medicine and "folk" medicine. The latter is also discussed as "alternative" medicine and sometimes "quackery" (Starr, 1982; Shryock, 1931). I choose to retain the terms "elite" and "popular" in order to convey the more detached sense that common terms, used in other arenas, help to maintain.

The claim of Science to have advanced human welfare through medical discovery is one of the most telling arguments for the idea of progress in the twentieth century. Civilization, through scientific research, has protected us against disease and deterioration and lengthened life while making it more comfortable. It is in the development of knowledge and technical equipment that health can be produced and extended. Contemporary institutional, professional medicine rests on the belief that there is a special body of knowledge and technical skill such that only those trained in it can help to cure sickness and prevent illness. This is a definition of the medical institution. Specially accredited persons, doctors and nurses, and specially equipped arenas (clinics and hospitals) represent the institutionalized form of scientific medicine. It is to these persons and these spaces that legitimate medicine should be practiced and only there that health can be achieved (Parsons 1951: Ch. 10).

The triumphs of scientific research advanced and supported the claim of the professional to know more and be more skilled in prevention, diagnosis, and treatment of disease than the layperson who lacked the training and the technology. Without the progress that science has made, the claims of a medical elite to legitimate authority would lack credibility and trust.

The medical institution and professional medicine emerge as attributes of Culture; products of an historical development in which Nature is overcome and improved upon. Popular medicine is a claim to achieve health without doctors, apart from the activities of medical institutions. Within this contrast, health is not an attribute of scientific knowledge, dependent upon an elite of professionals, but is within the grasp of the ordinary person. It needs no special training or expensive equipment. The populace, Everyman, the untrained, non-professionalized, are their own physicians, their own healers. The "natural man" is as much an authority in matters of health as is the Ph.D. and the M.D. If elite medicine is conceptualized as the legitimate institution then popular medicine can be considered a counter-medicine and part of a counter-culture.

It is unwarranted to sum up all of popular medicine in any single, easy description. Its populist idea is inherent in the description of popular medicine as the medicine of the nonprofessional. This is a unifying sentiment in much, though not all and not in same manner, among the dissenting medical reform movements of the nineteenth and much of the alternative medicine of the twentieth centuries. In that respect the situation is not unlike that expressed by the sectarian leader of the botanic medicine of the early nineteenth century, Samuel Thomson. The study of medicine, he wrote, was "no more necessary to mankind at large, to qualify them to administer relief from pain and sickness, than to a cook in preparing food to satisfy hunger" (Quoted in Starr, p. 52).

This distinction between popular and elite medicine marks a boundary essential to the understanding of natural foods movements. Such movements are a constituent of popular medicine and need to be seen in contrasts to practices and philosophies of medicine as conducted within elite institutions.

Food as Social Symbol and Metaphor

My use of culture and its embodiment in food is a perspective focused on the understanding of meanings. From this viewpoint, culture can be seen as symbol systems with which life is organized into an understandable set of actions and events (Gusfield, 1981). Clifford Geertz has stated this in an excellent fashion:

> Both so-called cognitive and so-called expressive symbols or symbol-systems have, then, at least one thing in common: they are extrinsic sources of information in terms of which human life can be patterned—extrapersonal mechanisms for the perception, understanding, judgment and manipulation of the world. Culture patterns...are "programs"; they provide a template or blueprint for the organization of social and psychological processes. (Geertz, 1973: 216)

That food and drink are used as symbols of social position and status is an old theme in sociology. Thorstein Veblen's classic study of conspicuous consumption and status symbols created a mode of analysis which has been the staple of sociological studies of consumer behavior since its original publication in 1899 (Veblen, 1934). More recently, the study of food and drink has been as attentive to the text—the content of consumption—as to its context-the setting and the participants (M. Douglas, *Food in the Social Order*, 1984: 1-39). Mary Douglas, probably the leading figure in this reinterest in an anthropology of food, makes the distinction between the interest in food as material and as symbolic by referring to eating as a "field of action. It is a medium in which other levels of categorization become manifest" (M. Douglas, 1984: 30). In her own analyses of British meals and of the Judaic rules of *kashruth* she has demonstrated how what is eaten and how it is eaten constitute a mode of communication and can be read as a cultural object, embodying the attributes of social organization or general culture (M. Douglas, 1975).

Others have made use of somewhat similar orientations to the study of food. Sahlin's distinction between animals that are improper to eat and those proper to eat in Western societies laid emphasis on the "human-like" qualities attributed to "pets," such as dogs, horses, and cats as compared to those perceived as less than human, such as pigs, sheep, and cattle (Sahlins, 1976). Barthes analysis of steak as a male food or sugar as symbolic of a "sweet time" again show the use of food as a system of signs and symbols capable of being read for their meaning for what they say as well as what they denote as material sustenance (Barthes, 1973; 1979; also see Farb and Armelagos, 1980: Ch. 5). Lévi-Strauss' *The Raw and the Cooked* is, perhaps, the seminal work in this approach to the study of food as a symbol and as a medium of communication (Lévi-Strauss, 1969).

In his analysis of taste and social structure, Pierre Bourdieu presents both an empirical study of consumer habits and an interpretive theory which, applied to food and drink, sees in the content of meals and foods, the communication and representation of more general orientations to life styles. In his surveys of the French population, Bourdieu found sharp differences in both the foods eaten and the nature of meals among various classes and occupational groups. Among the working classes, the emphasis in eating is on the material and the familial. Guests not closely related to the household are seldom invited. The sequence of courses is unimportant. The changing of plates is minimal. The food itself is heavy and filling, a focus on plenty. There is a sharp division between male food and female food and a lack of concern for food as creating health or beauty of body. Among petite-bourgeoisie and the bourgeoisie, the opposite is the case. The meal is an occasion for social interaction; it is regulated in manners and sequences; it is preoccupied with considerations of health and aesthetic consequences (Bourdieu, 1984: 177-200).

Bourdieu reads these empirical differences as the existence of distinctive class-based tastes, part of fundamental and deep-seated styles of life. In emphasizing the meal as an occasion of social relationships, the bourgeoisie deny the primary, material function of eating and maintain the integration of familial with the more disciplined areas of life. Order, restraint, and propriety may not be abandoned. In this they express a dimension of the bourgeois orientation to society as a matter of refinement and regulation, of a "stylization of life" which "tends to shift the emphasis from substance and function to form and manner, and so to deny the crudely material reality of eating and of the things consumed or...the basely material vulgarity of those who indulge in the immediate satisfactions of food and drink" (Bourdieu, 1984: 196).

To describe a structural context is not to deduce the behavior from a social situation, as a direct response or solution to perceived social problems. Food and body can better be seen as possessing levels of meanings, as being polysemic (Turner, 1967; Leach ,1976; Gusfield and Michelowicz, 1984). On one level, they connote a literal, substantive meaning. The relation between food and health, at this level, is physiological. It does not connote an attitude toward social order. At other levels, however, it can be read as a language in which the experience of the user, of the author, creates a metaphorical level that symbolizes other domains of understanding with which the literal is connected (Douglas, 1975; 1984; Farb and Amelagos, 1980). To see steak as a food symbolic of masculinity is to observe the symbolic properties with which it has become invested in some modern societies (Barthes, 1973). The metaphorical attributes are connected by a common vision of the world, by a way of stylizing activity (Bourdieu, 1984). It is these diverse yet connected levels and domains of meaning that constitute the object of my analysis of natural foods movements.

The Natural Foods Movement: Sylvester Graham and the 1830s

The American "natural foods" movement has its origins as a movement in the 1830s, in a period of intensive religious reawakening and a deep concern over the immorality and crime associated with emergent urbanization (Nissenbaum, 1980; Sokolow, 1983; Schwartz, 1986). These were also the years in which a new public attitude toward sexuality was emerging as well as a transformation of public ideas about alcohol. It was also a period in which many were experiencing the transformation of American society from a traditional, hierarchical community to one of greater openness and individuality. The authority of past institutions, especially that of family, was seen as declining and generational conflict was enhanced as family and apprenticeship forms played less and less of a role in determining career. It was especially the demise of familial and church authority that spelled danger and fear among many, although it was also the source of satisfaction to others (Smith-Rosenberg, 1978; Rothman, 1971). It is against this background that the rise of the American natural foods movement in the 1830s can be understood.

Sylvester Graham is usually taken as the major figure in the development of the idea system associated with food avoidances and beliefs about the dangers to health from modern food technology. Graham, who was an ordained Presbyterian minister, was not a medical professional. He had, however, read and been influenced by two French physiologists, Bichat and Broussais, and by the American physician and health reformer, Benjamin Rush. While serving as an organizer for the American Temperance Society, he came to prominence in the early 1830s through his lectures on health in New York and Philadelphia during the cholera epidemic of 1832.

The physiological principles that Graham had received were coupled with an orientation toward modern life that emphasized the destructive impact of modern "refinements" on food, morality, and health. By the 1830s, Americans began to experience a transformation from self-sufficient farming, at least of their own food, toward a commercialization of foodstuffs. Graham was particularly appalled at the production of bread outside the home, in commercial bakeries. In seeking to appeal to the palates of their consumers, the refinement of flour produced a less grainy, less fibrous bread, one that was whiter than the coarse, dark bread with which Americans had been familiar in an earlier era. Graham was convinced that this loss of fiber was detrimental to health. In his lectures and writings he preached against the use of refined flour and against the consumption of white bread (Graham, 1839). He developed a form of bread that retained the natural fibrous qualities in a foodstuff called the "Graham cracker," still in use in American homes today.

Bread is, of course, a central part of the diet and, as a consequence, a frequent object of symbolization. The breaking of bread as a symbol of solidarity or the use of the wafer in the Eucharist are examples. In writing and speaking about the advantages of raw, unrefined flour, Graham waxed nostalgic over the associations of bread with home and hearth:

> Who that can look back 30 or 40 years to those blessed days of New England's prosperity and happiness, when our good mothers used to make the family bread, but can well remember how long and how patiently those excellent matrons stood over their bread troughs, kneading and molding their dough? And who with such recollections cannot also well remember the delicious bread that those mothers used invariably to set before them? There was a natural sweetness and richness in it which made it always desirable." (Graham, 1839, v. 2: 448-449)

But Graham and the Grahamites went much beyond an attack on refined flour. Graham's scheme for the understanding of ill health was built on an assumed relation between excitation and debility (Nissenbaum, 1980). The excitement that certain foods created was dangerous to the body. The refined flour produced in commercial agriculture deprived the body of needed coarse fiber. But it is not alone the direct effects of diet on the body that alarmed Graham. It was also the effects of sexual desire and sexual intercourse on health.

Limits to lust were essential to human health as were limits to gluttony. Meat, spices, sugar, coffee, tea, and alcohol, like sex, were other forms of excitation that were also deleterious to the body. So, too, was the nervousness created by the pace of urban life. The resulting stimulation risked destroying a natural health that previous generations, and primitive peoples, instinctually knew and followed.

Graham's view of the debilitating consequences of "excessive" sexual stimulation and intercourse should be seen against the growing Puritanism of American sexual norms. That Puritanism which Europeans frequently see as part of American culture does not emerge until the 1830s (Sokolow, 1983; Smith-Rosenberg, 1978). It is a product, in part, of the religious revivalism of the era, but also a response to the immoralities perceived in the rise of cities and the immigration of diverse populations. One study of Graham's influence and the rise of "Victorian" morality in America attributes it to an American response to modernization (Sokolow, 1983).

Whatever its origins, the period in which Graham came to public notice was also one of growing condemnation of American sexual morals. There was public admonition against masturbation and an expressed sense that sexual behavior and gluttony were out of control (Sokolow, 1983: Ch. 2; Schwartz, 1986: Ch. 2). Graham was himself one of the first public enunciators of the new sexual purity. His *Lectures to Young Men on Chastity* is among the early statements of the antimasturbation movement. The attitude toward masturbation and sex, in general, is significant to the nineteenth-century purity campaigns. The connection between diet and sexuality is important to the symbolic character of meanings implicit in each. Each involves a similar view of the body as a metaphor for social order and disorder in Graham's time. That connection is a central thread in my analysis.

Throughout his writing, and that of much of his followers, the contrast is drawn between a past of nature and a present of artificiality, of civilization. The processes by which food is grown, prepared, and processed for a commercial market of anonymous customers and the blandishments by which the consumer is induced into "luxury" are departures from a natural order of events. That natural order is healthier and safer than modern life, despite its technical additions. Graham was opposed to the then innovation of using manure as fertilizer. It was "unnatural." The process by which bread was baked from superfine flour, "tortured it into an unnatural state" (Nissenbaum, 1980: 7).

The heightening of sexual appetites under modern conditions contrasted with a natural propensity for self-control.

Graham's use of "nature" was not simply an equation between the absence of the modern and his contemporary world. His is both an anthropological and a religious sense, although he was no primitivist.[2] (Whorton, 1982; Schwartz, 1986). Nature is God's order, the laws of nature. That he finds them often followed where humans act instinctively, in primitive life, or in the immediate past of rural, farm life, does not mean that they may not also be disobeyed there as well. It is the disobeying of such laws of healthy living that constitute the danger to health. Mankind, he wrote, is unwilling to affirm that in "the higher order of God's works...human life and health, and thought and feeling are governed by laws as precise and fixed and immutable as those that hold the planets in their orbits." (*Lectures on the Science of Human Life*, Vol. 1, p. 20. Boston: Marsh, Capen, Lyon and Webb, 1839).

In this fashion, Graham was similar to many who thought about health in the nineteenth century. He equated the moral and the medical; good health and good character go together. By improving health, you improved moral capacities; by improving moral character you improved health. The body was not a neutral physiological object but a field of moral contention. The self-discipline demanded by healthy diet was itself an act of moral virtue. It was a paradigm common in the nineteenth century (Schwartz, 1986 Ch. 2; Rosenberg, 1962: Chs. 2, 7; Rosenberg and Smith-Rosenberg, 1985; Pivar, 1973, Ch. 1). Graham expressed it this way:

> While we continually violate the physiological laws of our nature, our systems will continue to be living volcanos of bad feelings and bad passions, which however correct our abstract principles of morality may be, will continually break out in immoral actions." (The Graham Journal of Health and Longevity 2, July 7, 1838; 212, 221. Quoted in Pivar, 1973: 38-39)

I dwell on Graham and his ideas far longer than seems warranted for a short paper. Two reasons prompt this attention. First, Sylvester Graham was among the leading medical reformers of his time. His ideas, and that of a number of other reformers and Grahamities, had much influence on American conceptions of health and illness in the uses of food. Not only did he spawn a number of journals but his conceptions of how to avoid the risks of ill health were embodied in a number of Grahamite resort hotels. He had much influence on the American religious group of Seventh Day Adventists. One of these Grahamite followers was John Harvey Kellogg, whose invented food, corn flakes, was an endeavor to provide a vegetarian, fibrous, and safer food for the American breakfast (Carson, 1957.

Second, and perhaps more important, Graham's ideas, both manifestly and in their latent meanings and symbolism, have much similarity with the current "natural foods" movement in the United States. How foods are perceived as sources of risk or safety and what they symbolize about the consumer and about his/her society are remarkably similar. For this reason, it is useful to analyze Graham's thought more closely.

I find it helpful to conceive of Graham's ideas in the form of two sets of contrasts. The first (below) is a contrast based on substances. The second (below) is based on the added meanings Graham utilizes, the symbolic attributions of his thought.

Substantive Table of Healthy and Unhealthy Foods

Healthy Foods	Unhealthy Foods
Unrefined	Refined
Coarse	Smooth
Pure	Additives
Raw	Cooked
Wheat bread	White bread
Organic	Fertilized
Water	Alcohol
Fruit juice	Tea, coffee
Chastity	Sexual Intercourse
Natural	Artificial

The table above is convertible into another table of contrasts symbolized through the meanings attached to substances that I have presented in discussing Graham's own writings and those of his disciples. Here the distinctions reflect a benign view of a natural order as conducive to health and a malignant perspective toward the social order (or disorder) as producing illness.

Symbolic Table of Healthy and Unhealthy Social Orders

Natural Order	*Social Order*
Temperance	Indulgence
Serenity	Excitement
Natural desires	Induced desires
Sufficiency	Luxury
Self-control	External control
Home	Commerce
Moral economy	Market economy
Health	Disease
Nature	Civilization

Social Contexts and Structural Meanings

The charts above relate the various substantive matters, such as a preference for unrefined flour, to the personal and moral characteristics which are symbolized by the recommended eating styles, such as temperance. These meanings, however, need also to be seen in the light of what the contrasts imply for social structure. At another level of analysis, Graham and his followers are proffering advice that relates to the social order of their times. It is here that culture and social structure come together to form contextualized meanings. It is here that the contrasts between substantive and symbolic aspects of meaning are turned into statements about social boundaries between valued and disvalued behaviors, between healthful and diseased people.

Graham has drawn us a picture of what it is that he finds objectionable and at the same time unhealthy in food and sex and in the social order emerging, in his view, in the America of the 1830s. With the market replacing the home as the source of production of food, the control of the individual and the family over their life stuff—their food—is passing into institutional hands—to commercial agriculture, to food technology, to impersonal, profit-oriented businesses. It is a market whose appeal to the consumer is that of taste and indulgence. With this transformation, a new kind of person is coming into existence—one who lacks the capacities for self-control. In the 1830s, there was a growing abundance of food and at the same time a growing denunciation of gluttony (Schwartz, 1986). It is in this social order that Graham finds the sources of risk to health and to morality.

There is, however, a contrast to be protected and to which the new being—the consumer—can cling for safety. It is the natural order that men and women have known and of which they are capable of following. It is not a Hobbesian but a Rousseauistic natural order. Human beings are not advantaged by the growth of a larger, more technologically integrated social order and the material progress it brings. Health is an attribute of the past, the unspoiled, unindulgent, and disciplined traditional American.

That this symbolism pervaded more than the Grahamites was evident in the Presidential election of 1840. Whig followers of William Henry Harrison used the distinction between the elite and the populace in drawing their candidate as a "log cabin" man in contrast to the elite and polished Martin Van Buren. In the discourse of the campaign, Van Buren's cuisine was contrasted to Harrison's plain and simple food, "chateau wine" against "log cabin cider": "The fable was the same. The simple, the home-grown, the coarse and blunt must triumph over the elegant, the manufactured, the refined and diplomatic" (Schwartz, 1986).

In his history of the Grahamite movement, Stephen Nissenbaum remarks on the irony that Graham's antipathy to the marketplace is coupled with a view of man as naturally capable of self-control. The latter tenet, he maintains, fits a "bourgeois philosophy" more consistent with the marketplace than a moral economy (Nissenbaum, 1982).

I would agree with Nissenbaum that Graham's doctrines symbolize a view of the commercial institutions of his day as detrimental to human beings and a natural order as superior and preferred to social order. But the contradiction is as deep within conceptions of a consistent bourgeois philosophy as in Graham (Levine, 1978). What our analysis of these ideas uncovers in the context of Graham's doctrine of health and risk is the individualism inherent in the glorification of natural man. As I will discuss below, Graham's view of the social order of his time is critical of the weakened forms of social control and the consequent need for principles of self-discipline made necessary in the 1830s. What the developing commercialism and the weakened role of familial, communal, and religious authority led to was the release of appetite—of passions, feelings, and desires. Gluttony and lust were the results and the source of disease and illness.

Here Graham's enunciation of sexual purity is significant. It is by no mean idiosyncratic to Graham. Others in the diet movement were similarly critical of American sexual practices and wrote various forms of advice to young men, including condemnations of masturbation and warnings about its ill and evil effects (Smith-Rosenberg, 1978). Among these were Graham's leading "competitor," William Alcott, in the early 1830s; Trall, in 1856; James Jackson, in 1862; John Harvey Kellogg, in 1888. Graham's published lectures on the subject were a way of fixing in print what he had been saying for two years in lectures to young men in colleges and in lyceums. He was addressing the young men away from home and open to the new, uncontrolled areas of urban life.

It is this young male, unattached to institutions of family or church, unapprenticed to occupational supervision, to whom Graham and others directed their message of sexual purity. It was the young male, the unattached adolescent, who constituted the sources of fear, a part of the "dangerous classes" who provided the disorders of urban crime and drunkenness. They were also the same population who were the potential victims of the temptations to which urban, modern life exposed them (Boyer, 1978; Schwartz, 1986). They were the objects of the awakened and unchained desires that surrounded them in the urban environments.

The message of Graham and other sexual reformers was substantially the same. Control thyself. Sex is intended for reproduction, not for recreation. Indulgence, hedonism, self-abuse contain the seeds of sickness, directly in poor health, even insanity, and indirectly in their impact on the future role of husband and father. Married couples, cautioned Graham, should limit intercourse to once a month. It is the stimulation and excitation that, within the scope of his physiological scheme, creates illness to the stomach and which diminishes the general vigor and fitness of the person.

It is here, in the concept of excitation, that I find a linkage between Graham's temperance, sexual and diet theories, and exhortations. In all of these, the temptations of indulgence and release surround the individual. The new foods, the sexual opportunities, the presence of alcohol are all damaging to the moral order of the community and the personal order of the individual. All the stimulation and arousal of desire have ill effects on health. The institutional controls of family, church, and work are declining.

The solution that Graham suggests is not a reformed institution but the emergence of heightened self-discipline and self-control. In the absence of authority, the social and moral order must depend on the internal mechanisms of discipline and order that the individual is capable of sustaining.

It is in this juncture of diverse programs at the nexus of self-control that I find the metaphorical, symbolic significance of natural foods in the nineteenth century. The linking concepts are "excitation" and "self-control." Excitation emanates from the outside, from the foods and markets and temptations available to the contemporary, urban population. In the inaugural issue of the *Graham Journal of Health and Longevity* (March 29, 1837), the editor writes:

> the mental movement of the present is retrograde...the vehemence of passion is subduing the vigor of thought....Vehemence and impetuousity are, indeed, the characteristics of the age....continual and inordinate craving and eager grasping after every species of moral as well as physical stimuli....everything adopted to excite and dissipate. (p. 1)

Such a description of contemporary society might have been written by Emile Durkheim as an example of *anomie*. It pictures a society in which communal, religious, and familial norms are either absent or unenforceable. In the consequent void anything is possible; everything is capable of realization. In such a society, the traditional institutional controls cannot be depended upon to insure righteous living. Discipline and control must depend on the self.

What is it that the body symbolizes as an object of health? Illness, like sexual immorality and intemperance, is both a sign and an effect of moral defection. It indicates the inability of the person to exercise resistance to physical desire and, at the same time, results in the debility and disease that constitutes illness. Here is the theme of Christian perfectionism exemplified. Immorality is also unhealthy. Illness is failure to observe God's law and a sign of theological dereliction. As James Whorton points out, stimulation was a term in Graham's time used as much in a moral as in a physiological context.

The determination to promote godliness by suppressing animal appetites and passions, the Victorian antipleasure principle, was sufficiently far advanced as to have branded overstimulation, or nervous and mental excitation, as morally evil, the first step of gradual descent into drunkenness and debauchery. (Whorton, 1982, p. 43)

The body is then an area of struggle between the tempting forces of market and city which draw the person into immediate physical gratifications and the laws of God and Nature from which the canons of good health and right living are derived. In a changed world of weakened tradition and institutional forces, it is to the self that one must look for sources of social and personal control.

This analysis of symbolic and metaphorical properties in the theory of health is not a form of reduction. I am not asserting that Graham and his disciples saw natural foods as a means to achieve sexual morality or a device for coping with urban crime and disorder. That is certainly not what the Grahamites assert. Rather what I am claiming is that the theory of illness and health and the body as an object can be understood as "making sense" to the Grahamites and their audiences because those theories are embedded in a view of reality that fits the experiences of their audiences. Such "root hypotheses" or paradigms are seen in the lectures and books on sex and temperance as they are on physiology. The body is seen metaphorically. They are what Christians experiencing the decline in communal and family controls could well have understood in those times. It is here, in the view of the body as a manifestation of moral order and immoral disorder, that culture operates. It is in perceiving the situation of the times, of loosened authority and increased temptations, that social structure operates to give specific, situated meaning to cultural categories.

Implicated in that paradigm is a particular view of the place of the person in the society of the time. In that paradigm, external social

controls cannot be depended upon to produce people of moral recti-
tude. They are absent or unworkable. As Harry Gene Levine, David
Rothman and others have pointed out, colonial America depended
on institutions, not persons, to enforce social rules (Levine, 1978;
Rothman, 1971). The nineteenth century could not do so. One response might have been to attempt to rebuild or reinforce such institutions. Rothman's analysis of mental asylums, poorhouses, peniten-
tiaries, and hospitals describes just such attempts. But in the natural
foods movements, and in health reform in general, there is no such
attempt. It is to the individual, to the self that Graham and his followers looked.

The Natural Foods Movement: Popular Medicine and Counter-Culture, 1950-1990.

Interest in natural foods and nutritional health by no means disappeared with the death of Graham nor did health faddist sects.
Graham influenced a number of disciples and out of his ideas about
grain cereals and the risks of meat-eating emerged a modern commercial industry-the breakfast cereals. John Harvey Kellogg and C.
W. Post both were self-styled disciples. Kellogg, a physician and
Seventh-Day Adventist, became director of a Grahamite sanitarium,
which he moved closer to conventional medical practice yet embodied Graham's principles of nutrition. He experimented with various grain products and, in 1900, invented the corn flake. Originat-
ing in a perceived threat from the market, it spawned a new industry. Kellogg was a most prolific writer during the almost fifty
years in which he played a significant role on the American health
scene. He wrote as well on matters of morals, continuing the sexual
purity theme which the earlier natural food advocates had also
espoused (Carson, 1957)[3].

Others continued the concerns for nutrition as an avenue toward
good health. Nevertheless, these efforts remain distinctly on the margins of medical institutions. Following the feats of bacteriological
immunization and sanitation and the organization of medicine into a
profession dominated by the paradigm of allopathy, the "natural
foods" movement remained marginal to the central forms of food
consumption in the United States (Gideon, 1948: 200-207; Cummings,
1940).

The Natural Foods Movement of the 1950s and After

Beginning sometime in the 1950s and continuing into the present there has been a quickening of interest in nutrition as a means to achieve good health and prevent illness.[4] It is evident in the increased publication of books espousing the value of "natural foods" and criticizing current American food habits. It is further evidenced in the considerable increase in journals devoted to the topic and in the proliferation of a new enterprise, the "health food" or "natural food" industry. In 1990, there were 108 retail outlets listed in the San Diego County telephone directory under the rubric "Health and Diet Foods-Retail." This represents approximately one such outlet for every 23,148 persons in the metropolitan area.

In referring to the movement, I recognize a wide range of organized and unorganized groups that include often quite diverse food advisories. It would include sectarian views, such as those of macrobiotic devotees and strict vegetarians. But it also includes the movement towards use of unrefined flours, use of vitamins, the appeal of organic food products, the disuse of foods containing additives and preservatives, and limits on the use of meats and sugar. At one location on some scale, there is the complete vegetarian, who avoids sugar, refined flours, all products raised through chemical fertilizers and containing additives and preservatives, reads the books and journals advocating natural diets and for whom diet is a central point in life (Kandel and Pelto, 1980; New and Priest, 1967). At the other end is the casual consumer who has come to adopt some aspects of the natural foods "programme" without seeing himself/herself as belonging or subscribing to any movement.

The spread of a "natural foods" orientation in American society is also evidenced in the adoption of certain foods into the commercial world of food distribution (Belasco, 1989). Granola was, for a long time, a cereal product obtainable only in specialized shops labeled "Health foods" or "natural foods." Sometime in the 1970s, American chain food shops, supermarkets, began to stock granola produced by small companies servicing "natural foods" stores. In the late 1970s, Granola was taken up as a product of conventional, large scale companies, such as Quaker Oats, and sold in supermarkets. In the last few years there has been some trend toward stocking cereals and other commodities in an unpackaged, bulk form, long a characteristic of the "natural foods" store as well as a characteristic of urban grocery shops before World War II.

The differences between the two forms of retail establishment is, perhaps, one clue to the symbolism of the current natural foods movement and, at the same time, evidence of the similarities to its nineteenth-century analogues. The movement of the 1830s shares much with that of the 1950s. Each finds risks and safeties in the same places and from highly similar vantage points. Each symbolizes safe and dangerous foods in the same framework or paradigm. While the differences between the two forms of distributing food have been somewhat attenuated in both directions, the differences do still persist. Knowing only that a store is "natural foods" rather than a conventional supermarket, you and I can well know what to expect.

One of the most striking aspects of the contemporary American health food or natural food store is the large number of products closer to the point of primary production—to the raw, natural, and unprocessed state. Spices, cereals, and dried fruits are more likely to be found in bulk than is the case at the supermarket. The absence of complex packaging in the natural foods store is clear. The customer is closer in time to the natural state of the products. And the variety of such products is again much greater. Not several brands of tea or honey but forty or fifty such. The varieties within standard categories are, in turn, large and varied. Nationally known brands do not dominate the shelves. The number of different spices is far greater than those found in conventional groceries. The contrast between localized, specific distribution and the mass production of the supermarket is evident.

Two products, or forms of product, are conspicuous by their absence or limited presence. One is animal products—meats, poultry, fish, but especially red meat. The other is canned goods. Both would have been symbols of progress in an earlier period—animal products, especially meat, because they are part of the diet of affluent populations and expensive to produce and transport. Canned goods have represented the triumph of technology over the quick-destroying powers of nature. It is almost superfluous to point out also the absence of frozen foods for immediate consumption and, especially, processed white bread, the great *bête blanc* of natural foods enthusiasts and the symbol, in its "sweet smoothness" of commercialized food industries and of modern civilization (Gideon, 1948: 200-207).

To a certain extent, walking into a "natural foods" store is a walk back into an earlier American form of merchandising. It gives the consumer a sense of greater closeness to, and control over, the product. Yet it demeans the very qualities of safe packaging, diminished fear of adulteration, high animal content, and long shelf life which had been heralded as the signs of a progressive food technology. It ascribes to these qualities, as well as to the signs of a progressive agriculture in chemical fertilizers and effective pesticides, qualities of risk. In other eyes, these are signs of safety and well being. The availability and approval of non-pasteurized milk is again a symbol of the superiority of the natural over the artificial and processed.

In another symbolism, the store and its merchandising hearkens back to an earlier era of a small-scale economy. Until recently, when major American food industries began to adopt "natural foods" and the country had become health-conscious and food-conscious, the necessary agricultural and merchandising groups had represented a wide variety of small producers who had either produced for a small and local market or had occupied a very marginal place in national distribution. It is quite true that the spread of the consumer movement to natural foods depended on the preexistence and generation of the natural foods industry (Miller, 1990). However, to some extent, these had been in existence prior to the 1950s.

The similarities between the nostalgic sense of a traditional America of Sylvester Graham and that of the contemporary health foods movement appears in the writings of leading gurus of the movement, as it does today in such journals as *Vegetarian Times, Holistic Health, Whole Earth News, New Age, East/West,* and *Prevention.* One of the most popular and widely read of gurus has been Adelle Davis, whose book, *Let's Eat Right and Keep Fit,* was first published in 1954, revised in a new edition in 1970, and is still in print and on sale at bookstores (Davis, 1970). Although there are differences in stress on certain foods and inclusion of others, and although there are differences in how authors apportion sources of blame, Davis's book is surprisingly akin in basic outlines to much of the "natural foods" movement's general programme and philosophy and to Graham's pronouncements in the 1830s. However, as developed below, while this is true at one level of meaning, it is not so at other levels of meaning and symbolism.

Like Graham, for Davis the appearance of a technology of refining, packaging, and preserving food has increased the risks of illness and disease. In the procedures of processing, of increasing agricultural yield, of preserving food beyond short periods to decay, in the service of commercial gain the natural qualities of food have been allowed to disappear. The fibers, vitamins, and minerals essential to physical and mental health are removed from our diet. It is up to the consumer to find ways, through improved diet, to restore them. All her flour, she writes, is stone-ground, whole wheat, organically grown. She bakes her own bread from flour purchased at a local health foods store. She believes that the refining machinery creates such friction that the flour is pre-cooked (Davis, 1970: 101).

The distinction between the safeties of the past and the risks produced by the present commercial and technological society are referred to at many points in Davis's book. The raising of hens in shaded cages diminishes the healthful properties of sunlight. So, too, frequent bathing robs the skin of oils that enable sunlight to work its healthful properties.

> Sunshine would be an excellent source of this vitamin (D) if it were not for the fact that people are surrounded by smog, wear clothes, live in houses and have bathtubs and hot-water heaters. (p. 139)

Davis does think that, despite the better health of primitives, Indians, and earlier American families, being bath-happy and soap-happy is progress. Yet her description has cast much doubt.

This broad distinction between the modern world of civilized, cultured, refined man and an earlier world of primitive, rural, rawer people is implicit and often explicit in Davis, as it was in Graham. The processes of working on the raw, the uncooked food in its original state—of adding modern technology and convenience to nature— is the source which accentuates the risk of illness. Whatever transforms food from its "natural" state is harmful (Belasco, 1989). "By wholesomeness I mean the kind of food our grandparents and all our ancestors before them ate at every meal. *Just plain food*" (Davis, 1970: 228 [italics mine]).

Davis uses research studies of nutritionists but she is also often skeptical of academics and medical personnel, seeing in the former people supported by the food industry in their research and in the latter people who ignore nutrition. The purpose of medicine is disease not health, she writes. "The purpose of medicine is to help the sick person get well....The purpose of nutrition is to maintain health and to prevent illness" (p. 18). Like other writers in this movement, she presents instances in which the "common man" knows better and is proven better than the wise doctors and professors. It is paradoxical, since she was herself a trained chemist and dietician.[5]

An ad in the *Vegetarian Times* presents the same message of the virtue of the primitive and natural as superior to the civilized and scientific. It describes Lavilin as "free of aluminums and other harsh chemicals," yet effective. It is described as having been developed by scientists who were alarmed by the wide use of aluminum in deodorants and who "re-discovered the herbal flowers Arnica and Calendula, known for centuries to be soothing and anti-bacterial" (p.1, May 1986). These "natural extracts" decrease the bacteria that create odors.

At this level of specific advice on what to eat and what to avoid, the current health foods movement is of a piece with its earlier analogues. It is advice to the individual on how to help himself and herself. Graham lived in an American society just beginning to recognize national and regional organization, one in which medicine was just beginning to assume licensure. Food was just beginning to pass from the self-sufficient producers of the family to the commercial and technological concerns of the marketplace. Those processes have come full-blown in our time yet the basic advice remains. In one sense, the glorification of natural foods is symbolic of efforts to carve out a niche of control over the forces of outside destruction, to find safety through our own means and not through dependence on the established social order of institutions. In its apolitical course, it differs considerably from the uses made of natural foods in the counter-culture movements of the sixties. Yet in its challenge to professional medicine and to the large and highly capital-intensive food industries, it projects both a counter-culture and a consumer revolt. To borrow a term used by Warren Belasco to describe the movements of the 1960s, the natural foods movement is a phase of counter-culture in creating and espousing a "counter-cuisine" (Belasco, 1989 passim).

The counter-cultural and counter-structural elements in the health and natural foods movements of the 1950 are made even more strident in the ideological symbolism of food in the counter-culture of the 1960s. During the 1960s, many elements of the natural foods syndrome were taken over by the cultural side of the counter-culture movements. Two differences mark this phase of the health foods movement. First, it was no longer primarily a health movement. The advisories about what to eat and what to avoid were set within the general ecological movement rather than appearing within the paradigm of advice on maintaining health and curing illness. Secondly, the symbolic character of the advice concerning health was given a general ideological tone as opposition to many aspects of American political and cultural life (Belasco, 1989). For example, the antipathy to white bread, a staple aspect of both nineteenth- and twentieth-century natural foods movements, carried with it often explicit meanings of opposition to white supremacy and political or cultural authority in general.

Now the symbolism became more explicit and pointed as a mode of expressing political opposition. While the health motif is sounded, it is embedded in a general concern for ecological reform and given a symbolic meaning which stresses the affinity of the speaker or writer with a more explicitly ideological movement. Lappe's book, *Diet for a Small Planet*, was widely read in this period (late 1960s) and sounded a theme common to many journals, such as the *Whole Earth Catalog*, which were popular in the movements of the 1960s. What was implicit in the 1950s has become explicitly a programmatic message of opposition to the food industries and to business interests that are seen as responsible for the destruction of the ecological balance of the earth. Thus states Frances Lappe in one of the most read books on food in the 1960s:

> Previously when I went to a supermarket, I felt at the mercy of our advertising culture. My tastes were manipulated. And food, instead of being my most direct link with the nurturing earth, had become mere merchandise by which I fulfilled my role as a 'good' consumer. (Lappe, 1971: 8)

Yet the 1950s movement persisted in its own form and is found today absorbed both within the medical institutions themselves and within other movements, such as New Age. The health consciousness of the 1980s has reflected a similar concern with nutrition supported by the medical institutions own work on the role of such elements as cholesterol, fiber, deleterious effects of red meat, and the effects of overweight on health. Here, too, as in holistic medicine, the movement is toward finding sources of illness in defective life styles and forms of eating (Lowenberg, 1989; Zola, 1978; Carlson, 1975).

Contexts of Meaning: The 1830s and the 1950s

There are two highly significant ways in which the current movement beginning in the 1950s differs, at least manifestly, from its nineteenth-century precursor. One is what I call its more evident popu-
lism. By this I mean the rejection and condemnation of professional
institutions to which Americans conventionally look for advice on
health. The philosophy of self-help is accompanied by a rejection of
medicine and often of academic and scientific writings. In its explicit
antipathy to institutionalized medicine and science the movement of
the 1950s manifests its counter-cultural character as an alternative
medicine.

The antipathy to organized, professional medicine was less strident
in Graham, although medicine was just beginning to become an organized profession. Graham was one among a number of medical sectar-
ians and reformers of his age. Part of their appeal was a response to
the harsh treatment and poor rates of success of professional medicine. As practiced, mid-nineteenth-century professional medicine was
often accompanied by "heroic" therapy—drugs that produced excessive discomfort and heavy amounts of bleeding (Starr, 1982: 94-102;
Shryock, 1931: 178-79).

A second difference between the current movement and the nineteenth century is the area of sexual behavior. Sex is not a source of
danger or sexual desire an avenue to disease. While there is a hint, as
in Davis, of a positive relation between good food habits and sexual
fulfillment, it is not a theme in the present movement. But at another
level the current movement is similar in demanding a rejection of
indulgence. As lust is to sex, so gluttony is to hunger. The food
industries surround us with a seduction through the hedonistic use of
food as pleasure with no regard for health. Sugar is an enemy, even in
its unrefined, raw form. Sweets are anathema: the source of illness
and bad teeth (Garten, 1978). Among the terms in use in American
life for pleasurable indulgence are symbols of sugar, "a sweet time."
In his paper on food as symbol, Roland Barthes recalls the American
popular song, "Sugar Time," as the expression of joy and pleasure
(Barthes, 1979).

To live well and be fit the natural food advocates are saying, requires, at symbolic levels, a self-oriented person, unswayed by the
institutional order and deaf to its lures. It requires self-control. A more

extreme advocate, writing in the holistic medicine journal, *The Well-Being Newsletter*, states this clearly, discussing the general rule to eat foods close to their natural state: "Is the Hygienic diet for you? Only you can answer this. It demands discipline and self-control, but it offers vigorous health and vitality" (Forrest, 1985).

The continuity between the nineteenth- and the twentieth-century movements appears to me to reflect an individualism that may be unique to the American cultural scene (Lukes, 1973). The imagined idyllic state of nature implies and leads to a rejection of social controls and social institutions. In this structure of thought, the human being is both capable of and is exhorted to depend on his own knowledge and on his abilities for self-control. He is warned against the advice of professionals and the supposed values of technological progress. He/she is not exhorted to mobilize with others to change the institutions. The behavior espoused is market-oriented, not politically directed. In the categories Albert Hirschman has used to describe consumers in a free market, his/her behavior is neither protest nor loyalty. It is exit (Hirschman, 1970).

The ideal of character is the independent consumer, uncontrolled by either the commercial market or the trained professional. The values and the knowledge of scientific professionals, of government, of food technology are distrusted. They are seen as enhancing risks to health. The industrial world and agricultural technology preach a gospel of indulgence and luxury. That way is danger. Health and safety depend on the individual and his capacity for self-control. Civilization produces risk while nature is the source of health.

It would be an error to see this philosophy as a form of amoral anarchism. While it emerges from a context of opposition to institutional structure, it also commands a code of moral discipline that is viewed as sterner and tighter than the hedonistic ideal that the market enjoins. To follow the diet of the "natural foods" movement is to engage in an exercise, a ritual, in the display to self and others of that moral character. The resultant health is the reward. In this respect, the affinity is to a past and a "hard primitivism" of moral and physical steadfastness with which, from time to time, Americans, and others, have built their adulation of the primitive and the past. The social order produces illness; the natural order creates health. Health is a product of "right living" and illness a sign of immorality, of a deficient life-style.

Where the two movements, that of the 1830s and that of the present, digress is at the direction toward institutional structure that forms the context for the positive evaluation and exhortation toward self-discipline and self-control. In the movements of the nineteenth century, the acts of eating and drinking and the diminished restraints on sexual practice are symbols of a social life in which the moral order has lost the authority to enforce what Nature, in God's law, demands. Illness is the outcome of the loosened social structure. The appeal to self-control is an appeal within the context of what is perceived to be a weakened and delegitimized set of social rules. The body, as well as the body social and politic, is out of control and only the will of the individual can bring it into boundaries.

In the contemporary movement the substantive message is remarkably similar but the context, and thus the meaning, is considerably diverse. It is the institutions and their power that are to be avoided. Medicine, science, the marketplace of food industries are too commanding, too powerful, and too much the source of conventional wisdom. They are distrusted and delegitimated in the movement's insistence on naturalness. What is signified and symbolized in the contemporary health movement is a return to control over one's body. What is signified and symbolized in the Grahamites and their disciples is the attempt to restore moral and scientific authority.

This alienation of natural foods users from the conventional and the dominant in eating is analogous to other related movements. Examining a variety of magazines with health foods concerns is to enter a world of holistic medicine, of the healing powers of quartz crystals, of yogic and tantric rites, of forms of non-professionalized psychotherapeutic self-transformation that are today grouped under the rubric of the "New Age." Both movements sought and seek a return to a past, but it is a different kind of past. For Graham and his followers the past was a traditional structure of well-observed and understood laws and the power vested in traditional authority. That past cannot be fully recovered because the institutions of authority cannot be redeveloped. But the laws they ensured are still applicable and a Christian perfectionism is possible, if not through institutions then through socializing the individual: A healthy mind, a healthy body, and a moral character.

For the contemporary movement, the past is more directly hallowed. What is envisioned is a world of individuals who carve out for themselves areas of detachment from the strong and overpowering institutions that surround them. Only in themselves and in their control over their life and their intake can they find the health and the political morality with which to prevent disease and illness. What the Grahamites sought, the contemporary movement sees as having been found and now lost.

But the nineteenth century was open to a view of nature as an ordered system for which religion provided both an understanding and a source of effective rules. Moral purity and physical purity were synonymous and the body the expression and symbol of the individual's fealty to both. In a world of limited embodiment of that ideal in institutions, the burden of health is thrown on the individual as is the burden of social behavior.

The contemporary movement is more secularized, less sacral in tone and content. We are faced with a world that both restrains and permits, that stimulates the appetites and provides the elites to treat the effects of appetite. Nature becomes the symbol of opposition. It describes a morality and a source of knowledge that stems from an instinctual and unsocialized self which civilization, in its appeals and hierarchies, seems to have lost. Modern life is thus the blameworthy form from which so much of evil arises.

The movements of the nineteenth and twentieth centuries are alike in some other respects. Most importantly both substitute a planned, ordered system of eating for one that is haphazard and spontaneous. Meals cannot be unplanned periods of gratification. What to eat, when to eat, and how to eat must all be thought through and deliberately chosen. The body, like the office, the factory, the home, is brought into the orbit of the rationalized soul, the central symbol of modern life and the modern social system. Here is the paradox of the anti-modernism of the health foods movement. Its counter-culture is committed to the dominant value of the modernist project.

For both movements, the organic, raw, grainy world of the uncooked, the unprocessed, the virginal and untouched has a hallowed aura around it. "Civilization" is a word that spells danger, disenchantment, and distrust. John Harvey Kellogg used the word to describe the origins of much that he thought ails us. In a phrase that both periods of natural foods enthusiasm would have found descriptive, he referred to certain illnesses as products of the "civilized colon" (Whorton, 1982: 221).

Notes

1. This paper is part of a chapter on health movements which, in turn, is part of a book in progress, tentatively titled, "The Idea of Regress: Studies in the Anti-Modern Temper."
2. "Graham was too little the Leatherstocking and too much the Presbyterian to embrace the primeval. He proposed rather a civilized rejection of civilization, a return not to the tribal primitive but to primitive Christianity" (Schwartz, 1986: 32).
3. John Harvey Kellogg and his brother William developed the cereal business bearing their family name. They quarreled over the character of the cereals. William wanted to improve the taste and market them without reference to their healthful propensities. John remained committed to the idea of natural foods as health foods. William was able to gain legal control of the business and moved the enterprise away from its Grahamite origins (Carson, 1957).
4. After the 1950s, the movement develops a number of derivative branches and additions to date. However, the central advice, even when supported by medical research, remains relatively unchanged. Its symbolic meanings, however, shift in accordance with the large movements with which it becomes associated.
5. The natural foods movements of the 1950s and the 1960s were denounced by many medical authorities and nutritionists as frauds, hucksters, or just plain wrong. For examples, including bibliographies, see Whalen and Stare, 1975, and Herbert, 1982.

References

Abrams, M. H. 1985. "Art-as-Such: The Sociology of Modern Aesthetics" *Bulletin of the American Academy of Arts and Sciences* 38, 8-33.

Aries, Phillipe. 1962. *Centuries of Childhood: A Social History of Family Life*. New York: Vintage Books.

Barthes, Roland. 1973. *Mythologies*. St. Albans, Herts: Paladin.

_____. 1979. "Toward a Psychosociology of Contemporary Food Consumption." In R. Forster and O. Ranum, eds., *Food and Drink in History*. Baltimore, MD: Johns Hopkins Press.

Belasco, Warren. 1989. *Appetite for Change: How the Counterculture Took on the Food Industry, 1966-1988*. New York: Pantheon.

Boas, George, and A. O. Lovejoy. 1935. *Primitivism and Related Ideas in Antiquity*. Baltimore, MD: Johns Hopkins Press.

Bourdieu, Pierre. 1984. *Distinction: A Social Critique of the Judgment of Taste*. Cambridge, MA: Harvard University Press.

Boyer, Paul. 1978. *Urban Masses and the Moral Order in America, 1820-1920*. Cambridge, MA: Harvard University Press.

Burke, Peter. 1970. *Popular Culture in Early Modern Europe*. London: Temple Church.

Carlson, Rick. 1975. *The End of Medicine*. New York: John Wiley and Sons.

Carson, Gerald. 1957. *Cornflake Crusade*. New York: Rinehart and Co.

Cummings, Richard O. 1940. *The American and His Food: A History of Food Habits in the United States*. Chicago: University of Chicago Press.

Davis, Adele. 1970. *Let's Eat Right to Keep Fit*. New York: Harcourt, Brace, Jovanivich

Douglas, Mary. 1984. "Standard Social Uses of Food: Introduction." In Mary Douglas, ed., *Food and the Social Order: Studies in Three American Communities*. New York: Russell Sage Foundation.

_____. 1975. "Deciphering a Meal." In Mary Douglas, ed., *Implicit Meanings*. London: Routledge and Kegan Paul.

Eliade, Mircea. 1971. *The Myth of the Eternal Return*. Princeton, NJ: Princeton University Press.

Farb, Peter, and George Armelagos. 1980. *Consuming Passions: The Anthropology of Eating*. New York: Pocket Books.

Forrest, Stephen. 1985. "Principles of Practical Nutrition." *Well-Being Newsletter* 2 (Nov.-Dec.): 5.

Frye, Northrop. 1957. *Anatomy of Criticism*. Princeton, NJ: Princeton University Press.

Gans, Herbert. 1974. *Popular Culture and High Culture*. New York: Basic Books.

Garten, Max, 1978. *"Civilized" Diseases and Their Circumvention*. San Jose, CA: MaxMillio Publishing.

Geertz. Clifford. 1973. "Ideology as a Cultural System." In Clifford Geertz, ed., *The Interpretation of Cultures*. New York: Basic Books.

Gideon, Siegfried. 1948. *Mechanization Takes Command*. New York: Oxford University Press.

Graham Journal of Health and Longevity. 1837.

Graham, Sylvester. 1839. *Lectures on the Science of Human Life*. 2 vol. Boston: Marsh, Capen, Lyon and Webb.

Herbert, Victor, and Stephen Barrett. 1982. *Vitamins and Health in Foods: The Great American Hustle*. Philadelphia: George F. Stickley Co.

Hirschman, Albert. 1970. *Exit, Voice and Loyalty*. Cambridge, MA: Harvard University Press.

Kandel, Randy, and Gretel Pelto. 1980. "The Health Food Movement." In N. Jerome, R. Kandel, and G. Pelto, eds., *Nutritional Anthropology*. Pleasantville, NY: Redgrave Publishing Co

Lappe, Frances M. 1971. *Diet for a Small Planet*. New York: Ballantine Books.

Leach, Edmund. 1976. *Culture and Communication*. Cambridge: Cambridge University Press.

Levine, Harry Gene. 1978. "Demon of the Middle Class: Liquor, Self-Control and Temperance Ideology in 19th-Century America." (Unpublished Ph. D. dissertation, Department of Sociology, University of California, Berkeley.)

Lévi-Strauss, Claude. 1969. *The Raw and the Cooked*. New York: Harper and Row.

Lowenberg, June. 1989. *Caring and Responsibility: The Crossroads Between Holistic Practice and Traditional Medicine*. Philadelphia: University of Pennsylvania Press.

Lukes, Steven. 1973. *Individualism*. Oxford: Basil Blackwell.

Miller, Laura. 1990. "The Commercialization of a Social Movement: The Natural Foods Movement as Lifestyle and Politics." (Unpublished paper prepared for Seminar in Social Movements, Department of Sociology, University of California, San Diego.

New, Peter, and Rhea Priest. 1967. "Food and Thought: A Sociological Study of Food Cultists." *Journal of the American Dietetic Association* 51: 13-18.

Nissenbaum, Stephen. 1980. *Sex, Diet and Debility in Jacksonian America: Sylvester Graham and Health Reform*. Westport, CT: Greenwood Press.

Parsons, Talcott. 1951. *The Social System*. Glencoe, IL: The Free Press.

Pivar, David. 1973. *Purity Crusade: Sexual Morality and Social Control, 1868-1890*. Westport, CT: Greenwood Press.

Rosenberg, Charles. 1962. *The Cholera Years: The United States in 1832, 1849 and 1866*. Chicago: University of Chicago Press.

Rosenberg, Charles, and Carroll Smith-Rosenberg. 1985. "Pietism and the Origins of the American Public Health Movement." In Judith Leavitt and Ronald Numbers, eds., *Sickness and Health in America*. Madison: University of Wisconsin Press.

Rosenzweig, Roy. 1983. *Eight Hours for What We Will*. Cambridge: Cambridge University Press.

Rothman, David. 1971. *The Discovery of the Asylum: Social Order and Disorder in the New Republic*. Boston: Little, Brown and Co.

Sahlins, Marshall. 1976. *Culture and Practical Reason*. Chicago: University of Chicago Press.

Schorer, Mark. 1959. *William Blake: The Politics of Vision*. New York: Vintage Books

Schutz, Alfred. 1967. *The Phenomenology of the Social World*. Evanston, IL: Northwestern University Press.

Schwartz, Hillel. 1986. *Never Satisfied: A Cultural History of Diets, Fantasies and Fat*. New York: Anchor Books, Doubleday.

Shryock, Richard. 1931 "Sylvester Graham and the Health Movement." *Mississippi Valley Historical Review* 18: 172-83.

Smith-Rosenberg, Carol. 1984. "Sex as Symbol in Victorian Piety." In John Demos, and Sarane Boocock, eds., *Turning Points: Historical and Sociological Essays on the Family*. Chicago: University of Chicago Press. *Sociological Review* 51: 273-86.

Sokolow, Jayme. 1983. *Eros and Modernization*. London and Toronto: Associated Universities Press.

Starr, Paul. 1982. *The Social Transformation of American Medicine*. New York: Basic Books.

Stephens, Leslie. 1927. *History of English Thought in the Eighteenth Century*. Vol. II. London: Putnam.

Stocking, Jr., George. 1989. "The Ethnographic Sensibility of the 1920s and the Dualism of the Anthropological Tradition." In George Stocking Jr., ed., *Romantic Motives: Essays on Anthropological Sensibility*. Madison: University of Wisconsin Press.

Swidler, Anne. 1986. "Culture in Action: Symbols and Strategies." *American Sociological Review* 51: 273-86.

Thompson, E. P. 1974. "Patrician Society, Plebian Culture" Past and Present." *Journal of Social History* 7: 382-405.

Turner, Victor. 1967. *The Forest of Symbols: Aspects of Ndembu Ritual*. Ithaca, NY: Cornell University Press.

Whalen, Elizabeth, and Frederick Stare. 1975. *Panic in the Pantry*. New York: Atheneum Press.

White, Hayden. 1972. "The Forms of Wildness: Archeology of an Idea." In Edward Dudley and Maximilian Novak, eds., *The Wild Man: An Image in Western Thought from the Renaissance to Romanticism*. Pittsburgh, PA: University of Pittsburgh Press.

Whorton, James. 1982. *Crusaders for Fitness: The History of American Health Reformers*. Princeton, NJ: Princeton University Press.

Zola, Irving. 1978. "Medicine as an Institution of Social Control." In John Ehrenreich, ed., *The Cultural Crisis of Modern Medicine*. New York: *Monthly Review Press*.

12

The Social Symbolism of
Smoking and Health

The mirror images of tobacco as harmful and immoral and smoking as harmless and innocently pleasurable have spiraled through Western history since tobacco was first brought to Europe in the wake of the discovery of the Americas by Columbus (Gottsegen, 1940; Best, 1979; Troyer and Markle, 1983). Though our economic, political, and legal institutions have often been dominated by one or another assessment, both positive and negative images of tobacco have been a part of American life. The two concerns of health and morality have appeared in the perception of tobacco and its uses. The pleasures of smoking have been countered at times by claims of its bad effects on health; at times by its perception as an evil habit associated with vicious living. Dual images and dual criteria have been embodied in institutional practices and the recurring interests of various segments of the American population. Neither the rejecting nor the appreciative view of smoking has entirely disappeared from American life.

Health and morality are by no means always, or even often, separate and unconnected domains. In the history of American medicine, matters of health and matters of illness have been construed as results of styles of life, of behavior that produces disease and illness for the behaving person (Zola, 1972; Crawford, 1977, 1979). How we eat, drive automobiles, accept stress, drink alcohol, exercise, conduct sexual relations,

From Robert L. Rabin and Stephen D. Sugarman, eds., *Smoking Policy: Law, Politics and Culture*. Copyright (c) 1993 by Oxford University Press. Used with permission of Oxford University Press, Inc. Donald Kelly provided able assitance.

lead sedentary lives, use drugs and smoke tobacco are widely understood today as important to the health of the individual.

A healthy life style and a moral one might seem unrelated to each other. It is logically possible to see each as separate, as different and distinct frames within which to interpret, assess, and adjudge human actions. What is logical is not, however, necessarily sociological. Prescriptions for healthful living, of which nonsmoking is now a part, are also prescriptions for being a particular kind of person leading a particular kind of life (Tesh, 1991; Glassner, 1989).

In this chapter, I assert that the frames of morality and health are not as divergent as they appear at first sight. The story of the antismoking movement in the past three decades is a story of its leadership by the elite of medical science supported by the official imprimatur of the national government as health agency. It is the credibility of the scientific research elite that is salient in any comparison with the antismoking movement of the early twentieth century in the United States. The antismoking campaigns of the early twentieth century were set in the frame of moral concerns. The present campaigns have been framed in the context of health, an appeal to rational thought devoid of moral judgments. As we will argue later in this paper, that has not eliminated the moral quality of the issue nor eradicated the significance of emerging social distinctions. The cigarette has been defined in a way different from the earlier movement yet not as different as appears on first sight. In the context of the health consciousness of the past three decades, smoking has taken on a symbolic meaning in which moral and social considerations are significant. What began as an appeal to considerations of the smoker's health has accrued meanings that make the smoker an object of moral as well as health concerns. With the rising interest in the environmental smoke produced by smokers, the moral condemnation of smoking has been accentuated.

I. The Moral Condemnation of Smoking

The Movement Against the "Tyrant in White"

The early campaign against smoking originated in the last twenty years of the nineteenth century. By 1890, twenty-six states had passed legislation prohibiting the sale of cigarettes to minors. By the end of

1909, seventeen states had prohibited the sale of cigarettes altogether. By 1917, the movement was clearly in retreat, yet even then there were still twelve states that maintained prohibitory laws (Gottsegen, 1940: 184; Troyer and Markle, 1983: 34-35).

Rather than at smoking in general, the movement, triggered by a great increase in consumption, was chiefly directed against the cigarette, an object that one writer in 1909 referred to as "the tyrant in white" (*New York Times*, October 2, 1909, p.580).

Hand-rolled cigarettes had been in use for several centuries, especially in Europe. However, it was not until the 1880s that a mass market was possible in the United States (Sobel, 1978: Chs.1, 2; Schudson, 1984, Ch. 5). Three developments made mass consumption feasible. One was the invention of the Bonsack cigarette-rolling machine in 1884 (Wagner, 1971; Sobel, 1978, Ch. 2).[1] The second was the invention of the portable and safe matchbook, in use by the 1890s (Sobel, 1978: 66-71; Whelan, 1984: 39-40). The third development was less technological than organizational. James Buchanan Duke organized the cigarette industry when in the 1880s he put together several companies to form the American Tobacco Company (Sobel, 1978: Ch. 2).

The production and consumption of cigarettes rose dramatically from the mid-1880s when the estimated per capita consumption of cigarettes was approximately 8.1. By 1900, it was approximately 34.7. By 1920, it had increased to approximately 470.5 (Gottsegen, cited in Troyer and Markle, 1983: 34). Until then, cigars, pipes, and chewing tobacco had been the dominant forms of smoking tobacco in the United States and adult men almost the entire market for tobacco products.

The cigarette introduced a new commodity and made possible a new set of meanings that smoking carried with it. It was distinctly smaller, easier to light, and milder than its competitors. As such, it created a greater opportunity for two groups for whom smoking had been under a restrictive taboo. One was women; the other was young people, especially boys. In this period, concerns for the harmful effects of cigarettes on health played a minor role. The moral and social consequences of smoking cigarettes loomed large in the themes that appeared in editorials, in news and magazine stories, quoting partisans of the antismoking organizations and in professional medical and scientific journals.[2] Cigarettes were gaining a meaning that spelled moral looseness coupled with a minimized respect for the authority of the male adult—the cigar and pipe smoker.

The following themes appeared in the public media of newspapers and magazines of the period. However, it would be misleading to impute a high level of consensus to this public discussion. Not only were different themes sounded by different people, but there was much disagreement, both within the ranks of nonsmokers and between smokers and nonsmokers.

1. The Threat to Male Dominance. During the nineteenth century in America, smoking was a major symbol and sign of the adult male in American life. The segregation of the genders and all that it implied was dramatically portrayed in the exclusivity of smoking as a masculine form of pleasure. Cigarettes, however, made it much easier for women to pursue the pleasures of smoking. Cigarettes could be easily hidden in purses and the newly invented safety match added to convenience and safety. The fact that women might begin to smoke reinforced the notion that cigarettes posed a social threat. It raised the fear that women might begin to smoke. Complaints of women smoking appeared in the newspapers in opposition to "continental habits" and in support of "good manners (*New York Times*, May 5, 1908, p.6). A New York assemblyman introducing his annual bill to prohibit the sale of cigarettes, expressed a sentiment appearing often in the public discourse of the period:

> "Do you know that any number of our High School girls, as well as boys, smoke cigarettes, and do you know that many foolish women are beginning to believe that it is real smart to learn to smoke cigarettes?
>
> Women in society have taken to smoking cigarettes and persons who are on the ragged edge of society think they have as much right. All roads to ruin are open when [boys and girls] begin to smoke." (*New York Times*, February 20, 1905)

It was not until several years after World War I that public smoking became acceptable for women (Schudson, 1984: Ch. 5). Cigarettes had already begun to be a symbol of equality between men and women. Whatever the intent of the smoker, the use of cigarettes assumed a political meaning.

As the cigar and pipe were symbolic of male power, the cigarette suffered among male consumers in the 1900s from identification with effeminacy. (I leave to more psychoanalytically oriented readers the obvious resemblance between the cigar and the penis.) That impediment to a more rapid development of the cigarette market among men was not to be overcome until after World War I.

2. The Moral Threat to Youth. With the beginnings of mass marketing of the cigarette, smoking was available to the adolescent. Characteristically, cigarettes were sold in packs of ten and it was sometimes possible to buy one at a time. In marketing them, especially for young men, Duke's advertisers often provided free cards with pictures of alluring young women (Sobel, 1978: Ch. 2).

Opponents associated cigarettes with depravity. The cigarette was described as an accompaniment to crime, lust, insobriety and a general looseness of social obligations. Some times this was attributed to the peers with whom the young smoker associated. Sometimes it was seen in the image of the "cigarette fiend" directly affected by the inhalation of smoke. This version was analogous to much current discussion of the effects of illegal drugs on the behavior of the addict (Inciardi, 1986, Chs. 3, 4). Occasionally the cigarette was portrayed in association with prostitutes and the woman user seen as a victim of loose morality brought about by the evil weed. Studies were cited establishing an association between cigarette smoking and crime (*Literary Digest*, 1914; Boyers, 1916; Hubbell, 1904). This theme is consistent with the constant fear of the "dangerous classes" and youth, which fill the nineteenth century and have continued to today (Gusfield, 1991; Kett, 1977; Monkkonen, 1975).

Illustrative of this view was the following from Charles Buckley Hubbell, President of the Board of Education of New York City:

> Boys of ten, twelve and fourteen years of age, naturally bright, were observed to be losing the power of concentration and application of mind....Further investigation disclosed the fact that very many of these boys stole money from their parents, or sold all sorts of articles that they could lay their hands on, in order that they could gratify an appetite that fed on its own indulgence." (Hubbell, 1904: 377)

3. Loss of Efficiency. The cigarette, some believed, caused a loss of productivity in the work force. Furthermore, it led to a decline in mental abilities. Studies were reported that indicated most students who smoked did poorly in their school grades (Carter, 1906: 488ff). Nonsmoking was seen as a prerequisite to an efficient school performance. The smoker was less likely to succeed; the nonsmoker had a head start in the game of life (This belief seems to have reappeared. Robb, 1991).

The themes of immorality, crime, and inefficiency sometimes appear together in the public discussions of cigarettes. Not everyone believed the assertions claiming responsibility of cigarettes for these problems. Nevertheless, they were sufficiently in the public discussion as "fact" that the social meanings of the cigarette were apparent. It conveyed a sense of challenge to authority, ranging from feared rebelliousness to a mild aura of naughtiness and "continental" sophistication.

4. *Polluting Effects of Smoking.* The traditional segregation of the genders when men smoked was defended as a concern for the sensibilities of women for whom smoke was assumed to be distasteful. The same argument, in reverse, was used by the Nonsmoker's Protective League to support laws that banned smoking in public buildings and transportation facilities. Such laws were passed in a number of localities. although their enforcement is less certain. Smoke was, for some, an impure substance and contact with it polluting. The cigarette smoker was portrayed as a physical threat to the nonsmoker.

5. *Medical Harm.* Physiologists and professors of medicine had begun to study the effects of smoking at the beginning of the twentieth century. They investigated the effects of smoking on blood pressure and on certain ailments of the eye (tobacco ambylopia) (Dunn, 1906; Bruce, Miller, and Hooker, 1909; *Journal of the American Medical Association*, 1909). Such studies were generally experimental and clinical and the results were mixed. No large-scale epidemiological study appeared during this period.

Several of the medical professors were scornful of intuitive judgments about health and morality found in the antismoking movements. Most, however, agreed that the prime focus was and should be on the cigarette. If for no other reason than that the smoker inhaled much more often than he did with other means of conveying smoke.

At no time in the early movement are health concerns at the center of the public discussion of cigarette smoking. There is no consensus, among medical researchers or the lay public, that the physiochemical consequences of cigarette smoking are very harmful to the health of the smoker.

By the entry of the United States into World War I all of the major themes in the contemporary antismoking movement were in place in some or most of the population. The popularity of the cigarette in post-World War II America owes little to a changed perception of its healthful or unhealthful properties that new research might have produced. While the use of cigarettes increased considerably among women, American men shifted their habit from cigars, pipes, and chewing tobacco to cigarettes. The total amount of tobacco in use in the United States remained stable between 1918 and 1940 while the sale of cigarettes increased greatly (Schudson, 1984: 182).

The Social Acceptance of the Cigarette

The antismoking movement collapsed in the wake of World War I. Many elements are associated with the rise of the cigarette habit and its acceptance by both genders of the American buying public. An adequate social history has not yet appeared although several elements of the story can be suggested. The carrying convenience of cigarettes , in contrast to pipes and cigars, supported their wide distribution to American soldiers. The association of the soldier with cigarette smoking did much to change the view among men that cigarettes were effeminate and also surrounded the cigarette with an aura of patriotism (Troyer and Markle, 1983: 40-47). The taboo against women smokers, which was weakened by the development of the cigarette, was further weakened as the cigarette came to be identified as a symbol of demand for equality of the sexes (Schudson, 1984: Ch. 5). By the early twenties, all of the state prohibitory legislation barring the sale of cigarettes to adults had been repealed.

The mildness of cigarettes, as compared to other forms of tobacco, aided its acceptance among women, as among men. During the 1920s, especially among urban, somewhat cosmopolitan and sophisticated women, smoking took on the symbolism of the modern. As Schudson expresses it, the cigarette was "connected to the young, the cosmopolitan and the naughty" (Schudson, 1984: 196) It is during the 1920s that smoking in public, although not yet on the streets, becomes acceptable conduct for women, especially in American cities.

In any understanding of the shift in smoking behavior in American life, it is clear that consciousness of health or illness played a small role, if any, prior to the 1950s. How this changed is a major part of this chapter.

Public Health: The Current Movement Against Smoking

Before 1964, an intuitive feeling that smoking was harmful existed among a number of Americans, but there was no widely accepted authority that settled the factual question of the healthfulness of smoking. Unlike the moral orientations of the earlier campaigns, the present movement has been oriented toward health and directed as an aspect of public health. The earlier movement was largely led by voluntary associations. The present movement has been sparked and directed primarily by public health agencies of government, especially the Federal government. It has found its authority in the research of medical science.

For much of its use in Western societies there has been some intuition that smoking is harmful but also some intuition that it is not. How great is the risk of disease from smoking? The individual citizen is no epidemiologist , experimental physiologist or medical clinician. Whatever his or her intuitive sense about cigarettes and the medical risks in its use, he or she must look to others to make such determinations. But what others? Who "owns" the cigarette question? [3]

By the late 1940s in the United States, cigarette smoking had become common in all classes and genders. Its possible negative effects on health were not a public issue and it could be said that cigarette smoking was not a public problem. By the mid-1960s, this was no longer the case. A public consensus had developed in the belief that smoking cigarettes is harmful to health, that it significantly heightens the risks of developing lung cancer, heart trouble, and other diseases. That consensus is largely the work of scientific research, governmental and news reporting, and the emergence and activity of voluntary medical organizations. It represents the hegemony of medical science over the culture of health.

Divisions often exist not only about the wisdom of public policies but also about the very facts that constitute the conditions of problems. As it operates in social actions, "reality" is not something given in the nature of things, plain for all to see and agree upon. Events and conditions have to be attended to and interpreted. The current American birth rate or the Gross National Product are instances of aggregated facts that cannot be directly perceived by individuals. We depend on institutions and persons that accumulate data and transmit them to an interested audience. It is in this sense that I consider the belief in the harmful effects of cigarettes as an example of "the social construction of reality" (Berger and Luckmann, 1967; Spector and Kitsuse, 1977).

In the early antismoking movement, the body of research on the negative effects of smoking was too scattered, too conflicting, and too unavailable to the public to serve as an authoritative guide to behavior, a guide that was difficult for the individual to ignore or to impeach. While surveys at the time indicated a public acceptance and appreciation of "Science" as an institution and scientists as disinterested investigators, there was little of the institutional structure of scientific research that has emerged over the past fifty years (LaFollette, 1990). Nor was the role of government in medical research as central as it became after World War II (Brandt, 1990). By the time the Surgeon General issued the now famed Report of 1964, conditions had come to be favorable to the transmission and credibility of medical science and the position of the Federal government as a source of authoritative advice and activity in the promotion of health.

The Emergence of a Scientific Elite

World War II was an enormous stimulus to the development of Science in the United States. The construction of the Lawrence Laboratory at UC Berkeley and the successful Manhattan Project to create the atomic bomb demonstrated what might be accomplished by governmental subsidization of scientists in large-scale projects (Davis, 1968; Nelkin, 1987). Although there had been earlier instances of such subsidization, as a general policy of the Federal government it is largely a creature of the recent past.

By 1964, a structure of science had emerged that made possible the development of a range of medical studies and their dissemination to a public that was attentive to them. Large-scale epidemiological research was itself a relatively new development in medical science. The language with which the smoking problem was discussed and the institutions responsible for developing and disseminating knowledge about it were those charged with the functions of maintaining and improving the health of the nation. Among these, the Public Health Service and the Surgeon General's Office of the Federal government were preeminent.

Findings of research were now more easily transmitted to the general public. By 1964, science reporting had become a part of journalism and the science reporter a specialist on many newspapers and newsmagazines. William Laurence of the *New York Times* and Milton Silverman of the *San Francisco Chronicle*, pioneers in the field, had begun their careers as science reporters in the late 1930s. This meant that some reporters now read certain scientific journals regularly and were attentive to work they saw as significant for their readers.[4] In the medical field this meant that the reports published in the *Journal of the*

American Medical Association, the *New England Journal of Medicine*, *Lancet* and several other journals for published studies were now accessible to the public. The *Reader's Digest* played a significant role as well in reporting the medical research on smoking, especially in the 1950s. The public was better educated than in the past and was now exposed to television as well as print media (Nelkin, 1987; Pfohl, 1984).

Since the early antismoking movement, a non-professional medical establishment has developed in the form of organizations that support research and seek to persuade the public of healthful forms of living. Among these are the American Cancer Society, the American Heart Association, and the American Lung Association. The ACS was the major source of funds for some of the most widely cited epidemiological studies of smoking prior to 1964 and since.

Lastly, the federal government became a major player in the game of health promotion. The Department of Health, Education and Welfare was not established in the United States until the 1950s. Medicine was not conceptualized as a major concern of the federal government earlier, even though government sanitary engineers had played a paramount role in public health activities that greatly improved the country's resistance to major infectious diseases. That the Surgeon General's Report was received with a high degree of credibility suggests the trust that government and science possessed in 1964.

Of course, medical science in the past had often played a large role in affecting personal behavior and public action. The discovery of germ-produced disease, the spread of immunizing vaccinations, and the work of sanitary engineers are all highly significant developments in the relations between medical science, government, and the individual. What is new, however, is the great increase in health-consciousness in a public fed daily by a multitude of accounts in newspapers, magazines, and television of the latest scientific research, the newest discovery, the most recent advice on how to prevent illness and improve health. Such material is a major part of the more general concern for healthy living characterized as the "health fitness movement" (see below).

Medical Science and the Health Effects of Smoking

The modern study of the health effects of smoking might be dated from 1900, from 1925, or from 1938 (Wagner, 1971: 69ff). Such studies however made little dent on the public. A sense of harm con-

nected with tobacco smoking in all forms was present in the nineteenth century and earlier (Wagner, 1971; Best, 1979). That intuition
was strengthened by the first antismoking movement and continued as
an element in American culture after the movement ceased to be an
active force in public policy. During the 1930s and 1940s, there was a
growing consciousness that smoking was unhealthy. Several studies
found a strong statistical association between heavy cigarette smoking
and the incidence of lung cancer which was on the rise in the United
States (Brandt, 1990). These studies rang alarms but too softly to be
heard. It was finally in the fifties that a number of prospective epidemiological studies on the risks of smoking were undertaken, especially in the United States, in Canada, and in England. By the late
1950s, these studies had developed in importance so that major news
magazines reported their findings in featured studies, sometimes with
critics as well (*Consumer Reports*, December 1958: 628-36; *Cort, The
Nation*, August 15, 1959: 69-71; *Newsweek*, December 21, 1959: 80-
81; *Time*, June 13,1955: 67-69; May 5, 1958: 61; April 27, 1959: 73;
U.S. News and World Report, June 17, 1955: 45-47; August 2, 1957:
84-86; July 26, 1957: 56-75). The demand for a governmental review
of this material was growing. In December of 1959, Surgeon General
Burney issued a statement condemning smoking as unhealthy
(*Newsweek*, December 7, 1959: 66).

The studies of the 1950s formed the major bases for the conclusions of the Surgeon General's Report of 1964. Issued in January of
that year and accompanied by a televised press conference, it marked
the definitive beginning of a medical and public consensus that tobacco is harmful to health (U.S Department of Health, Education and
Welfare, 1964a).

1964: The Emergence of Consensus

The alacrity with which the Surgeon General's Report of 1964, and
subsequent reports, were accepted as reality, as true conclusions, is
indicative of the legitimacy of the scientific and the governmental
medical agencies in American life. Once issued, the mass media treated
the conclusions of the Report as certain and authoritative. In 1959,
Newsweek, in its medicine section, described the question of the harmful
effects of cigarette smoking as still awaiting "a final, undebatable
medical answer" (*Newsweek*, July 27, 1959: 80). In 1962, the maga-

zine began a story of the announcement that the Surgeon General would review the question with the phrase, "No one can say with certainty that cigarettes cause cancer" (*Newsweek*, June 18, 1962: 74).

In a later issue, *Newsweek* described the steps in developing that report as "an attempt to settle one of medicine's most controversial questions,..." (*Newsweek*, November 19, 1962). When the report did appear, in January 1964, *Newsweek* gave it two and one-half pages and implicitly criticized the long wait before the government agreed with other countries and American health agencies. However, *Newsweek* now described the belief in the health hazard of smoking as having "the full weight " of U.S. authority. It referred to the report itself as "the official judgment" (*Newsweek*, January 20, 1964: 48).

The conclusions of the Surgeon General were reported elsewhere by the press in similarly definitive terms. The *New York Times* began an editorial with the statement, "Now it is official" (*New York Times*, January 12, 1964). In the same edition, on the front page, the *Times* stated that the report " found no doubt about the role of cigarette smoking in causing cancer of the lungs" (Sullivan, 1964). *Time* magazine stressed the way in which the "impartial committee of top experts" unanimously supported what was already known about the harmful effects of smoking (*Time*, January 17, 1964).

That the report was quickly accepted by public segments is seen by the decline in cigarette sales and numbers of Americans who said, in surveys, that they had stopped smoking. 1964 was a watershed year. Per capita consumption of tobacco in the United States decreased continuously from a high of 4,345 cigarettes in 1963 to 3,971 in 1969 (U.S. Department of Agriculture, 1990: 100, 106). Surveys of the American population also show a continuous decline in the percentage of smokers since 1965 (U.S Department of Health and Human Services, 1986: 19-20; 1988: 565-66).

Medical Knowledge and the Public

To refer to the hegemony of science is to call attention to the way in which the institution of science, medical science in this instance, creates a believable reality, based on scientific research. Scientists may have to convince each other of the "facts," but they do not have to go far to be the source of the construction of the "real" character of smoking and health. The very attention of the news media is itself an important element in the definition of the truth about smoking. The construction of that reality is an important part of the role that medical science plays.

What is the status of the knowledge of the medical consequences of smoking? David Bloor makes a distinction between "high status knowledge" and "low status knowledge" (Bloor, 1992). For much of the public that has been aware of the Surgeon General's reports, the condemnation of smoking rests on the certainty of verified knowledge. Such knowledge is the property of those uninvolved in the complexities of the investigations. It is low-status knowledge. For those involved in the production of the knowledge, the result of research is more complex. It is "high status knowledge." Probability, revision, and qualification are more the rule in epidemiological studies that depend on talking to human beings or utilizing records produced by human beings. The 1964 Surgeon General's Report is no different in that respect. It rested its claims heavily on epidemiological studies, although clinical and experimental research were taken into account (U.S. Department of Health, Education and Welfare, 1964).

The epidemiological studies on which the writers of the report based much of their conclusions were seven prospective studies, ones in which data on smoking habits are drawn from a population and the same population followed over a period of years. (Sociologists would call these "longitudinal" studies.) Despite consistent findings, the studies presented problems in interpretation. Some of these are recognized and dealt with in the Report. The authors themselves suggest four major deficiencies in the study populations on which the research was based (USDHEW, 1964: 94-96). First, the samples were entirely men and not representative of the total populations of American, British or Canadian men studied. The samples of respondents were better educated than the total populations from which they were drawn. Second, reporting of deaths was incomplete, especially where they depended on volunteers' reports. Third, even though smokers had higher death rates than nonsmokers, the death rates of both groups, corrected for age, was below the national average, especially so for nonsmokers. As the authors of the report point out, this suggests that the nonsmokers were an especially healthy group. Lastly, the study populations did not include people in hospitals, who would have probably increased the numbers of those who died during the sampled periods. In addition, the almost exclusive use of volunteers in gathering data in two of the largest studies (70 percent of the total populations studied) led to ignorance of the number and character of non-respondents or how a large part of the population was sampled. A number of other criticisms and qualifications have been made in medical and other journals where the validity of public health conclusions about smoking have been debated (Burch, 1983; 1984; Eysenck, 1989; Sterling, 1975; Lilienfield, 1983; Weiss; 1975).

What I wish to convey by this discussion is the distinction between conclusions derived from wise, informed judgments and those very rare conclusions in human studies that can be presented with certainty.[5] The authors of the report were aware of many of the defects of the studies. They write, at one point, that "Any answer to the question to what general population of men can the results be applied must involve an element of unverifiable judgment" (p. 94).

An essential part of the report's conclusions is developed around a specific perspective toward the concept of causation. Given that most smokers do not develop lung cancer and that some nonsmokers do develop lung cancer, the concept of a single linear cause, necessary or sufficient, is rejected. Indeed, the authors of the report developed a complex view of cause, which was itself, an innovation in epidemiology (Burch, 1983; Brandt, 1990). It utilized criteria based on consistency, strength, specificity, temporality, and coherence of the statistical associations between smoking and death rates. No single criterion or study is sufficient but a number of different criteria, taken together, establish a test (pp. 181-89):

> As already stated, statistical methods cannot establish proof of a causal relationship in an association. The causal significance of an association is a matter of judgment which goes beyond any statement of statistical probability. (p. 182)

The authors of the report, aware of the immense difficulties in achieving certainty, defend their conclusions and recommendations by stressing the interrelated elements of the consistency, strength, specificity, temporality and coherence of the associations found in the various studies (pp. 183-86). Thus, despite their differences, all of the studies found similar relative risks for lung cancer. All report a dose-effect phenomenon: heavy smokers were more likely to die earlier and of lung cancer than were lighter smokers; lighter smokers more than ex-smokers and ex-smokers more than nonsmokers.

Medical research operating in the ownership of public problems has the dilemma of waiting for the almost never occurrence of certainty of proof or not addressing themselves to a public eager to know the best advice. An editorial in the *American Journal of Public Health* makes the case. While the precise importance of smoking can be debated, wrote the editor,

> there can be no question that widespread cessation of smoking would result in more good than harm. To dilute the importance of smoking is to foolishly divert us from an important goal. (Ibrahim, 1976: 133)

The summary of the Report, published nine months later, cautiously stated:

> On the basis of prolonged study and evaluation of many lines of converging evidence, the Committee makes the following judgment:
> CIGARETTE SMOKING IS A HEALTH HAZARD OF SUFFICENT IMPORTANCE IN THE UNITED STATES TO WARRANT APPROPRIATE REMEDIAL ACTION. (USDHEW, September 1964: 6)

In discussing the possible causative role of smoking in coronary disease, the report finds such a role, though not proven, strongly enough suspected to warrant countermeasures. They conclude:

> IT IS ALSO MORE PRUDENT TO ASSUME THAT THE ESTABLISHED ASSOCIATION BETWEEN CIGARETTE SMOKING AND CORONARY DISEASE HAS CAUSATIVE MEANING THAN TO SUSPEND JUDGMENT UNTIL NO UNCERTAINTY REMAINS. (p. 10)

In public discourse, however, the distinction between the guarded character of "judgment" and the certainty of "cause" gets lost. In the arena of public knowledge, qualifications and conceptual difficulties gave way to consensus and certainty. The *San Diego Union* began its front-page story on the 1964 report with the sentence, "Heavy cigarette smoking is the principal cause of cancer of the lungs (*San Diego Union*, January 12, 1964: 1). American Cancer Society materials currently use several different terms. Sometimes they refer to smoking being "responsible" for harm; sometimes to "cause" and sometimes to "may cause" (American Cancer Society, 1982; 1987a, b). A statement mandated to be placed on the walls of California hotels and restaurants that permit smoking reads: "WARNING: This Facility Permits Smoking and Tobacco Smoke is Known to the State of California to Cause Cancer." In these forms, public discourse is informed by a more ordered and certain perception of harm than given by the necessarily fragile and limited character of wise judgment.

The Culture of Healthful Living

The Surgeon General's reports and the media's reporting were couched in the language of health. While such language does not disappear, in the three decades since the report a distinct moral tone has been added; the individual's responsibility to follow the advice of medical science becomes a significant element in health or illness. To some extent, we have returned to the moral rhetoric of the earlier movement.

The Meanings of Illness

The Surgeon General's reports on smoking, published annually since 1964, do not occur in a vacuum. They are congruent with and add to a more general shift in the perception of health and medicine, which was, and still is, occurring in American life. In the remainder of this chapter, I want to consider divergent conceptions of health and medicine and the place of smoking in them.

The smoking issue may be described in more general terms in order to highlight the idea of health as an aspect of morality. Illness may be, and has been, seen as a sign of deficient moral character, that epidemics can become symbols of communal malfeasance. This Sodom and Gomorrah story is especially clear in illnesses such as venereal disease and AIDS. Here the source of disease includes human behavior. This viewpoint is to be contrasted with that perspective in which medical science focuses on the non-purposive, non-human forms of disease instigation. Illness is seen as a result of factors external to individual character or behavior (Tesh, 1991). The individual's health is less a result of harmful living than of chance, genetics, and environment. Attention is thus directed toward treatment of disease rather than toward educating the public toward changed styles of behavior.

While the search for a cure for cancer is still dominated by the latter view, in cases of smoking and lung cancer and coronary disease, styles of living and personal habits have assumed great importance as ways of preventing illness. To see cancer or heart trouble as consequent on a style of living is to shift, to some degree, the nature of the disease and responsibility for its occurrence onto the person. In this fashion, medicine comes to emphasize prevention of diseases by proper living, by who you are, rather than treatment by chemical or physical means.

Who then is the healthful person? What is the life style enjoined by the transformation of health from the domain of the medical institution to the domain of the individual? Since the 1970s, the public has been exposed to the idea that the healthful person incorporates the pursuit of good health into his or her daily life, at work and at leisure. He or she eats nutritiously, avoiding excess fats, watching caloric intake and aiming at weight reduction. Exercise is a part of leisure; jogging, fitness activity, cycling are all aspects of daily routine. Drinking alcohol is risky behavior and should be limited or eliminated. Smoking is a foolish risk and should not be a part of life. "Safe sex" should be the rule. Health is not the absence of illness but something pursued in the very way we behave (Stone, 1986; Zola, 1972; Gusfield, 1992). This emphasis on the adoption of healthful styles of living can be considered a social movement—the health-fitness movement (Goldstein, 1991). It has been advocated and supported by work of the health "establishment," including government and voluntary medical associations such the American Health Association (U.S. Department of Health, Education and Welfare, 1979).

The individual becomes the focus of responsibility for his or her own health. A further example is found in the rise of the nutritional approach to health, an approach which was met with skepticism and resistance by medical science in the 1950s and early 1960s, but which has become a major element in American orientations toward good health (Belasco, 1989; Gusfield, forthcoming; Schwartz, 1986, Goldstein, 1991). What we eat and how much we eat has come to be viewed as a major element in preventing or developing illness.

The role of government in this endeavor at preventive medicine is furthered by the increased role of federal and state governments in financing medical care and the greatly enhanced costs of physician and hospital services. Preventive medicine has virtues for public finance when compared to the one-on-one costs of treating and hospitalizing ill patients.

The Smoker as Responsible Victim

The advice of the health organizations, including government, has been a major part of the health-fitness movement. That advice includes the underlying "moral message" of the movement. In its focus on preventive behavior, the rhetoric of the advice distinguishes between responsible and irresponsible people. Smokers are foolish, ignorant, or lacking in the kind of character necessary for healthfulness. The reward of a healthful life-style is long life; the punishment of unhealthy living is early death. The avoidance of risk is a virtue; the acceptance of risk is vice.

The Surgeon General's annual reports on smoking, from 1964 until the early 1980s, and the news coverage that transmitted them, are largely addressed to a public who is to be persuaded to stop smoking or never to begin to smoke. Their rhetoric makes an appeal to a disciplined self-control. The person is asked to act in a rational fashion by developing habits that minimize risk and to give up habits that maximize risk. It is assumed that sensible people will desire a longer and more healthful life. Only fools or foolish addicts will begin smoking or make no efforts to stop. The person who persists in smoking is a victim of his or her own ignorance, stupidity, or lack of self-control. Either way the smoker falls short of the character enjoined by authoritative medical science.

The Healthful Public

In describing the public response to the Surgeon General's Reports I have not differentiated parts of the population from one another. The image of the healthful citizen as a model to be followed above is however more prevalent in some segments of the population than others. Not everyone is a follower of medical news in the popular culture of contemporary America.[6] Not everyone places the trust in science described above. Not everyone makes health the cornerstone of life depicted in the model of the healthful citizen.

Our knowledge of the segments of population that are attuned to medical science and incorporate health recommendations into their lives is still meager. Nevertheless, all studies report that the college-educated public are the prime recipients and appreciators of health news and advice (USDHSS, 1989: Ch. 5; USDHSS, 1986; Schoenborn and Boyd, 1989; Pierce, Fiore, et al., 1989; Fiore, Novotny, et al., 1989). Lesser, but significant, differences exist between income levels (Goldstein, 1991; Williams, 1990; Fuchs, 1979). Smoking is similar to other forms of a healthy life-style.

In the years since the 1964 Surgeon General's Reports, these surveys have consistently presented three important findings in respect to smoking:

1. The cessation of smoking and absence of initiation into smoking is more often found among better educated than less educated persons. This is especially true of the gap between college-educated and non-college-educated persons. It is also truer of men than of women. (This latter finding is reversed in other forms of health behavior in the health-fitness movement such as alcohol use and dieting, where women are more responsive to health advice.)

2. That difference has been continuous and has increased over the years since 1964. White-collar workers are less likely to smoke than are blue-collar workers and employed workers more likely to smoke than unemployed workers. High school students expecting to attend four-year colleges are less likely to smoke than are students not expecting to continue education past high school. These indices of smoking and cessation from smoking show the close association between compliance with health advice and markers of social class and status. While studies indicate a high level of knowledge of the harmful effects of smoking at all social levels, the response to health information is structured along lines of social stratification.

3. While both men and women have decreased in their usage of cigarettes, the decrease has been considerably greater among men than women. At present the prevalence of smoking among women is only slightly less than among men. Considering new smokers, women are beginning to smoke in larger percentages than are men.

The Social Symbolism of Commodities

These styles of daily living are part of the person's "cultural capital" (Bourdieu, 1977; 1984). By marking him or her as someone of a specific style they are signs of membership in networks of people of like styles. In Veblen's terms, they are signs that the claimant to a status and to a group membership is a person of worth and not someone of a different and less valuable culture (Veblen, 1899).

To refrain from smoking becomes necessary to the style of the health-oriented, rational, risk-aversive person. Following the prescriptions of medical science also displays to oneself that he or she is a person of virtue. It shows that the person takes a measured, self-controlled attitude toward his or her life and behavior. He and she are persons who have heard the calls of medical research and have the will to avoid the indulgences toward which a consumer-oriented market beckons their participation. To cease smoking demonstrates the capacity for self-control that has so often been a mark of American self-help movements.

Creating Moral Boundaries: Smokers as Victims and Villains

In the health-fitness movement, smoking has been described as a habit hurting the smoker. Since the early 1980s, however, this situation has changed. With the research and publicity about passive smoking, the smoker has become troubling to others, to nonsmokers, as well as to himself or herself.

The appearance of research on passive smoking, its dissemination to the antismoking public and the recent wave of legislative and administrative polices based on conceptions of passive smoking have widened the distinctions between the smoker and nonsmoker. By the 1990s, the smoker was not only a foolish victim of his or her habit, but also an obnoxious and uncivil source of danger, pollution, and illness to others. The early movement against the cigarette and the current movement against smoking take on growing similarities.

Smoking and the Creation of Moral Boundaries

In a recent case challenging the use of gender as a screening device in health insurance rates, the Supreme Court judge gave voice to the now more common usage of the unhealthy life style as a point of differentiation between Americans:

> when insurance risks are grouped together, the better risks always subsidize the poorer risks. Healthy persons subsidize benefits for the less healthy...persons who eat, drink or smoke to excess may subsidize pension benefits for persons whose habits are more temperate....To insure the flabby and the fit as though they were equivalent risks may be more common than treating men and women alike. (City of Los Angeles Department of Water and Power vs. Manhart, 435 US 702, 710:1978)

What is noteworthy in this opinion is the consciousness of healthful and unhealthful life styles as bases for boundaries of significance in American society. "Excess" and "temperate" are used in this context as terms of opprobrium and approval as are "flabby" and "fit."

Before the emergence of the antismoking movement, the issue of smoking did not warrant enough significance to make it a part of descriptions of people. While parents may have cautioned their teen-aged children against it, smoking occupied the same status as drink-ing: an adult pleasure which children might be expected to experiment with before adulthood. It might be a chastised act among teenagers, but by itself was an ambiguous dereliction. This has changed and smoking has become a matter of note, of distinction. Even in personal, singles ads today modes of eating, drinking, and smoking are ele-ments of self-description (*New York Review of Books*, 1991). Smoking or nonsmoking has become an issue, a behavior toward which a stand must be taken. As a source of social distinctions it has been given a moral status. "Substance abuse" has added smoking to form a new trinity: alcohol, cigarettes, and drugs.

For Americans in the middle years (25-60), lower class and less educated people have higher death and illness rates than their oppo-sites (House, et al., 1990). There is evidence that differences in life styles, perhaps more than access to medical care, explain such class differences in health (Williams, 1990). It is beyond the scope of this chapter to disentangle the ways in which differences in class affect styles of health behavior. A credible argument can be made for the view that income, education, and occupation create a social milieu which deeply influences access to information, dispositions to self-control, and exposure to smoke and to smoking pressures (Navarro, 1976; Tesh, 1991).

I do not want to overstate the differences between life styles and social groups. For one thing, according to the NIH surveys for 1987 in all educational levels today most people are nonsmokers. In 1985, smokers made up approximately 18 percent of those with sixteen or more years of education, but they only made up approximately 34 percent of those with less than twelve years of education (Pierce, Fiore, et al., 1989). Neither are class and education levels fully con-gruent. In American society, as compared to other nations, such as France, the cultures of classes and other groups are only loosely ho-mogeneous (Lamont, forthcoming).

A better way to think about the boundaries developing in American society is to think about health habits and fitness as emergent criteria by which people judge each other, with smoking behavior serving as an important indicator (Troyer and Markle, 1983). In this respect, consciousness of smoking as a boundary marker is more likely to be shared in the professional, college-educated, expert-oriented upper middle class than in social classes with opposite attributes.

Passive Smoking: The Smoker as Pariah

During the early 1980s, the public became aware of research on what is known as "involuntary smoking" or "passive smoking." This research, carried out in several countries, has investigated the effect on the health of nonsmokers of being in the presence of smokers (USDHHS, 1986: Ch. 2; Repace, 1985: Ch. 1).The dominant research has consisted of epidemiological studies of the children of smokers and the nonsmoking spouses of smokers. While the effects of different periods and different circumstances of exposure to smoke by non-smokers is still undergoing debate, discussion, and further investigations, it has already had a profound impact on the antismoking movement and on the moral meanings of smoking and smokers. Scientific support for belief in the danger of smoking for nonsmokers has been the intellectual basis for legislation and policy to prohibit smoking in many public areas and to segregate smokers from nonsmokers in many public and work areas.[7]

Before the 1980s, the smokers had been viewed in public discourse as people who should be troubling to themselves. Now they were becoming people troubling to others as well. In this fashion, smokers have become similar in the public eye to users of alcohol and illicit drugs (Gusfield, 1991).

The emergence of research into passive smoking has turned the distaste of smoke into a positive source of exclusion. The smoker is on the defensive as the act of smoking is increasingly banished from many social circles and the smoker so frequently admonished not to smoke. The mandatory exclusion of smoking from public places, including outdoor seating areas in stadia, furthers the public definition of the smoker as pariah.

As we have seen in the materials on the early antismoking movement, a belief in the polluting effects of smoking and a distaste for proximity to smoke has been a part of American culture for a long time. In public discourse and policy, it remained in the background until recent years. Now it is forcefully and often legally revived. Cigarettes have come to assume the status of "dangerous object." The *New*

York Times, in an editorial sounding the theme of the shift in the status of the smoker, wrote:

> What a difference a few years and a few Surgeon General's Reports can make. Only yesterday the nonsmoker was perceived as odd man (or woman) out. Today it's the smoker who stands out. Only 30 per cent of adults smoke now, and they may be feeling a bit hounded. (*New York Times*, December 19, 1984: A38)

Public policy cannot wait until scientific criticism has been answered. It draws on the already present intuitive sense of the polluting character of smoke to which the twenty-five years of the contemporary antismoking movement has been added. The resulting pressure for legal measures to segregate smoking and its absence has produced a still continuing set of local and state measures banning and/or limiting smoking in public areas.

In recent years, a variety of policies have been put in place that implicitly and symbolically create the definition of the smoker as pariah, someone to be excluded from casual sociability unless he or she abides by the rules of nonsmoking (Shauffler, 1993; Sugarman, 1993). Individual life insurance and hospitalization-health insurance now require higher premiums for the smoker than the nonsmoker (Stone, 1986). The physical segregation of the smoker on airplanes is now supplanted by the elimination of smoking from all domestic flights in the United States. Increasingly smoking is bracketed with other vices such as drinking and drug abuse. When New York City recently outlawed smoking in public places, the law exempted bars from its provisions, again associating smoking with marginally acceptable areas of behavior. Norms of civility in many social circles now restrict the smoker from smoking in the presence of others (Skolnick and Kagan, 1993). Smoking is an indulgence if granted at all by hosts, and often requires the smoker to exclude himself or herself temporarily from sociability.

The moral boundaries between smokers and nonsmokers are now widened by actual physical boundaries. Whenever the smoker steps outside to smoke he or she acts out the symbolism of the pariah being cast from the community. As smoking takes on the attributes of social deviance, of unsocial action, it is even more able to play the role of a social divider. It symbolizes the inability to be aware of or to respect medical science—a sign of the less educated person.

Public Health and the Individual

The antismoking campaigns and the health fitness movement have raised again the issues of paternalism and civil liberties. Such issues have always dogged public health efforts to create an environment that would minimize risks entailed to the individual by unhealthy behavior (Beauchamp, 1988). Whether public policy should intervene in the free market of business supply and consumer choice has been a question in the movement against the cigarette as it has in other similar public health activities. The developing norms of smoking act to segregate smoking rather than prohibit it entirely (Skolnick and Kagan, 1993). To smoke or not to smoke, to cease or not to cease, are still consumer choices.

The effort to eradicate the cigarette in American life is another stage in the public and self-control of individual life through science and reason. It is in this sense that the health movement and the component promotion of nonsmoking are a facet of modernization. The extension of discipline and forethought to the body as a continuation of the self presupposes and reinforces an image of the noble person. As eating, drinking, smoking, physical movement, and leisure are objects of expert, professional advice and law, the individual who shuns the hegemony of the health elite risks both early death and social censure.

By contrast, the resistance by some to the advice of medical science and public health reflects a distrust of law, social norms and other constraints on individual action. This resistance is a facet of the glorification of the uniqueness and expressiveness of the authentic person in American culture. It symbolizes an individualism which has long been seen as accentuated in the United States as compared to other democratic and modernized societies (Beauchamp. 1988: Ch. 5; Lukes, 1973; Riesman, 1950; Bellah, et al., 1985).

In the context of that cultural tension between the individual and the public, the cigarette becomes a symbol of rebellion and individuality. A recent movie, *The Fabulous Baker Boys*, illustrates the point. This is the story of two brothers who work as a dual piano team playing popular music in nightclubs and cocktail lounges. The film is set in the present. The bourgeois brother lives in the suburbs with his family. The other lives in sleazier quarters in the city. The cigarette smoking of the less conformist brother is an issue between the two of them. A female singer, who hints of a past as a prostitute, joins the duo. Her smoking and that of the more "outcast" brother establishes a contrast to the conventional brother. In the end, the bohemian brother gives up his job playing the kind of popular music he hates to devote himself to the jazz world of his black friends. The "hero" has opted for the authenticity of impulse and risk. Smoking is a sign of his identity: a symbol of his opposition to convention and comfort. The cigarette has been given an "heroic" meaning.

From a standpoint of rational concern with health, such attitudes may appear frivolous, foolish, romantic, and hedonistic. What medical science advises is a disciplined orientation toward the body based on avoidance of risk. The rational person seeks to maximize life at an acceptable level of bodily comfort. The costs of indulgence in harmful behavior clearly outweigh whatever may be the transient benefits of bodily neglect. A rational orientation toward life and leisure consists in constant consciousness of how each action contributes to health and longevity. Instant gratification, impulsive behavior, habit-forming activities are a threat to wellness.

The contrast in perspectives is also illustrated in the necessarily public, aggregated character of the research material on smoking. In almost all of the material on the risks of smoking, the differences in death rates between smokers and nonsmokers are stated in relative rather than absolute terms. Thus we know that the chances of a smoker dying of lung cancer during the period studied for the 1964 report was approximately ten times that of a nonsmoker. This way of reporting the data tells us nothing about the absolute chance of dying of lung cancer. For example, in the data of the 1964 report, for the sample studied, that chance, calculated by myself, was approximately 1/357 for smokers; 1/3807 for nonsmokers.[8] From the standpoint of the total nation that difference in risk is very important. In a large population it adds up to a magnitude of considerable importance. From the standpoint of the individual its significance is less clear (Beauchamp, 1988: Ch. 5). Will he or she be that one? That is compounded out of all the elements known and unknown that determine who will contract lung cancer. Smoking is a significant addition to those elements, to be sure, but its importance is accentuated from the perspective of the total population. It is the public character of the risk rather than its application to specific persons that forms the basis for environmental control and individual advice.

The contemporary place of the cigarette in American life is a distant shout from its accepted position in the 1950s. Despite the opposition of the tobacco industry, the public health campaigns of the past three decades have brought about a remarkable change in attitudes and meanings toward smoking. The health movement has produced a cultural shift in the meaning of health and patterns of living that would have seemed impossible thirty years ago. A new reality has superseded an older one. The current meaning of smoking is by no means a mirror image of the early twentieth-century antismoking movement in the United States, nor is it a complete contrast to the 1950s. But it now includes some important similarities. Although in the 1960s the findings of medical science reversed the accepted place of smoking in American life, by the 1990s smoking has become a moral as well as a medical issue.

We live in a world of symbols in which commodities can both represent ourselves to others and to ourselves, in which the measures taken to improve or ignore healthful acts are immersed in a society that defines the virtuous, the villainous, the foolish, and the romantic. Like most acts of human beings, smoking is not aloof from a culture where meanings dilute the boundaries of medicine, morality, and science.

Notes

1. Both books, by Wagner and Sobel, are lacking adequate documentation. Wagner's has neither footnotes nor bibliographical references, although there are frequent quotations. Sobel's has a bibliographical note, but does not document specific assertions or quotations.
2. Virtually all materials on smoking listed in the *Reader's Guide* and in the *Index Medica* prior to 1945 and available in the University of California, San Diego library were read. We excluded figures on tobacco production, voting on anticigarette bills in state legislatures, letters to the editors and articles about other uses of tobacco (e. g., nicotine as a natural insecticide). After 1930, the evils of tobacco were discounted and almost no information was listed in the *Reader's Guide*.
3. For a fuller discussion of the concept of "the ownership of social problems," see Gusfield, 1981.
4. I am indebted to Milton Silverman, formerly of the *San Francisco Chronicle*, and to David Perlman, currently science reporter for the *Chronicle*, for informative conversations on the history and current functioning of science reporters.
5. "In sum, *any scientific estimate is likely to be based on incomplete knowledge combined with assumptions, each of which is a source of uncertainty that limits the accuracy that should be assigned to the estimate"* (National Research Council, 1988: 44).
6. As David Perlman, science reporter for the *San Francisco Chronicle* put it in an interview: "If I write an article about AIDS most everyone in the gay community will read it but very few drug users will do so."

7. This chapter was completed and in press before the appearance of the widely publicized report on passive smoking of the U.S. Environmental Protection Agency in December 1992 (U.S. EPA, 1992). Its general conclusion, that "environmental tobacco smoke in the United States presents a serious and substantial health impact" (p.1-1), rests chiefly on sources also reviewed for this chapter. The report appears to have already increased support for restrictions on smoking in public places.

8. This figure of absolute risks differs from that of Viscusi who reported the risk of lung cancer death for smokers in a range of .05-.10. He used lung cancer rates per year and thus a much longer period of time in which outcomes of smoking were manifest. He also assumed that 85 percent of lung cancer deaths were due to smoking. He does not report the absolute rate of lung cancer deaths over the same period for nonsmokers. The research reported in the Surgeon General's 1964 report referred to a specific population over a period of approximately 10-15 years (Viscusi, 1990).

References

American Cancer Society. 1982. "The Most Often Asked Questions about Smoking, Tobacco and Health and....The Answers." Sections 4, 24, 26.

_____. 1987a. "Facts on Lung Cancer."

_____. 1987b. "The Truth about Alcohol Use—Statistics, Facts and Figures."

Beauchamp, Dan. 1980. *Beyond Alcoholism: Alcohol and Public Health Policy*. Philadelphia: Temple University Press.

Belasco, Warren. 1989. *Appetite for Change: How the Counterculture Took on the Food Industry, 1966-1988*. New York: Pantheon.

Berger, Peter, and Luckman, Thomas. 1967. *The Social Construction of Reality: A Treatise on the Sociology of Knowledge*. Garden City, NY: Anchor Books/Doubleday.

Best, Joel. 1979. "Economic Interests and the Vindication of Deviance: Tobacco in Seventeenth Century Europe." *The Sociological Quarterly* 20 (spring): 171-82.

Bourdieu, Pierre. 1984. *Distinction: A Social Critique of the Judgment of Taste*. Cambridge, MA: Harvard University Press.

Boyers, Charles. 1916. "A City Fights the Cigarette Habit." *The American City*, Vol. 14, No. 4 (April): 369-70.

Brandt, Allen. 1990. "The Cigarette, Risk, and American Culture." *Daedalus* 19: 155-76.

Bruce, James, James Miller, and Donald Hooker. 1909. The Effect of Smoking Upon the Blood Pressures and Upon the Volume of the Hand." *American Journal of Physiology* 24: 104-16.

Burch, P. R. J. 1983. "The Surgeon General's 'Epidemiologic Criteria for Causality': A Critique." *Journal of Chronic Diseases* 36: 821-36.

_____. 1984, "The Surgeon-General's 'Epidemiologic Criteria for Causality': Reply to Lillienfeld.", *Journal of Chronic Diseases* 37: 148-57.

Carter, R. Brudenell. 1906. "Alcohol and Tobacco." *The Living Age* v.32. (August 25): 479-93.

Conrad, Peter, and Joseph Schneider. 1980. *Deviance and Medicalization: From Badness to Sickness*. St. Louis: C. V. Mosby Co.

Consumer Reports. 1958. "Cigarettes." (December): 628-36

Cort, David. 1959. "Cigarettes, Cancer and the Campus." *The Nation* (August 15): 69-71.

Crawford, Robert. 1977. "You Are Dangerous to Your Health: The Ideology and Politics of Victim Blaming." *International Journal of Health Services* 7: 663-80.

_____. 1979. "Individual Responsibility and Health Politics in the 1970s." In Susan Reverby and David Rosner, eds., *Health Care in America*. Philadelphia: Temple University Press.

Davis, Noel Pharr. 1968. *Lawrence and Oppenheimer*. New York: Simon and Schuster.

Dunn, Percy. 1906. "Tobacco Amblyopia." *The Lancet* (December 1): 1491-1493.

Eysenck, Hans J. 1986. "Smoking and Health." In Robert Tollison, ed. *Smoking and Society*. Lexington, MA: Lexington Books.

Fiore, Michael; Thomas Novotny, John Pierce, Evridiki Hatzandrieu, Kantilal Patel, and Ronald Davis. 1989. "Trends in Cigarette Smoking: The Changing Influence of Gender and Race." *Journal of the American Medical Association*, 261: 49-55.

Ford, Henry. 1916. *The Case Against the Little White Slaver*. Detroit: Henry Ford.

Glassner, Barry. 1989, "Fitness and the Post-Modern Self. *Journal of Health and Social Behavior* 30 (June): 180-91.

Goldstein, Michael. 1991. *The Health Movement: Promoting Fitness in America*. Boston: Twayne Publishers.

Gottsegen, Jack J. 1940. *Tobacco: A Study of Its Consumption in the United States*. New York: Pitman.

Gusfield, Joseph. 1980. *Symbolic Crusade: Status Politics and the American Temperance Movement*. Urbana: University of Illinois Press.

_____.1980. *The Culture of Public Problems: Drinking-Driving and the Symbolic Order*. Chicago: University of Chicago Press.

_____. 1992. "Nature's Body and the Metaphors of Food and Health." In Michel Fourier and Michelle Lamont, eds. *Cultivating Differences: Symbolic Boundaries and the Making of Inequality*. Chicago: University of Chicago Press

_____. 1991. "Benevolent Repression: Popular Culture, Social Structure and the Control of Drinking." In Susanna Barrows and Robin Room, eds. *Drinking: Behavior and Belief in Modern History*. Berkeley and Los Angeles: University of California Press.

House, James, Ronald Kessler, A. Regula Herzog. 1990. "Age, Socioeconomic Status and Health" *Milbank Quarterly* 68, No. 3: 383-411.

Hubbell, Charles. 1904. "The Cigaret Habit—A New Peril." *The Independent* v. 56: 375-78.

Ibrahim, Michel. 1976, "The Cigarette Smoking/ Lung Cancer Hypothesis." *American Journal of Public Health* (February): 132-33.

Inciardi, James. 1986. *The War on Drugs: Heroin, Cocaine, Crime and Public Policy*. Mountain View, CA: Mayfield Publishing Co.

Journal of the American Medical Association. 1909. Editorial. "The Pharmacology of Tobacco Smoke." Vol. 52, No. 5 (January 30).

Kett, Joseph. 1977. *Rites of Passage: Adolescence in America*. New York: Basic Books.

LaFollette, Marcel. 1990. *Making Science Our Own: Public Images of Science, 1910-1955*. Chicago: University of Chicago Press.

Lamont, Michelle. Forthcoming. *Money, Morals and Manners*. Chicago: University of Chicago Press.

Lillienfeld, Abraham. 1983. "The Surgeon General's 'Epidemiologic Criteria for Causality': A Criticism of Burch's Critique." *Journal of Chronic Diseases*, 36: 837-45.

Literary Digest. 1914. Editorial. "Some Cigaret Figures." Vol. 49 (August 8).

McMurtrey, J. E. 1968. "Tobacco." *Encyclopedia Britannica*, Vol. 22: 263-67.

Millman, Marcia. 1980. *Such a Pretty Face*. New York: W.W. Norton and Co.

Monkkonen, Eric. 1975. *The Dangerous Class*. Cambridge, MA: Harvard University Press.

National Research Council. 1989, *Improving Risk Communication*. Washington, DC: National Academy Press.

Navarro, Vincente. 1976: "The Underdevelopment of Health of Working Americans: Causes, Consequences and Possible Solutions." *American Journal of Public Health* 66: 538-47.

Nelkin, Dorothy. 1987. *Selling Science: How the Press Covers Science and Technology*. New York: W. H. Freeman.

Newsweek. 1959. "Dr, Burney's Alarm." (December 7): 66.

_____. 1959. "Do They-or Don't They?" (December 21): 80-81.

New York Review of Books. 1991. "Classified Ads-Personal." (July 18): 47.

New York Times. 1905. "Says Schoolgirls Smoke." (February 20): 12.

_____. 1908. Editorial. "A Good Beginning." (May 5): 6.

_____. 1909. "A Counterblast Against Tobacco." (October 2).

_____. 1964. Editorial. "The Smoking Report." IV. (January 12): 12.

_____. 1984. Editorial. "Clearing the Air for Nonsmokers." (December 19): A38.

Pfohl, Stephen. 1984. "The Discovery of Child Abuse." *Social Problems* 24: 310-23.

Pierce, John; Michael Fiore, Thomas Novotny, Evridiki Hatzandreu, and Ronald Davis. 1989. "Trends in Cigarette Smoking in the United States: Educational Differences are Increasing." *Journal of the American Medical Association* 261 (January 6): 56-60.

Repace, James. 1985. "Risks of Passive Smoking." In Mary Gibson, ed. *To Breathe Freely: Risk, Consent, and Air*. Totowa, NJ: Rowman and Allanheld.

Robb, Christina. 1991. "Child Deficits Tied to Smoke Breathed by Mothers At Work." *Boston Globe* (July 17): 1, 17.

Rosenberg, Charles. 1962. *The Cholera Years*. Chicago: University of Chicago Press.

San Diego Union. 1964. "Cigarettes Called Peril To Health." (January 12): 1.

Schoenborn, Charlotte, and Gayle Boyd. 1989. "Smoking and Other Tobacco Use, 1987." *National Center for Health Statistics: Vital Health Statistics* 10 (69).

Schudson, Michael. 1984. *Advertising: The Uneasy Persuasion*. New York: Basic Books.

Schwartz, Hillel. 1986. *Never Satisfied: The Cultural History of Diets, Fantasies and Fat*. New York: The Free Press.

Scott, Janny. 1991. "'Smoker's Rights' Asserted Under New Job Bias Laws." *Los Angeles Times* (July 23): A5.

Sobel, Robert. 1978. *They Satisfy: The Cigarette in American Life*. Garden City, NY: Anchor Books/Doubleday.

Starr, Paul. 1982. *The Social Transformation of American Medicine*. New York: Basic Books.

Sterling, Theodore. 1975. "A Critical Reassessment of the Evidence Bearing on Smoking as the Cause of Lung Cancer." *American Journal of Public Health* 65 (September): 939-53.

Stone, Dorothy. 1986. "The Resistible Rise of Preventive Medicine." *Journal of Health Politics, Policy and Law* 11: 671-95.

Sullivan, Walter. 1964. "Cigarettes Peril Health, U.S. Report Concludes." *New York Times* (January 12): I, 1.

Tesh, Sylvia. 1991. *Hidden Arguments: Political Ideology and Disease Prevention Policy*. New Brunswick, NJ: Rutgers University Press.

Time Magazine. 1955. "Smoking and Cancer." (June 13): 67-69.

_____. 1958. "Smoking and Cancer (Cont'd)." (May 5): 61.

_____. 1959. "Smoking and Cancer (Cont'd)."(April 27): 73.

Troyer, Ronald J., and Gerald Markle. 1983. *Cigarettes: The Battle Over Smoking.* New Brunswick. NJ: Rutgers University Press.

U.S. Department of Health and Human Services, Public Health Service. 1988. *The Health Consequences of Smoking: Nicotine Addiction* (A Report of the Surgeon General). Washington, DC: Government Printing Office.

U.S. Department of Health and Human Services, Office on Smoking and Health. 1986. *Smoking and Health: A National Status Report.* Rockville, MD: Government Printing Office.

U.S. Department of Agriculture. 1990. *Agricultural Statistics.* Washington, DC: Government Printing Office.

U.S. Department of Health, Education and Welfare. January 1964a. *Smoking and Health. Report of the Advisory Committee to the Surgeon General of the Public Health Service.* Washington, DC: Government Printing Office.

_____. September 1964 b. *Summary of the Report of the Surgeon General's Advisory Committee on Smoking and Health.* (Public Health Service Publication, No. 1103-D) Washington, DC: Government Printing Office.

USDHEW. 1979. *Healthy People: The Surgeon General's Report on Health Promotion and Disease Prevention.* Washington, DC: U.S. Government Printing Office.

USDHHS. 1989. *Reducing the Health Consequences of Smoking: 25 Years of Progress. (A Report of the Surgeon General).* Washington, DC: U.S. Government Printing Office.

U.S. News and World Report. 1955. "Latest on Smoking and Cancer." (June 17): 45-47.

_____. 1957. "What Britons Are Told About Lung Cancer and Tobacco." (August 2): 84-86.

_____. 1957. "What is Known and Unknown About Smoking and Cancer." (July 26): 56-75.

Veblen, Thorstein. 1934. (orig. pub. 1899). *The Theory of the Leisure Class.* New York: The Modern Library, Inc.

Wagner, Susan. 1971. *Cigarette Country.* New York: Prager Publishers.

Weiss, William. 1975. "Smoking and Cancer: A Rebuttal." *American Journal of Public Health* 65 (September): 954-55.

Whelan, Elizabeth. 1984. A Smoking Gun: *How the Tobacco Industry Gets Away with Murder.* Philadelphia: George F. Stickley Co.

Whorton, James. 1982. *Crusaders for Fitness: The History of American Health Reformers.* Princeton, NJ: Princeton University Press.

Williams, David. 1990. "Socioeconomic Differentials in Health: A Review and Redirection." *Social Psychological Quarterly* 53: 81-99.

Zola, Irving. 1972. "Medicine as an Institution of Social Control." *Sociological Review* 20: 487-504.

13

The Social Meanings of Meals:
Hierarchy and Equality in the
American "Potluck"

Human behavior is capable of interpretation and understanding at different levels and in diverse dimensions. In recent decades, under the influence of semiotics, structuralism and the general analysis of behavior as text, anthropologists and sociologists have engaged in much insightful examination of varying levels of meaning of action (Geertz, 1973; Schwartz, 1986; M. Douglas, 1975; Bourdieu, 1984). Such examinations involve the sociologist in treating behavior as a text-that is as something to be "read" for its meanings as well as for its ostensible ends (Riceour, 1979; Geertz, 1973).

In his paper, "Deep Play," Clifford Geertz has developed the art of such interpretive analysis into a classic model. He utilized the cock-fight as a prism through which to find aspects of Balinese culture both reflected and reinforced (Geertz, 1973: 412-54). In her paper on the Hebrew doctrine of *kashruth*, Mary Douglas used the laws forbidding certain foods as a vehicle through which to explicate subtle and non-obvious aspects of ancient Hebrew culture (Douglas, 1975: 249-275). Geertz interpreted the cockfight as a "metasocial commentary" and as "a means of saying something of something" (Geertz, 1973: 448). Douglas's approach is similar in speaking of "the language of food" (Douglas 1975: 250).

Reprinted from Gerald Platt and Chad Gordon, eds., *Self, Collective Behavior and Society: Essays Honoring the Contribution of Ralph H. Turner*, 1994, pp. 297-306. Reprinted with permission of JAI Press, Inc., Greenwich, CT, and London, England.

It is possible then to examine patterns of food use as microcultures—recurring situations that display meanings. It is possible also that the meanings of the specific form of activity is expressive of patterns of human relationships that transcend the immediate form and which constitute a macroculture. In this sense, we can "read" behavior for what we can learn and interpret about more general attributes of a social group.

That is what I am doing in this paper. On one level it is about a recurrent event—the American form of shared meals called the potluck. On another level, it is about hierarchy and equality as aspects of American life. A more formal mode of hosting persists in American life as well. Both are forms of sociable sharing of meals, but each is set in a complex of different assumptions and obligations about hospitality and the role of persons toward each other. The texts of human behavior, like literary texts, are capable of diverse meanings. In this sense, they are polysemic (V. Turner, 1967: Ch. 1). However, meanings often take on a dimension as contrasts. In this paper, I assert that one meaning of the potluck lies in its contrast to formal modes of meal presentation to visitors. That contrast provides useful insights into American forms of hierarchy and equality emerging in contemporary American life.

Friends of mine in England relate the following experience. After completing several years of graduate work in a California university, they returned to their native England and to a position in a provincial city. They had become appreciatively accustomed to American informality and invited colleagues to their home for a "potluck" meal. My friends were surprised at the disapproval that this mode of entertainment generated. It was seen as decidedly stingy and inhospitable. Too many years of living in America had given them a very different conception of the proprieties in hosting. What they had thought would be seen as fun was taken as dereliction of social duty.

The "potluck" has become an accepted part of the possible forms of home entertainment among many circles in American life. Its appearance in the homes of upper-middle and even upper classes in the United States is the occasion for this paper. The term "potluck" refers in this context to a meal in which the contents—the prepared food—is the contribution of each guest to a common meal. Both the cost and the cooking are the obligations of guests and hostess. It is not the same as some picnics, where each family brings its own meal. The potluck is a meal in which each guest has the food that he or she and all the other guests and the hostess have provided. (The term has been in use for some time also to refer to whatever is being prepared for a family meal. In this context an impromptu invitation to a hostess's home for potluck could mean that the meal would not be as if for a special, formal occasion but "whatever we're having that night.")

I use the term "hostess" to refer to the hosting person because of the greater obligations placed on women for this service in American life. It should be recognized, however, that this does not imply the absence of participation and distinct duties on the part of the male host.

The Formal Meal: Hierarchy and Structure

It is a sound rule in understanding the meanings of human actions to recognize principles of contrast (Leach, 1976; M. Douglas, 1976).The symbolism of the potluck is unclear unless we recognize its contrast with the formal, hostessed meal, which has been conventional in upper-middle classes and is still a frequent form of entertaining guests. It is in its differentiation from the formal meal that the significance of the potluck can be found.

The formal meal, almost always the dinner, is the crown of the evening. It constitutes the central event of the program for that occasion. Everything that occurs is framed around the meal. The before and after events have their meaning in relation to the timing and service of the meal. Drinks and hors d'oeuvres are served before the meal and in a different space. Conversation may take place after the meal around the table, but usually there is a movement back to another space. The arrival time is set in relation to the meal and all guests arrive at approximately the same time and leave at close to a uniform hour.

The meal begins and ends in a definitive fashion. It takes place around a table and all the guests, the host, and the hostess begin at the same time and end at approximately the same time. The meal is marked by defined courses in a uniform, standard way (M. Douglas, 1975). Soup precedes the entree; dessert is at the end. Salad may precede or follow the entree but never before the soup or after the dessert. A liqueur or brandy may be served, but not during the meal. Once begun, the meal is not to be interrupted, although dessert and coffee may be taken in another space. Guests and hostesses eat each course at the same time and they remain seated. They do not get up, walk about, or eat part of the meal in a standing position, part in a seated form. While there are individual and situational variations the formal meal is a structured affair. It follows a settled scenario and distributes understood roles to the players.

A significant element in that structure is its hierarchical character. The distinction between host, hostess, and guest is clear and governs the event from beginning to end. The hostess selects the meal, prepares it, and serves it, with or without assistance. It is the hostess who determines the beginning of the meal, the pacing of the courses, the movement in and through the space of the home.

The hostess is the provider; the guests are the recipients. The meal, and the evening program, is entirely the production of the hostess. Whatever status honor or dishonor accrues it is to the hostess and not to the guests. Power over the evening and obligation to provide the hierarchical character of the event is plain. The choice of food, mode of preparation, form of service are all outside the province of the guest role, although clearing of the table may be cooperative.

The formal meal must also be seen as a contrast, quite patently to the informal, daily meal of the household. In terms Erving Goffman has made so well known, it is "front-stage"; not "backstage" (Goffman, 1976: Ch 3).The plates and the cutlery are often not those in everyday use. The place of service—customarily a dining room or dining space— is not that where daily meals are served. The rigid structure of the formal meal and the pre-meal service of drinks and hors d' oeuvres (literally "outside the main work") contrast to the more utilitarian character of the daily meal, as does the cost and elaborate preparation of the hostessed meal. Even the clothing of both hostess and guest is different, more ostentatious, formal, and different from daily use. The "backstage" meal is further differentiated from the "front-stage" by the looser character of the home; less tidy, less polished, and more "lived in." So, too, the members of the family are expected to behave with greater cooperation in the daily meal and its after-operations. "Don't be a guest in your own home."

The Potluck: Spatial and Temporal Diffusion

Where the formal meal is tightly structured, the potluck is loosely arranged. Where the formal meal is "front-stage," the potluck moves us closer to the back. Two aspects in which this is clearly displayed are in the different uses of space and of time.

The potluck meal is usually served buffet style. Guests take their food from the table and proceed to parts of the house. There is a separation between the serving place and the eating place that requires guests to move through parts of the house. Since the appearance of food depends on the arrival time of guests there is much milling about, as new foods arrive or guests return for "seconds." The sense of moving to and from the meal in unison, as in the framing of the meal at the formal dinner, is less in appearance. However, the place of the food is still the center of the occasion.

There is another important way in which space opens up and contributes to the "backstage" quality of the potluck. The kitchen is now more available as a meeting and conversing area than is the case in the formal meal. The last stages of food preparation may require the guest to be in the kitchen to complete the warming of food, the tossing of a salad or the finishing touches to a decorative platter. While in the formal meal the kitchen, especially before and during the meal, is off limits to guests, in the potluck this is not at all the case.

It is in the temporal sequencing, however, that the most significant contrasts emerge. Characteristically, the potluck is served to a larger group than is the formal meal. This makes the meal often one of great variety: several varieties of each course—several salads, several entrees, several desserts. Since the meal has a less clear beginning and end, there is less compulsion for the guests to arrive at the same time and for the others to wait for them. The sampling of the varieties of food is part of the pattern of the meal and each new arrival may be sampled. This means that the sense of courses separate in time is lacking. Someone's salad may arrive after the guest has moved on to the entrees, but that does not prevent him or her from returning to sample the new entrant on the table. Since all the courses remain on the table, it becomes possible to move back and forth across the menu with little regard for the temporal sequencing of the formal meal.

The Disappearance of Hierarchy

In a paper on sociability published some years ago, David Riesman and his associates reported on a study of parties in which they concluded that there is a trend toward the disappearance of the hostess as a central governing and pace-setting center to parties (Riesman, Potter, and Watson, 1960).The potluck goes even further in eliminating the hostess as the provider of food. Along with the disappearance of structure in the timing and spatial elements of the dinner, the hostess has given up the rights and duties to manage the interaction between guests, to make introductions, determine the flow of conversation, and assume responsibility for the "good time" of guests.

In such an egalitarian gathering no one assumes the role of management and social authority. Each guest is left to his or her own capacities and aspirations. Even the flow of drinks, so often a major mood-setter, is both open to the unbounded wishes of the guest and closed to the scrutiny of the watchful eye of a hostessing management. The same is true of the gluttonous or abstemious appetites of the eaters. The synchronization of food and drink is lessened and the experiences of the guests less homogeneous, less similar than is the case in the formal dinner party.

With the disappearance of the hierarchy that separates hostess from guest there is also the disappearance of the guest. The obligations to observe a necessary civility and feigned interest in others, to observe standards of arrival and departure and to engage in activities that focus the assembled diners around a common topic are also visibly absent. The dinner itself, the clear focus of the formal dinner party, loses its continuous and continuing cement of the evening as the guests no longer sit at a common table.

In many respects, the "backstage" character of the meal and the evening contribute to a sense of family. Even the cutlery and plates (which may be paper on these occasions) create that sense of closeness. It heightens the informality of the event and, rather than drawing people into a solidarity, enables each person or small group, like so many American families, to "do their own thing." It becomes more possible than at the formal dinner for people to go through the entire evening and speak only to those they already know.

Some of these elements are aspects of size. The formal dinner party is necessarily constrained by the size of the table. That ,in turn, is necessary to the commitment that the formal party has undertaken in the first place, whether it involves the wish or need of a hostess to bring together this array of people, to demonstrate their skills at hostessing or the elegance of their material objects or the sophistication of their culinary tastes and abilities. But the emergence of the "potluck" is the opportunity to combine both the dinner party and the larger size. It stimulates the move to the larger party and away from the conversation-oriented formal dinner party with its focus on the more intimate interaction, often among previously unacquainted guests.

The Potluck and the Communitarian Impulse

But there is another side and another sense to the contribution of the potluck to the social rhythm and significance of the dinner party. Two matters stand out. First, that it is a communal meal, one in which each person (or couple) joins in providing food and the preparation of it. Secondly, that it is apparently experienced as a joyful and festive event; it sets a tone that is both light and appreciated. In these respects the potluck dinner party is distinguished from the large party as well as from the smaller formal dinner.

The very existence of the buffet table provides a distinctive focus unlike the large cocktail party or after-dinner event. Getting the meal is a more labored and less casual process than the snacks and hors d'oeuvres of the large gathering. It forces the assembled guests into an ecology that puts them in interaction with each other: standing in line, discussing the food, helping each other. In that sense, it constitutes an "ice-breaker" function.

Here the lack of a clear time structure serves to overcome some of the problems raised by the disappearance of hostesses and guest hierarchies. New food, new guests, and returning eaters are arriving at the buffet table, sometimes for two or three hours. The appearance of new foods provides the occasion for the return of earlier arrivals to see what the new ones have brought. Where the formal dinner party has a certain static character and the large party becomes shapeless and fragmented, the potluck develops a flow that breaks up the continuity of small groups and provides a way of meeting others in the assemblage.

The communal form of the meal constitutes a focus in still another fashion, neither spatial nor temporal. It constitutes a source of conversation that can cut across divergences among the guests. The foods brought to the meal are a continuous topic of conversation. Each is capable of being commented upon and the taste, skills, and sophistication of the donors are assessed. Since the donors are not universally known by their contributions they can be a "safe" topic. In fact, such contributions are an expression and a display that reflects on the status of the contributor, a form of conspicuous production. They may be inappropriate or inadequate. (Who brought the "store-bought' cole slaw and potato salad?!) They may add to the good repute of the skilled cook. (Who brought that marvelous chocolate mousse?) It is not unusual for such comments, especially where favorable, to appear months later. ("You remember her? She brought the pepper steak.")

The Spirit of Communitas

The potluck is still comparatively new in the circles where the formal dinner party had been a requirement of decent hostessing. As an innovation it has about it an aura of the unstructured. To this is added the elements of flow and loose structure already described. The result is somewhat akin to the interaction about which Victor Turner has written so much. (V. Turner, 1974). It is an ungoverned and unstructured situation, mixed with danger, adventure and appeal. The atmosphere, for partygoers, is tinged with a greater festiveness than either the formal dinner or the large party.

Both the communality of the meal and the lack of clear structure for the evening throw people back upon each other, emphasizing their common levels and their mutual interests and appetites in food. The formal dinner party does not permit such lingering on the food as a topic without becoming a comment on the hostess's preparation for the dinner of the evening.

The sense of communitas as distinct from hierarchy may be displayed as well in the transfer of managerial functions from the host and hostess to the guests. At one pole is the great threat that the evening will fragment into small groups of like souls. The age and sex and work differences of the guests will emerge as stronger than other considerations. But, as often also happens, the assemblage begins to assume responsibility for perpetuating and expanding the mood of communality and festivity once it has begun. The party ceases to be the product of the host and hostess and is taken over by the guests as their product. The pride or failure that a hostess knows is then transferred to the assemblage.

The Decline of Formal Hospitality

The decline of formalism in entertaining needs little documentation here. In understanding it, more is to be said than general remarks about American informality or the role of women in the labor force. To be sure, as so many women now participate in the labor force, the degree of home care, culinary preparation, and wardrobe maintenance required by older forms of hospitality now seems excessive. When middle-class women of all ages have a work life as well as a home life, the potluck and other forms of communal preparation are a gladly accepted alternative.

The potluck draws support as well from the antipathies that formalism engenders in contemporary American life. As is so often the case with hierarchies, they seem to work most effortlessly when they are experienced less as illegitimate domination than as reciprocal rights and duties. The formal dinner party demands that guests are both willing and able to help the hostess in her role as manager of appropriate conversation and timing. Otherwise everyone reaches for talk to fill empty space, age levels and sexes disperse, and the evening is seen as constraining, stiff, and damned boring.

The formal dinner party may bring together a group of friends already accustomed to each other, who need no hostess to provide the social glue for easy and stimulating dialogue. Classically, however, the dinner party has appeared as the opposite—bringing together people who know each other slightly or not at all and who are pulled together into a evening of brilliance and insight by the work of the hostess. Her talent for selecting the proper mix and finding the points of convergence and the means for the environment that produces that mix is a product of experience or socialization or both.

The social circles about which I am writing are those most familiar to me—of professional or academic people. Typically, though not always, they are drawn from members of the same organization, such as a university or hospital. In such circles there is a felt need to support the work life with a social life, to bring the new member into the social circles of the established members. This means, however, that generational differences must be ignored and differences of rank temporarily suspended in the atmosphere of sociability. As so often happens, however, the evening descends into the only matters of commonality—the intellectual and organizational shop—talk of the "workers". Wives or husbands who are not part of the common work life are implicitly excluded and left to daydreaming or to the chitchat of weather, children, hometown, and shopping.

As an appendage to the organizational and work life, the formal dinner party too readily and too often becomes an extension of work and becomes experienced as work, as effortful and other than "fun." Both for the hostess and the guests it requires more than they can cope with after a busy and tense day. Lacking the easy graces of experience and filled with the tensions of organizational interactions, the hostess is not well equipped for the art or the energy of competent hostessing.

Nevertheless, the needs for visiting reciprocity, for establishing work-related acquaintanceships, for developing the eventful evening persist. With it there is a prevailing mood of American life that is impatient with too close a relation between work and leisure. Here the potluck is experienced, as my British friends testify, as a release from the role-playing and self-consciousness and regulation of organizational existence. The "backstage" quality makes the experience of "fun" more possible than the formal dinner. Even the possibility of exclusiveness and retreat, impossible in the formal dinner party, is more welcomed than the regulated character of hostess control.

Despite the outward show of seemingly egalitarian forms, Americans find the mix of ages, sexes, and occupational diversities a difficult context in which to find enjoyment. In a world of ethnic and racial strains, of generational conflicts and organizational levels, it is difficult to sustain a sociability that ignores these. The potluck is part of our continuing search for how to be both many and one.

References

Bourdieu, Pierre. 1984. *Distinction*. Cambridge, MA: Harvard University Press.

Douglas, Mary. 1966. *Purity and Danger*. London: Routledge and Kegan Paul.

_____. 1975. "Deciphering A Meal." In *Implicit Meanings*. London: Routledge and Kegan Paul.

Goffman, Erving. 1956. *The Presentation of the Self in Everyday Life*. Edinburgh: University of Edinburgh Social Science Center.

Leach, Edmund. 1976. *Culture and Communication*. Cambridge: Cambridge University Press,.

Ricoeur, Paul. 1979. "The Model of the Text: Meaningful Action Considered as a Text." In Paul Rabinow and William Sullivan, eds., *Interpretive Social Science*. Berkeley and Los Angeles: University of California Press.

Riesman, David, Robert Potter, and Jeanne Watson. 1960. "The Vanishing Host." *Human Organization*. 19:17-27.

Schwartz, Hillel. 1986. *Never Satisfied: A Cultural History of Diets, Fantasies and Fat.* New York: The Free Press.

Turner, Victor. 1967. *The Forest of Symbols.* Ithaca, NY: Cornell University Press.

_____. 1974. *The Ritual Process.* London: Penguin Books.

14

"Buddy, Can You Paradigm?"
The Crisis of Theory in the Welfare State

Having some small cachet as an historical sociologist, I prepared for this evening's pontifical remarks by scanning the addresses of my past twenty predecessors, as well as Emory Bogardus's inaugural address in 1930. It was a sobering task. In most cases these were forgotten papers. While each journal issue containing these addresses usually contained one or more papers that continue to play an active scholarly role, the presidential address was seldom among them. I concluded, as I had suspected earlier, that these remarks must be interpreted in the ritual sense in which I shall give them. The inferred rules of the ritual are that the paper must be long enough to dignify the status of the office but short enough to keep the occupant from being beheaded by bored and angered audiences. It must sound significant by tackling a profound and broad topic but must not do so in any manner that might stimulate profound thought or intense intellectual conflict, since such responses are best undertaken on empty rather than full stomachs. Lastly, as I have begun doing, it must unite the sacred and the profane. Hence this beginning, which raises a skeptical and demeaning attitude toward the evening's event, lest too sacred a tone be thought to raise the speaker to an oracular height overlooking an audience of his or her peers.

This article was prepared as the Presidential Address at the annual meeting of the Pacific Sociological Association, Spokane, WA, April 15, 1978. Published in the *Pacific Sociological Review* 22:1(January 1979):3–22. With permission of JAI Press, Inc., Greenwich, CT, and London, England.

Having made these necessary obeisances to intellectual equality, I can move into a more pious mode. The twenty presidential papers have no unifying theme. Bogardus's initial paper, I was surprised to discover, was a very matter-of-fact one about sociological tools of research, devoid of hortatory hopes for a bright future. The others, however, are somewhat more visionary. While some dwell on specific topics, such as Frank Miyamotos's reexamination of the concept "social act," others are global and synoptic, dealing with major perspectives or issues, such as Harry Alpert's discussion of some defects in contemporary sociology.

Most of my predecessors accepted the vision of a sociological enterprise that is worth the candle—that is, on the way toward useful and virtuous knowledge. Alpert, despite some misgivings about sociological practices, concludes his paper of 1963 by saying, "I have no doubts about the future of our discipline. A science is, after all, a self-correcting system." Carl Backman, in 1970, put it even more hopefully: "We can anticipate a tremendous period of growth....Who knows, before the end of the century we may finally assume our predicted place in Comte's hierarchy of the sciences." What these addresses do reflect is a positive and cheerful sense of the importance of sociology to society. Only Jack Gibbs sounds a discordant note, in the discordant year of 1968, warning that sociology has not achieved a consensus on vital principles and continues to be an arena in which sociologists achieve eminence by writing for special audiences of those who share their principles. I shall be closer to Gibbs than to my other predecessors.

Sociology has often presented one or another version of *Star Wars*; theory against theory and theorist against theorist;...the Marxians against the Durkheimians; the Meadians against the Parsonians; the Simmelites against the Freudians. Contemporary sociology is, however, a veritable canyon of fissures in which basic orientations to method and to perspectives about human behavior call into doubt the paradigms or underlying frameworks of thought which have given a degree of consistency and unity to a discipline historically plagued by intellectual conflict and self-doubt. This is a period of search without seizure in which method, theory, philosophy are centers of attention; in which sects abound, denominations are becoming more fractured, and a conventional wisdom no longer adheres for novitiates to pray to or for dissidents to curse at.

Sometimes I see contemporary sociology as a gigantic cafeteria in which the patrons are choosing from a great menu of immense variety. There are two kinds of pasta: micro-roni and macro-roni. They are both noodles, but for those who consume one, the other gives indigestion. The structural-functionalists are carefully following a neatly balanced diet with four courses, cooked on a middle range. The Marxists focus their attention only on proletarian chili and turn quickly away from the seductive odors of bourgeois Beef Wellington. The symbolic interactionists pay no attention whatever to the menu. They move down the cafeteria line nervously devouring the labels. The ethnomethodologists pay no heed to anyone else since they are not interested in eating at all. Their hunger is adequately satisfied by listening to other people *talk* about food. The eclectics take a little of this and a little of that and turn the whole dinner into a stew. All argue violently about their just desserts.

This fanciful smorgasbord is a prologue to a more careful discussion of the impact of the current intellectual conflict in sociology on a society in which some very specific interests exist in the production of theoretical and empirical certainty. Louis Wirth, in the preface of his and Edward Shils's translation of Karl Mannheim's *Ideology and Utopia*, wrote that "The distinctive character of social science discourse is to be sought in the fact that every assertion, no matter how objective it may be, has ramifications extending beyond the limits of the science itself" (p. xvii).

For Wirth this premise to the sociology of knowledge meant that every time a fact was asserted it challenged the interests of some group and supported the interests of some other. My focus in this paper is not upon the implications of this or that empirical fact or theory, for this or that group, but rather on the role of social science theorizing for group direction and activity. It is the weakening capacity of sociological discourse to provide compelling believable theories and facts that I am examining.

This last half of the twentieth century is indeed an age of sociology. There is no longer a major university without some unit of sociology. It is a part of the college education of a great many students. Its studies are a feature of the popular culture of news and television. But that optimism about the significance of sociology and the social sciences to generate an authoritative intellectual base to the society is dim. Belief in the function of scientific method to provide the author-

ity for intellectual synthesis, political direction, and institutional technology is no longer the article of faith it was even two decades ago.

That this is an age of sociological interest is largely a reflection of
the rise of that kind of social engineering and political action that is
summed up in the term "the Welfare State." To a substantial degree,
the Welfare State has emerged out of the failure of a free market to
meet social and economic problems at a level deemed adequate (Briggs,
1961). It has meant the effort of government to achieve control over
social and economic institutions and arenas in two forms. First, in
seeing and acting toward "society" as if it were a unitary object which
could be the recipient of policies and plans. Secondly, in fashioning
social technologies for acting upon such problems through personnel,
programs, and political supports. Both of these have necessitated a
theoretical base of grand and middle-range levels and a version of
reality and fact that is believable and authoritative as a public commitment. The image of science as a validator of reality plays an important
role in this process of public authority.

Sociology in America has been an offspring of the Welfare State.
Its position in the educational marketplace, its role in the training of
professions and occupations, and the demand for its research have
largely reflected the concerns of a society and a state wishing to
alleviate the inadequacies of a market economy. The demand for new
programs and personnel with skills in influencing, manipulating, and
understanding human behavior has been the base of the immense expansion of sociology in the postwar period. The loss of faith in the
market as a model of social and political understanding action has
contributed, as well, to the intellectual rise of sociology and to sociologists as progenitors of social visions and political directions. The
failure of the capitalist society to disappear into history and the historically unique character of the welfare society have presented the
major problem of sociology in its role as critic and guide.

Both of these trends, one institutional, one political, have rested on
the demand for a kind of certitude in human affairs for which the
model of science as a source of valid and general knowledge has been
dominant in this century. The claim of sociology, vis-à-vis the past
humanistic disciplines of philosophy, literature, history and political
science, has been its presentation as a form of valid and credible
science, a way out of endless polemics and vain opinion. Its differentiation from economics has come in rejecting the market as an intel-

lectual basis for understanding and interpreting society and human behavior. It is as a branch of science and as a user of scientific method that sociology has staked its claim to intellectual authority, as an empirical and not as an analytical method, as theory rather than as history.

Conventionally, we have expected different things from sociologists than we have expected from historians. History has been uncomfortable with generalizations. It has adopted a mode of speech and a framework in which the study of past events yields no propositions about the future. Sociology has separated itself from this tradition and attempted, in one form or another, to go beyond the instant; to develop theories and propositions on the model of a science. As a rule of thumb, sociologists write books with concluding chapters, summarizing and generalizing. Historians write books with final chapters that offer few conclusions. How often do we say of some piece of sociological work that it is interesting in a descriptive sense but that it lacks theoretical value?

I will point to three uses of theories and theorizing—three functions, if I can be permitted to adopt one paradigm for a moment. The first is *intellectual*. Theories, and their underlying paradigmatic assumptions, enable us to turn what William James called "the buzzing, blooming confusion" of raw reality and sensation into an ordered and consistent pattern. Weber's *Protestant Ethic and the Spirit of Capitalism* is not just about the historical development of capitalistic institutions. It creates an interpretation of economic action. It makes it understandable and explainable. Marx's theory is by no means the same, but it too counteracts an uncertain and fragmented perspective about a unitary object-capitalism. Both make the world a rational, understandable place.

As sociologists, we are in the business of making the world not a safe place to live in but a sane one. We generate and disseminate explanations; we manufacture theories; we create realities. The image of the sociologist as soothsayer, prophet, and sage has, as my colleague Bennett Berger (1957) pointed out a few years ago, supplanted the literary and the religious moralist as the interpreter of events, as the creator of public frameworks for analyzing and understanding. I am still shaking from the remark of a student in my undergraduate class in social stratification a number of years ago. We were reading W. Lloyd Warner's Yankee City series, and I had asked her to identify the class position of her family. When she said she couldn't do it, I probed and asked her how she would go about doing it, expecting an answer in terms of Warner's methods of classification. Instead she replied, "I'd ask a sociologist."

This intellectual function is, of course, a limiting and constraining one. If it creates certainty and direction, it also obscures and blinds us to whole orders of phenomena. As Paul Feyerabend (1975:38–39) documents in his engaging book, *Against Method*, theories provide the framework which makes some phenomena fact but lead us to ignore others. Yet, without theorizing, we are unable to typify and order events. The objects of our thought in sociology are arranged and structured by virtue of paradigms and theories. To talk about "American society," for example, is to adopt a frame of thinking which grants objective reality to a set of separate events. It is to think about these phenomena *as if* they were integrated and unified. Such intellectual functions are deeply ingrained in the perspectives of sociology and are part of the cultural apparatus that we disseminate. In the deepest sense, we have been rationalizers.

A second function of theorizing is *political*. Here, as Marxists and other sociologists of knowledge are quick to point out, we have been *ideologues*. In constructing society as an object of thought and assertion, sociological theories have reflected conceptions of political values and made an impact on the ways in which Americans conceptualize that society. The dominant theories of the 1930s conveyed a view of social change and the impediments to change which provided an intellectual basis for the reformism of that period. William Fielding Ogburn's (1922) view of change enunciated in his theory of the cultural lag and Lynds' (1937) depiction of the conservatism of Middletown provided the support of sociology for an entire orientation toward the dynamics of American life: The political sociology of American sociologists of the 1950s and early 1960s projected a general liberal pluralism, sometimes countered by a more dissident and radical perspective of a C. Wright Mills. The sociological theories of Talcott Parsons, whatever their intent, did present an America that had achieved a high measure of consensual harmony. In a brilliant paper, Richard Hovard (1977) has recently acutely analyzed the premises of the collective behavior school of Park, Blumer, and their followers with a view to understanding their work as a support for an abiding commitment to the value of popular participation in a liberal-democratic framework.

Such assertions about theory only point to how theories enable us to take attitudes toward a total society—to provide an attitude to political judgment and evaluation. They do so because they attempt to understand where the society is going. Every theory is then a utopia or an ideology.

But ideologies serve in *institutional* as well as societal contexts. In this is their third function. They enable us to carry out activities in institutions. Some of this is evident in our own action as sociologists in academic institutions. Theories teach is to create an organized intellectual world. Students must take examinations, and we must distort the disorganization and confusion of raw experience in order to create the ordered world that constitutes the myth of introductory sociology and the advanced myths of advanced work. Graduate students, uncertain of their capacities, need the comfort of an identity and a perspective that enables them to have answers to questions, to find problems, to criticize and appreciate. To be a Weberian or a Parsonian or a Marxist is to have that identity. Further, the sectarianism and solidarity which adherence to theory provides has some tangible economic values, as well. It grants the adherent sponsorship, contacts, possible journal access. The more the theoretical sects abound, the more departments feel it incumbent upon them to have "one of them and one of those" to make a balanced department, lest graduate students stray into other territory.

It is especially in its institutional importance that sociological theorizing impinges on the second side of my title—the Welfare State. Here the existence of theories provided by academic institutions is the basis for the authority of practicing occupations and a major source of educational and organizational demand for sociologists. As modern economies have been less and less primary and secondary goods-producing and increasingly service economies, doing things to or for people has become the daily occupation of large components of the industrial enterprise (Gartner and Reissman, 1974:19; Wolfbein, 1971:46). It is in these areas of economic life that sociology has played a significant role as a source of those cognitive and moral ideas that have enabled new professional groups to claim a mandate to practice. This is especially the case in areas of education connected with human behavior and in those occupations sometimes called the "troubled persons" industries or "human resources" occupations.

In his brilliant and seminal essay, "Social Problems That Are No More," the late Ian Weinberg (1974) suggested that the proliferation of public or social problems was a characteristic feature of modern societies rather than a product of their disorganization or malaise. Earlier societies, and those dedicated to a laissez-faire market economy, lacked the referral structure that enables us to turn private woes into public welfare programs. Weinberg (1974:41) wrote, "In a modern society it is accepted that the family has not the human material or organizational resources to deal with problems such as illness or crime. The educable, the sick, the criminal quickly become public and social problems."

The emergence of occupations in which knowledge is used to solve human problems is then a part of the "social problems" orientation of contemporary societies and their public politics. People viewed as "troubled" or "deviant" or "needing" are the object of others' activities. The "troubled persons" industries are a vital source of the new professionals. They have no clear designation but certainly include such people as social workers, counselors, community organizers, race relations specialists, clinical psychologists, psychiatrists, educational guidance personnel, medical health workers, alcohol treatment and prevention personnel, substance abuse specialists, and those who teach and train them. They claim a mandate to advise, plan, and treat on the basis of an expertise that rests on a "state of the art" or a body of fact and theory of ascertained and valid form. It is the source of their claim to skill and knowledge. The gerontologist, for example, purports to address a world in which there is a body of knowledge and skills making up gerontology and providing his or her source of professional claim to treat, plan, and advise, to create and evaluate policy about the aging.

Such applied knowledge owes much to basic academic disciplines such as sociology. They provide a methodology that grants credibility to the research on which application is based. They contribute a theory of society that provides a way of understanding and interpreting behavior as well as a set of ideas, which identify the importance of the occupational mission. Both cognitively, as a set of beliefs, and morally, as a definition of mission, they enable an aggregate of persons to earn a living through the acceptance of their mandate to be specialists. As has been said of the missionaries to Hawaii, they came to do good and they stayed and did well.

Like other areas in the production of culture, sociology exists at two levels: that of the elite or cognoscenti, and that of the popular user. The virtuosi religion and the popular religion, Weber called it, talking about another arena of the sacred. For the cognoscenti, who examine, criticize, and produce the paradigms, theories, and facts of what Robert Redfield (1956) called "the great tradition," their knowledge is always less than certain and more than complex. For the populace, the practitioners who use it, it is more than certain and less than complex.

Relations between these two are seldom secure and consensual. The elite, though they produce a rational and ordered reality, see the popular versions of their culture as crude and simplistic. Those who teach a revealed or accepted truth or use the interpretations of the elite to ground their practices ignore the niceties of hesitant scholarship. Such scholarship is too hesitant for legitimating action, too demanding of technical knowledge or broad erudition. The virtuosi of sociological theories appear to them arcane, aloof, and picayune. The situation is not unlike Gibbon's description of the source of Roman tolerance for religions: "To the populace all religions were equally true; to the philosophers all were equally false; and to the magistrates all were equally useful."

Nevertheless, these two have managed to coexist enough for one to project a sufficiently rationally ordered world that the other could use, with students, with "clients," with a public needing to be convinced that they, the practitioners, have a right to practice and prevent those who lack the specialized training from preempting their grounds.

In the remainder of this paper, I assert that these two levels—the constituencies of sociology in the popular studies and the human-services industries, one level; and the high culture of the intellectual scholarship of sociology, the other level—are moving further and further apart. The ordered, consistent, and definitive perspective toward human behavior, which has been the goal and object of sociology, seems further away. The competing paradigms of contemporary intellectual life strike at the capacity of sociological theory to provide a valid and ordered reality to intellectual, political, and institutional life. They describe a sociology more inward, self-contained, hesitant, and unsure of its basic premises than in the past, and less willing or able to construct substantive theory.

It is not that sociology, unlike many of the "hard" sciences, is an arena of diverse and opposing viewpoints. That has been a constant feature of theories and the theory scene at least since sociologists began to conduct empirical studies. What is more salient is the growing disenchantment with the basic paradigm of science as a model on which to build the discipline. The current competition is not only between this or that theory—between exchangists, structural-functionalists, Marxists, or symbolic interactionists. It is also between those for whom the old vision of a science of society, discovering the vital laws and principles of human action, is still a guiding vision and those for whom such goals are either fruitless or even vicious. The longing for a social science Newton still exists, writes Anthony Giddens (1977:13) in his *New Rules of Sociological Method*. However, as he puts it, "Those who still wait for a Newton are not only waiting for a train that won't arrive, they're in the wrong station altogether."

In my judgment, there are three crucial intellectual movements which operate today as forces that make the tasks of theorizing and the generation of a propositional science capable of infusing thought less feasible today than in past generations of American sociology. The most significant of these is the revolution in thought fostered by the philosophical critiques of natural science and the emergence of structuralistic and linguistic concerns. Many names can be cited: Chomsky and Lévi-Strauss in linguistics and anthropology; Michael Polanyi and Ludwig Wittgenstein in philosophy; Thomas Kuhn in the history of science; Alfred Schutz in sociology; and the Marxist critical theorists as well. These have made us sensitive to the presuppositions of seemingly presuppositionless science. They have laid the basis for a view of human action that is less deterministic, more situational, and more creative than given by the paradigm of a generalizing social science. They make us hesitant to offer theories and generalizations with the compelling certainty of a neutral, detached, and valid science, with the ring of an authoritative elite.

What this has meant for sociologists has been the renaissance of micro-level orientations: the tendency to discount and even dismiss the major, overarching perspective of sociology; the belief in the externality of "social facts." I used to consider a sentence from Marx's (1932) *The German Ideology* the seminal, summatory statement of sociology: "It is not the consciousness of Man that determines his life but his life that determines his consciousness." That view of a real institutional world to which people *had* to respond has been the basic assumption of sociology. To find it and elucidate it has been the goal. "Our primary aim," wrote Robert Merton (1949:125–126) in "Social Structure and Anomie," "is to discover how some social structures exert a definite pressure upon certain persons in the society to engage in nonconformist rather than conformist conduct." Even the symbolic interactionists, the more micro-, less scientistic, and more humanistic side of sociology, had accepted what Herbert Blumer (1969:22–23) refers to as the "obdurate facts" of social life.

The appearance of a strong phenomenological criticism of social science seems to me an intellectual movement of great significance. Works such as Berger and Luckmann's *Social Construction of Reality*, Harold Garfinkel's *Studies in Ethnomethodology*, Aaron Cicourel's *Cognitive Sociology*, and Erving Goffman's *Frame Analysis* display the impact of Alfred Schutz and reflexive concerns upon our understanding and acceptance of a factual world as the basis for discovery. They make us aware of how social facts are themselves, in whole or in part, constructions of social actors.

The effect of these intellectual currents is to make us warier about the very tools of analysis and the language with which we can act to wrest certainty from a world of confusion. We are now in the midst of a rash of works, like Spector and Kitsuse's (1977) excellent *Constructing Social Problems*, in which the solution to problems is less central to the concern of the sociologist than is the procedure by which the "problem" is itself defined. In this intellectual process the factual validity of the problem is itself weakened. The sociologist's concern shifts from the problem as a situation to be solved to the problem as the datum to be explained. Pressed to the wall to provide solutions to human problems, my last gasp is to say, "Why do you ask?"

Armed with this new skepticism about science, with a reflexive awareness of sociology as only one of other "folk" methodologies, with a sense of the situational rather than institutional elements in human action, sociology is less certain, less propositional, and more historical. "[T]hough the inquirer begins with the object to be known as the object upon which theorizing will reflect, this very beginning is an achievement of theorizing itself…what we display through an apprehension of the principles is a re-cognition of self" (Blum, 1974:100).

The two other intellectual currents are also significant in diminishing the ability and willingness of sociology to provide that political and/or institutional mission with its ideological base. The most prominent of these is the renaissance of Marxism as a major source of grand theory among American sociologists. Parsonian functionalism had provided a sense of mission and a direction to American sociology as an intellectual and political theory of *the* society. It enabled sociologists to "see" the United States as a unit, as a system. Its decline has left us without a macro-theory with which to assess the totality of the society and the drifts of social and technological change. As Alvin Gouldner (1970: Ch. 2) points out in his brilliant analysis of American sociological theory, social theories are shaped by domain assumptions of partially intellectualized beliefs. It is this character of theories that makes them able to express felt sentiments of their shapers and their hearers. If Parsonian theory expressed an age of acceptance of American society and its direction, the rise of a renascent Marxism expresses the opposite. Both, however, share the character of grand theory and affect a vision of the political that builds on an intellectual effort to create an integrated and authoritative sense of American society, deeply sought after the 1960s had left liberalism in shambles.

The new Marxism, however, both here and in Europe, is far from immune from the corroding impact of the academic disputes over method, language, and philosophical assumptions. As Paul Attewell has pointed out to me, it is a new Marxism in that it is drawn from and addresses academic audiences: Marxists and non-Marxists who earn their living by teaching and writing in universities and colleges. Here too the divisions and splits that characterize competing paradigms emerge. There are many Marxisms, and the homogeneity and force that the doctrine had possessed are diluted in the intensity of arguments about the autonomy or dependence of ideology. The issues of structure and superstructure recreate the basic argument about culture, consciousness, and social structure that exists in non-Marxian sociology as well. So, too, does the argument about the possibility of a social science (Bauman, 1976; Habermas, 1968; Gouldner, 1973: Ch. 16). Marxists have not solved the critical issues and grounded theory in empirical reality any better than bourgeois scientists. That failure continues to limit its claims to a compelling authority.

The renaissance of Marxism has again made sociologists reflexively aware of their own biases and assumptions that shape the character of their research. It is also turned, as well, toward Marxism itself. This sense of suspended conclusion, of a skeptical and tentative air to ideas and data, accentuates the distinctions between a sophisticated and a vulgar Marxism. In its endless convolutions and permutations, European Marxism is, as Perry Anderson (1976: Ch. 2) reminds us, a Marxism of the Chair—the products of academic minds. But Marxist sociology, although a profound influence within sociology, has no connecting point in political action to govern and constrain its fragmenting tendencies. It is sophisticated without a vulgate to talk to. Like its opposite in conventional sociology, it, too, is obsessed with philosophical as much as with substantive issues. The critique of a market society is not sufficient, per se, for a political theory of the welfare society of the 1970s.

The last of the currents of theory and research is the standby of "bread and butter" sociology—the quantitative empirical work that seemed the hope of sociology to construct a technology that would serve institutional needs. Paul Lazerfeld, the Bureau of Applied Social Research, and the fourfold table were the symbols of that postwar development. Whatever its merits or demerits as methodology, it did create a sense that through technical advances social problems could be solved. It assumed that there is a social technology. The adherents provided clear statements of the realities of the social world: effective maps and recipes for action. That orientation to an integrated view, in partial areas and institutions, has given way to more and more refined multivariate analyses (Hirschi and Selvin, 1967). The more refined our techniques, the less we have to say. The depictions of pathways and analyses of variance have given us greatly advanced tools for analyzing the play and interplay of variables. At the same time they have frequently ended in the view that everything is relevant and everything causes everything else. What is good science may not be very helpful to active policy or functioning theory.

A more critical and sophisticated attitude toward data and the modes of data collection has not provided us with a better set of propositions to give to a hungry audience. In contrast, it has made the sociologist more skeptical, less sure, and more tentative than in a less critical period. I cite as one example a recent ASR article on race and crime— a subject of much study for the past two decades. The author quotes approvingly the statement of Gwynn Nettler on the subject: "It is difficult to make comparisons today of the relative importance of the alleged causes of any differences in observed behaviors" (Hindelang, 1978:107).

The bright hope had been that sociology, by the logic of its theories and the power of its empirical findings, would provide the insights and generalizations enabling governments to frame policies, and professionals to engineer programs, that could solve the exigent problems of the society and help intellectuals to direct understanding and criticism. Our record has not been very good. In area after area—gerontology, crime, mental health, race relations, poverty—we have become doubtful that the technology claimed is adequate to the demand. We are skeptical that the problems exist in the direct fashion that policies and programs presuppose. Posited as political issues, as matters of total system or institutional change, we are unconvinced that a science can point the way to a compelling conclusion on which effective policies can be generated. It is not that conflicting interests lead groups to ignore social science. It is rather that our belief in the legitimacy of our knowledge is itself in doubt. Our failure to anticipate or still to explain the 1960s is clear.

It is ironic that, in an age of sociology, the enterprise itself falters in its aspiration to play the role of elite—to be the governing intellectual force that underpins a popular technology, a common politics, and an occupational mission. Yet the sentiments that seek an intellectual resolution are there in popular aspirations; the effort to understand and evaluate the politics of an egalitarian thrust and a centralized national government; the need for occupations of social engineering to project a mission and a sense of authority. Between those two arenas—the rarefied atmosphere of academic sociology and the active world of work and politics—there is a growing distance. Each sees the other as either irrelevant or simple. In this is the crisis of sociological theory and competing paradigms in contemporary society. We are passionate about our ideas, our schools of thought, our theoretical rivalries, but the enterprise itself is more sectarian, more scholastic than it was in the era of Robert Park and Robert Lynd. We are less willing to examine the empirical world unless our theoretical presuppositions and methodological techniques are flawless. This intense concentration on philosophical premises marks a tendency toward self-paralysis, a "failure of nerve," as Gilbert Murray describes ancient Greece in its decline.

At this point I will reveal my hidden agenda—not a way out of the crisis of legitimating sociology as a cultural enterprise but an avowal of it as a worthy activity of human thought and creativity, part of social studies rather than social science. One of the apocryphal sayings of Robert Park was that, "sociology is at best a pedagogical exercise." But that is not a little goal to aim toward. As my student in the stratification class recognized, the sociologist has made an impact on the imagery and language of American life. Even its vocabulary, barbarous as it often seems, has seeped into ordinary language: *anomie, charisma, alienation, power structure.* All of these carry theoretical perspectives in their images of a particular kind of social arrangement and its consequences. The technical methods and the formalized theories and propositions have had less impact than the specific works of sociologists that create models, metaphors, and images for perceiving human behavior and institutions. It is in the works that seek significance and insight, that dare to ignore the demand for closure and accuracy, that sociology has made its greatest effects. Would deTocqueville have passed a Ph.D. thesis committee's scrutiny of his methods? Works like *The Gold Coast and the Slum, Street-Corner Society, The Power Elite, The Lonely Crowd, Asylums, Social Origins of Dictatorship and Democracy* are deeply flawed when compared to any model of rigorous empirical science or a grand, formal deductive theory. They do not tell us what is absolutely there, but they make us aware of what is possible and plausible. They do not avoid reflecting on their limits by examining, testing, and learning from immersion into the confusion of an empirical world.

We are, at our best, part science, part art, part journalism, part contemporary historians—scholars not researchers. That is, in my judgment, a reflection of the nature of our datum in human beings. Because they, and this includes ourselves as sociologists as well, are reactive and reflexive beings, they interpret their world, infuse it with meaning and bring creative and innovative elements into the structure of life. This humanistic view of human beings is not a substitution for the operations of observation, analysis, and self-criticism that marks scientific attitudes. It recognizes the danger of theories that lack the ground of understanding that comes from close encounters of the empirical kind.

Our crisis of legitimacy is, in part, of our own choosing. The competition of paradigms that infuses contemporary sociology is deeply threatening to those for whom a model of science as a closed system is essential; for whom it is imperative that victory, defeat, or syntheses emerge. If we face our limits and our opportunities, we recognize that our discipline is not, and may never be, the source of a new physics; that is, crucial and valuable work can come in the fusion of the empirical discipline of science and the interpretive skill of humanistic studies. We cannot give to the welfare state the authority of science for its institutional actions or achieve a compelling validity to the political criticism of it. The modest place that I see is valuable in undercutting the "enslavement through science" by which institutions and institutional personnel build hierarchies of expertise. Hopefully, such a view provides a mission more sensitive to the illusory authority in alleged scientific theory. It will, I hope, make us recognize the wider and ultimately political conflicts and ambiguities that science cannot bypass. It has done so already in the critical examination of medical models in psychiatry, to give one example.

This will not satisfy those who seek a place of certitude from which to lecture the world or those who wish a firm and secure basis for work and action. It is not consoling for those who seek jobs, bigger budgets, or more power or for those who wish to rest their political critiques or defenses on the authority of a factual science. It does, however, give a firmer mission that recognizes that controversy and competition are the permanent hallmarks of human behavior and human study, that a contemplative and critical detachment is a worthy model of scholarship. What David Riesman, inverting Gilbert Murray, calls "the nerve of failure" is a better guide than the constant demand for absolute success, for political or institutional expertise.

I shall abjure the temptation to prophesy the state of things twenty years from now, after another twenty presidential addresses have gone into deserved obscurity. Ritual occasions like these meetings are as important for what they signify as for what they contain. That "quality" of "occasionness" is not revealed in the printed accounts of past such addresses, but it is, nevertheless, the thread of continuity that makes this a Durkheimian ceremony instead of a lonely crowd.

References

Anderson, Perry. 1976. *Conditions of Western Marxism*. London: NLB.

Bauman, Zygmunt. 1976. *Socialism: The Active Utopia*. New York: Holmes and Meier.

Berger, Bennett. 1957. "Sociology and the Intellectuals." *Antioch Rev.* 17:275–290.

Blum, Allen. 1974. *Theorizing*. London: Heinemann.

Blumer, Herbert. 1969. *Symbolic Interactionism*. Englewood Cliffs, NJ: Prentice-Hall.

Briggs, Asa. 1961. "The Welfare State in Historical Perspectives." *Archives of European Sociology* 11:221–258.

Feyerabend, Paul. 1975. *Against Method*. London: Humanities Press.

Gartner, Alan, and Frank Reissman. 1974. *The Service Society and the Consumer Vanguard*. New York: Harper and Row.

Giddens, Anthony. 1977. *New Rules of Sociological Method*. New York: Basic Books.

Gouldner, Alvin. 1970. *The Coming Crisis in Western Sociology*. New York: Basic Books.

_____. 1973. *For Sociology*. New York: Basic Books.

Habermas, Jurgen. 1968. *Knowledge and Human Interests*. Boston: Beacon Press.

Hindelang, Michael. 1978. "Race and Involvement in Crimes." *American Sociological Review* 43 (February):93–109.

Hirschi, Travis, and Hannan Selvin, 1967. *Delinquency Research*. New York: The Free Press.

Hovard, Richard. 1977. "The Interactionist Paradigm: The Collective Behavioral and Pluralist Conceptualization of Politics and Society." Paper presented to the annual meeting of the American Sociological Association.

Kitsuse, John, and Malcolm Spector. 1977. *Constructing Social Problems*. Menlo Park, CA: Cummings.

Lynd, Robert, and Helen Lynd. 1937. *Middletown in Transition*. New York: Harcourt Brace.

Mannheim, Karl. n.d. *Ideology and Utopia*. London: Routledge and Kegan Paul.

Marx, Karl. 1932. *Capital and Other Writings*. New York: Modern Library.

Merton, Robert. 1949. *Social Theory and Social Structure*. Glencoe, IL: Free Press.

Ogburn, William Fielding. 1922. *Social Change*. New York: Viking.

Redfield, Robert. 1956. *Peasant Society and Culture*. Chicago: University of Chicago Press.

Weinberg, Ian. 1974. "Social Problems That Are No More." In E. Smigel (ed.), *Handbook of Social Problems*. Chicago: Rand McNally.

Wolfbein, Sidney. 1971. *Work in American Society*. Glenview, IL: Scot

Index